BLACK COFFEE LIGHTNING

David Lynch Returns to Twin Peaks

BLACK COFFEE LIGHTNING

David Lynch Returns to Twin Peaks

Greg Olson

Author of ***Beautiful Dark***

Black Coffee Lightning: David Lynch Returns to Twin Peaks

Photo courtesy of Showtime/CBS
Book cover and interior design by Scott Ryan

Published in the USA by Fayetteville Mafia Press
Columbus, Ohio

Contact Information
Email: fayettevillemafiapress@gmail.com
Website: TuckerDSPress.com
Instagram: @fayettevillemafiapress
Twitter:@fmpbooks

ISBN: 9781949024623
eBook ISBN: 9781949024630

Come now,
my child,
if we were planning
to harm you, do you think
we'd be lurking here
beside the path
in the very dark-
est part of
the forest?
–Kenneth Patchen, *But Even So*

He had imagined that as a policeman he would be granted a special kind of knowledge. He would learn things that other people didn't know, things of life and, far more significantly, things of death, and dying. A foolish expectation, of course—to live was to live, to die was to die. It was what everyone did. What was there for a detective to detect that other people weren't privy to?
–John Banville, *Snow*

We suppose a case, and put ourselves into it, and hence are in two cases at the same time, and it is doubly difficult to get out.
–Henry David Thoreau, *Walden*

CONTENTS

–FOREWORD–

DARK AND BOLD, WITH HINTS OF SPICE AND EARTH

Most of us, when we watch a movie, see it from a remove. The movie plays on a screen in front of us—over there, some distance away. We watch, and we react, and if it's a good movie, we might find ourselves absorbed, even seduced. For many of us, that's as far as our relationship goes. The movie ends, and we delight in our newly formed thoughts and emotions.

For some of us, that's not enough. Moved by powerful art, stimulated by the visions of singular artists, we want to know more. We want to know how a film was made, what inspired the director or screenwriter, how a particular actor came to embody a role. We dig deeper into the work, watching it again, reading about its history, seeking other works by the same creators. Invigorated, we shape our minds around it.

For a rare few of us, even that's not enough. Great art reconfigures our worlds, propels our lives in unexpected directions. We actively pursue a relationship with the art that moves us. We speak publicly about it; we interview those involved with making it; we write books about how the work came to be and why it succeeded.

That brings us to Greg Olson and *Black Coffee Lightning*. What you have before you is a product of love and devotion, a book that, because Greg reveres the art of David Lynch, lovingly and diligently explores the world of Twin Peaks—specifically that world's latest iteration, *Twin Peaks: The Return*.

I've admired Greg Olson's work for a long time. His previous book, *Beautiful Dark*, provides valuable insight into the films and life of director David Lynch. Whether Greg is recounting his on-set experiences with the film *Fire Walk With Me* or relating his intimate, in-person conversations with Lynch and his team of artists or puzzling through Lynch's challenging narratives, he always gives you something fascinating to think about. He opens doors and guides you through dark passages.

Now Greg is exploring David Lynch's longest, most demanding work. In *Black Coffee Lightning*, Greg examines every chapter of *Twin Peaks: The Return*. He dives deep, exploring the various nooks and crannies of this sprawling, eighteen-hour television series. More than that (and not surprisingly), Greg tells us about *The Return*'s background, the years leading up to the show's 2017 premiere, the secretive filming in Washington State in 2015, the importance of Mark Frost's 2016 novel, *The Secret History of Twin Peaks*. By doing so, Greg contextualizes *The Return*, showing us the many dynamic pieces that contributed to the final work.

That's not surprising. Greg Olson is a wide-screen writer. Sure, he tells you about the action happening at the center of the picture—the immediacy of the story as it unfolds—but he also tells you what's happening on the edge: the background detail, the nondescript set dressing or curious dialog that holds a fascinating story all its own. Greg doesn't sit and watch a film from his seat; he stands up and gets closer. He looks at the margins of the screen, and he even peers behind it.

Twin Peaks is an elusive work; it holds its secrets close and is stingy with its clues. Those who have struggled with the work know how challenging it can be. Fortunately, Greg has the patience, intuition, and the right amount of courage to navigate his way through.

In the pages of *Black Coffee Lightning*, you'll find secrets and truths. Notions to ponder on those long, dark drives.

Greg Olson is serving you a rich brew. Drink full and descend.

John Thorne
August 10, 2023

For Linda Bowers (1947-2017)

–CHAPTER ONE–

SEE YOU IN THE TREES

A dimly lit space. An oval table top with a glass of wine. Touching the stem, the hand of a beautiful woman. Blonde, wrapped in a long dark coat, a half smile on her lips.

I tell her I watched her make a movie twenty-five years ago. Late, on a cold autumn night in the deep woods above a small Northwest town. A narrow logging road, a black motorcycle, her character, and the boy she loves. They are desperate and tormented. Matters of life and death are at stake. They're pulled together and apart all at once; they weep and plead, she slaps him and gives him the finger to his face, she glimpses something in the empty black air and screams in terror. These moments are scary and unbearably intimate to witness so close. Because of the narrow road, the film crew and I have our backs up against the bristling foliage behind us. I tell the actress I was just barely out of camera range that night; I could have reached out and touched her shoulder. As the camera rolled, I kept telling myself, "These are actors, this isn't real," but they were human beings pouring their hearts out, their breath clouds in front of my face, and I instinctively averted my eyes from the scene. In my peripheral vision I could see that most of the crew was also studying the dirt, until David Lynch softly said, "Cut. That was so *beautiful*."

The actress with her wine touched my arm and said, with earnest intensity, "I'm so glad you told me this. You know, I haven't watched *Twin Peaks: Fire Walk With Me* in twenty-five years. I just couldn't, but I did, knowing I was coming up here. Seeing it again, I was amazed. I realized I had blacked it out of my mind."

Actress Sheryl Lee was "up here" in Seattle from Los Angeles in the spring of 2017 to appear at the Seattle Art Museum with her 1992 film. The event sold out overnight. The lovely, open, blue-eyed, beneficent face in front of me was an icon of popular culture.

In the spring of 1990, 34.5 million American TV viewers were entranced by the premiere of David Lynch and Mark Frost's *Twin Peaks*, and the haunting emblem of the show was a homecoming queen portrait photograph of high school sweetheart Laura Palmer, played by Sheryl Lee. From a golden picture frame, the golden girl radiated glorious innocence and love, resplendent in her white gown and sparkling crown. But dwelling in the Lynchian world of doubleness, *Twin Peaks* presented a second iconic image of Laura, a cold, gray-blue corpse face, dead on the shore of a lake, beach sand on her brow, raped and murdered.

Lee was studying acting in Seattle in 1989 when Lynch and company shot the Northwest-based *Twin Peaks* pilot. Lynch's artistic process relies on intuition, what he calls "thinking and feeling together," and he spontaneously chose Lee just for the purpose of playing the murdered girl by the lake for a few hours. But Lynch, struck by the genuineness of Lee's presence and emotive power, made her a major part of the show, embodying all the light and darkness of the human soul, rather than just someone who died and isn't here anymore.

Laura's absence, her sudden violent loss, convulsed her loving community in a paroxysm of extended grief. But Lynch and Frost, both mystically inclined, made Laura both dead and alive, in the town's heart and in the air, where you couldn't/sometimes could see her. David Lynch listens to what sensations, vibrations, drifting thoughts, electrical hums, and night winds say to him and, with his dream logic filmmaking, makes us see and hear and feel them too, to the depths of our being. In *Twin Peaks,* Laura could be both gone and "glowing in the dark woods," known intimately by the community yet "full of secrets."

Lynch, a daily meditator since the mid-1970s, understands the multilayered nature of consciousness, the many selves we contain, and *Twin Peaks,* like all of his moving image work, dwells in doubleness: the reality of the surface, and of the hidden. Laura is virtually the town's idol, a sunny paragon of beneficence, but she's also the night girl of drugs, promiscuous sex, and prostitution. And Sheryl Lee portrayed both Laura and her lookalike cousin Maddy, who are slain by the same man, Laura's father Leland (Ray Wise). Leland also exhibits doubleness: he has a dark passenger he wasn't born with, Bob (Frank Silva), a demonic extradimensional entity who uses Leland's body to penetrate Laura sexually and finally knife her to death.

Over the 1990-1991 course of the TV *Twin Peaks* and the 1992 feature film *Twin Peaks: Fire Walk With Me*, Lynch and Sheryl Lee took Laura's character to heartrending levels of suffering and spiritual depth, making her death a self-sacrifice that is redeemed with a floating Christian angel attending, as is a handsome man in a black FBI suit.

The suit isn't stipulated in the bureau's regulation manual, but it's part of Lynch's culture, in his off-screen life and on-screen when he portrays Deputy Director Gordon Cole in *Twin Peaks.* The man standing watch over Laura in her post-death spiritual transition period is FBI Special Agent Dale Cooper (Kyle MacLachlan), and if Laura's face, alive and vivacious or drained of life, is *Twin Peaks*'s female icon, then stalwart Dale Cooper, standing tall in his black suit, is the male. So much so that when Lynch, who left the show for a period to make his film *Wild at Heart*, returned to find Cooper gone casual in a plaid flannel shirt, he raised a ruckus. Lynch has a way of blasting out "NO, NO, NO" like the machine-gun fire of the weapons he used to draw as a kid.

As a boy growing up in the Pacific Northwest (Montana, Washington, Idaho), David Lynch had an awestruck sensitivity to the world around him, learning that that tall, wide, green thing was "tree," that life was sitting in a puddle squishing mud between his fingers, that "the whole world was two blocks long." Lynch's father, Donald, a Forest Service research scientist, was a great example to his son, carefully studying the natural world with a questioning mind and drawing conclusions from considered evidence, like a detective. Donald inadvertently gave David this key metaphor of his art. In the midst of a beautiful forest that could have come from a fairy tale, there were dark, invisible forces at work, hidden pockets of disease that Donald probed for beneath the surfaces of pine trees. Lynch has loving, blissful memories of his all-American childhood, but even as a youngster he sensed "a force of wild pain and decay" gnawing at the world. And he was sensitized to surreal scenes that violated the normality of a Norman Rockwell picture: labeled insects in a room in the midst of a forest or a naked, bloody-mouthed woman walking down a residential Spokane street a few blocks from the Lynches' house.

Lynch, like all of us, expends energy trying to make coherent sense of the images, actions, and sounds that he perceives. But as he grew up, and even now in his seventh decade, he doesn't strive for a comforting cause-and-effect narrative interpretation of life; he's registering abstractions of thought and feeling, painterly contrasts, slow streams and sudden surges of empathy, absurdity, beauty, magic, and the fluctuating ways that time and space are orchestrated. Encouraged and supported by his parents to express his mind artistically, young David made drawings and paintings while his brother and sister pursued, and excelled at, more conventional vocations. Lynch's visions were recognized and rewarded. And visions is the word: he sees things we don't, until he shows them to us. One night he was working on a painting of a dark garden with a figure, and as he told me, "I heard a wind, and the figure moved a little." In the Indian Vedic scriptures, which Lynch studies as an adult, Desire and Motion were generative forces in the creation of the universe, and young Lynch fulfilled his desire to make more moving figures in short, 16mm films. These films (*The Alphabet*, 1968; *The Grandmother*, 1970) deftly merged drawn and painted animation and stylized live action that manipulates real people so that they eerily seem like animation. The films were impressive in technique and theme, and earned Lynch an American Film Institute grant to study at its Beverly Hills Conservatory for Advanced Film Studies, which in turn spawned the stunning feature-length *Eraserhead* (1977). And Lynch kept climbing the ladder: *The Elephant Man*, *Dune*, *Blue Velvet*, *The Cowboy and the Frenchman*, *Industrial Symphony No. 1: The Dream of the Brokenhearted*, *Twin Peaks*, *Wild at Heart*, *Twin Peaks: Fire Walk With Me*, *On the Air* (TV), *Hotel Room* (TV), *Premonition Following an Evil Deed*, *Lost Highway*, *The Straight Story*, *Mulholland Drive*, *Rabbits*, *Dumbland*, and *INLAND EMPIRE*. Lynch, who believes in karma, must be doing something right.

Now in his upper seventies, Lynch maintains a childlike sense of wonder at the worlds of nature, human beings, and spirit. And his decades of faithfully practiced meditation have deepened his access to the inspirations of his subconscious. Many of us have waking dreams, but Lynch can conjure his into cinema of unparalleled power and style, giving us emotional-cerebral-visceral experiences that shake us and materialize us within the mysteries of life and death. In Lynchworld, something can be scary and funny all at once, banal and profound, awkward and elegant, disturbing and instructive. Puzzlements and dualities abound, but between two things that are polar opposites, there's "a secret door" to cosmic grace. All this Lynchness is an artistic heat signature like no other, and it grips some people like a fever.

In the spring of 2017, the hundreds of people in the Seattle Art Museum audience were certainly fired up. Twenty-six years earlier, in 1991, the TV audience for *Twin Peaks* had cooled and dwindled once Lynch and Frost, bowing to network pressure, revealed that Leland Palmer had violated and killed his own daughter. The show's two creators had wanted this central mystery to extend into some far-off future, so new plot lines with far less resonance, and more melodrama than Laura's story were hastily introduced. And worst of all, after the cancellation was announced, the last episode left the post-death Laura in the mysterious, otherworldly Red Room and Agent Cooper possessed by the evil Bob, who grinned back at Coop from his bathroom mirror. There had been a sense of conjoined destiny for Laura and Cooper, a poetic kind of love, that now would never come true.

After the TV series was canceled, the film *Fire Walk With Me* (1992) kept the world of *Twin Peaks* alive for one more year, but it was a financial failure. That was that; the sets were disassembled, the props were sold, and David Lynch and Mark Frost, their actors and crew moved on to other projects with a real sense of loss. But the show, the idea, feeling, and spirit of *Twin Peaks*, lived on in the hearts and minds and work of book and masters thesis writers, TV and film artists susceptible to the show's mesmerizing influence, cultural critics, video tape and DVD watchers, filming site tourists, fan festival attendees, Japanese teens who gave Laura a mock funeral, people who grinned when they consumed the show's mythic cherry pie and black coffee.

The passionate hordes who swarmed into the Seattle Art Museum to be in the presence of Sheryl Lee/Laura Palmer were certainly in the *Twin Peaks* groove. When I introduced her to the audience, there were cheers, then a reverent silence. An hour away from where the show was filmed, I said, "Tonight, *Twin Peaks* is right in this room," and there she was, the one who is "dead, and yet I live." And soon, that would be proven true.

–CHAPTER TWO–

A WIND STIRS

Actor Ray Wise, who'd masterfully portrayed one of TV and movies' most disturbing and complex malefactors, the father who raped and killed his daughter, Laura Palmer, was causing more trouble early in 2012. Twenty years after playing Leland for the last time in *Fire Walk With Me*, he was quoted as saying that "David Lynch is thinking about making more episodes of *Twin Peaks*." Lynch's inner circle, including his daughter Jennifer Lynch, who'd written the best-selling *The Secret Diary of Laura Palmer* (1990), forcefully said, "There won't be any more *Twin Peaks*." But then Laura Dern, Lynch's friend, close neighbor, and star actress (*Blue Velvet*, *Wild at Heart*, *INLAND EMPIRE*), said, "David's cooking up something wonderful for me." Knowing Lynch, the something cooking could be an Indian Ayurvedic meal of quinoa, but Dern's statement sent a little jolt through Lynch watchers.

In Lynch's fictions, characters are often devoted to their undying obsessions, and in 2005 he mused that "I couldn't get myself to lose the world of *Twin Peaks*. I was in love with Laura Palmer and her contradictions: radiant on the surface but dying inside. I wanted to see her live, move, and talk. I was in love with that world and I hadn't finished with it." He was talking about the period between the cancellation of TV's *Twin Peaks* and the making of *Fire Walk With Me* in 1992, but in 2012, Laura Palmer, her town, and its denizens were still vibrantly alive in Lynch's psyche.

If Lynch was still enthralled by the Passion of Laura, Mark Frost was more philosophical. When I interviewed Frost for my book *David Lynch: Beautiful Dark* (2008, 2011), he was deeply proud of his partnership with Lynch and their *Twin Peaks* achievement. It had been "something special and meaningful in our lives and in our work." Past tense, but what about the future? In the final TV episode, written by Frost and directed by Lynch in 1991, Laura Palmer, consigned with Agent Cooper to the other-dimensional Red Room, whispered in his ear, "I'll see you in twenty-five years." Could Laura and Cooper's creators abandon their Schoolgirl of the Sorrows and her Champion, suspended in an indecipherable zone of flickering time and space, their souls prey to all the darkness of the universe?

Over the twenty-five years since *Twin Peaks*'s demise, Frost had been busy writing novels, screenplays, producing and directing TV and film. In recent decades, Lynch had international exhibits of his artwork, was a peace ambassador for his Transcendental Meditation-based David Lynch Foundation, made records of his music (composition, instruments, and vocals), got married, and had a towheaded daughter, Lula, named after Laura Dern's strong, spirited character in *Wild at Heart.*

Twin Peaks is a world of multiple, shifting time streams. In 1989, two years before cancellation and the last episode airing on TV, Lynch and Frost had to satisfy the European home video market by combining the pilot episode with some new material to create a fully resolved ending, a self-contained movie with closure. They decided to go into the mysterious Lynch-devised Red Room, which would appear in some of the TV episodes. For European consumption, the Red Room scene was subtitled "Twenty-Five Years Later," and Laura whispered something in Cooper's ear. When the full series was broadcast worldwide, Episode Twenty-Nine, the finale, let us hear what Laura had whispered: "I'll see you in twenty-five years."

In 1989-1991, Lynch and Frost didn't make a twenty-five-years-down-the-road marketing scheme to try to revive *Twin Peaks* in the 2000s. Over the years since the show's debut, it's been fully acknowledged that *Twin Peaks* opened the door for the rush of smart, imaginative, deeply engaging, and cinematic television that we now enjoy. In 1990, *Twin Peaks* story editor and writer Robert Engels realized that "*Twin Peaks* is perched on mighty fertile turf." In the 2000s, Mark Frost, with his background and expertise in TV production, didn't need reminding of *Twin Peaks*'s magical glow and groundbreaking status. As he watched *Mad Men*, *Breaking Bad*, and *Fargo*, his creative and competitive instincts stirred. He heard Laura's whisper, and so did Lynch. Soon the two were having lunch at Hollywood's venerable Musso & Frank restaurant, itself a kind of time machine, to answer the call of a dead girl.

After dreaming and writing, Lynch and Frost came up with a solid proposal and approached an original-participant member of the *Twin Peaks* extended family. Showtime cable network's head of programming, Gary Levine, had been in the room at ABC in 1988 when Lynch and Frost presented their first *Twin Peaks* ideas. Levine was predisposed to appreciate his friends' concept of a *Twin Peaks* return, and Showtime's head, David Nevins, was a major Lynch fan, but what really swung the deal was a painting. Prominently displayed in Nevins's office was a painting of an unbalanced bookcase that looked like it might tip over onto a little girl. A touch of surrealism, a threat of danger in a seemingly orderly world, always makes Lynch feel at home, and he felt attuned to Nevins's sensibility. Lynch believes in karma and fate: "Sometimes the lights are red, sometimes they're green." The "Go" signs in the Showtime offices were being dusted off, but there were obstacles ahead on the road to Oz.

The minds seemed to have met, and in October of 2014 Lynch and Frost simultaneously tweeted, "Dear Friends: That gum you like is going to come back in style!" (this phrase being one of the series's otherworldly Man from Another Place's cryptic pronouncements). Lynch and Frost would write, and Lynch would direct, nine episodes revisiting *Twin Peaks* twenty-five years later. Their four-hundred-page screenplay would be shot as one long movie, then divided into segments for weekly Showtime TV presentations.

All seemed well, but over the months Lynch announced that he was dropping out of the project for financial reasons. He wasn't angling to fatten his own bank account: he felt that "not enough money was offered to do the script the way it needed to be done." The network's business office wanted to fit Lynch into its "This is the way things have always been done" box, but head man Nevins didn't want *Twin Peaks* without David Lynch.

In *Twin Peaks* culture, and the cultural history of the world, caffeine, comfort food, and baked goodies help foster interpersonal harmony. In the original series, Agent Cooper tells Sheriff Truman, "Every day, give yourself a present," like pie, coffee, doughnuts. David Nevins and Gary Levine ascended the serpentine roads to Lynch's Hollywood Hills house bearing cookies and goodwill. Lynch added coffee and his "Let's do this!" attitude to the mix. Nevins always felt that Lynch was an artistic genius, and he was soon convinced of the auteur's sense of financial responsibility. In the warm, golden light of a Los Angeles spring, Lynch announced, "The rumors are not what they seem. . . . It is!!! Happening again," referencing *Twin Peaks*'s themes of deceptive surface appearances and the cyclical nature of reality. There would be not nine new hours of the show, but eighteen, done just the way Lynch and Frost wanted them to be. Actor Kyle MacLachlan, Agent Cooper himself, said, "I'm taking my black suit out of the closet." The world would get to see if "that gum you like" still had some flavor left.

–CHAPTER THREE–

VALLEY OF SHADOWS

Before he started his grocery business in the 1950s, my father, Carl Olson, was a Swedish emigrant lumberjack in the woods of Washington State's Snoqualmie Valley, a cradle of Native American spirit tales and the site of the small towns of Snoqualmie and North Bend, known to the world as *Twin Peaks*. As a 1960s high schooler, I got my first driver's license in North Bend, and landmarks of my youth became *Twin Peaks*'s Double R diner, Packard Sawmill, Great Northern hotel, Roadhouse, sheriff's station, White Tail and Blue Pine Mountains, and White Tail Falls.

The spiritual resonance of this region, the way that my father and Lynch's father had been woodsmen, Lynch's mindset that "we're all detectives," the way that an artist who'd fascinated me since 1970 came to my home turf to craft one of his seminal works prompted me to pursue Lynch and his mysteries in my book *David Lynch: Beautiful Dark*. By chance and stealthy design, I watched the month of *Fire Walk With Me*'s filming in 1991, which enabled me to chat with Sheryl Lee in 2017 about Laura's wrenching scenes with James on the last night of her life.

Linda Bowers, my romantic partner since the early 1980s, was skeptical about my desire to represent the full spectrum of Lynch's personal and artistic sensibility on the printed page. More than once, I heard, "Now why do you want to write about this guy? He's so disturbing." Linda was independent "to the max," as Lynch would say, so trying to convert her to my cause was fruitless. But gradually Linda became intrigued by Lynch's work and personhood, eventually being awestruck sitting in Lynch's painting studio watching him float clouds of cigarette smoke around his head, talking to him about his deep understanding of women, and sitting in the dark as Lynch played a tape of Rebekah Del Rio singing "No Stars" before it came out on record. Even though Linda was somewhat resistant to Lynch's world initially, she became friends with Lynch's first wife, Peggy Reavey (whom Lynch remained close to after their divorce), and her husband, Tom. Linda became close enough with them that we spent time together at their San Pedro home, and I awoke on the morning of my sixtieth birthday at the Reaveys', jammed with Linda into Jennifer Lynch's former bed.

Not surprisingly, the highest percentage of *Twin Peaks* viewers was in the Seattle, Snoqualmie, North Bend area, and the region kept the show's spirit alive in a low-key Northwesty way. Tourists and locals frequented the Double R diner and took a few photos at the filming sites they could find. And the upscale Salish Lodge & Spa (Great Northern hotel) offered a couple of *Twin Peaks*-related cards and mugs amid its elegant high-end fare. In town there were no public commemorative photos, plaques, or banners to be seen. But some locals fondly remembered when Hollywood had come to their north woods and transformed it into a mythic locus of wonder and fear. As rumors of a third, long-awaited *Twin Peaks* season mushroomed, speculation sparked in the chilly air. "Will Cooper become himself and defeat Bob and brighten Laura's world?" "Surely there'll be a new murder mystery, some new woman in danger." "Since Frank Silva's dead, who will play Bob, the creepiest villain ever, who just *has* to look like Frank?" "Which characters will be coming back?" "All the actors will be so old." "Will they even come back up here to film—they can do everything with computers now."

Given my history with Lynch and company, I was curious too. I live in the suburbs of Seattle, with the Snoqualmie Valley forty-five minutes further out. One Saturday I stopped at the North Bend Library. The female librarian was very Northwest-natural looking, with no makeup, unstyled utilitarian brown haircut, and wan, earth-toned clothing. When I asked if the new *Twin Peaks* was going to be filming in town, she said, "Oh, are they doing more of that?" Twede's Café (the show's Double R diner), with its fresh coffee and pastry smells, was far cheerier. The blonde counter woman sported a vibrant blue Seattle Seahawks jersey and said, "Someone from a production company called our boss last week."

David Lynch believes that we're all detectives, paying close attention, looking for signs and clues to what's going on, right here and throughout the cosmos. One night a North Bend woman said goodbye to her husband, as she did every night, as he headed out for his evening walk with their dog. When he returned he had a strange look on his face. He said he'd followed his familiar trail and, as usual, gone beyond it into the deep woods. Amid the dim tree shapes he'd come upon some people, measuring with tapes, taking photos and notes: "It was the damndest thing." Weeks later, north of Seattle in the city of Everett, location of Laura Palmer's house, the police posted a notice on a residential street: "There may be dramatic screams on Friday night." And in a few days, David Lynch was spotted enjoying a chocolate ice cream cone in North Bend. As Agent Cooper once said, "I believe these occurrences are complimentary verses of the same song." Without a doubt, *Twin Peaks* had come home.

–CHAPTER FOUR–

PICTURES IN A CAVE

At six feet two inches, 185 pounds, I was too big to miss, but if David Lynch spotted me, he let it pass. In the Snoqualmie Valley fall of 1991, I strode into the bustling *Fire Walk With Me* production as if I belonged there. Lynch's assistant, Gaye Pope, came up to me and asked why I was taking notes. I said I had a connection at *Film Comment* magazine and might write up my impressions of the day. A few days later, a friend of mine who worked at *Entertainment Weekly*'s New York office proposed a set visit to Gaye and was told, "Don't even think about getting on that plane." There wasn't a security-guard-enforced perimeter around the filmmakers, and interested townsfolk were allowed to watch daytime shooting from a respectful distance. I wondered if media representatives had been warned off; at any rate, they weren't here.

I bonded with Gaye over our mutual love of legendary British director Michael Powell's films (*The Red Shoes*, *Black Narcissus*), and I showed her a photo I'd taken of Michael standing on the spot where James Hurley had sat with his motorcycle brooding over the valley view, Michael having been there a year before the world had even heard of *Twin Peaks*. Lynch notices, and seems to generate, such synchronicities. When driving he spots his initials on license plates. And years ago, knowing that his favorite number had changed from nine to seven, I told him that out of over two hundred possible Seattle Art Museum staff key numbers, mine was seven. Nothing unusual there; he said, "See, there you go."

When my 1991-1992 *Film Comment* articles on watching the *Fire Walk With Me* filming, and my interpretation of the finished film, came out, Gaye Pope told me, "David really liked your articles; you really nailed it." Having been influenced by Lynch's belief in the significance of signs, I took Gaye's/Lynch's words as an indicator that I should write a book about the man and his art. With all the multiyear gaps between Lynch's films, the book came out seventeen years later. I know authors who've published books and articles on Lynch and never heard any response from him. Lynch's first wife and great friend, Peggy Reavey, told me that "David read every word" of my 733 pages, which was significant, since those close to Lynch always say he's not an avid reader.

Lynch and his cadre of professional colleagues, friends, and parents, and me the appreciative inquisitor, had formed an energized circuit, a golden circle. Because of my *Film Comment* writing, Lynch felt I was on his wavelength enough to talk to me, and then to trust me. People close to Lynch are deeply loyal, and before talking to me they would need to get the go-ahead from David, which he always gave. When Lynch's best friend, Jack Fisk asked him about participating in my project, Lynch told him, "No holds barred"; in other words, "Talk freely."

In addition to his major part in making my book happen, Lynch was a generous participant in my film curating job at the Seattle Art Museum. The first, 1992 Twin Peaks Festival premiered *Fire Walk With Me* at the North Bend Theater. Lynch flew in from Los Angeles, introduced the cast, left the screening after the film started, and flew home. The second, 1993 Twin Peaks Festival had no film screening planned, so I called Gaye Pope and offered my services at the museum. Lynch had recently bought back the rights to *Eraserhead*, and had refurbished it with the help of cinematographer Frederick Elmes and sound wizard Alan Splet. When I heard that Lynch would ship the film up to me, I called Catherine E. Coulson. She would be in the Snoqualmie Valley for the Twin Peaks Festival, forty-five minutes from Seattle, but she warmed to the idea of coming to the museum to talk about working on *Eraserhead* in the days when she was married to its star, Jack Nance, whose *Twin Peaks* character, Pete Martell, discovered Laura Palmer's body in the 1990 *Twin Peaks* pilot.

Coulson's professional and personal bond with Lynch ran deep. They were close personal friends, and she was deeply immersed in the film that launched his cinema career. Plus, he saved her life. One morning during the *Eraserhead* production, in the kitchen, in front of Lynch, she fell to the floor in a seizure and began ebbing away. Lynch called an ambulance, cradled her head, and kept saying, "Don't go to sleep, stay with me, keep repeating your mantra (they had both recently taken up Transcendental Meditation.") At the hospital, she went into cardiac arrest, but the doctors stabilized her and told her that she'd be dead without Lynch's help. For the rest of her life, she phoned Lynch on her birthday to thank him. And she spoke reassuringly to me about her near-death spirit journey: "I saw the long tunnel stretching ahead, the welcoming bright light at its end. There's nothing to be afraid of; it was like I was going on a tropical vacation. Peace and golden light."

Like the Log Lady she played on *Twin Peaks*, Catherine wanted her words to be meaningful when she spoke about *Eraserhead* at the museum, so she visited Lynch one night to bone up on their moviemaking history of two decades previous. Lynch's artistic world is a place of light and darkness, and when Catherine left Lynch's house after their chat, the light over his back stairs had burnt out, and she tumbled down. When I drove up to the Salish Lodge (the Great Northern hotel) to pick her up for the drive to Seattle, she had a big smile, a swollen, bandaged ankle, a cane, and a bottle of pain pills. Trouper that she was, she limped to the museum stage and charmed the audience with tales of Lynch using a strange tangle of oily, hairy stuff that he'd found on a nocturnal roadside as a design feature of Henry's apartment room. Like the Log Lady might, she cryptically referenced the character played by Lynch's friend Jack Fisk, simply saying, "He *is* the Man in the Planet," meaning he's God, or the mate of Mother Nature, or a dark force controlling Henry? And as with everyone associated with *Eraserhead* over the years, she didn't say a word about what the bizarre, disturbing Baby was made of, or had been born from.

By the end of the evening Catherine's ankle and foot throbbed with fire, so she took a couple of pills, and two tall people that we were, we contorted ourselves into my little VW Rabbit. She was wearing a long dress, but we managed to get her leg and foot up onto the car's dashboard to elevate the pain source and still enable me to see out the windshield. We pulled into the Salish Lodge's arrival area, where Audrey Horne had taken her limousine to school. It was late on a chilly night, and before the lodge's valet emerged to open the VW's doors, Catherine E. Coulson, married woman, leaned over and gave me a big kiss on the mouth. "Thanks for a wonderful evening," she said, and I, thrilled in all ways possible, said, "Thank you!"

Like the Log Lady, Catherine was my guide when I started my book project, connecting me with Peggy Reavey and so many others who helped me portray Lynch's life and art. And after the *Eraserhead* night, Lynch kept lighting up my museum screenings over the years, letting me show, before they were available on home video, his early short films, his commercials, special projects like *The Cowboy and the Frenchman,* and his personal, one-of-a-kind 35mm print of the *Twin Peaks* Pilot, plus the 35mm reel of the European ending. To introduce my Lynch film evenings, he sent me videotaped weather reports ("It's clear in LA, seventy-three degrees, and tonight at the Seattle Art Museum . . . ") and an audio intro with his voice and *Twin Peaks* music that slowly faded into a wind sound. And in the most golden of gestures, in 2008 he made a five-minute film for me to show. A Red Room in black and white: dark curtain, zigzag floor, two chairs facing forward, a dead girl, a female effigy figure motionless on the floor. Lynch, in black suit and buttoned white shirt, slowly wanders into the space, looking around like it's a strange new place to him. He tries to sit in the left chair, but there's some invisible disturbance, and he has to twist and contort before settling in. In Red Room-style backward speech, he advises us to stay strong in our convictions and to buy a raincoat. The dead-girl figure materializes in the empty chair next to Lynch. He stands, and as "Laura Palmer's Theme" swells, he bends and kisses her on the forehead, then faces forward, the beam of a circular spotlight transforming his head into a glowing white orb. The film was a heartfelt abstraction: it was Lynch himself and Dale Cooper, Laura Palmer and Sheryl Lee, his love for the *Twin Peaks* world he and Mark Frost had created, an illustration of the human capacity for enlightenment, a head full of white light—and he'd choreographed and performed it all backward in a single camera take! He wanted to hear from me as soon as I'd seen it. My words added up to "Bless your heart, David."

Lynch invited Linda and me to the cast-and-crew screening of *Mulholland Drive* at the Directors Guild on Sunset Boulevard, and the next morning he responded warmly to my overall impression, but when I brought up structural elements like his use of silence, his flow stopped with "There are three silent parts." Lynch follows his intuitions in life and art, and in not revealing his own interpretations of what he creates, he lets our minds range freely on an analytical field day. My intuitions and sense of Lynch's personhood and aesthetic sensibility guided my interpretations of his work, and some of my key readings jibed with those of Lynch's intimate associates like Gaye Pope and his *Twin Peaks* partner Mark Frost. Jack Fisk told me, "You're the perfect person to write this book." They offered their responses to what I was doing; I didn't ask for them.

Lynch's favorite of his own films has always been his first feature, the cryptic *Eraserhead*. He's always been silent about one of its mysteries: What happens to Henry at the end? Once when Lynch and I were talking, about not *Eraserhead* but his Vedic belief in the blissful undifferentiated field of enlightened consciousness, which he called "the big home of everything," I had a split-second brainwave. I said, "Is that where Henry is?" Without a pause he said, "You bet." Since my mission in *David Lynch: Beautiful Dark* was to interpret Lynch and his work as I saw them, it was gratifying to know that some of my readings synchronized with Lynch's perceptions. Maybe they were too close to home. In 2014, I heard that Lynch "had an issue with your book, even though there are multiple copies of it at his house." Some people who participated in my book, like Naomi Watts, wanted to read their parts before publication. But Lynch, believing in the artist's right to final cut, set no conditions on my project. I called David's first wife, Peggy Reavey, who said that Lynch was steamed up "because since he gave you so much time and access, readers will think that he's endorsing your interpretations of his work." Peggy added that this was what he said some years back. "He may feel differently now." Obviously, I'm biased, but I found it hard to see how the book provided evidence to support Lynch's impression. At a key point in the book, he even said, in response to my pointing out some recurring theme or motif, "You would see that, but I wouldn't." I've told a few people, including authors of other books on Lynch and *Twin Peaks*, about Lynch's misgivings, and they're as surprised as I was.

At any rate, when Lynch and his *Twin Peaks* crew returned to our area in 2015, I didn't want to try crashing their party, or even wave from across the street. I wanted Lynch and Frost to create something fabulous that would again enthrall the world, and I felt no need to even be on the periphery of their process. But Lynch, with his mastery of a multivalenced tone, knows it's possible to feel at least two ways about a topic. Temptation can be as fierce as Bob, and one Saturday Linda and I drove out to the Snoqualmie Valley with a mind to visit the Twin Peaks Sheriff's Station (Weyerhaeuser Mill office), where she had once snapped a picture of me while I stood on the front steps. And if we just happened to run into the production . . . At the top of the narrow road down to the old mill property, a sign was planted: "Rancho Rosa." Linda was driving, and she coasted down further to two security guards standing on my side. I rolled down the window. One of the unsmiling men asked, "How did you find us? Are you lost?" I said, "No, I don't think so." I thought he might chuckle, but his face was grim as he said, "We're shooting a commercial. Have a nice day." That was that. We backed up the road, and when we passed Twede's Café, I noticed a new painted stripe on its façade that said "RR to Go." Rancho Rosa? Hints about the new *Twin Peaks* were close to invisible.

Media coverage of the production was rare as snow in July. All that the *Seattle Times*'s Jack Stone Truitt could find on the production's fringe "was a rotting deer leg on the forest floor." Self-described paparazzo Tim Ryan, hoping to make "serious cash" from telephoto lens production images, instead tangled with crew members who blocked his shots. Later, cocooned in thorny blackberry bushes, he got to see "a van carrying David Lynch!" go by.

Lynch wants to present his creations precisely when he wants to. He's never been one to reveal much about a project while it's being made, or even after it's completed. In our era, private emails, personal bank accounts, and political campaigns are invaded by hostile cyber forces, and episodes of popular TV shows are stolen and leaked weeks before their scheduled broadcast release. Understandably, there was a stone wall around the *Twin Peaks* production, but there was a cleft in the rock. A cave.

A breeze of Tibetan Buddhism wafted through the original *Twin Peaks*, and in Tibetan Tantric thought, a cave is the female genetic opening, the vagina and birth canal, the path into the womb, where primal knowledge, the code of energy and matter, sparks to life and surges into the world. In *Twin Peaks*'s Owl Cave, an ancient Native American wall painting of a tree circle, a giant being, sun moon and fire, was a map to concrete places and things and to invisible realms of immeasurable power that shaped peoples' lives.

The number of Lynch's world is seven, and seven months before *Twin Peaks* would fill our TV screens, the show's executives, writers, director, actors, and technicians were upholding the code of Silencio. But there were pictures on a cave wall to read and interpret: Mark Frost, *Twin Peaks*'s chief scribe and literary light, had published *The Secret History of Twin Peaks.*

–CHAPTER FIVE–

PEN AND PAINTBRUSH

One hopes that Mark Frost doesn't wince when, for the seven-thousand-five-hundred-fifty-eighth time, he hears the words "David Lynch's *Twin Peaks*." The show's lush, quirky, imaginative, cinematic visuals, its mesmerizing sound design and music, offbeat characters with non sequitous dialogue, trance-like pacing, and intimate and visceral familiarity with suffering and transcendence were recognizably Lynchian. But there's a misguided stereotype that Lynch was the artistic genius and Frost kept the production running smoothly; Lynch = poetry, Frost = prose. True enough, Frost had excelled in the world of writing and producing mainstream TV series (*Hill Street Blues*, *Buddy Faro*), while Lynch was painting abstractions of thought and feeling on-screen that a fair number of cinemagoers couldn't decipher. But Frost created one of *Twin Peaks*'s most resonant image-concepts, the town traffic light at night, swinging in an eerie wind, changing from green to red and holding the red as though the demonic color of fire was painting the town. And because Lynch's interest in Asian spirituality was more well-known, people incorrectly assumed the he, not Frost, wrote the renowned, pivotal scene in which Agent Cooper comforts the dying Leland Palmer and guides him into the light of an afterdeath spiritual journey. And Frost's childhood may have spawned the germinal idea of the *Twin Peaks* saga, for Frost's grandmother told him about Hazel Drew, a young girl whose corpse was discovered in a pond in upstate New York, and about spirits haunting the woods near the grandmother's home.

In Lynch's childhood, his neural pathways were being shaped by drawing and painting images. He had time for drifting thoughts, sensations, moods that gradually or suddenly formed a seed idea. In Lynch's thinking and films, inside and outside comingle. Inner states of mind and emotion can be visualized as other people, places, objects; Lynch's artistic ideas can be caught like swimming fish outside himself, or seeds sprouting inside his head. In Lynch's decades-deep Vedic philosophy, we are all simultaneously separate individuals and at one with the All of being, the one indivisible universal consciousness.

As a painter, Lynch manifests his mind with complete freedom, growing his initial idea, deepening a background wash of gray-brown, letting the pale canvas show through on the left, making dark strokes center-right, adding a vague figure—what is it doing? He adds elements; he acts and then reacts to what he's done. It's "creation and destruction"; sometimes he rubs parts out, pushes in another direction, lets an accidental move guide him. He knows the moment when it's done. He's expressed himself fully and, gloriously, he has the final cut.

The inner visions and sounds Lynch perceives are intensely meaningful to him; they are "correct," and he wants to "stay true to them." When he spoke to a graduating college class in 2017, his all-inclusive advice was "Have final cut." In the mid-1970s, Lynch devoted years of his life to making *Eraserhead,* a deeply personal, independent film that's as intimate as an X-ray of his nervous system. In the mid-1980s, he spent years writing and directing the gargantuan, multimillion-dollar studio production *Dune*. Lynch calls *Eraserhead* his "perfect film," but *Dune* was a soul-killing experience in which he had to compromise his best instincts, shaping the film according to others' wishes, and, worst of all, talking himself into feeling okay about it all. *Dune* remains a toxic, wounding life lesson for the artist.

When Lynch paints, his mind and hands control the process, as do Mark Frost's faculties and fingers when he types words on a page. Each activity primarily lights up a different part of the brain. There's a golden circle, a circuit of energy flowing between their heads, their means of expression, around and around. Of course Lynch can write potent dialogue and Frost can compose evocative images, but at a primal level, Lynch is the master of atmosphere and flowing visuals and Frost the eloquent wordsmith: the yin and yang of *Twin Peaks*.

Lynch and Frost would agree with American transcendentalist Henry David Thoreau that "the spiritual assists the natural eye." When the partners conjured up the original *Twin Peaks*, Frost felt that "David provided a sense of spiritual mystery through his presence on the set, the way he directed. His ability to suggest moods and feelings visually. David is great at showing rather than telling with words. A tremendous amount gets communicated in his silent passages. We were both in love with secrets hidden and revealed. We were determined that there wasn't any reason why a television show shouldn't have a sense of mystery and spirituality as one of its major components, residing side by side with reality."

Frost's contributions to the *Twin Peaks* mystery train, often scripted, are derived from existing, traditional myth systems: Theosophy (multidimensionality, the Black and White Lodges), Sherlock Holmes, Arthurian legends, Druids, UFOs. While Lynch's brain produces his own mythology: the Red Room, Bob, the backward talking dancing little man, the Log Lady, the Giant, creamed corn as the dark cosmic mana garmonbozia, electricity. Elements which, arguably, contributed most to *Twin Peaks'* poetic otherness.

Lynch had famously thrown out the Mark Frost-Harley Peyton-Robert Engels-scripted conclusion to the original *Twin Peaks*'s last episode and intuitively crafted a haunting Red Room phantasmagoric finale. And throughout the two years of production Frost commented that Lynch would disregard established structural guidelines and do his own thing. So what would Mark Frost's 362-page *The Secret History of Twin Peaks* tell us about Frost's *Twin Peaks* sensibility, unadulterated, 100 percent pure, final cut?

The residents of Seattle read more books than the citizens of any other American city. And on a crisp night in late October 2016, hordes of them crowded into the Elliott Bay Book Company to hear Mark Frost present his new tome. He'd spoken here before over the years when some of his mystery novels and golf books had come out. And Lynch collaborator Barry Gifford (*Wild at Heart, Lost Highway*) had also visited the store. The main floor was abuzz with anticipation before Frost's arrival. The chairs and any standing room were quickly filled, and I noticed a few young Agent Coopers in their black suits.

Standing in line for the coffee bar, I was surrounded by small tables where folks were spending a mellow Saturday night with their friends, laptops, or a book. Right in front of me, ten feet away, sat a beautiful woman with center-parted long brown-blonde hair, wearing an elegant dove–gray pantsuit, rather than a turquoise waitress outfit. The turquoise outfit popped into my brain because she looked, really looked, like Mädchen Amick, who played *Twin Peaks*'s Double R diner waitress and romantic player Shelly Johnson. Amick doesn't live in the Northwest, and Frost is solo on his book tour, so?

I let a *Twin Peaks* fog of ambiguity curtail my analysis and took my seat, but as Mark took the stage, I noticed the Woman in Gray standing at the edge of the crowd taking phone photos. Frost looked relaxed in a sweater and plaid shirt, his gray hair swept back from his tall forehead, his wire-rim glasses gleaming. He had the air of the wise, bemused, accessible college professor we all wished we'd had, or of a favorite uncle, teller of tales full of fear and delight.

In *Twin Peaks*, the Bookhouse Boys are a small core group dedicated to the good, the true, and the legal, upholders of the town's better nature who liked to gather in a little cabin to read, muse, and strategize. Standing in the Elliott Bay Book Company with soaring rough-hewn beams above, surrounded by 250,000 books printed on paper, Mark Frost was Bookhouse Boy Number One, keeper of *Twin Peaks*'s literary flame, prophet of a secular Church of the Word. With Lynch he'd created the future, and when he said, referring to the new *Twin Peaks* just months away, "We're counting the days," all us readers cheered.

All his life Frost has had mysteries and stories on his mind, and the gift of expressing and sharing them. Inspired by the great mythologist Joseph Campbell, Frost chose the path of art and myth over a dedication to financial gain. "When writers plug into the subconscious powerhouse that Campbell describes, they can move past entertainment and sensationalism to provide the kind of nourishment that people have sought from stories since the days of the first shamans. We need writers to help make sense of who we are and the strange place we find ourselves. They help us see, through the strivings and failings of fictional characters, what our own lives are trying to tell us. That's the writer's high purpose, and they should embrace and honor it."

I'm sure no one expected Frost to reveal specific details about the new *Twin Peaks*, but there was the question of whether his brand-new book would—one assumed gatekeeper Lynch had weighed the story-leak potential of every word. Regarding whether the book contained conscious clues or not, Frost cataloged some of its elements: Washington State's Native American heritage, the state's role in creating the first atomic bomb, the Roswell UFO crash story, following characters through time, aging and dying, the way the mind can offer an escape when there are things we don't want to see, mysteries that sustain us versus secrets that hold power over others, the common good versus ruthless dominators, the way glasses with one red lens and one blue one integrate both halves of the brain.

As the store employees got ready to sell the books that Frost would sign, he came to his conclusion. As a committed artist and humble man, he said that "a book is something you leave by the side of the road for someone to find." And he added, "For you writers out there, don't tell everything at once" (the *Twin Peaks* house style is more like "Don't tell everything, ever"). Frost, a passionate anti-Donald Trump tweeter, had one more thought: "Vote on November 8!" Then, that beautiful woman in gray was standing next to him: "Mädchen Amick was filming up in Vancouver and came down to be with us tonight." In the Church of the Word, *Twin Peaks* State of Mind, beaming waitress Shelly Johnson gave the final benediction: "We love you!"

The fiction-loving bookstore community that felt at home in an imaginary small woodsy town exited into the urban Saturday night. The Elliott Bay Book Company is located in the heart of Seattle's Capitol Hill neighborhood, long known for its secure, thriving gay community, affordable housing, art students, a main street called Broadway, a statue of Jimi Hendrix playing the lost chord. As I walked block after block to my car (the horror stories about Seattle traffic and parking are true), the sidewalk teemed with young and old, aroused desire and high spirits. I felt a wave of that 1960s-early 1970s "free to be you and me" euphoria, when the Kinks' Ray Davies sang, "Girls will be boys and boys will be girls," and liberal values were going to reshape the world. But a sober moment later I remembered that now rich young techies were gentrifying soulful old enclaves like Capitol Hill, forcing out folks who couldn't pay ever-raising high rents. Frat boy types were coming in on weekends to beat up "weirdos" for sport, and Seattle cops were getting known for using excessive force against minorities. The 2016 presidential election season was revealing disturbing currents of racist, fascist, misogynistic thought and behavior in my fellow Americans. But of course, Hillary Clinton was going to defeat Donald Trump; those in my tribe would carry the day. And no matter what, as Ray Davies also sang, "I live in a museum, so I'm okay." Just how much of America in the late 2010s would Frost and Lynch let seep into their twenty-five-year-old *Twin Peaks*-in-a-bubble?

–CHAPTER SIX–

BOOK OF REVELATIONS

Imaginative in word and image, *The Secret History of Twin Peaks* is the sort of work you'd expect from Mark Frost: an engaging overstory comprising fascinating parts, a long view of history and philosophy, characters with idiosyncratic voices, some questions answered, and other mysteries deepened. And throughout, the conjecture-stimulating possibility/likelihood that some, all, or none of the book will be realized on-screen in *Twin Peaks: The Return.*

The book is like an alluring vault containing writings from 1805 to 1989, photos old and new, hospital records, passports and redacted FBI files, a memorial service memento, a café menu, and unexplained symbols: a dossier FBI head Gordon Cole (played by Lynch in all versions of *Twin Peaks*) gives to agent "TP" in 2016. It was found at a crime scene and seems to relate to the missing Agent Cooper and the closed Laura Palmer case of twenty-seven years ago. Cole needs to know who compiled the dossier, and with profound urgency: "We need to know yesterday." A fine, straightforward statement, but *Twin Peaks* is a zone of multiple meanings, and these words also convey *The Return*'s the-past-is-the-key-to-the-future dynamic.

Agent TP sees that the material was compiled by an anonymous "Archivist," who has annotated various pages. So immediately we know that the dossier relates to *Twin Peaks* mysteries, and that the identity of agent TP and the Archivist are unknown. Mark Frost, via the Archivist's notes, underscores the book's main point: "Mystery is the most essential ingredient of life," for it stimulates curiosity, the desire to know, to derive meaning from chaos. In an "indifferent universe," myths and stories and our limited scientific knowledge can be seen as a single activity: seeking.

And Frost finds the need to pursue truth within mystery ingrained in the American character, Thomas Jefferson having chosen Meriweather Lewis and his partner William Clark to lead a Corps of Discovery mission into the uncharted west. Frost, like a true detective/seeker-creator, presents Lewis' story through a progression of information fragments that were amassed by an Archivist and are being presented to us by an FBI person who's adding their own margin comments. If Lynch feels "we're the same inside as when we were little," Frost must feel he's had the old soul of a scholar inside him. With his fluency in interrelating and layering thoughts, it makes perfect sense that he saw himself, and *Twin Peaks*, in the term "meta" when he first heard it years ago. Frost's storytelling is so compelling, his complex of "evidence" so convincing, that it's easy, and enjoyable, to believe that in the early 1800s, the historical Meriweather Lewis had for a time possessed the green jade ring that in a future century Laura Palmer would put on her finger in *Fire Walk With Me*.

In *Blue Velvet* (1986), MacLachlan played a detective figure in a woodsy town of neighborhoods, where bad things are happening. The film had the air of Lynch's beloved 1950s: the way people dressed and combed their hair, the vibe of well-mannered teens in love, vintage songs, safe and secure family life, homey living rooms, an old-style café—but there were late-model cars on the streets and computers in the police station. This is Lynch's genius, to subtly tease our brains with uncertainty and open us to suggestiveness, to give us a shiver of dislocation and immerse us in a reflection of reality/realities, where the clock on the wall is a melting Salvador Dali watch: dreamtime.

Twin Peaks exists in "future past," especially after *Fire Walk With Me*, which Lynch wrote with Robert Engels, not Mark Frost. Laura Palmer, in the last seven days leading up to her murder, has a dream in which Agent Cooper, in the other-dimensional Red Room days after her death, tells her not to "take the ring," the jade ring inscribed with a symbol from the Owl Cave petroglyph (a diamond shape between two peaks). A few nights later, in an act of self-sacrificing heroism, she chooses to slip on the jade ring and be stabbed to death by her Bob-possessed father. In the "real" world, Agent Cooper hasn't even come to Twin Peaks yet, but after dying, Laura joins him in the Red Room. So the ring can both mark you for death and transport you across time and space.

In *The Secret History of Twin Peaks*, Mark Frost isn't saying that Meriweather Lewis puts on the ring and suddenly appears next to presidential candidate Donald Trump and lectures him on truth-telling and honorable behavior, though Frost is an anti-Trump partisan. By 2016, the twenty-seventh year of the *Twin Peaks* saga, the jade ring and the slipperiness of time and space were fundamental principles of the *Twin Peaks* universe, like the Red Room, cherry pie, coffee, electricity, wind, people, and beings with multiple identities, the wisdom of intuition. In Frost's book, the ring didn't transport Meriweather Lewis anywhere; in fact, it was stolen from him. But Frost's linkage of a nineteenth-century historical figure with a mystical-power object we've seen only in our time just fits in the world of *Twin Peaks*. We read it and think, Of course. And our second thought is, What would have happened if Lewis had slipped the ring on?

Frost's historical/fictional Lewis reinforces the idea that strange, dark forces have haunted the Northwest woods throughout recorded time, and beyond, a major thematic thread that Native American Deputy Hawk and Sheriff Truman introduced early in *Twin Peaks*. Frost's Archivist surmises that Lewis's mission, in addition to blazing a Northwest Passage (the original title of *Twin Peaks*) to the west coast, was to secretly investigate Northwest mysteries like a tribe of "white Indians," "quasi-mythical beasts," and a "race of giants." Frost reproduces a weathered journal entry of Lewis's "vision quest" at "the place by the falls and the twin mountains." Following the directions of a Native American, and perhaps in the grip of a fever, Lewis experiences "Lights from the sky, the silvery spheres . . . music, like some heavenly choir . . . fire that burns but does not consume . . . colors flowing from all things . . . gold, bright, and shiny . . . the secret deep within the color red." He also refers to classical statuary and black lines (like in the Red Room) and Ben Franklin's "mysterious force" (electricity), an encounter with a "silent man," and "a warning." In summation: Frost's Northwest Passage immerses us in the *mysterium* of *Twin Peaks.*

Our brains seem made to discern meaningful patterns in gathered bits of data, to seek knowledge. The most ancient narrative about gaining the power of knowledge is the eighth-century BC account of the Greek farmer-poet Hesiod, who wrote of the demigod Prometheus stealing fire from the ultimate god, Zeus. The fire has been interpreted as mechanical skills, science, language, imagination, consciousness itself. Prometheus's defiant, heroic effort enabled humankind to thrive in bliss and harmony, but our benefactor paid with his life. Then Zeus, still angry, created Pandora and sent her to earth, with a mysterious box. She couldn't suppress her burning desire to know what was inside, so she lifted the lid, and storm and fury, care and woe, and all possible manifestations of evil surged into our world.

Did you get the message, humankind? Don't question or provoke the Divine Order, the political overlord, the status quo wisdom. Accept the way the maps have been drawn, the boundary lines established, the physics calculated, what the Warren Report concluded. You know all you need to know, the facts are the facts, the truth the truth. Live with it, or there'll be trouble.

But as Lynch wrote in the 1990s' *Twin Peaks,* "The magician longs to see." He and Frost, in their psyches and their creations, venture forth, beyond the way things have always been, into the mysteries. They're spiritual seekers who believe that gaining knowledge and determining what is true (these days there are fake "facts" and gradations of "truth") ultimately lead to planetary wisdom and enlightenment, the meaning of all the meanings.

In real life, Meriweather Lewis heroically trekked to the western edge of the country, saw sights no white American man had ever seen, wrote about them, and returned to civilization, where Thomas Jefferson praised his "luminous intellect." Jefferson's further words lauding Lewis's sterling qualities could be describing Agent Dale Cooper: "his firmness and perseverance of purpose which nothing but impossibilities could divert from its direction" (though Cooper's through-line mission will suffer some setbacks in *The Return*). Lewis was not diverted, but he died a mysterious death, either by his own hand or an assassin's bullet. Frost's narrative hints at a shadowy conspiracy that wanted to keep a lid on some of the things that Lewis discovered in the Northwest or that saw Lewis as a threat to their financial aspirations and power schemes. Having used an historical figure to introduce the tension between knowledge seekers and the forces ready to suppress them, Frost branches the theme forward closer to our time.

In ways delightful/irritating/confounding, the new *Twin Peaks* could foil our expectations. In his book, the nimble Mark Frost makes aged sensualist buffoon Dougie Milford—who died on the night of his wedding to a teenage gold-digging vixen in the original series—our guide into the Unknown. In his years with the Boy Scouts, Dougie had seen "a giant" and a "walking owl tall as a man" in the forest around Twin Peaks. In the series, the Log Lady had warned that "the owls are not what they seem," and Frost's book hints that the tall owls with their big eyes are the familiar extraterrestrial "grays" of UFO encounter accounts and films like *Close Encounters of the Third Kind.*

Through a collage of documents, Frost's book chronicles the fascinating life Dougie led after leaving Twin Peaks as a "wayward, black sheep" young man. He worked in New Mexico on the Manhattan Project developing the first atomic bomb. He was at Roswell when the "UFO crash" and possible cover-up occurred and saw something that reminded him of his "large walking owl" experience. In our real-world history, two weeks before the Roswell incident, an Idaho pilot flying over Washington State's Mount Rainier spotted nine flashing objects flying "like a saucer would if you skipped it over water." This was the beginning of the modern flying saucer era and culture. Centuries ago, the Old Testament book of Ezekiel spoke of paranormal beings and their wheel floating in the air. Ezekiel uses the ancient Hebrew term "hashmal" to describe the amber, burnished-brass, glowing radiance of this vision/visitation. In modern Hebrew, "hashmal" means electricity, an organizing principle of David Lynch's mystical cosmology.

Frost's book goes on to tell us that Dougie Milford was recruited into the ranks of the knowledge suppressors, the anonymous Men in Black who intimidated UFO witnesses into silence. Then Frost, good dramatist that he is, reverses direction and has Milford himself experience the first close encounter of the third kind near Twin Peaks, in the same area where, as a youth twenty years earlier, he'd seen the Owl Cave pictographs and the "owl that walked like a man." Young Milford had also seen a flying craft abduct two children, who grew up to be the Log Lady and Fat Trout Trailer Park manager Carl Rodd who, in *Fire Walk With Me,* with a haunted, burned-out look, says, "I don't want to go anywhere; I've already been places." Frost introduces the idea of "masking memories." Shadowy government elites try to contain and cover up paranormal happenings, but the human mind that's had a traumatic, uncanny experience may create its own mask, a numbing fog of forgetting or a new protective narrative of reality to bury some horror. Lynch explored this idea in *Lost Highway,* his 1997 film, in which a murderer unconsciously makes himself into a new, innocent man. The idea of thought-created physical beings will be a key part of *The Return.*

Frost's book is a pulsing, decades-spanning electromagnetic network of paranormal, unexplained happenings. Its + and – poles are mystery and wonder/

fear and secrecy and power-grabbing, its magnetic north the Northwest. In the 1800s, in the area that will become Twin Peaks, we find Native American Chief Joseph (historical), who (fiction) obtains power from the Sky People so that he can confuse his enemies with moving clouds of smoke. He has metaphysical "congress" with the "'Great Spirit Chief' who rules above." But he can't prevent the white men from stealing tribal territory. This evildoing awakens a "powerful medicine," and it is known that "there will come a reckoning." There are malevolent Lemurians living underground beneath Mount Rainier (when Frost and Lynch first met in the 1980s, they talked about doing a Lemurian-centric series) who war with benevolent Teros who visit from the stars. Washington State provides the plutonium for the first New Mexico Manhattan Project atom bomb (historical), and a few years later, the bomb's horrendous killing power has decimated Hiroshima and Nagasaki, and we're in the desert again for another dark process.

Jack Parsons (all details historical), Pasadena rocketry wizard and founder of the Jet Propulsion Lab, was an acolyte of the notorious British occultist Aleister Crowley, who led his lodge followers, including Parsons, in anti-Christian, sex-and-drugs-fueled black magical practices in a wealthy Pasadena neighborhood. Parsons also associated with science fiction author L. Ron Hubbard, who would found his own religion, Scientology. In Frost's fiction, Dougie Milford interviewed Parsons, and when he heard of Parsons and Hubbard's paranormal endeavors, he got a shivery reminder of his own strange experiences as a youth in Twin Peaks. (Historical to end of paragraph): Parsons and Hubbard attempted to open a portal that would give the Book of Revelations's evil "Whore of Babylon" access to our world. Later Parsons met and married Marjorie Cameron, painter of haunted landscapes and monsters who saw herself as "Babalon" and portrayed the dark entity in underground filmmaker Kenneth Anger's *Lucifer Rising* (1964). After a life of extreme ups and downs, explosives expert Parsons blew himself up, by accident or on purpose, in a Pasadena carriage house. (I've been fascinated by Parsons's saga for years; Linda and I visited the California sites of his story.)

Back to Frost's fiction: Dougie Milford's adventures link to the mystery of JFK's assassination (a mutual interest of Frost and Lynch) and a big reveal about tricky Dick Nixon: the forty-sixth president knew that UFOs and alien visitations were real, and he urged Milford to "dig" and keep an open mind in his pursuit of the truth. And the truth might not come just from other planets, for young Margaret Lanterman, after her lost-time disappearance and return, spoke of "life from other places," other dimensions. The idea arises that high government officials not only knew about alien visitations, they struck a deal with the supremely powerful visitors after being presented with two choices. We, Earth, could give up our nuclear weapons and all would be good, or we could keep our nuclear firepower if we gave the visitors human genetic material for their own purposes. Call it a devil's bargain—we chose the latter.

We learn that FBI Deputy Director Gordon Cole (David Lynch) and Agent Phillip Jeffries (David Bowie in *Fire Walk With Me*) were the most gifted graduates of the FBI Academy. And that Major Briggs (Don Davis), whose secret array of scanning technology, hidden in the wooded mountains of Twin Peaks, was seeking to detect signs of intelligent nonhuman life in space and on Earth. Briggs had inherited the post of quester number one from Dougie Milford. Briggs is the Archivist of Frost's book, and he's ready to hand the bulging dossier over to his replacement, Agent Dale Cooper.

It's the next day, after *Twin Peaks*'s last 1991 episode. The good Cooper's trapped in the Red Room/Black Lodge with post-death Laura Palmer. The Bad Cooper, possessed by Bob, is out in the world, and he comes to get the dossier from Briggs. The major can sense that "something's wrong" (the idea/abstraction/words "something bad is happening"), so he heads for his mountain listening station with an emergency strategy in mind.

Agent TP, whose margin notes we've read throughout *The Secret History of Twin Peaks*, is revealed to be FBI Agent Tamara Preston, who muses on Gordon Cole's thought that life is "waiting for the right moment," implying volitional agency, willful human action. But Lynch has told me that "things happen when they're supposed to." Human volition, being proactive, fate, karma, the will of the gods—who's running the Big Show, anyway?

Frost's book, which some took to be the first, written, part of *The Return*, was lauded for its deep immersion in historical/metaphysical/paranormal themes and hints of possible new storylines. But some devotees of 1990-91's *Twin Peaks* were dismayed by Frost's treatment of certain familiar town residents' stories: some established timelines and character points were different in the book. Frost, the vocabulary master's response was, "Reality is fungible," meaning "one instance or portion may be replaced by another." As Sailor Ripley (Nicolas Cage) pointedly said in Lynch's *Wild at Heart*: "Uh-oh." We remember the charges thrown at the original *Twin Peaks*: "Anything goes," "They're making it up as they go along," "They're putting in weird stuff just for the sake of being different."

Given the abiding cultural presence of the 1990-91 *Twin Peaks, Fire Walk With Me*, and almost three decades of fan chatter, analytical books, media interest, documentary films, Mark Frost's book, and the anticipation for *The Return*, we are arguably more aware of the show's creators, the two men behind the camera with their script pages (that sometimes get thrown away) than for any other show in TV history. So, "Reality is fungible." So now they're going to be monkeying with fixed elements of the story and characters we know and love? Altering and interchanging parts of the way things are? How can Lynch, as he likes to do, float us into a dream that blossoms organically if we hear the disruptive pounding hammers of story-building? What if we can't stop thinking about the puppet masters pulling the strings? Is Frost's book the new normal, the template for *The Return*?

At a March, 2017 TV Critics Association conference, Lynch was asked what he thought of his *Twin Peaks* co-creator partner's book, published five months earlier. He said, "I haven't read it. It's his history of Twin Peaks." Traveling through the *Twin Peaks* forest, Lynch and Frost may be on forking paths. We each live within the bubble of our own subjective consciousness, our version of reality; wars are fought over the inability to perceive common ground, shared purpose. Frost has said,"It's our prerogative to change reality," as individuals and as showrunners. Flux, change, metamorphosis, relativity will be core themes of *The Return*.

–CHAPTER SEVEN–

THE EVENING STAR

I don't have cable TV, so my longtime friends Janice and Paul invited me over for *The Return*'s May 21, 2017, debut. A projector TV set-up, an eleven-foot-wide screen, full Dolby sound, comfortable couch, friendly cats, home-cooked food—is this not living? Over the hiss and scent of frying onions, Janice asked in a tender voice, "Would Linda be here tonight?" Meaning, if Linda were alive would she be as excited about the new *Twin Peaks* as Janice and I were.

As if to illustrate the *Twin Peaks* theme of individuals having multiple personae, Linda and I, for thirty-five years, had been friends, lovers, resentful combatants, and happy traveling companions, all under the sign of love and deep intimacy. We lived apart, but were truly together. Decades ago, she had evaded the cancer that tried to possess her, but in 2016 it was back, and hungry. After a year of medical procedures and interventions, Linda chose not to "rage against the dying of the light," but to "go gentle into that good night." Gentleness is a relative term: she endured fear and pain and her body's every indignity. But being Linda, she cared about how all of us caregivers were bearing up: "I *would* have to do this at Christmas time."

From the *pilot* episode onward, Linda and I had watched the 1990-91 *Twin Peaks* together, and the scene in which Cooper helps ease the dying Leland out of this world crossed my mind when I sat on Linda's bed holding *The Tibetan Book of the Dead*. Linda read widely in a multitude of spiritual traditions, but she was a no-nonsense "when the brain dies, it's all over" girl, whereas I'm an afterlife hopeful. Still, she listened intently as I read aloud about what outlives the body: "the indestructible drop of the subtlest wind-energies coordinated with the clear light transparency intuition, the subtlest mind and seed of enlightenment."

Near the end, she was setting her emotional house in order and atoning "for some of the shit I've done." On a rare bright and sunny winter day in Seattle, she looked from the light falling in from the window up to the sky and some luminous clouds and said, "It would be nice to be up there in the warmth and the light and be part of the energy, something that flows on."

The number of words she spoke dwindled, but her small voice remained focused and impassioned: "I'm sorry," "Thank you," "I love you," the latter being her second-to-last words. Her final word was "pajamas," meaning time for bed. Linda loved Christmas, but it was too sad for both of us to hear the seasonal music when we were together at the end. Still, I had the radio music on a lot when I was by myself. The first time I turned it on after she died, Ringo was singing the John Lennon-penned hymn "Good night, good night; good night, sleep tight, dream sweet dreams for me." I will try.

Linda once gave a public presentation on the transcendent glory of David Lynch's *Mulholland Drive*. On another night in a backstage green room, she'd talked brassiere brands with Lynch's ex-lover Isabella Rossellini as they changed clothes. And in Lynch's Hollywood Hills house next to Mulholland Drive, he'd looked Linda in the eyes and said, "I love the female psyche." Yes, Linda would have been with us for the premiere of *The Return*, the further story of a dead woman who lives.

Going over Linda's belongings, I came upon something she'd left for me to find, a book of poems by Louise Glück. There was a bookmark at the poem *The Evening Star*. As the earth darkened, "the first star seemed to increase in brilliance." Its "light, which was the light of death, seemed to restore to earth its power to console." The light is "enough to make my thought visible again." I'll be on the lookout, Sweetie.

–CHAPTER EIGHT–

NOW IT'S DARK
(PARTS ONE AND TWO)

Out of darkness our seeking eyes ride a wind sound, fast, jolting left-right across the Red Room's zigzag black-and-white floor, dizzily tipping-falling into the red curtains. David Lynch masters contrast, cutting directly to visual calm, the inner heart of the Red Room, one of the most evocative spaces in art history. Watching in the present, we are experiencing the past, a key passage from the original, 1990-91 *Twin Peaks* (hereafter referred to as *Twin Peaks*). Agent Dale Cooper and Laura Palmer, icons when separate and paired, sit in dark chairs before the curtains' ruddy glow, he in his black suit, she golden in a black gown. Still coquettish after death, she gives him a wink and says (in garbled backward speech), "I'll see you again in twenty-five years. Meanwhile . . . " Then she poses her hands in a graceful gesture that suggests curvaceous musical notes. In *Twin Peaks,* Frost and Lynch's personal spiritual interests cast deathly matters in a Tibetan Buddhist radiance, having Cooper guide the dying Leland Palmer "into the light" and, without using the term, implying that Laura is in a post-death Bardo state in the Red Room, a "waiting room" between incarnations. Laura's hand pose suggests the gestures of Tibetan monks, who move their hands gracefully in the air, feeling currents of spirit energy. In our culture, Laura's hand pose is a womanly gesture, a marker of curving beauty and a reminder of the female energies that have aided Cooper's quest to right wrongs and restore order, energies that David Lynch reveres. He believes there's a primal female spiritual power abiding at the heart of time, so "Meanwhile. . . " is now and forever. From the 1990-91 *Twin Peaks* onward, Laura has been "full of secrets," and perhaps Lynch included this older footage in *The Return* to stress Laura's personification of mystery. For Laura's hand pose echoes a moment in *Fire Walk With Me* (which Lynch considers required homework for fully experiencing *The Return*) when highschooler Laura, alone in her bedroom, lifts her ceramic desk lamp. Holding the lamp, her hands are in the "Meanwhile. . . " gesture position, and she's lifting the lamp to retrieve the key to her secret diary, her hidden life. The lamp is not lit, but she is on a path to spiritual illumination, though she doesn't know it.

After speaking to Cooper and posing her hands, Laura snaps her fingers in the air, making a clicking sound like a light switch. Twenty-seven years later, in *The Return*, Lynch's sound design melds the inorganic and the organic in a mechanical click that sounds like a fragment of garbled speech; perhaps this is the Voice of the *Twin Peaks* saga's highest power. In the 1940s, visionary author-thinker Philip K. Dick (1928-1982) was taking a high-stakes physics exam in order to be accepted for college. He needed a single answer but went blank, frozen with anxiety. All was lost when a voice with a mechanical quality "clicked on" and gave him the answer.

Over his seven decades of life, David Lynch has had to shoulder many grown-up responsibilities, but in terms of the occupation of his life, what he faces every morning when he gets up (with the alarm set for a time that adds up to seven), he's still a school kid, sensitive to what the world will show and tell him. He retains a touch of his childhood agoraphobia (the world out there can be scary), he's drawn to things that give him "an air of euphoria" (peachy keen), he's on the lookout for license plates with his DKL initials when driving (very carefully). Thrilled by the mystery of it all, he is looking for signs and meanings that will help him survive and thrive today and tomorrow, while in his deep self he's on alert for the coordinates of eternity. In *The Return*, he has eighteen hours to immerse us in his primal concerns, to show us a confounding, challenging, and revealing way to look at existence and consciousness, a chance to open our eyes and minds and grow a bunch of new neurons just to keep up.

Twenty-five years ago in the Red Room, Laura's hands form a graceful primordial feminine gesture. Then her image fades and blends with a golden orb in a mist of radiant light, and we're looking down from high above Twin Peaks's forests. A girl runs screaming the day Laura died, then Laura's close-up golden homecoming queen photograph mists away, and we're traveling over rocky ground, which drops out from under us. We're vertiginously hanging in the air looking straight down at the torrent of White Tail Falls, falling from foreground to deep below, where the surging white cascade strikes calm, dark-blue river water. While the opening credits roll, we stare at the falling water's pulsing white spray, ever-blossoming like a blue rose. The flower shape becomes the red curtains, guttering like fires of desire and danger, then the optic maelstrom of the zigzag floor as it lurches between suggesting jagged mountain peaks and hungry teeth that can tear and devour.

The opening moments of the original *Twin Peaks* were more earthbound and tranquil, a welcoming nest of a Northwest place: a bird on a bough, lazy smoke from sawmill stacks, the falls in a picture postcard view, ducks on a serene pond. The beginning of *The Return* feels disquieting and aggressive; the energies at work unstable, intense. The high aerial perspective of the forest suggests new horizons far beyond the town borders, our familiar dimension and some other one/ones blending and tipping and flying into our faces. We'd better hang on tight for this ride. Perhaps the abiding golden spirit of Laura will help us keep our bearings, the smiling, laughing Laura, transcendent after death.

But Laura's grace-manifesting luminescence is out of reach: Lynch puts us in a black-and-white place. (Black and white, darkness and light, the primal dynamic of Lynch's moral universe and a mainstay of his aesthetic: *Eraserhead*, *The Elephant Man*, still photos, drawings and prints, his and Agent Cooper's iconic attire.) Cooper is sitting in a dark space in a dark chair opposite the Giant (Carel Stuycken) in a similar chair. In *Twin Peaks*, the Giant (a David Lynch character-story idea) could appear out of thin air to give Cooper cryptic hints that aided his investigation of Laura Palmer's murder. Lynch and Frost, obsessed with the existential mysteries of human/cosmic consciousness, have created a fictional universe with its own paranormal structure of time and space and behavior, where immensely powerful, enigmatic forces and entities are seeking what they want, and their desires can wound and destroy human bodies and minds. The dark forces are almost overwhelming; the people resisting and confronting them are frail in comparison, even a supremely gifted and brave man like Cooper often feels like he's lost all human agency. To navigate the *Twin Peaks* world, he needs some compass that hasn't been invented yet. And it's Lynch and Frost's genius to make us feel as wind-whipped by confusion and dismay as Cooper; like our special agent, we must gather clues where we may.

In *The Return*, the Giant is called the Fireman and is a more powerful upholder of goodness who seeks to quell and extinguish the metaphorical fires that consume souls. (The phrase "Fire walk with me," from the original *Twin Peaks*, evokes the devilish flames of dark magic.) In his black-and-white realm, the Fireman has brought Cooper to him for some schooling (a physical manifestation of the idea "Get the truth down in black and white.") From the funnel-shaped horn of an ancient gramophone comes a mechanical/organic click sound that suggests garbled speech, in seven short bursts (Lynch's favorite number, seven, will add Pythagorean structure to *The Return*). We feel that the sounds (the Voice) carry a heavy metaphysical weight, perhaps resonating matters of life and death and afterlife, and that the Fireman understands them, but they are unintelligible to Cooper. Perhaps they are, as nineteenth-century English visionary poet-artist William Blake said, "portions of eternity too great" for the interpretive senses of humankind. Or maybe they're vital secrets that Cooper can comprehend only in a more evolved state of consciousness. There aren't posted road signs for the natural laws of this place, but the Fireman has some solid information. "Remember 430" (it adds up to 7), "Richard and Linda," "Two birds with one stone." Cooper says, "I understand." We don't understand, but Lynch and Frost know that early in *The Return*, they've planted major seeds that will activate our perceptive and detective skills. The Fireman makes Cooper flicker in his chair, and vanish.

Cooper and the Giant/Fireman's sit-down is the first we've seen of these two in over two decades, and now, once again, we're back in Twin Peaks, the familiar mountains and the woods, where a red truck is backing slowly through the evergreens. After it makes its delivery, it will retrace its path going forward: a primal metaphor for the flow of time and space in *The Return*. The truck stops next to Dr. Jacoby's (Russ Tamblyn) funky trailer in the trees, and the driver and Jacoby exchange a few words as they offload boxes of brand-new shovels. Lynch's staging and editing of this scene make it feel like real time, in other words, a long time compared with standard TV scene pacing. As long as he's been making films and TV shows, Lynch has said he wants to float us into a dream, to leave us room and time to dream. For viewers who can relax their reflexive impatience and sink into a more contemplative narrative time flow, *The Return* will indeed be an immersion in dreamland. There's no big-size, medium-size, or small-size drama in Jacoby's scene, but it shows Lynch's sensitivity to, and reverence for, the things of everyday life. And characteristically, the director does not break up the flow of the scene by cutting in for close-ups; we watch at a distance, figures in a landscape, like one of Lynch's paintings. And the director makes a wonderfully subtle, evocative choice. He frames the delivery truck and Jacoby small in the background between the trunks of two big evergreen trees, large in the foreground. As the scene progresses, Lynch's camera (our point of view), almost imperceptibly, drifts slightly to the right, pauses between the trees, and drifts back left. Almost subliminally, Lynch has made us sense an invisible presence or force at work in this world, a watcher in the woods.

Lynch always says that sound generates at least half of the power of the moving image arts, and beginning with his late-1960s short films, he's taken as much care with his sound design as he does composing and lighting images. Leading up to the premiere of *The Return*, there was much pleasurable anticipation of the lush Angelo Badalamenti music that would blanket the new eighteen hours as it did the original series. But aside from the beginning use of the "Twin Peaks Theme," hardly a note is heard for vast stretches of screen time. (Along with *The Return*'s slow pacing, this was a point of disgruntlement for some viewers/commentators.) In many ways, *The Return* will tip the known world on its axis, and not having the consistent comfort zone of Badalamenti's music is a disruptive lurch in that direction. Instead there are Lynch's sounds, which are as hard to put names on as the clickvoice of the Fireman's gramophone. The director feels that putting a name on something diminishes its power, but it can be said that through a fusion of natural, mechanical, and electrical sounds, he invades our ears and minds with atmospheres of wonder and dread, piped in from a steam-driven factory outside of time.

Following his law of juxtaposed contrasts, Lynch jumps us from the soft morning breeze of Dr. Jacoby's woods to the metropolitan roar of the city that never sleeps, New York, lit up at night. Surrounded by glowing steel skyscrapers is a big brick building oddly without lights, and an ominous rumble gets louder as the camera climbs up that structure's exterior. A blister of glass protrudes from the top floor, then we're through it and inside: Lynch always makes us aware of two or more worlds, and the passage between them.

Inside, the glass forms a massive cube structure sitting atop a black tangle of humming machines and cables—this must be where the building's electricity is going. The cube sits in a large warehouse space that's a subtle marvel of Lynchian design: beige-gray concrete walls, black metal accents, brown cardboard boxes strewn around the floor. Spotlights on black stalks are symmetrically placed around the cube. It's the center of attention, and young Sam Colby (Ben Rosenfield) is paid to watch it and change the batteries and computer cards of high-tech recording devices. An anonymous billionaire is funding this experimental project, and the guy who previously had Sam's job said that once "something" did appear in the box.

Sam's dedicated focus on the box and the circular aperture that connects it to the exterior glass blister builds tense anticipation. Surely something will appear; will something appear? There are electronic locks between the room and the smaller room where the security guard sits. When the guard isn't at his post, Sam sneaks his friend Tracey (Madeline Zima) in (she's wearing a camel-colored coat to harmonize with the cube room). In a Lynchian twinning tableau, the two sit opposite the cube and sip coffee in unison. Then Tracey's coat and black panties are on the floor, and she's straddling naked Sam and moaning with pleasure. We're holding our breath, and Sam, who can see the box behind her, says, "Stop," and she looks over her shoulder (at us). Across the space the cube darkens and a black-and-white image of a blurry pale figure appears, a naked woman with a blob head, featureless except for a gaping mouth hole. Is it some kind of hologram, an electronic illusion? Are we willing what happens next to happen? Of course, the glass shatters, Tracey and Sam scream as the creature's point of view (now ours) dives onto them, its head-mouth thrashing and thrusting at an insane speed: composition in beige-gray, black and white, flesh and blood. And perhaps a cautionary tale for us viewers: watching the glass box (TV and all our screens) can be dangerous—or was it the sex that aroused the hungry demon? Is this entity the ultimate form of evil in the *Twin Peaks* universe? Or some very powerful underling, kin to Bob or a grade above or below him? Perhaps for Lynch, she's a Raksasa, a female demon from the Hindu tales he studies.

Essays and books have been written about how we viewers can abhor violence in real life and do everything in our power to prevent it, yet we lap it up on-screen. The atavistic, reptilian part of our brain (I must live, I'm hungry, I want sex, you must die if you threaten me) likes to be fed, and vicariously through art, the civilized angel of our natures enjoys the meal and gets a transgressive, cathartic thrill. As Freud said, in our subconscious, we're all rapists and murderers. Lynch's violence is always powerful, but it's generally on the I stab you/I shoot you level. He says that in his art "I like to go deep," and in his canon the visceral horror of the cube room feeding frenzy is surpassed only by *Eraserhead*'s Henry cutting open his mutant, yet human, baby.

The cube room episode is one of the great sequences of Lynch's career: its physical sparseness and minimal-drama buildup, the interplay between silence and subtle hums and drones, the hip/cool flirting of Sam and Tracey conveyed in body language and few words. We immediately like these kids, and then they're shredded by Otherness, some nameless horror we've never seen before. Could Lynch and Frost make a stronger statement that the world is not a safe place? That curiosity killed the cat?

In the eleven years since his last film, *INLAND EMPIRE*, Lynch has been an international peace ambassador for Transcendental Meditation and his David

Lynch Foundation, which teaches TM to traumatized war veterans and at-risk underprivileged youths. For most of his life Lynch has seen the world from a Hindu/Vedic perspective: the multifarious world, the trees, the cars, the people and cherry pies are all manifestations of oneness (Brahman), the All underlying everything, the one that displays as many. Twice daily, through meditation, Lynch taps into this single-point awareness and transcends the fear and anger and negativity of temporal life. He feels the expansive unity, the interconnectedness of all things, and is better able to radiate harmony and positivity into the world.

Thirty-one years ago, in the furor over the sexualized violence of *Blue Velvet*, some saw Lynch as an exploitive, almost satanic perpetrator of toxic darkness, a dangerous male who, according to a panel of feminists, was a threat to women and should never be allowed to make another film. The great poet Allen Ginsberg once said that to truly represent humankind, the artist must have supper with both God and the Devil. Just because Lynch can put soul-wrenching darkness on screen like nobody else doesn't mean that he's trying to extinguish the light. In darkness, the light shines brighter; it's a blessed treasure to seek. As he once said to me, "Let's pump some coherence into the world and get on with a beautiful life."

My book *David Lynch: Beautiful Dark* was defensive on Lynch's behalf, an effort to present the full spectrum of his humanity and his art. Today his artistic genius and personal beneficence are status quo knowledge, and his portrayal of FBI Director Gordon Cole in *The Return* (for more screen time than we expected) underscores his capacity for empathy and goodwill. Lynch's warmth toward longtime friends and collaborators Catherine Coulson (the Log Lady), Harry Dean Stanton (Carl Rodd), and Miguel Ferrer (Albert Rosenfield), all of whom barley outlived their performances, is palpable. And *The Return* honors Lynch's friends and masters in the art world that he's devoted his life to. The sympathetic character Bushnell Mullins (Don Murray) is named for Bushnell Keeler (1925-1987), the man who inspired and furthered young Lynch's art-making journey. In the 1960s, when Lynch was embarking on his Art Life, as he calls it, his eyes and mind were blasted by the work of British painter Francis Bacon (1909-1992), who's had more influence on Lynch's imagery than any other artist. Lynch appreciated the quirky ideas and creations of the European Surrealists and the bold, spontaneous intuitions in action of the American abstract expressionists, but Bacon's paintings were magical. This artist treated human flesh like a moldable, sculptural material, much as when, in *The Return*, Bad Cooper (Kyle MacLachlan) grips a man's face with his hand and slowly kneads and pushes it around like it was putty. As a child, Lynch felt "a wild pain and decay" inside people and things, and Bacon seemed to feel it too, giving it painterly expression in contorted bodies and faces twisting in existential anguish or slipping into dark, atavistic/animalistic contours. There are no weapons in Bacon's paintings, but they emanate emotional violence and mutilated spirits. Bacon often played off the soft, rounded curves of his disturbingly mutating figures and faces against a geometric tracery of faint white lines that enclosed the organic forms. The geometric lines joined at ninety-degree corners, so the organic forms floated within a cube shape, like the demon within Lynch's glass cube. And the entities within both artists' cube forms have heads that are mostly mouth holes. Bacon's mouths gasp in horror, or scream. Lynch's tear and suck and liquify.

Twin Peaks makes us feel the darkness and fear, but what about light and love? An archetype of life and art: an heroic man risks his life to rescue a beautiful woman from the clutches of evil, thus banishing or destroying the evil. Whether it's his karma in action or just his damn fine set of values and skills, Dale Cooper is such a man. At the end of the original *Twin Peaks*, he risked body and soul, entering the otherworldly Black Lodge/Red Room to save his love Annie Blackburn (Heather Graham). We saw Cooper and Annie emerge in the woods, free of the lodge. But we soon learned that this Cooper was the dark half of Cooper's psyche, possessed by Bob, while the "good" Dale is trapped in the Black Lodge/Red Room, unbeknown to the world at large.

Now, twenty-five years after Cooper sat in the Red Room across from the spiritually radiant post-death Laura Palmer, he sits in his familiar dark chair opposite the One-Armed Man (Al Strobel), a member of the otherworldly crew of spirits that includes the Man from Another Place (Michael J. Anderson) and Bob (Frank Silva). Bob is perpetual evil, as foundational as darkness, whereas the One-Armed Man and the Man from Another Place are more complex, at various times helping or hindering the forces of good. Alternating, wavering, being this way now, that way then, or presenting as one but being two. Since childhood, Lynch has been fascinated by electricity, seeing it as a magical invisible force within the walls of houses, and it's a key conceptual and aesthetic theme of *The Return*. The seeming singleness of the electrical flow that powers the world is actually the enlivened alternation of energy between negative and positive poles: doubleness. In Lynchworld, electricity can throw bright, rational light on a subject or be a free-ride conduit for wild, infernal powers and entities. Lynch links the uncanny trio of Bob, the Man from Another Place, and the One-Armed Man with electrical forces, and at various times the Man from Another Place and the One-Armed Man pointedly say "E-lec-tricity!" like a mantra. These two can warm you or zap you, but in *The Return*, the One-Armed Man is solid-state on Cooper's side and, like the Fireman, gives him cryptic guidance.

In the Red Room, the One-Armed Man asks Cooper *The Return*'s seminal question: "Is it future, or is it past?" This is new, 2015 footage, as was the earlier scene of Cooper getting instructions from the Fireman, but which really came first? Will *The Return* present itself in chronological order, or will it be steered by Lynch's love of the way, In *Fire Walk With Me*, Dale Cooper somehow interacts with the dead-yet-alive Laura Palmer before he first comes to Twin Peaks to investigate her murder. The director makes us get the point twice, as the One-Armed Man repeats, "Is it future or is it past?" A primal idea to tweak our minds as we watch.

The One-Armed Man vanishes from the Red Room, and at last: the eternal feminine, the lost and found soul, the Homecoming Queen of the Night, Laura Palmer. *Fire Walk With Me* showed us her last seven days, her body and spirit debased by drugs and prostitution, anguished and terrified by the realization that the Bob who rapes her at night is inhabiting her father's body and that Bob wants to possess her completely. A young woman who loved life and her friends and the men she chose to be with feels reduced to ashes and dust. But an angelic spark is still alive within her, and in order to contain Bob's deep evil, to keep herself from spreading its contagion to those dear to her, she lets herself be killed. She's taken on her community's sins, and after death, in the Red Room, she's blessed by a floating Christian angel and smiles and laughs in bliss. As Cherubini's Requiem in C minor chorus swells on the soundtrack, Laura enjoys a Christian transcendence. (Lynch was raised Presbyterian and believes in actual angels). The good Dale Cooper (as opposed to the Bob-possessed one out in the world), with his air of Asian wisdom and Tibetan spirituality, stands at Laura's side. (Lynch studies Hindu scriptures and believes in karma and reincarnation, and the Red Room, which is his invention, is a "waiting room" between incarnations.) So this scene projects the full spectrum of Lynch's spiritual nature, stirred by a prevailing breeze from the East.

From the beginnings of recorded human life and thought, mystery has reigned supreme. There have always been more questions than answers from scientists, religious believers, and everyday dreamers. Are we just bundles of cells and atoms who get up striving forward every day just so the human race can reproduce itself? Have gods/God set us in motion on a self-improvement course that can span many lifetimes? Are we pawns in a cosmic battle that will someday conclude and then start all over again? Lynch and Frost envelope us in the *Twin Peaks* universe, which has its own physics and natural laws, and it's up to us to make our ways through its mysterious maze. It's a place of vertical hierarchies. FBI is above local law enforcement, mystical FBI (Dale Cooper, Gordon Cole, Phillip Jeffries) is above regular FBI, Major Briggs has an overview above theirs, and on a higher, esoteric, unquantifiable plane, the Giant of goodness, the Fireman. Then, perhaps in the fullness of time, the spirit of Laura Palmer as female godhead, the Bringer of Light. On the dark side, local criminals are beneath Windom Earle, psychotic former FBI partner of Dale Cooper, master of mayhem and seeker of supernatural power—but Bob can, at will, vaporize Earle's soul. Because Lynch and Frost leave us in the dark about Bob's origins and ultimate aims, and limit our experience of him, we see him as primal evil, and our primal fear, personified. He's one of the scariest things to ever haunt the moving image arts.

This is the basic power structure of *Twin Peaks*, the map of its known/semi known world. But if Laura Palmer is "the One," as the Log Lady reminds us, who is or can become the goddess of goodness, then there's a gap on the dark side. Something needs to appear in the glass cube. Having talked to Lynch as much as I have since the early 1990s, I've absorbed his belief in intuition. Over the years I sensed that Bob was not the highest power of evil in *Twin Peaks*, and in 2008 I suggested in print (*David Lynch: Beautiful Dark*, page 392) that the Judy that's mentioned in *Fire Walk With Me* is a malevolent mother goddess above Bob: she's "the ultimate authority/ spiritual figure" of his realm. In the ten years leading up to *The Return*, I didn't encounter anyone else positing the Judy/dark goddess idea, so when the demonic female figure appeared in the glass cube and went into horrific action, I was more than electrified.

In *The Return*, when Lynch first took us to Twin Peaks and Dr. Jacoby's woodsy domain, he showed us an introductory place-identifying shot of the forested mountains, and later we quickly knew where we were coasting over New York at night. Now we're in no place, our point of view floating through the mystery of night, headlight beams thrusting out ahead as we advance down a dark road, on and on. The night road we're traveling isn't a paved highway like in *Wild at Heart* or *Lost Highway*; it's a dirt snake slithering through wilderness. The archetypal feeling of our point of view moving forward through the dark in silence is hypnotic—but Lynch shatters the flow with heavy drumbeats like gunshots, and a voice. Not the Fireman's click-sound voice from beyond: this is someone forcing song from a voice drowning in whisky, forcing unintelligible, aggressive words through a mouthful of smashed teeth and swollen tongue, malice as guttural sludge.

Lynch cuts to the sleek, dark car pulling its hungry mouth up into our faces. There is no license plate. This driver's aim is to find and feed on what he wants, and to not register on the screen of anyone who could slow him down. Of course, it has to be: Bad Cooper (Kyle MacLachlan), the Bob-inhabited shadow side of Agent Cooper, the better Cooper remaining trapped in the Red Room, as shown in *Twin Peaks*'s finale and *Fire Walk With Me*. Bad Cooper (Mr. C, as his criminal cohorts call him) is in the mode of the Lynchian badass: *The Elephant Man*'s Bytes, Sting's Feyd-Rautha in *Dune*, *Blue Velvet*'s Frank Booth, *Twin Peaks* and *Fire Walk With Me*'s Bobby Briggs, Bobby Peru in *Wild at Heart*. As a youth, Lynch was tempted by, but turned away from, the corrupting influence of bad company and behavior, but it swaggers through his work. Before *The Return* aired, some wondered if Lynch and Frost, with their love of characters having secrets, would present the possessed Cooper (Mr. C) as, outwardly, the good Dale that the community knew and loved, with his evil dark passenger hidden inside. He could move through the world as a handsome, bright, stylish, charismatic man clandestinely causing mayhem. But no, they have Mr. C dwell on Bob's jeans-and-long-greasy-hair level: backwoods shacks, out-of-work truckers, sleazy motels, women who hold a drink in one hand and a gun in the other while his hand explores between their thighs.

Mr. C wears the requisite black leather jacket (the classic talisman of bad boys from Lynch's 1950s youth onward) and black pants. Pulled back from his face, his black hair is long and rather stiff, perhaps held in place by the blood mist from point-blank killings. His eyes are black orbs (if the eyes are the windows of the soul), his unsmiling face stony. Sober and unemotional, Mr. C completely lacks Cooper's characteristic joie de vivre. He's an unholy mixture of Cooper's mental and physical prowess and Bob's devouring desire. He uses less than a third of his brain power to run a small-town South Dakota criminal operation with his low-life minions, sampling their women when he feels like it. The majority of his mental energy is devoted to seeking some hidden ultimate knowledge. He's familiar with metaphysical realms and beings, but there's something above and beyond him that he wants and can't reach.

Two decades ago, Lynch expressed his poetic gift for imagistic condensation in the phrase "Fire walk with me," an evocation of flaming dark powers and those who seek them. Mr. C carries a playing card that signifies the same message. It's a one-of-a-kind ace of spades. The little spade signs at the corners are disquieting in themselves: black inversions of the red heart, which is a symbol of love and illumination. Instead of a large spade sign/black heart occupying the card's center, there's a whorl of black energy, an irregular-bordered circular shape with little horn-like ears on top. The image is like a synthesis of Lynch's monoprint *Untitled (aces), 1997* (black oval head with gaping mouth) and collograph *Small dog with human head, 1998* (dog with black oval humanoid head, open mouth, horn-like ears). Mr. C, smart man, kills for strategic reasons, and before he offs a woman who plotted to have him killed, he shows her the card, emphasizing, "This is what I want," as in Life Goal. Traditionally the ace of spades is "the death card," an ominous omen of impending doom, and for Mr. C it has literal and esoteric meaning. The singular image on the card is truly disturbing: as David Lynch said of the traffic light stuck on red in the 1990s *Twin Peaks*, "It gives you the willies!" A simple form that's humanlike and bestial all at once, a sucking cosmic black hole and the devouring mouth of the demon in the New York glass box. The form has no name, we've never seen it before, but our psych knows enough to be terrified. Maybe the image is Mr C's mirror, showing him the pure monster he aspires to be, all the way to Bob and beyond, master of powers beyond imagining.

Bob's supernatural energies may course through Mr. C's body and mind, but he still has to live in, and negotiate with, the realm of human beings. He has to struggle. There are forces out to get him. The FBI Agent Phillip Jeffries he talks to on the phone may be an imposter. Can he even trust his neighborhood criminal allies? Mr. C wants what the black ace card represents, but he can't get there without some mysterious coordinates, and he has to rely on weaselly Ray Monroe (George Griffith) for that puzzle piece. Ray has sway with the secretary of high school Principal Bill Hastings, a man who will open up new, mysterious story vistas.

David Lynch is head-centric. He's spent at least six hundred fifty-seven thousand hours meditating. He feels that our bodies exist to carry our minds around, and the expressions of his mind have brought him worldwide acclaim and three properties in the Hollywood Hills. He likes to stay home, in a compound where he's got "a good setup." He can think and feel, discover ideas and write, and make music, paintings, and films. Aside from his private TM mantra, his motto is "Have final cut." Guard the sovereignty of your mind and its sacred products; have as much control as possible. Out in the uncontrollable world, Lynch can feel vulnerable. As his daughter Jennifer says, "He's got to put on some kind of actual armor. He's afraid of things coming at him, rather than him being able to observe them." Lynch's work portrays a correspondence between the head and the home, and both are places easily invaded and wounded, where, as he's told me, "things can go wrong." Physical trauma, of course, but most terrifying is realizing that invisible thought entities that aren't you—or maybe they are—dwell within you.

We already like short-haired Bill Hastings (Matthew Lillard), Buckhorn High School principal, because he reminds us of the short-haired principal of Twin Peaks High School, who announced the death of Laura Palmer to his student body, then broke down in wracking sobs. (The evil entity Bob had invaded Leland Palmer's head and house, so he could violate and kill Laura, metaphorically invading the whole-town house of Twin Peaks.) Bill Hastings is enjoying an afternoon in his cozy middle-class home when there's a knock on the door. It's the police. They arrest Bill and take him away in handcuffs. Lynch and Frost, masters of complex tonalities, add humor to emotional trauma as Bill's wife Phyllis says, "But the Morgans are coming for dinner tonight."

How bad can it be? The cops have found a slice of human tissue in Bill's Volvo, and his fingerprints are all over the apartment of Ruth Davenport (Mary Stofle), the town librarian, who's just a nodding acquaintance to Bill. Ruth's severed head is resting on her pillow, but the body lying under the covers belongs to some headless man. The tableau of the body (lumpy haunch prominent, all white, black and red) is another Lynch homage to Francis Bacon's paintings. And Lynch projects his own aesthetic by lighting the dark hallway leading to the horrific bedroom with reflected camera flashes from the forensic photographer just around the corner, evoking the blue-white electricity that's an otherworldly energy pulse in the *Twin Peaks* universe.

The Return is wall-to-wall with superb acting, but Matthew Lillard as Bill being interrogated by his fishing buddy police Detective Dave Macklay (Brent Briscoe) is outstanding. In a small, gray room they sit opposite each other, and we, Lynch's camera, and Dave are intent on Bill's face. Minute after minute, his face and voice communicating disbelief, nervous energy, growing fear as he forgets, then remembers everyday details (did he just pretend to forget?), Lynch doesn't cut away from the two men, so we sense Bill's growing anguish. When he looks to the side thinking, Isn't somebody out there going to help me? we feel his poignant separation from the free people just outside that room. Bill is so likable, so sincere—but does he know his own mind? He's genuinely shocked when he's told Ruth's been murdered, that his prints pepper her rooms. But strangely, he'd had a dream that he was in her apartment, "just a dream."

In 1987, I was in a large Seattle room with psychiatrists, psychologists, and assorted mental health professionals. We'd just watched *Blue Velvet*, and the scholarly moderator of the evening said, "I'm not familiar with David Lynch or his work, but this man has an understanding of human psychology that's at the genius level." Lynch's understanding of human nature comes from his life experiences, intuitions, and imagination, not book learning, and it deeply marks his work. He's fascinated by identity crises, secret selves, "things that are one way, and then you see that they're another way." (*Lynch on Lynch*). In *Twin Peaks*, the inhabiting spirit Bob makes Leland Palmer violate his own daughter for years, unconscious of his predator self. In *The Elephant Man*, the good, humane Dr. Treves wonders if he's actually selfishly exploiting the deformed John Merrick. *Lost Highway*'s Fred and *Mulholland Drive*'s

Diane commit acts so heinous that they become the innocents Pete and Betty so they can live with themselves. Does Bill know if he's telling the truth? Is he in some predator protection program within his own mind? This being Lynchworld, there may be forces beyond human agency at work, for down the row from Bill's jail cell we glimpse a charcoal-encrusted male figure whose body fades away as his black smudge of a head floats ceiling ward. Perhaps he's kin to the elemental encrusted dark being in *Mulholland Drive* who scared a man to death: "the one who's causing all the fear."

The fear, anxiety, worry, and concern that have always occupied the consciousness of *Twin Peaks* are well represented in *The Return*'s opening night. Hotel owner Benjamin Horne's (Richard Beymer) brow is permanently furrowed over the doings of his brother, Jerry (David Patrick Kelly), who looks like a garden gnome come to life), and is perpetually high on his homegrown grass (a nod to marijuana's legality in Washington State). The Log Lady (dear Catherine Coulson, frail with cancer but wearing large, far-seeing glasses) perceives a larger cosmic picture than anyone else in Twin Peaks and is troubled that "something is missing" regarding Dale Cooper. Mr. C/Bob, wanting to stay in our world, defying the cosmic plan for him to return to the Black Lodge when Dale Cooper comes out, realizes that his criminal associates want to kill him. And a powerful man in a banquet room-sized Las Vegas office suite speaks with controlled hysteria of having "someone like him" (a creepily nameless who?) in his life. The worried man is played by Patrick Fischler, who drops dead from fear in *Mulholland Drive*.

Viewer and media responses to the original *Twin Peaks* often mentioned a lurking sense of dread, source unspecified, something oppressive in the air. We'll eventually see the very specific lethal threat that's in the Las Vegas man's life, but at this stage there's great resonance in the hovering mystery. In *Mulholland Drive*, Fischler's character encounters a primordial dark street denizen behind an LA diner, and the very sight kills him. The figure, called the Bum in Lynch's screenplay, is a primal force, "the one who's causing all the fear," like *Twin Peaks*'s Bob, whom Lynch calls "an abstraction in human form." (*Lynch on Lynch*). In the dark metaphysical gridwork that underlies *Mulholland*'s LA. the Bum is also linked to heroine Diane, and drives her to suicide. Lynch and Frost are adept at characterizing states of mind and spirit, like evil, in inspired ways. Frost has even mused that the doings of *The Return*'s wicked frog-moth creature, still to come, are tantamount to Trumpism (*Conversations With Mark Frost*).

Presented on the opening night of *The Return,* Cooper and Laura in the Red Room, suspended beyond time in a Lynchian ecstacy of silent gazes back and forth, are the welcome home ambassadors of the *Twin Peaks* universe. Their comforting mutual gazes bespeak worlds, higher powers, purpose, and goodwill. She's dead/a spirit, he's a corporeal man, but maybe someday on some plane of being they'll mate and raise godlike children. The Red Room is a particular, delineated space that expands into mystery: micro-and-macro-, inside and outside, above and below. When Cooper and Laura sit and look at each other without speaking, the air

At the end of *Fire Walk With Me*, Laura was a recipient of angelic Christian grace. Now, twenty-five years later, her spiritual evolution has proceeded to a point where when she says, "I am dead, yet I live," it's natural to think of Christ's resurrection. Striking in her more mature beauty and statuesque in her long black gown, Laura is a formidable figure of self-knowledge and agency: she removes her face like a mask to show that she's a being of clear white light. And she's the one who tells Cooper when he can leave the Red Room. Surely she will join him in some inevitable showdown with Bob, Mr. C, and dark forces as yet unnamed. But Lynch and Frost won't let us become complacent, thinking we've figured things out so early, for some invading, invisible force makes her shake and scream—and she's whisked away, up and out of the Red Room. Who's in charge here? Who's running things? *The Return* puts everything in flux, subject to change. The original *Twin Peaks* dream of restoring a stable, wholesome 1950s American order to a sweet little Northwest town now seems as remote as the Norman Rockwell cover painting on a dusty old *Saturday Evening Post* magazine.

A major component and signifier of the old-home *Twin Peaks* feeling is missing: the Red Room's homebody, the Man from Another Place (Michael J. Anderson), the thirty-seven-inch-tall man in the red suit, who bop-danced and finger-snapped across the zigzag floor, backward-speaking enigmatic epigrams to Cooper with a sweet, mischievous, sometimes malevolent grin. In Lynch's biological-spiritual matrix, the Man is the evolved form of the One-Armed Man's arm. Fellow dark spirits from somewhere beyond, the One-Armed Man, as Mike (Phillip Gerard), and Bob used to raise hell together in a "golden circle of appetite and satisfaction," with souls as food. But Mike "saw the face of God" and "took the arm off." Lynch's visual sense of painterly, compositional balance sparked a narrative concept: the little man can be the wicked arm of the regular-sized, reformed, now-one-armed man. The arm/Man from Another Place can be spritely and charming (and Michael J. Anderson's performance is an enchantment), but his motives are suspect, whereas the serious-mannered One-Armed Man is on Cooper's side.

Michael J. Anderson has a muscular-skeletal condition that's necessitated many surgeries; he isn't a midget or a dwarf, but his "odd" persona in *Twin Peaks* made him a star. I've spoken of the hierarchies of power, good and bad, in Lynch's work. In *Mulholland Drive* (2001) the director had Anderson (with prosthetics) play a six-foot-tall man who's one of the controlling overlords who pulls the strings in Hollywood. In the lobby of the screening of the film for cast and crew, Anderson spoke to me glowingly of Lynch's artistry, warmth, and generosity. Anderson went on to happily portray a little person in the TV series *Carnivale*, but he's not in *The Return*. Bits of information in recent years indicate a falling out between Anderson and Lynch, with Anderson making unfounded, rather paranoid accusations not worth repeating in our era of lightning-fast fake news.

Lynch had the creative chops to transmute his rejected *Mulholland Drive* TV show into one of his film masterpieces, so why not evolve the Man From Another Place into . . . an electric tree with barren branches? The Northwest where Lynch grew up was lush with evergreen foliage, so a tree leafless from disease or death was singular, skeletal, mysterious. Lynch began expressing himself artistically at a young age, and over the years denuded trees have appeared in his drawings, paintings, prints, photos, *The Grandmother*, *Eraserhead*, a promotional video for Michael Jackson's *Dangerous* album, and the *Twin Peaks* forest near the entrance to the Black Lodge. *The Return*'s tree (the Arm, the Man from Another Place) is a striking manifestation of Lynchian surrealism, its bare thin trunk and gently swaying branches pulsing with blue-white light against the red curtains, emitting a sound composed of crackling electricity and soft rain. And it has a voice, for atop the taller-than-Cooper tree is a featureless, broad-crowned head (reminiscent of Anderson's), a pale blob of organic matter. Lynch has said he thinks that a wad of chewed gum looks organic, and in the late 1980s he molded some gum into a blobby head that he mounted on a plastic male figurine and photographed. And he has photographed snowmen whose heads are vaguely human but melting into something strangely other. We've noted Lynch's fascination for the plasticity and malleability of Francis Bacon's painted heads, and the electric tree's "flesh" head is in that family. Unlike the similarly blob-headed female glass-box demon with its big, gaping, and devouring mouth, the tree head has a small speaking hole at its base.

Lynch has said that the Red Room is "slippery," and negotiating its fluctuating ways is a constant living experience for resident Cooper. When he asked Laura Palmer, "Who are you?" she said, "Laura Palmer," but not when he first asked "Are you Laura Palmer?" And when Cooper traverses the curtain-walled hallways, he's sometimes stopped by a clicking sound like an invisible electronic doorway that won't open. But the click lets him proceed after he encounters Leland Palmer, who underscores Cooper's twenty-five-year mission to "Find laura." Before she was whisked out of the Red Room dimension, Laura had told Cooper, "You can go out now," and she whispered something in his ear that made him pause for thought. Now the Arm/electric tree emphasizes (in subtitled backward-speech), "253. Time and time again," and orders Cooper, "Go now!" Our senses are occupied with the moment's high drama, but does some part of our brain remember that in the earlier time of *Fire Walk With Me*, when Laura was under extreme duress, the clock on the wall seemed stuck at 2:53? In *The Return* the reference point 253 as time stamp and metaphysical-spiritual principle will be a signifier of sustained instability, a circuit that needs to be closed.

It's like the matrix of the Red Room contains/is acted upon by shifting force fields/intelligences that contend with each other, sometimes dominating, sometimes yielding or being overpowered. It's a realm of varying metaphysical chemical combinations and reactions, wavering pressure gradients, alternating stable and unstable atomic structures, wild tsunamis of gravitational waves, symmetry and asymmetry.

The polarities of the Red Room lurch from stable to unstable. Cooper is assaulted by the good electric tree's evil doppelgänger, which has a gaping black mouth hole in its blob head, and the One-Armed Man voices a key Lynchian theme: "Something's wrong!" in the household of the Red Room. Indeed it is. The cosmic stakes are at a new, intensely high level. Through a slit in the red curtains, Cooper sees that Mr. C, instead of coming back in, has gone desperado, blasting down a sunny highway in a big black outlaw car. In the world of *Twin Peaks*, the physical integrity of the Red Room is never breached. But when Laura was gripped by invisible forces and whisked away, a dark wind ruffled the red curtains, and we saw, beyond the curtains' boundary, that the zigzag floor vectored off into ultimate blackness. Now the evil tree lashes its crackling limbs at Cooper, and the floor bucks and heaves beneath his feet. The floor splits, revealing black water, and as Cooper drops down into the unknown, the tree says, "Non-exis-tent!" This monumental threshold crossing is comparable to the moment when Cooper first chose to step forward and enter the Black Lodge/Red Room. Now, in *The Return*, Cooper doesn't choose to plunge into the water: the floor drops out from under him. But whether by choice or "chance," it's his destiny to travel esoteric paths. While experiencing *The Return*, it's helpful to remember that Lynch has a deep belief in ancient Hindu concepts like the three gunas. These qualities of being—darkness, light, and the motivational energy between—were perfectly balanced before the universe manifested, but now, within us and everything, they are ever shifting, seeking to rebalance, like Lynch composing a painting or an eighteen-hour film for television. The three-gunas idea existed thousands of years before Albert Einstein, but it bears a striking resemblance to his relativity theory: "All the masses and lengths and times change based on the relative motions of everything to everything else in the universe." We seem to have agency in the world. I reach out, grab my cup of coffee, but maybe we're just riding along on shifting forces. Lynch applies the words "balance," "relativity," and "ninety percent of the time I don't know why I'm making my choices" to *The Return*. And he's told me more than once, "Things happen when they're supposed to."

"Non-exis-tent!" Will Cooper's DNA strands be pulled apart and swept into an eternal void and incinerate in the cold fire of a black sun? Not yet, anyway: he's a small figure falling through blackness studded with white specks (stars, subatomic particles? Lynch's macro/micro perception encompasses both possibilities). He lands on the outside of the New York glass box, then floats inside it. This links to the time passage we saw early in *The Return* premiere, when Sam and Tracy were out of the room before coming back and being shredded, giving us an idea of how Lynch and Frost are delivering story elements when they want to, not according to a standard B-follows-A plot playbook.

It seems that Mr. C's decision not to come back into the Black Lodge as he's supposed to has sent a shock wave through the space-time continuum, frightening the One-Armed Man, empowering the evil tree, and sending Dale Cooper into the dark dimensional current that will deposit the demon in the glass box. But Cooper's in it now, and some vibration of goodness encloses him in a small cube form and sends him on his way, leaving the space open for the demon's arrival. Maybe the Fireman is able to monitor Cooper's journey and intervene on his behalf according to the physics rule book of wherever it is that we are.

Cooper falls on and on through the white-specked blackness, so maybe this matrix is more neutral than dark, and it was an evil dimensional suction that pulled him into the glass box for a few moments. Maybe Mr. C's driving-free disruption of cosmic order boosted the glass box demon's voltage so she could break out of the box to feed on Sam and Tracey's New York states of mind.

By the end of the first night of *The Return*, the show's icons, Laura Palmer and Dale Cooper, have been sent headlong into the uncanny, futures unknown. The show's creators have sampled intriguing tales from coast to coast, dazzling our senses and minds. But as the minutes tick by, it's time to get home, to Twin Peaks. And what a home: Sarah Palmer (Grace Zabriskie) sits in her dim living room, her daughter and husband dead and gone. She seems burnt out by the metaphysical fires that took her loved ones, her life a haze of alcohol, cigarettes, and TV. Her television casts a bluish light, the color of enigmatic FBI Blue Rose cases and the electromagnetic energies that brought the predatory, death-dealing horror of Bob into their lives. Sarah's watching one of those nature-porn shows in which some animal is eating another animal alive, the agony of blood and screams. Lynch's shot shows both the TV and its reflection in the mirror above Sarah's head, linking with the moment in the original *Twin Peaks* when Bob's image (not a TV image reflection) was in the mirror, a secret resident in Sarah's house, and in her.

Deliver us from creepy! Give us a beer and a band and the Twin Peaks Roadhouse. With perfect jugment, Lynch and Frost end night one of *The Return* at the town watering hole, where young and old hang out, sip a few and gab about what's going on with everybody else's love life. In strolls James (James Marshall), the soulful biker boy who loved Laura desperately and from whom she fled twenty-five years ago to accept, and meet, her doom. And there's Laura's gorgeous friend Shelly (Mädchen Amick), who was partial to bad boys and is now exchanging flirty looks with some new, dangerous-looking guy in town.

James was the most decent and pure-hearted of Laura's men; as Laura's best friend Donna (Moira Kelly) put it, "the one with the everlasting love." After Laura's horrendous murder, James and Donna united in grief and love and sought to discover her killer. Laura's gone, but her spirit abides and is evoked by Laura's cousin Maddy, who looks like Laura's twin and is played by Sheryl Lee. The plot enabled Maddy to complete the illusion when she put on a blonde wig and pretended to be Laura in a video. Viewers and commentators with an ironic bent sometimes don't credit the tender, heartfelt sincerity of Lynch's expressions. For some, a certain 1990 scene with James and a guitar still raises derisive snickers. James shows up with his guitar at Donna's living room, where Maddy's visiting. He's also brought a tape recorder and an amp to give his sound more resonance. He's got a microphone for himself and one for the girls. James is a romantic, quiet kind of guy with deep feelings, and Lynch's lyrics sound like James penned them. The kids take a few sips of Coke, turn on the tape, and earnest feelings float dreamily in the air: "Just you / And I / Just you / And I / Together forever / In love." Lynch knows that an upholding spiritual warmth is all around us, and he gives us and his characters a few stolen moments of innocent pop song communion, of grace, a little glimpse of everyday heaven, in the midst of a terrorized town. But it's just a few moments, for tension erupts when Donna notices that James is looking longingly at Maddy, who's the very image of Laura

James sang "Just you" in a haunting high voice, a tonal range that throughout musical history has evoked an angelic chorus, the music of the spheres. When Lynch works with female singers he often chooses those who can produce lofty, ethereal sounds, like Julee Cruise, the archetypal *Twin Peaks* songbird.

Now, in *The Return*, James has no female companion, no Donna. What's happened to her? He's suffered through some hard times (and actor James Marshall has had crises over the years), but he's a survivor. He gives a yearning look to Renee (Jessica Szohr), who's sitting with Shelly and some other women, but she doesn't acknowledge his gaze. On the Roadhouse stage, Ruth Radelet of the Chromatics, bathed in blue light, her long platinum hair electric blue, is singing in her high voice of shadows and lost love. She and her now-departed love once "pretending that we'll leave this town," recalling James's last moments with Laura: "Let's run away, James." Futile words in the wind; her doom was waiting, he couldn't save her. Tonight in the Roadhouse, Ruth Radelet keeps repeating, "For the last time," as James turns his face away from Renee in the booth with Shelly. James has had plenty of last times and lost times. But he's here tonight, and there will be other nights. He's a man of feeling who knows his feelings, and that's not nothing. One of the booth women says James "is weird," but Shelly knows better: "James is cool. He's always been cool."

In terms of being there and doing the work and doing it well, James, and Lynch and Frost, and maybe me with my grief over Linda's loss, we're all at it again.

The premiere of *Twin Peaks: The Return* is over; it's late when I'm driving home and unseasonably warm for Seattle. The sidewalks and shops are deserted on this Sunday night, the street lights glowing peach rose, no other cars. I catch green after green. I'm floating with Baudelaire, who celebrated intoxication: "With wine, with poetry or with virtue, as you please. But be drunken."

–CHAPTER NINE–

THE PINK LADY
(PARTS THREE AND FOUR)

Falling down. Laura Palmer contributed dark energy to her own spiritual downfall, but she ascended after her sacrificial death to a quasi-Tibetan heaven in the Red Room, where she radiantly waited for her incarnational evolution. Even when some force pulled her screaming from the Red Room, she rose up and out of the top of the frame.

Cooper is falling down. Lynch knows we're all *homoduplex*. Cooper is a paragon of goodness, but his dark side of fear and guilt over his affair with his FBI partner's wife, causing her murder, made him vulnerable to Bob and has kept him in the Red Room—till now. Something invisible jolted and convulsed the place, confusing and scaring the One-Armed Man, and as the electric tree's evil double assaulted Cooper, it intoned, "Non-exis-tent" as our agent fell through a split in the floor, down, down, down. Like a rag doll gripped and wildly shaken by a big black dog, Cooper's body and close-up face are taking a pounding, trembling and jittering around the frame. We see Cooper small in the frame, his black-and-white form recalling the similarly clad Boy in Lynch's *The Grandmother* (1970). Forty-seven years ago, Lynch moved the Boy's hand-painted, animated, black-and-white figure around the frame. Now, thanks to computer animation, Lynch moves a photographed Kyle MacLachlan in the frame in accordance with his painterly vision.

We hear the roar of cosmic winds whipping Cooper as he falls forward from us into what looks like black sky and white star specks (the intense quivering of the frame puts a hazy blur on everything). Then, from Cooper's point of view, we're moving through pink air currents, and a roundish shape of dark pink clouds churns into our faces. We see massive, simple, block-form architecture with a central balcony and a single window that looks like a dark door and Cooper, small in the frame, dropping in like a tossed doll and landing on the balcony. The huge structure, and Cooper when he stands to look out from his perch, glow with a pink sheen. Like images from the beginnings of color still photography or early hand-tinted motion pictures, Cooper's skin, his black suit, and the balcony wall have a warm soft-focus aura, as though the light reflected off of objects extends slightly beyond their physical surface. It's as if the light has to try extra hard to manifest. Is it night? Is the light source a deep-scarlet sun? Or the waning phosphorescence of that pink cloud? This enchanted light is one of Lynch's most magical conjurings.

From a position behind Cooper on the balcony, we look with him, from a great height, out over a vast, dark, deep-purple sea. This moment mirrors a scene in Lynch's *Dune* (1984), for which he wrote the screenplay from Frank Herbert's novel. In a scene Lynch created, that's not in the book, Paul Atreides (Kyle MacLachlan) and his father Duke Leto (Jürgen Prochnow) are on a balcony looking out over the sea of their watery home world before leaving forever and moving to the desert planet of Dune. The sea is in their bones and their culture, but wise Leto knows that "we need new experiences that jar something deep within us, allowing us to grow. Without change, something sleeps inside us. The sleeper must awaken." A collage of elements and thoughts—a wet, physical sea; awakening to the Vedic Upanishads' "one unbounded ocean of consciousness" within/without; the book *Catching the Big Fish: Meditation, Consciousness, Creativity* by David Lynch (2006)—we're at a point where the artistic and spiritual stars of Lynch's universe are aligning. Cooper needs to awaken, to become fully himself, able to save Laura and defeat Bob and to understand the vast cosmic power grid that he is a part of. Where Cooper has landed, things emanate photon energy, light, electrified air. The dark-purple sea upon which Cooper gazes seems unbounded, timeless, a metaphor for Lynch's ground-of-being unified field. In the Hindu cosmos, the tension between being and nonbeing manifests the world. The electric tree intoning "Non-exis-tent" evokes the Vedic Rig Veda's Creation Hymn, which speaks of an initial void of nothingness: "Not non-existent was it nor existent was it"; there was darkness, and a sea; the germ of all things was born, and desire arose, "the link between the existent and the non-existent."

Lynch is hyperaware of duality, of binary perception. He knows in his mind and in his gut that "we live in a world of opposites, of extreme evil and violence opposed to goodness and peace." (*David Lynch*). For him. finding "a mysterious door right at the balance point" is the answer that thinkers, spiritual teachers, artists, and scientists have struggled to find for centuries. Lynch's balancing point is his head, meditating, knowing that opposing forces, positive and negative poles, so solidly separate, are at base a manifestation of oneness. When he's meditating, he's in the deep waters of unbounded consciousness, the all-in-one. But outside of his meditation room, he chooses to vote for Bernie Sanders instead of Hillary Clinton, and he knows that though he and a Cadillac are both universal spirit, he'd better not step in front of a speeding Caddy.

Ever since childhood, Lynch has sought to secure a state of living in the world where he can let his mind roam freely, no coloring between the lines, by the book, to the sound of a nine-to-five timeclock. What a feat in America: a bright, gifted man with artistic perceptions and skills devoted to finding and, through his art providing, "room to dream." Has anyone seen the ghost of Walt Whitman?

Room to ponder, feel, embrace the subconscious. To be the detective gathering bits and pieces of evidence, following hunches, forming fragments into a collage of meaning, providing coherence and order. David Lynch tries to do this in his life, Dale Cooper in his, we in ours. Lynch knows it's not easy, but it's the great human adventure, and the thrill of confusion yielding to understanding is euphoric, a tiny taste of ultimate enlightenment. He doesn't have all the answers; he can't erect a big neon sign that says, "This Is It." But his strobe-like mind gives us flashes, poetic indications, images and words that form abstractions of his deep concerns and beliefs. Cooper needs to "wake up," to get back to familiar surroundings so "the Twin Peaks story" can proceed. But along the way, by conscious design or intuitive expression, Lynch is communicating a broader picture.

Lynch has said that "doors and corridors can take you into another world," and when Cooper makes his way inside the massive edifice above the dark sea (which Lynch calls the Mansion and which resembles his 2012 artwork *Modern House*), he enters one of those iconic Lynchian spaces like the Red Room. The Red Room is bright and vibrantly electric, generating a tension between the soft vertical curtains and the harsh horizontal zigzag floor, and the chairs, Venus statue, and torchère lamps sit on that floor with the uncanny presence of surrealist objects. The Mansion's Living Room is warmly dim, its colorless dark walls lit by the glow from a fireplace; a banquette curves in front of the fire beneath a curving arched ceiling. It's a womb-like, feminine place, and on the banquette sits a dark-haired Asian woman in a ruby red gown. The flesh of her face covers her eyes as though they've been sewn shut—a creepy, discordant note in this harmonious space. She's gesturing urgently at Cooper and making whimpering sounds that aren't understandable as words but convey intense concern (Lynch knows that words can't say everything). When Cooper sits next to her on the banquette, they're joined on a common surface rather than in separate chairs (and shots) like Cooper and Laura in the Red Room and Cooper and the Fireman at the Fireman's abode. The woman is named Naido (Nae Yuuki) in the closing credits, and her dress is the color of Dorothy's transportive, homebound ruby red slippers in Lynch's beloved *The Wizard of Oz*. Can Naido, in deeper senses than we know at this point, help get Cooper home? She emanates the "broken beauty" that so moves Lynch. She can't speak, but her body language conveys her passion and desire to help Cooper along on his journey.

In the Living Room, Cooper's and Naido's flesh glow soft pink, the symbolic color of compassion, nurturing, and love. Pink is composed of red and white, and in ancient alchemy, the red/white axis sublimated the antagonistic black/white opposition. The Bible's "Song of Songs" proclaims that "My beloved is white and ruddy"; in the history of mystical thought, the rose and the lily are essential symbols. Lynch is giving us the building blocks of "a knowing" that we're not conscious of. In the Hindu belief system that Lynch studies, the universe's energy of being, its creative urge, is composed of red (female) and white (male) sub-energies. The Buddha's symbol is a pink lotus.

As I write this, I'm looking at a book cover, black with a shaft of pink light illuminating the words *The Divine Madness of Philip K. Dick* by Kyle Arnold. Like young David Lynch, whose mind was opened to fantasy by *The Wizard of Oz* film, young Philip K. Dick (1928-1982) relished the fantasy of the *Oz* books. Lynch and Frost may be paying homage to *Oz* author Frank L. Baum (1856-1919) by basing major Mr. C story threads in South Dakota. Baum held séances in his South Dakota home, embraced Theosophy's multidimensional, astral-traveling teachings, believed in reincarnation, and held the Hindu-like thought that "all of nature is alive, including the air." Philip K. Dick, one of the most imaginative writers of the twentieth century (the films *Blade Runner, Total Recall,* and *Minority Report* and TV's *The Man in the High Castle* were made from his novels), was a deep philosophical thinker who wrote of holographic layers of reality, parallel universes, the illusion of time, and altered states of selfhood. He'd written twenty-nine books in nineteen years when he had a pink-light visionary experience. The pink rays entered his eyes and brain and "resynthesized, reprogrammed" him. The light was literal and metaphysical, a divine invasion by a superconsciousness of universal intelligence, "electromagnetic and alive." The light beamed languages (Greek, Hebrew, Sanskrit) and knowledge of the ancient religions of Egypt, India, Persia, Greece, and Rome into the California writer. Just as Lynch, who follows the promptings of his subconscious while creating and retroactively can see the resonant depth and structure of what he's made, Philip K. Dick's pink-light mystical experience showed him the deep meaning of his yearslong creative journey. On fire with inspiration, Dick wrote eight thousand pages of notes on his visions and explorations of February and March of 1974, which he referred to as "2-3-74." Via the esoteric process of magical addition, which Lynch believes in, 2 + 3 + 7 + 4 = 16 (1 + 6 = 7), seven being Lynch's favorite number, and a structural element in *The Return.*

Dick's fertile brain launched many mind-bending concepts. He felt that time devolves toward disorder, but that God/the Divine (meaning the ultimate spiritual reality of all religions) is a counterforce for order. This supernal agent, the female intelligence force and champion Sophia, time travels back and reshapes past negative, chaotic realities into stepping stones to a spiritual paradise. In *The Return,* the One-Armed Man asks, "Is this future, or is it past?" and before the series is over, Cooper will try to make the past into a new future.

Dick saw this divine reforming of reality to create a utopia as a metaphor for the artist/writer, editing and adding to past images and storylines to make something new and better, as Lynch and Frost are attempting in *The Return.* Are they aware of Dick's ideas and work? Three decades before *Twin Peaks,* Dick was pondering and questioning the nature of reality in his philosophical fiction. In the basic Dick narrative, a protagonist spots discrepancies in the reality that he's used to and gradually discovers that there's a hidden/forgotten reality, the real world, beneath the fake one he's been experiencing. What appeared real is the true reality's double. The protagonist reveals this conjuring trick and tries to find out who's perpetuating it: "Who is that man behind the curtain?" (to link *The Wizard of Oz,* Dick, and Lynch).

Throughout history, great minds have thought alike and artists have explored similar paths while being, or not being, aware of one another. There are some fascinating parallels between the world of *Twin Peaks* and Dick's 1957 novel *The Cosmic Puppets*, set in a small Virginia valley town surrounded by evergreen woods. A man named Barton grew up in this town, and the pull of nostalgia compels him to visit it years later. He has many strong, detailed memories of his youth, but when he gets there, Millgate is "all strange, alien." The buildings are the same, but they're run down, decrepit, and they've got different names. Disturbed, Barton goes to leave, but there's an ancient rusted logging truck tipped over across the road, its dumped logs forming a chaotic barrier. Barton stays, and makes disturbing discoveries: "Forces are operating here, powers that don't seem bounded." Lynch loves the idea of strange, malevolent forces hiding beneath the surface of a wholesome everyday reality. In Millgate, a dark fog of erasure hides the golden town that Barton remembers, that other townsfolk don't recall. "As above, so below" is one of Lynch's dictums, and Barton learns that Millgate is a microcosm of the eternal cosmic war between good and evil. The opposing forces manifest over the town, the head of goodness a "radiant orb, pulsing with life and brilliance" like the spiritually evolved Laura's light-radiating face in the Red Room and her pictorial presentation within an orb in the opening credits of each weekly Part of *The Return*. Dick doesn't call the warring powers "gods," but the one upholding order and truth is "He, Ormazd," and the dark one is "Ahriman, sterile darkness, silence, cold, immobility, death."

Ormazd versus Ahriman: even before the pink light downloaded massive quantities of information into Dick's brain, the writer was aware of the opposing deities of the Zoroastrian religion. Zoroaster lived in Southwest Asia seven hundred years before Christ, in the time of Buddha, Confucius, and the Hebrew prophet Jeremiah. Zoroaster rejected the orthodoxy of a vast pantheon of gods and declared there were two: Ormazd and Ahriman, locked in combat, influencing the actions of human beings and determining the fates of their souls. In *The Cosmic Puppets*, Ormazd's spirit of goodness animated the original Millgate that Barton knew, but Ahriman crept in and spread wickedness, much as in *Twin Peaks*, Bob slithers into Leland Palmer and sends dark ripples through the community. Millgate citizens take part in both sides of the cosmic battle. Barton fights evil with a "humming electrical cone," and at one point he's in space, "head downward, twisting and turning in a billowing sea of luminous particles," like Cooper's space-trip fall from the Red Room.

The forces of good prevail, and the town returns to its better self, but the cosmic battle goes on, with only the two combatants "seeing it as it's really waged." Zoroaster prophesied that someday Ormazd would defeat Ahriman, vanquishing evil forces forever, restoring Earth to paradise, just as, in Christian belief, Adam and Eve would find their way back to Eden, and Philip K. Dick, in his personal mythology, would break out of the Black Iron Prison and regain the Palm Garden. Just as, in Lynchworld, *Blue Velvet*'s Sandy says returning robins will bring light and love to a darkened earth, and even *Lost Highway*'s benighted sinner Fred Madison will find a road to salvation. For Lynch, it's a road of karmic improvement and reincarnation. For Barton, on the last pages of *The Cosmic Puppets*, it's a literal road leading onward from the redeemed town, a road past "two swelling mountains, identical peaks glowing warmly in the late-afternoon sun."

The Cosmic Puppets and *Twin Peaks*: multiple layers of reality in small woodsy towns; invading dark cosmic powers; hidden, secret realities; human and supernatural good and evil agents in conflict; logging trucks and humming electricity; higher knowledge that can be rewarding or dangerous; twin mountain peaks. Both fictions have doppelgängers and *The Return* will explore that doubling concept in a more nuanced way than the original *Twin Peaks*. In *The Cosmic Puppets*, Dick conveys what it feels like when a person's consciousness, within a single body, is doubled, a situation we will encounter in *The Return*. In a final note of correspondence, Mark Frost, in his book *Twin Peaks: The Final Dossier*, published after *The Return* aired, posits that the show's timeless entity of ultimate evil hailed from the Middle Eastern region of the Tigris and Euphrates rivers, which is where ancient Zoroaster told his tales of the evil Ahriman, *The Cosmic Puppets*' original malefactor.

Since Mark Frost's pursuit and expression of esoterica has been allied with reading to a greater degree than Lynch's, it would be more likely that he read *The Cosmic Puppets* at some point in time or that he would be more familiar with Zoroastrianism, or not. The conjuring of creative inspiration is as mysterious as worlds of gods and monsters. In Lynch's *Lost Highway*, a detective says, "There's no such thing as a bad coincidence." And in Lynch and Frost's *Twin Peaks*, Cooper says, "Coincidence and fate figure largely in our lives."

Throughout his artistic life Lynch has had mainline access to the deep waters of his subconscious, without intervening, self-analyzing words. And for decades he's bathed in the meditative sea of universal consciousness. Lynch hasn't spent a lot of time studying the ideas of Carl Jung, but *Dune* author Frank Herbert did, and Lynch absorbed some key Jungian thoughts while spending years writing and directing his 1984 *Dune* film. Jung's universal sea was humankind's collective unconscious, "which contains the archetypes of all ideas," like scholar-philosopher Joseph Campbell's pancultural, questing-hero myth. In *Lost Highway*, David Bowie sings, "Funny how secrets travel." Ideas too. As an old Chinese proverb says, "No coincidence, no story."

From its opening credits, *The Return* promises wider horizons, and Cooper's time in the huge cliffside mansion above the purple sea takes us there. When directing Cooper's journey from the Red Room to the Mansion, Lynch used the words "space" and "infinity" interchangeably: the director's ever-present cosmic consciousness of the space-time continuum. Still glowing pink, Cooper and Naido leave the emotional warmth of the Living Room as she, groping without sight, leads him onto the building's roof. Their bonding, nesting moments are short-lived because Cooper's forward progress must continue—and there is a threatening pounding that dents the Living Room's metal door. In Lynchland, devils, as well as angels, hover close.

The iconography of Tibetan Buddhism represents the Buddha (the Awakened

One) with a pink lotus, and when Naido and Cooper emerge on the Mansion's roof, their pinkness is gone, like a lost promise of togetherness, love, and enlightenment. Also gone, or severely altered, is our and Cooper's sense of where we are. Lynch instinctively goes to the spatial-architectural place of combined opposites, transcendent thought as paradox. The first time I talked to Lynch, decades ago, we bonded over the idea that you can be in a small space, a nutshell, yet feel boundless, perceiving the macrocosm within the microcosm. In *Eraserhead*, the man in the little room with his levers can be in Henry's brain, pulling strings, but also controlling the universe. Since Cooper left the Red Room, Lynch has emphasized bigness: the dark-purple sea and sky that go on forever, Cooper's smallness juxtaposed with the Mansion's imposing façade and balcony, the Living Room's heavenward ceiling arch, and an electrical outlet larger than Cooper. Naido and Cooper climb a metal ladder to the roof and emerge in one of Lynch's most mind-blowing aesthetic-conceptual images. From a high angle, we look down at the pair standing on a metal box that's just a fraction of the size of the grand spaces we've seen them occupy a moment ago, a box that somehow contains the sea, the cliff, the Mansion, a box floating in the starry universe.

Lynch's camera angle of vision is similar to the one with which, in *Eraserhead*, he approached the little structure that housed the man pulling the significant levers. And a large, dark, vertically elongated bell shape next to Naido has levers. Cooper is like a spectator watching the strange process that furthers his journey; trying to understand it at this point is fruitless. This is a time to go with the flow. With an unspoken note of poignance between her and Cooper, Naido throws the levers and puts her hands on the bell that's throbbing with electricity. Her body shakes, and she's thrown off in a beautiful ruby-red arc, falling away and vanishing in space. We notice that Cooper's and Naido's pink glow faded up on the roof, but the misty soft focus remained until Naido fell away. Their special aura is gone, and Cooper's is now in sharp focus.

A small exterior structure that's bigger on the inside: the purple sea, the tall cliff, and the Mansion, all contained within a box smaller than a ranch house. Many pop culture fans first encountered this paradox of scale concept in the *Doctor Who* TV series that launched in 1963. The structure the Doctor dealt with was a British police call box, like a phone booth, that contained an expansive time-travel control center. The box and its interior are called the TARDIS (Time and Relative Dimension in Space). As *The Encyclopedia of TV Science Fiction* says, it's "dimensionally transcendent": the outside is in a different dimension from the interior. Is that the case with *The Return*'s star-floating box? *Doctor Who*'s box and interior don't share common signifiers, but *The Return*'s box and interior comprise an electrical circuit: the Mansion's buzzing electrical socket and the space box's electrical bell machine with lever. Electricity does link and bridge dimensions in *The Return*, so how about the directionality of the way each show presents the bigger-inside-smaller-outside idea. As consumers of fiction and nonfiction, we are more used to the smaller-to-larger progression: the small cave opening that leads to underground cathedrals of stone, Pandora's box unleashing a world of hurt, a small jar releasing an immense genie, a wardrobe closet opening onto the universe of Narnia, miniscule fissioning atoms blossoming into gargantuan destruction, the small iceberg hiding its depth beneath the water, the finite human body that can conceive of the infinite, David Lynch's emotional-spiritual cinema that can, as he once told me, "capture a bigger thing than you are perceiving," from limitation to liberation. *The Return*'s contrary progression, from the limitless purple sea to the cliff to the Mansion to the box, strikes our kinaesthetic senses as atypical, surprising, magical.

Back inside, everything's as big as it was—the Living Room, the electrical socket—and there's a different woman, American Girl (Phoebe Augustine), without a glow and that special something that Cooper and Naido had. She can talk (backward in subtitles) and tells Cooper to hurry, it's almost 2:53. And she emphasizes, "When you get there, you'll already be there." When Cooper fell from the Red Room, the One-Armed Man sensed a dangerous disruption of the Lodge's exit plan for Cooper. But things seem to be back on track; after Naido threw the switch and fell from the roof, Cooper saw an image of Major Briggs (floating in the stars like Henry in *Eraserhead*) reiterating Cooper's esoteric mission: "Blue rose." He just has to get back to himself, with his mental, physical, and spiritual abilities at full strength if he is to find Laura, save her, defeat Bob and the inevitable challenges that he can't see coming. To get there, he's got to go forward, even if the electrified air hums and throbs with a rising pulse as he approaches the giant wall socket. His hair smokes and his forehead widens and stretches as the socket pulls at him. Even though Cooper is following the One-Armed Man's prescribed travel route, is in a homelike setting, and has been helped by two women concerned with his progress, horror and evil are part of the picture. A dark female force is pounding on the door again, and American Girl warns, "Mother's coming."

As Cooper feeds himself into the crackling socket, Lynch emphasizes the oppositional yet conjoined natures of Cooper and Mr. C by cutting directly to Mr. C barreling down the highway. (Lynch subtly stresses the doubleness idea by placing his camera on the center line of the highway, with Mr. C roaring toward us on the left, the road empty on the right: we don't know what space good Cooper will be filling next.) Cooper is doing what he's supposed to at 2:53, but Mr. C, a minute or two before 2:53, is going rogue. His black leather clothes and black speeding car, on a deserted road through desert hills, are a "Fuck You!" finger raised to the cosmic powers that be. Is there a more potent symbol of freedom than a black car, pedal to the metal, alone on a sunny American road? But Lynch believes in karma: choices and behavior have consequences, as a character will point out later in *The Return.*

Mr. C is wracked by invisible waves of physical pain and existential nausea. He grips the wheel, which seems to be wrapped with black electrical tape, and rocks back and forth in his seat. The road blurs and doubles, he swerves, hits the embankment, and the car flips and grinds to a stop. Through the cracked windshield, he sees the Red Room curtain—it's almost time. In *The Return*'s eighteen hours, Lynch and Frost give us more OMG/WTF moments than we can count. Now we see Cooper—

can it be Cooper?—with longer, browner hair and white shirt in bed with a naked African American prostitute in an empty desert tract house. She (Jade, played by Nafessa Williams) calls him Dougie and goes to take a shower. Has Cooper taken an alias? Paunchy Dougie puts on a gold blazer and doubles over in pain. He vomits some yellow goop onto the carpet, and we see that he's wearing the Owl Cave ring associated with the Red Room and esoteric transports. The Red Room curtains materialize, and Dougie vanishes. Mr. C., through his cracked windshield, sees Dougie sitting in a chair in the Red Room. As 2:53 is reached, Mr. C vomits gallons of a yellow substance (garmonbozia, the food of the extradimensional entities, which was introduced in *Fire Walk With Me*), and his car trembles with electromagnetic energy. Part of his dashboard becomes a glowing electrical socket, but he is *not* going back to the Red Room. He sees Dougie in the Red Room vanish, and the curtains fade. We assume that Mr. C's Bob energy, his extradimensional kinship, allows him to perceive these glimpses of his tribe's realm. In the Red Room, Dougie sits in the chair, feeling woozy and strange, and the One-Armed Man tells him he was "manufactured for a purpose that's been fulfilled." Dougie's body shrinks away, leaving a black smoke smudge where his head was. All that's left is a small gold ball and the jade ring, which the One-Armed Man returns to the *Fire Walk With Me* black marble table, where it awaits future use.

As in *Fire Walk With Me*, Lynch practices his electrical magic, implying that the essence of beings or souls travels through powerlines. In the Las Vegas tract house, while Jade showers, a black smoky stream flows from a wall socket, elongates across the beige carpet, and becomes the long, prone form of Dale Cooper, with Dougie's yellow vomit mound near his head. He's landed, and as his Mansion Living Room girl guide said, "When you get there you'll already be there." So Dougie was a pretty-close-look-alike "manufactured" placeholder for Cooper, someone with an established Las Vegas life that Cooper could now assume—but why? And manufactured by whom? The preceding resonant five minutes of *The Return* is the only time the three iterations of Cooper (he, Mr. C., and Dougie) appear in proximity, and they emphasize that the saga of Cooper's soul is the show's humming power plant.

The fact that Dougie is wearing the Owl Cave ring before he's whisked to the Red Room is a major clue. At the end of the original *Twin Peaks*, Cooper's current love, Annie Blackburn (Heather Graham), somehow ended up in the woods outside of the Red Room, in a dazed trance. She was wearing the ring. In a deleted scene from *Fire Walk With Me*, released in 2014, a nurse at the hospital where Annie was being examined stole the mystical trinket. We can surmise that Bad Cooper, leaving Good Cooper trapped in the Red Room as he escapes and possessing some of Bob's esoteric knowledge, understands the ring's powerful capabilities, steals it from the nurse, and uses it in manufacturing Dougie. Dougie, who can be a vessel for a Cooper stripped of his powers and made remarkably vulnerable, a Cooper who should be easy to attack and kill. And when he created Dougie years earlier, Mr. C may have thought this being could at some point be a camouflage identity in which he could hide. Between Dougie's behavior (we've witnessed with a prostitute) and, as we will see, his wife Janey-E's (Naomi Watts) angry, fed-up attitude toward him, we sense that Dougie's prone to waywardness: a watered-down Mr. C. When Mr. C, in his wrecked car, sees the Red Room view of Dougie materializing, he may think this means that he is coming back in to replace him as Cooper has left, all at 2:53. However, Cooper's true, Bob-possessed shadow self was supposed to return, not a shadow of a shadow self. The One-Armed Man is frustrated: there's a testy, scornful note to the way he enunciates "someone" when he tells the bewildered, recently arrived Dougie in the Red Room, "Someone created you." Further, he later tries to communicate with Cooper-as-Dougie that "You were tricked"—the bad aspect of the electric tree made Cooper leave the Red Room before Bad Cooper (Mr. C) came back in, as was mandated by cosmic law. Cooper and his shadow self now exist in the same world: "One of you must die." The game is on. And since the One-Armed Man is on good Cooper's side, he will try to help Cooper-as-Dougie as much as he can, considering that they're positioned in different dimensions.

The conventional wisdom is that Mr. C created Dougie, and I lean toward that interpretation, but could Major Briggs, presumed dead for over two decades, be enacting a master strategy that involved creating Dougie as a soft landing for Cooper after he was battered by dark forces on his harrowing trip from the Red Room? A form in which Cooper can rest, recuperate, and regain his full powers so that he can pursue his mission, and a way for single-man Cooper to gain a wife-and-son family, like Briggs with his wife and son? Garland Briggs was a stalwart military man with a brilliant mind, depths of heart and soul, and a questing spirit who secretly tracked signals from deep space and experienced paranormal dimensions. He knew about the Black Lodge and that Cooper was trapped there, knew that "fear and love open the doors" and that Cooper must "protect the queen," a chess term meaning guard and help Laura Palmer's spirit. After Cooper fell from the Red Room and encountered the warm, helpful Naido at the mansion by the purple sea, he saw Major Briggs's huge face (black-and-white like in the Fireman's positive-force realm) floating in space saying "blue rose." Just minutes later, inside the Mansion's electrical socket room, Cooper saw a blue rose in a vase as the socket was pulling him into the electromagnetic birth canal towards becoming Dougie. Is Major Briggs an ethereal spirit guide for Cooper or a prescient planner with physical agency? From the Pentagon we learn that Briggs's fingerprints have been found sixteen times at various locations in the twenty-five years since he's been gone. In *Twin Peaks*, you can be gone and still be.

Two-fifty-eight, the big cosmic moment, has passed. The proper exchange did not happen. Mr. C and Cooper are breathing American air, and we relish the prospect of a final, major (decisive?) battle ahead between the factions of Cooper's split psyche.

We remember that Cooper, despite his virtues and strengths, was weak enough to be trapped in the Red Room. Does he have the emotional/spiritual will to kill his double, a man with his face and DNA, his living shadow, when the time comes? The doubleness that human beings feel inside has been explored in philosophy and art for centuries. The fictional splitting of a person's consciousness into light and dark characters at odds with each other flourished in the nineteenth century with Edgar Allan Poe's "William Wilson" (1839) and Robert Louis Stevenson's *The Strange Case of Dr. Jekyll and Mr. Hyde* (1886). And these writings inspired Paul Wegener's German Expressionist film *The Student of Prague* (1913). Cooper will face a profound existential challenge when he faces Mr. C: in all three of the early doppelgänger tales, killing the bad man also kills the good one.

Kill Mr. C? Jade has to put on Dougie's (Cooper's) shoes for him and tie them. When he walks to her Jeep, he takes little shuffling steps like someone new to locomotion. He's dazed, stupefied, silent, experiencing the most mundane objects and actions that we take for granted with his eyes and body at a newborn's skill level. It's like the roaring-hot fire of Cooper's brilliant mind has been reduced to a burnt matchstick. A dismal situation for our hero, but a perspective of value. Lynch the lifelong artist has maintained a childlike sense of wonder, attuned to the world's magic, that's enhanced by his deep, meditative exploration of the garden in his mind and at his doorstep. The tagline for *The Return* could be "Slow down and smell the Blue Rose."

Two of Lynch's bywords are texture and depth, and it takes time to truly experience both. He counsels his actors to slow down, sink into their characters, and enact them at an organic, measured pace. Lynch loves the unhurried, reverie-conjuring aestheticism of French culture. He would surely understand novelist Gustave Flaubert's (1821-1880) sense of being immersed in the *Madame Bovary* narrative he was creating, of being at one with his characters: "I rode in a forest on an afternoon under the yellow leaves and I was also the horses, the leaves, the wind, the words my people uttered, even the red sun that almost made them close their love-drowned eyes." When Lynch explains even just a fragment of a scene to his actors, he gets passionately immersed in the narrative as if he's living it, and he wants us to be too, entranced by his slow-cinema dreaminess.

But America is a 24/7 multitasking, ASAP, hurry-up culture: get your submarine sandwich/particular car color/coffee drink/online date just the way you want it—right now! This is the habitual rate at which Americans consume life. By the law of opposites, and following the advice of *Dune*'s Duke Leto to his son, we grow when we're jolted from our same-old routines and perceptions; we wake up. So the radical slowness of Dougie and his doings should be a refreshing change for viewers, a chance to empathize with a most unusual, outsider's point of view, to look at the world afresh and humbly appreciate some essential human values. As author-philosopher Jack Keruoac(1922-1969), who wrote *On the Road*, said, "You have to bow your head to understand life."

Another tagline for *The Return* could be "Remembrance of Things Past," in reference to Marcel Proust's (1871-1922) seven-volume epic novel in which the taste of a madeleine cookie dipped in lime tea evokes a man's childhood and the meaningful happenings and people of his life. Proust like Lynch, took time to provide a deep experience for his audience. He famously used thirty pages to convey every sensation and thought of a boy falling asleep. And one of Proust's sentences could wind seventeen times around the base of one of the wine bottles that Lynch and his character Gordon Cole like to drink. On the way to Las Vegas in Jade's Jeep, Dougie sees a Sycamore Street sign, which reminds us of the Sycamore trees in *Twin Peaks*'s woods outside the Red Room entrance. And when Jade says, "You can get out now, Dougie," he sees a flash of when Laura Palmer in the Red Room told him, "You can go now," but this doesn't expand his consciousness and revive him; he remains dumbfounded by the world and how to proceed in it. Jade thinks his strange condition may be the result of a small stroke. She gives him some of the money that he paid her for sex and drops him off, saying, "You can call for help." In the original *Twin Peaks*, Lynch and Frost knew that the most psychologically/emotionally resonant person to be Laura's rapist and killer would be her father. And in *The Return*, they know that we are all calling for help, we all want to go home. Years ago Lynch confirmed to me that "the big home of everything" is where *Eraserhead*'s Henry ended up after the "dream of dark and troubling things" that was his life. *The Return* will be a homeward journey for Cooper, and Laura, and Lynch and Frost want us to fully experience every step of the way.

Cooper-as-Dougie journeys forward like a monk unintentionally modeling innocence, compassion, and simplicity to the world, but does the world get, or want, the message?

To reference the French again, a key principle of Surrealism (André Breton: "I believe in the resolution of two states [in appearance so contradictory] dream and reality, into a sort of absolute reality; Surréalité.") is dislocation, an image composed of contradictory elements. And Agent Cooper (Dougie), elegant in his black suit, a spiritual, mystical, cultured gentleman standing mutely like a lost waif in front of a huge, gaudy, loud, exploitive money-sucking powerhouse of a Las Vegas casino, is a surreal image. And as Cooper tentatively moves forward and gets tangled up in the casino's revolving door before making it inside, where he starts pulling slot machine handles, he evokes the absurdist spirit of French filmmaker Jacques Tati (1907-1982), one of Lynch's favorite directors. Tati's films center on Monsieur Hulot (or a Hulot-like character), whose bumbling, confused, naive ways, his humorous encounters with the shortcomings of modern technology, consumerism, and status-seeking, spotlight the essential comedy of being human. Would Tati have plunked M. Hulot down in Las Vegas, with its fake, small-scale Eiffel Tower? Mais, oui!

Cooper-as-Dougie may be Hulot-like, but gentle Hulot never faced a world so harsh that it wanted to rub him out. When Jade is driving Dougie into town, a bad guy with a long-range scope rifle is positioned to shoot him as the Jeep comes by. But Dougie, having found a strange key in the pocket of Cooper's suit that he's wearing, drops it and bends low to pick it up, so it looks like only Jade is in the Jeep: no target to shoot at. The rifleman's cohort is stationed near the tract house Dougie and Jade left, and Dougie's white car's still there, so the bad guy attaches a bomb under it. Right across the street, a curious little boy sees the man put something underneath the car—and here comes the final French reference, for a while. The boy's mother is a burnt-out husk of a person, her world reduced to a card table top littered with booze, pills, and cigarettes. All she says is, "One-one-nine, one-one-nine," a coded, garbled expression of the 911 tragedy (thanks for the clue, Mark Frost). Lynch, Naomi Watts, and company had been screening the director's new film *Mulholland Drive* at the Toronto International Film Festival when the terrorists struck, and Lynch, devastated, felt that the world had shifted, immeasurably, to the dark side. Shortly thereafter, in a video for Lynch and John Neff's song "Thank You Judge," Lynch appeared as a creepy masked figure with 911 on his shirt. So in *The Return*, we have a single mother in the Southwestern desert evoking the memory of monstrous explosions, nihilism, the hungry death force: seems like Lynch and Frost might be foreshadowing something big coming at us a few episodes in the future. So what's French?

Prominent behind the mother in the bedraggled tract house is a red balloon, sitting on the floor, not floating free in the air. If this haunted woman and her spent balloon are a Lynchian negative polarity, then Albert Lamorisse's 1956 silent French film *The Red Balloon* is the positive pole. In this charming thirty-four-minute (adds to seven) film, a little Parisian boy is befriended by a floating red balloon (the life force), and the two enjoy adventures until some wicked kids burst the balloon. Lamorisse, like Lynch, knows that hope and transcendence are always possible, and the young Parisian is rescued by a big happy cloud of balloons. Like a spiritual barometer, more red balloons will appear in *The Return*. The spiritual barometer reading in the Rancho Rosa mother and child's house: low pressure, bad weather.

It doesn't seem like any angelic cloud of balloons is going to help the mother and her boy anytime soon. But just as Laura Palmer was helped by her guardian angel in *Fire Walk With Me*, a supernatural entity is making what few moves he can to help Dougie/Cooper. Somehow, the One-Armed Man can monitor what Dougie is up to, which is pulling the casino slot machine arms again and again, with no payoff. But suddenly Dougie sees a little glowing Red Room symbol with a golden aura in the air above one of the machines. The symbol reads mostly as red and gold, and it's interesting to note that Philip K. Dick received, in addition to his pink-light revelations, visions of a red-and-gold intelligence, and that Tibetan monks wear red-and-gold robes. Dougie tries the indicated machine, then sing-songs, "Hell-oh-oh" like a delighted child as the slot machine pours out a megajackpot of coins. Lynch himself is in a delirium of absurdist joy as he has Dougie keep winning and "Hello"-ing wherever the symbol appears, on and on and on: thirty megajackpots total.

Dougie, in his personality/mentality-depleted state, is silent and virtually affectless, but he smiles slightly when he lets an ancient, downtrodden, white-haired female slot addict (Jane Porter) win on one of the machines symbol-chosen for him. When the casino teller had given Dougie money for the slots, she noticed his impaired state and touched her heart as he walked away. That gesture, and the look between the white-haired woman and generous Dougie, are little surges of empathy and goodwill that will grow into a strong current as *The Return* progresses. But why was the One-Armed Man helping Dougie beat the one-armed bandit so resoundingly? To punish the casino for exploiting gullible tourists and hard-core gambling addicts? As the One-Armed Man said, years ago "someone" established a Las Vegas life for Cooper to inhabit once he left the Red Room, so maybe pre-Cooper Dougie was in financial trouble and needs a cash infusion; we already know someone wants him dead.

And his wife, Janey-E (Naomi Watts), is ready to spew fury at him. He's been gone for three days, and when Dougie, with his sack of casino winnings, finally figures out how to find his house (he does everything very, very slowly) late at night, Janey-E bursts out of the red front door and slaps his face. In *Mulholland Drive*, Watts showed Lynch she could project a coldly burning rage, and later, in the video for Lynch and John Neff's song "Thank You Judge," she was a housewife volcanically aggrieved. A consummate actress, Watts projects the full spectrum of Janey-E's aroused emotions. Lynch and I once discussed how fear can be expressed as anger, and moment to moment, we feel Janey-E's worry, concern, frustration, and love for her very strange husband. Sure enough, Dougie does owe a lot of money, no doubt to nefarious parties, and the $450,000 in Dougie's casino sack helps Janey-E relax—a little. She's still angry that Dougie missed their young son's birthday. As she berates him, there's a red balloon of potential harmony and happiness from the party floating between them, unlike the dejected red balloon on the "one-one-nine, one-one-nine" woman's floor. It seems that Cooper, in his depleted, disempowered state, is incapable of much thinking, but we realize that being Dougie has given him a wife, a son, and a home, which is not inconsiderable given his rocky, tragic romantic history. Janey-E and Sonny Jim are minuscule collateral factors in *The Return*'s grand cosmic battle, but they're giants in Dougie's world.

In Lynch's world of doubles, it's as though Janey-E experiences in effect, without realizing it, two husbands: one without Cooper's deep soul and one with, though it will take them both considerable time to realize it, much like the spiritual progression toward enlightenment, which Laura will also experience. Does the spiritually attuned Lynch feel souls around him reincarnating as he moves through his day, individual karmas regressing or surging forward toward the light, each lifetime like a frame of film? Is *The Return* a metaphor, an eighteen-hour Lynchian abstraction of multiple lifetimes and reincarnations? Lynch has called the Red Room a "waiting room"; it's like Tibetan Buddhism's Bardo state between incarnations. Early in *The Return*, Laura was whisked away from her further soul journey, leaving Cooper with the red curtains. Lynch has said the Red Room changes depending on who's experiencing it, it's like a karmic mirror. And in the Bardo state, one confronts the worst and best of themselves. Cooper's flawed nature, his fear, confusion, culpability in the death of a dear love, got him trapped in the Red Room. He may have been sitting and meditating for twenty-five years, but he's still got dark karma, which threatens him in the form of the bad electric tree and disrupts his smooth exit from the Red Room, dropping him into a terrifying fall. He lands in the shadow realm of the glass box demon but is pulled out of it and put back on track (perhaps by the Fireman) and reborn as Dougie the holy fool.

Dougie is Cooper the Good, unadulterated, uncorrupted, childlike, regarding everything he encounters with innocent wonder, an adult living in a world of first-time experiences. He's a weird, frail, passive grown-up: he doesn't generate his own words, but occasionally he repeats a word someone else just said. He's out of it, touched in the head; he can't negotiate the world half as well as "his" six-year-old son and wouldn't understand what was going on in a kindergarten class. He needs so much help.

Like the first Sunday broadcast of *The Return*, the second week comprises two episodes seamlessly joined, and in number four Lynch and Frost firmly embrace the basics of human beings living together. Cooper as Dougie came "home" to Janey-E and Sonny Jim at night. (Sunny Jim was a Seattle peanut butter manufacturer of the 1950s whose motto was "We've got underground peanuts with a flavor that's out of sight.") Now it's a sunny school and work day, and Janey-E is bustling around getting her boys ready. Since Dougie is clutching his crotch in agony, she has to show him how to go into the bathroom and use the toilet. His groan of immense pleasure as he releases gallons of urine is very Cooper-like: the thrill of a small, commonplace treat. Janey-E goes to fix breakfast, and Lynch gives us our first look at Sonny Jim (Pierce Gagnon; Lynch loves French touchstones). The grinning little boy is standing in a passageway, the hallway between bedrooms, silently emphasizing the journey to family that Cooper has made, or that has been made for him. Seeing the boy and struck by a wave of love, Dougie strangely grips his own stomach in an abstraction of dark karma, guilt, and emotional pain. Cooper's stomach, where his partner Windom Earle once stabbed him. Cooper had been having an affair with Windom's wife, Caroline, and she did not survive her husband's slashing blade. But Lynch, without an editing cut that would have broken the moment, converts Dougie's dark, stomach-touching abstraction into *Twin Peaks*'s sunniest symbol—Dougie's hearty thumbs-up, which Sonny Jim instinctively returns. Lynch believes that in our current lives, and over a span of multiple lives, and in terms of all the life on the planet, sour lemons can become sweet lemonade.

At the breakfast table, Sonny Jim has to show Dougie how to sit down, use a fork, and pour syrup on his pancakes, but when Janey-E brings his coffee, he can manage by himself, sort of. Coffee, like the thumbs-up gesture, is part of *Twin Peaks*'s secular religion, an elixir of the life force. But Dougie doesn't know enough to check its hotness before he drinks, and with a scalded gasp and grimacing grin, he spits it out but exclaims, "Hi!" Any thought that "a good cup of Joe " might snap Cooper back to himself is out the window, but there's a warm sense of wordless bonding between Dougie and Sonny Jim, a feeling that the child will help guide the existentially challenged man. And there's no doubt that Janey-E has two kids on her hands.

Lynch keeps presenting polarities. In Twin Peaks at the Sheriff's Department receptionist Lucy Moran-Brennan (Kimmy Robertson) and her husband Deputy Andy Brennan (Harry Goaz), are having a special moment with their son, the self-named Wally Brando (Michael Cera). The Dougie-Janey-E-Sonny Jim family reunion took place in a sunny Southwestern kitchen; the Andy-Lucy-Wally Brando meeting is at night in a chilly Northwest parking lot. Parking lot-black asphalt that leads to the great American road. Just as Mr. C defied his 2:53 report-for-duty orders by blasting down a US highway, Wally Brando seeks freedom on his Harley-Davidson motorcycle. Wally wears black leather like Mr. C, but that's where the resemblance stops. Mr. C is a bone-deep badass, while Wally just tries to look like one. His rebel biker gear evokes Marlon Brando in *The Wild One* (1953), the archetypal disillusioned, alienated road burner rebelling against "Whaddya got?" Wally wears the same black jacket and motorcycle cap as Brando, but his cap tilts at the angle of a French existentialist's beret. In *The Wild One*, the beefy Brando looks ready to rumble, but Wally is played by Michael Cera, a less imposing, more mild-mannered, much lighter fellow known for playing nerds. Lynch and Frost are having fun with the name Wally Brando, since Brando's best friend was actor Wally Cox, a slight, light, bland, nerdy fellow who starred in TV's *Mr. Peepers* (1952-1955). And no, it wasn't about a Peeping Tom.

Often called the first modern cinematic antihero, Brando's nameless outlaw biker helped power the first wave of the youthful counterculture, which smacked baby boomers like Lynch and Frost right in the heart and mind. Look at what the adults had made of the world: the horrors of World War II, the Holocaust, the atom bomb, a soul-killing corporate-consumerist culture, frenzied status-seeking. After the war, a few men dropped out and chose to spend their days riding surfboards and motorcycles, splattering paint onto canvas, messing around with electric guitars, writing prose that sounded like bebop jazz. The writer riffing coolest on finding moment-to-moment freedom was Jack Kerouac, in his novel *On the Road*: "We were all delighted, we all realized we were leaving confusion and nonsense behind and performing our one and noble function of the time, move." Kerouac studied Buddhism and learned that he could travel in his mind as well as in a gas-powered vehicle. Being in motion, simultaneously on the path of personal fulfillment and universal ultimate reality, was the way to be. This was the noble way of Kerouac's spiritual father, poet Walt Whitman (1819-1892): "To know the universe itself as a road–as many roads–as roads for traveling souls." *Twin Peaks*, anyone? In Kerouac's parlance the thought was "I mean, man, whither goest thou? Whither goest thou, America, in thy shiny car in the night?"

Kerouac went to the high mountains of Washington State, where he manned a forest fire lookout station, alone, a tiny speck amid the vast grandeur of volcanic stone, snow, and ice. (The station is now a shrine visited by worldwide seekers.) Kerouac sought to perceive the oneness of nature's sights-sounds-smells; he read his Buddhist texts and contemplated his dharma, his personal truth path within the cosmic order. His thoughts were deep/airy and egoless: "Dharma law/Say/All things is made /of the same thing/which is nothing." The passion of Jack Kerouac and his friend poet Gary Snyder for Asian wisdom has inspired generations, including Lynch and Frost, and Kerouac's novel *The Dharma Bums* (1958) became a bible for the nascent 1960s counterculture. Over the years, Lynch and Frost have clearly mastered Kerouac's aim to "unleash the inner life in an art-method."

In the parking lot at night, Wally Brando stands by his motorcycle, his proud parents, Andy and Lucy, framing him left and right, touching his shoulders. Sheriff Frank Truman, played by Robert Forster (our familiar Sheriff Truman, Harry, is gravely ill at home), stands silently regarding the Brennan family tableau. Wally, with the ardent seriousness of a thoughtful youth, says he's stopped off at his home town to honor his parents, Sheriff Truman, and the place where he grew up. He puts his hand on his heart and says, "The road is my dharma." And to Truman, with an expansive gesture that takes in the night, the woods, the town, and all its people, Wally says, "This is your dharma." Wally's path, his calling, is to move, seek, explore, and perhaps achieve the transcendent, mystical subject-object melding of Kerouac's *On the Road* character Dean Moriarty: "This road drives me!" Sheriff Truman stays home, upholds law and order, does his duty. The ancient Sanskrit root of the word "dharma" connotes both traditional pattern-maintaining and pattern-transcending. In *The Return* Truman,, his colleagues Hawk and Bobby Briggs, Andy and Lucy, and the FBI's Denise Bryson are all essentially maintainers, while Cooper, Gordon Cole, Phillip Jeffries. Albert Rosenfield, and Tammy Preston vault past law-maintaining norms, entering territory that's beyond classified information and the "official version," diving to the depths of evil, traversing uncharted states of mind, seeking the never-never land of the soul.

Those who have read Mark Frost's *The Secret History of Twin Peaks* know that Tammy Preston is TP, finally revealed as the agent presenting Major Briggs's (the Archivist) dossier chronicling centuries of American involvement in investigating and suppressing esoteric happenings, centering on Twin Peaks. In *The Return* we meet Tammy when she shows Gordon Cole and Albert Rosenfield photos of the New York glass box massacre: pale neck stalks topped with unholy blooms, red petals of flayed flesh, the insides of young heads. And one of the box-viewing cameras caught something: the spectral female thing with the hungry mouth. Lynch, as the actor being Gordon Cole (deaf with two hearing aids), gives the photo-viewing moment the classic Lynch/Cole treatment, barking a very loud, "What the hell?" Hell indeed, hell on earth. *The Return* doesn't mention any dossier, but it does include Meriwether Lewis, a major character in Frost's book, in Wally Brando's speech about the exploratory freedom of crossing frontiers.

As we noted at the start of *The Return*'s Part One, the scope of this *Twin Peaks* is broader and deeper, geographically and metaphysically, in Lynch and Frost's expanded conception of the show, and in Lynch's portrayal of Gordon Cole. In the original series, Lynch had strong feelings about the specifics of Agent Cooper's character and his attire and was angered when they were violated, as he says in *Room to Dream*, by writers and directors other than "Mark and me." Clearly Gordon Cole is exactly as Lynch wants him to be, from the photo mural of an atomic bomb blast in Cole's office to seventy-something Gordon's eye for the ladies: "Those raging hormones!" (testosterone-supplemented?). He doesn't just sit behind his desk; he's in the field, on the move, at the edge of known reality, where the air is tinted blue rose, trying to dismantle the core reactor that powers darkness itself. His suit isn't James Bond skinny; it's baggy and black, his pants held up by suspenders. He doesn't run and jump; he thinks and drinks coffee, contemplates what he knows and doesn't know, listens to what others have to say (thanks to his two hearing aids), and says just a few things himself, loudly. In the film *Amadeus*, a rival of the composer Mozart criticizes him for using too many notes; Gordon Cole never uses too many words. Perhaps aided by his decades of self-centering meditation, Lynch has a solid, captivating presence on screen: We're not watching the writer-director pretending to be somebody; we're watching Gordon Cole. In the earlier *Twin Peaks*, Cole's mishearing of what others were saying was funny, and his too-loud responses were funny, and they still are. But the seriousness of his mission, and his passionate dedication to it, combined with Lynch's advancing age, gives Cole a deeply sympathetic gravitas. There's something magical about seeing him walk and talk in the unique fictional world he's created, like having Willy Wonka show us his chocolate factory. *The Return* presents characters with a more fully rounded humanity: we learn that even FBI masterminds can be forgetful and fallible.

In Part One, the golden, beatified Laura Palmer was torn out of the Red Room by who, or what? As in the original *Twin Peaks*, her tragedy, the shadow of her absence, is always with us. We experienced Dale Cooper's and Gordon Cole's entwined stories, their warm alliance, because of Laura's death, and for almost thirty years Cole has lived with the mystery of Cooper's disappearance. Now, in Part Four, just after Tammy Preston has shown Gordon and Albert the New York glass box massacre photos, a phone call comes in. The receptionist's voice says, "It's Cooper." In *Twin Peaks*, proper communication is often hard to attain, the path to establishing it circuitous. Gordon, Albert, and Tammy leave the conference room and go to Cole's office, where they form a stunning tableau. The wall behind Gordon's desk is a black-and-white photo mural of an atomic bomb blast: a mushroom cloud situated at the heart of FBI headquarters. Lynch frames the shot so that the lethal/beautiful/somehow-alluring nuclear cloud is central, with Cole on the right, Albert on the left, and Tammy visible left of Albert, with a photo of Franz Kafka (author of *Metamorphosis*, one of Lynch's artistic icons) on her left. The call, from a South Dakota prison, comes through to Cole. Lynch has dangled the plum of a Cole-Cooper conversation before us, but not so fast. Cole listens on his desk phone, says, "Are you sure it's him?" and then "What do you mean, trouble?" as the nuclear cloud looms over the moment and Lynch's artistry is in high gear. The elements: the atom bomb image, Cooper (we know it's the Bob-harboring one; Cole doesn't), trouble, the FBI. Lynch the writer-director is subtly prefiguring one of the *Twin Peaks* saga's major reveals: the linkage of nuclear fire, Bob, and the origin of evil. The reveal comes in Part Eight; we're in Part Four. It's not that we'll necessarily think of the images and words of the Cole office scene when we're experiencing the Part Eight reveal, but it's a sketch, an indicator, an abstraction that Lynch has planted in our brains. As the Wicked Witch in Lynch's beloved *The Wizard of Oz* says, "I've sent a little insect on ahead to soften them up."

Cole finishes the phone call, having made a 9:00 a.m. South Dakota date for himself, Albert, and Tammy to interrogate Cooper. True to the rhythms of *The*

Return, and the principles of suspense building, Lynch and Frost don't hop right ahead to the much anticipated meeting; they check in with some old friends, like transgendered FBI Director Denise Bryson (David Duchovny). Denis/Denise had been a revolutionary idea and presence in a 1990 network TV show. The 2017 night I presented Sheryl Lee, Gary Hershberger, and Wendy Robie at the Seattle Art Museum, a woman in the audience said she'd gone into the field of transgender scholarship because of Denise. The original *Twin Peaks* stressed Denis/Denise's crime-fighting abilities, whereas in *The Return*, her, and Cole's, sexuality is the topic. Throughout his life Lynch has sought to express his authentic self, and his Gordon Cole wants freedom within the law for everyone. He reminds Denise that when Denis transformed into her, Cole firmly told anyone in the bureau who might disapprove or mock, "Fix your hearts or die" (one of *The Return*'s sublime dialogue moments). Lynch performs Cole as a self-contained man of few, deeply sincere, powerful words, with a deadpan delivery. He speaks the essentials: regarding his support and respect for Denise, there's no question that the man means business.

Their talk veers in a personal direction: Denise refers to "raging hormones," and Cole winces and makes a "Don't go there" gesture. It's clear that Denise takes estrogen to maintain her womanliness, so maybe Cole's strong reaction means he uses testosterone supplements. While *The Return* was in production, he joked that "I used to be a young stud, and now I can barely walk." Decades ago, in the original *Twin Peaks*, Lynch created a scene in which he, as Gordon Cole, could kiss gorgeous young waitress Shelly (Mädchen Amick). Their tete-a-tete had a sweet touch of magic realism, since she was the only person he could hear without his hearing aid (a single one then, two now). But still, Cole (and Lynch) was a much older man in a power position enjoying the attentions/physical contact of a much younger woman. I'm not knocking his behavior. I'm Lynch's age; I'm probably envious. In his personal life and acting roles, he's evolved from choosing partners nearer his age to those much younger. Lynch's wife, Emily, and Chrysta Bell, who plays *The Return*'s Tammy, are both three decades younger than Lynch. Ace agent Denise knows Gordon's pattern, and he's concerned that Cole wants Tammy close at hand for her youth and beauty rather than her FBI skills. But Gordon's a stalwart professional and, speaking charmingly to include Denise, says, "It's possible to be both a solid agent and a beautiful woman." Denise catches the compliment and, flustered, fans her blushing face as Cole leaves. So in *The Return*, David Lynch gets to charm women of all ages, and one who used to be a man; maybe he's practicing for a date with Judy.

Cole tells Albert and Tammy they're off to not Oz, but the Black Hills, and in the South Dakota prison they see, behind a rising steel curtain, not the wizard (good, old Cooper) but the thing, the pretender, the ghastly Other. Their senses and level of knowledge tell them this is Cooper, the one and only, but separated from Cole, Albert, and Tammy by a glass barrier, he's eerie, strange. He's like a gray corpse of Cooper animated by some alien intelligence that can't properly perform his bonding ritual with his human colleagues. Director Lynch uses technology to slightly slow MacLachlan's speech, giving it a creepy edge. And when "Cooper" says,

"Very, very good to see you, Gordon," the first "very" is spoken backward ("yrev"), Red Room style. "Cooper's" thumbs-up salute is sloppy, not crisp. He tells Cole that he's been working undercover with agent Phillip Jeffries (who's been missing for years) and that he was coming to fill Cole in when he had his car crash (but Cole knows Cooper's car was heading west, not east, toward FBI headquarters). "Cooper" bizarrely says his words about the car crash a second time and musters a crooked, painted-on smile as the curtain comes down. Gordon Cole seems to have an iron psychological constitution, but the black abyss between the Cooper he once knew and this soulless ghost behind the curtain has shaken him, as conveyed by Lynch's subtle body language. How can this be? This must be Cooper but, also, not Cooper.

Interacting with Cooper has been a significant part of Cole's and Albert's lives, and they're deeply disturbed by this encounter with him. They need to talk alone, so Cole sends Tammy to wait for them in a restaurant. Albert's feeling queasy, but watching Tammy walk away, in a medium-close shot, her tight gray business suit accentuating her luscious, curvaceous form, he says, "I feel better already." If we were in France, or any other country not puritanical about sensual beauty, I wouldn't have to defend this shot, which some viewers feel objectifies her character by emphasizing her physicality. Clearly, her physicality is right there on the screen, but she's already been characterized as a rounded human being in *The Return*'s story; she's not some anonymous body. How is it a sin to notice the shapely way Tammy rocks her knee-length suit or the way this fashion model-tall woman has to arrange her long legs whenever she sits? How does the fact of Chrysta Bell's lissome beauty diminish Tammy's character? Does the low-cut dark gown Laura Palmer wears in *The Return* define her as nothing more than a sex object? If we're thinking this way, then we have to say that in *The Return* Laura Palmer is defined by her alluring looks: she's got a minuscule number of dialogue lines compared with Tammy Preston. Lynch chooses actors partly for the way they look: actors, and their characters, are bodies and faces and minds and spirits, indivisible. Lynch isn't going to stop pointing his camera at fetching women, and anyone who's of a mind to be offended by this should start keeping count of all the shapely legs in high heels that we're going to encounter. As *Archie Comics*'s Miss Grundy says, "Shameful!"

Twin Peaks reminds us that reality is layered; we consciously/unconsciously absorb multiple planes of data. Our eyes, the organs closest to the brain, teach us this lesson ("the mind's eye"). In a single moment, we see the coffee cup on the table in sharp focus while in soft focus we see the bright shape of light coming through the window and misty forms fading off to the far left and right, above and below, and we hear a dog barking outside. It's a foreground/background world, this and that, me and not me. No wonder that we perceive dualities everywhere, think in categories, and organize ourselves in tribes.

Even the FBI is not a monolith. There are clear, concrete messages as well as communications "off the radio," "official" and "unofficial" versions of happenings, transparencies and stone walls, revelations and secrets. The bureau isn't a machine; it's human, fallible, and forgetful, like Albert and Gordon Cole. With the good Cooper in electromagnetic shell shock as the befuddled Dougie, Albert and Cole loom large as our special agents of truth and goodness. They've been through the metaphysical wars together, and Miguel Ferrer and David Lynch do a subtle, emotionally moving job of conveying their warm bond of understated respect and affection.

In one of *The Return*'s most affecting scenes, the two men stand alone in the blue air, their faces close together, eye to eye. Director Lynch makes the perfect choice of having Cole crank his hearing aids way up, so Lynch the actor can speak in his warm, soft tones, in massive contrast to Cole's loud bark. The camera's on Cole, and he just says, "Albert," tenderly, meaning, "I love you, buddy." Then, in silence, Cole's blue eyes search his partner's face, meaning, "But something's up with you." Something big happened years ago that Albert hasn't told Gordon about. Agent Phillip Jeffries had contacted Albert on behalf of Cooper (only we know it was the bad one), who urgently needed to know who our agent in Columbia was. Soon thereafter, that man was killed. What a putrid meal for Gordon to digest: Phillip and Albert secretly sharing bureau info/intel; Cooper a colleague-killer. In one of those entrancing suspended-time passages that Lynch is a master of, Cole whispers, "Albert," pause, "Albert," pause, pause, pause, "Albert" as Cole seems to explore Albert's soul. As his eyes scan his partner's face, a faint high tone, a manifestation of Cole's perhaps mystical truth-gathering process, rises and falls away. Image, sound, acting have produced a haiku of intimacy, doubt, and trust affirmed. Together again, they agree that they're deep in the Blue Rose Zone of mystery, and they need a certain person, who's a drinker, to look at Cooper and size him up.

In *Twin Peaks*, the coffee's always hot, the cherry pie tasty, and there are sweet words of love whispered in the night. But there are also tears and pain and suffering. The air can be metaphysically blue, but also plain old lowdown can't-escape-it blue. In *Blue Velvet*, Issabella Rossellini sings of lost love and tears as the Blue Lady, and singer Julee Cruise mourns, "How can love die?" in *Fire Walk With Me*. Lynch has suffered physical, emotional, and spiritual anguish, and he's sensitized to those who do. His David Lynch Foundation teaches the balm of meditation to military veterans and at-risk youths. He can feel that it's a world of hurt: a deep river of sadness flows through *Twin Peaks*, things lost, teardrops, blue notes. After my Linda died, and I was struggling through one day at a time, I realized I was seeking out things that would make me feel as bad as possible, like the film *Manchester by the Sea* (2016), a dirge of romantic and family loss. Somehow wallowing in the dark sadness made me feel a hair better, and I realized why blues culture is a time-honored treasure.

Gordon Cole's personal and professional compadre Albert has just told Cole that he's kept something from him for years, something that resulted in the murder of an FBI man. Cole thinks he can trust Albert in the future, but can he really? And Bobby Briggs, now white-haired and a sheriff's deputy, having outgrown his defiant, bad-boy youth, is suddenly pierced with sobs. He comes into the office conference room where Sheriff Truman and Hawk are examining case files on a big table and sees, for the first time in years, Twin Peaks's heart-wound icon of suffering and loss, the golden-girl homecoming queen photo of Laura Palmer—the woman whose life line was tightly entwined with Bobby's until it was violently cut, cut but not erased. Gasping with his tears, Bobby, trying to compose himself in front of his sympathetic colleagues, says, "Man, brings back the memories," perhaps realizing for the first time that Laura is both not here and here.

With another nod to *La Belle France*, Lynch ends Part Four with the female trio Au Revoir Simone singing at the Roadhouse. Some of the musical numbers in *The Return* are more classically *Twin Peaks* than others, and the trio's song "Lark" cuts a perfect melancholy groove. The women's synth chords are warm, but their words are sad. A woman "want[s] to be enough" for someone, but "there's not enough of me." Whatever she/they have tried to build together, "it's done no good." We think of Laura Palmer's fragmented self, never able to be whole and solid in her love for James, having to hide her shameful, degrading double life that was sparked by the demonic spirit Bob, who has used her father's body to rape her for years. It's a hellish torment to keep herself together through another day, let alone to be the woman James thinks she is—if only she could! But her salvation is to run from James, to embrace death. In death she is whole again, no wicked parts, glorified by angels, a being filled with light.

But in *The Return*, Laura is torn away to who knows where. When will she find peace, a stable home? The woman in "Lark," who can't be enough for the one who wants and loves her, tells them, "I'll point you to a better time/A safer place to be." Through poetic happenstance, Au Revoir Simone has put the ultimate dynamic of *The Return* into words.

–CHAPTER TEN–

COORDINATES

In *The Return*, the bad guys and the good guys want the coordinates, the numbers representing the point in space and time where/when the mysterious "great whatsit?" they're seeking can be found.

On February 13, 2018, I wrote the ending of Chapter Nine of this book, talking about Au Revoir Simone's song "Lark," the lines "I'll point you to a better time/A safer place to be." I was at home, sixteen miles closer than Seattle to where Lynch filmed *Twin Peaks*. On February 14, at night on Valentine's Day, I'd read numbers and followed a map and was in a space I'd never been before, the sanctuary of Temple De Hirsch Sinai, Seattle's largest synagogue. The warm, sweet, sad sound of "Lark" and other *Return* music was softly playing. I was sitting with a thousand other people waiting to see David Lynch.

I'd last seen Lynch when I'd introduced him and done the Q & A at the Seattle premiere of *INLAND EMPIRE* at Paul Allen's huge Jetsons-modern Cinerama Theater. David and I had greeted each other with warm hugs. Tonight he might throw a brick at me. The *INLAND EMPIRE* night was two years before my book *David Lynch: Beautiful Dark* came out.

In his meditation, his thinking, his art and spirituality, Lynch dwells within and goes deep, and that's where I wanted to go with *Beautiful Dark*. I wrote with respect and affection, but I knew that David could perceive the book as an intrusion, an invasion. Lynch's first wife, Peggy Reavey, told me he'd "read every word" and had a few minor quibbles about biographical details. In the summer of 2018, Lynch would tell us his own story in his autobiography, *Room to Dream*. He won't be saying anything about what his own often dark and mysterious work means to him or why he made various artistic choices. He says he likes to hear all our impressions and theories about those matters, but for him, mum's the word. He wants to leave us "room to dream" our own responses.

In recent years, I've sensed more heat and energy in Lynch's reaction to my book;

I've heard "he's got an issue with it" from those close to him. I'm friends with Peggy Reavey, Lynch's first wife, who remains close to her ex. She told me that Lynch was steamed because, since he gave me so much time and access, readers will get the idea that he, who scrupulously doesn't say anything about his own work, is endorsing my detailed interpretations of that work.

In the years when I was interviewing Lynch for my book, I asked him about the five dots he makes beneath his signature. He said, "It's anger." (Another example of his natural mode of expressing states of emotion and mind with a physical abstraction.).He told me that years before, he'd treated some people to dinner, and when the bill came, it was way higher than he'd expected. He was furious, and when he signed the check, his hand stuttered with anger beneath his name and made five dot-like marks.

Jack Fisk, Lynch's best friend and art-making buddy since their youth, told me, "If David didn't have his art, someone would be dead by now." The intense power of darkness in Lynch's work is a measure of his personal animus. When he took up Transcendental Meditation in the early 1970s, he wanted to become less angry, to quit being jerked around by his own pissed-off-teenager response to things. Over the years, he's let characters in his paintings and comic strips ("The Angriest Dog in the World") and animated cartoons (*Dumbland*) and films act out all that negative energy. Lynch to self: Be aware of all the darkness in the world, but turn on the light; be an international ambassador for peace and expanded consciousness through Transcendental Meditation. Speak of art-making and life as "action and reaction"; know that you've created some bad karma and tons of good. You're the one who keeps the balance.

I don't know what it feels like to bare one's psyche publicly for decades like Lynch has done. He believes that karma prompts his choices, and his public and private life are in a happy balance. He puts up barriers when he needs to, and he may now see me as an enemy agent.

On Valentine's Day night, after his meditation talk, the long line of people with books for Lynch to sign curves around the synagogue's perimeter in the shape of a question mark, with Lynch at the dot point, sitting at a table, pen in hand. I hand him my hardbound *Catching the Big Fish*, bristling with blue Post-it note markers, sticking out at odd angles. We shake hands, our eyes meet—does he recognize me? My friend who was in line behind me says Lynch gave a startled reaction. I say, "Hi, David, Greg Olson." A little smile, he says, "It's been a long time." "Yeah, every ten years or so." We both chuckle. His head bends down as he signs and I say to his hair, "Will you be touring with *Room to Dream* when it comes out?" "Not sure, we're working that out." He hands me the book. I'm half-turned away; I point at him and say, "You're Mr. Jackpots," referencing Dougie's *The Return* winning streak. He grins, "Okay."

His signature on the medium-gray title page is in dark-blue felt tip. I see that he pushed harder on the five anger dots than the dot above the i of David.

–CHAPTER ELEVEN–

IN A NAME
(PART FIVE)

Part Five of *The Return*, the first episode presented singly by Showtime, serves up a tasty portion of *Twin Peaks* homefeeling.

Six night ago (when I'd called Lynch "Mr. Jackpots," and he'd answered, "Okay"), before he'd done his book signing, he'd spoken to a thousand people about growing up in the Northwest. To him as a child, and now, "The forest was like a cathedral." Lynch is sensitive to the physical reality, the forest's beauty, and its emotional and spiritual emanations. Lynch's favorite films have that physical-and-intangible sense of place that "takes you into another world": *The Wizard of Oz, Sunset Boulevard, Monsieur Hulot's Holiday*. And Lynch masterfully creates such worlds.

Before filming of *The Return* began in the Snoqualmie Valley, Lynch meticulously resurrected the look and feel of the Mar-T Café/Double R diner as it appeared decades ago in the original series. Now, having watched five hours of *The Return*, we're finally inside, where we discover that Lynch chose the exact shade of turquoise waitress uniforms to counterpoint the honey-gold wood walls, where Cooper once enjoyed pie and coffee, romances tangled and unraveled, gossip flowed, high school temptress Audrey Horne (Sherilyn Fenn) did a dreamy dance like she was on some spectral plane, and Major Briggs told his troublesome son Bobby that he envisioned a rewarding, righteous future for the wayward youth.

The diner's a welcoming, consoling place, and it's reassuring to feel the camera floating up to a booth, where owner Norma (Peggy Lipton) has her daily business spread out like on a kitchen table, coffee mug at hand. She and Shelly are in their uniforms, and it's impossible to say which woman is more beautiful. If, on balance, the rough-and-ready, after-dark Roadhouse is testosterone driven, the diner is a sanctuary of estrogen energy. Norma and Shelly have been through business and romantic ups and downs together, and now they're overseeing the emotional entanglements of Shelly's daughter, Becky (Amanda Seyfried).

Becky. "A lovely little blue-eyed creature with yellow hair." Maybe that rather archaic "creature" is a clue: These words aren't from *The Return*'s script; they were written in 1867. They describe *The Return*'s Becky; they describe Laura Palmer. Mark Twain wrote them to characterize Becky Thatcher, Tom Sawyer's love interest. Twain based his Becky on Laura, his boyhood girlfriend. In Lynch's world, will the echoes and reflections ever stop? *The Return*'s Becky's boyfriend/husband Steven (Caleb Landry Jones), like Tom Sawyer, is not the town's "model boy." Both Steven and Tom show up unkempt in attire and grooming for proper occasions. Both openly declare their love to their blondes, spin tales about their potential financial wherewithal, and make their beloveds cry because they have other girlfriends. But Tom saves the life of his Becky, while Steven might be capable of snuffing his out.

We know that Laura Palmer was named for Otto Preminger's 1944 film noir *Laura*, in which a detective investigating the murder of a beautiful woman falls in love with her intangible presence, the memory of her that lives on in those who knew her. Lynch has spoken of how, in the original *Twin Peaks*, we barely see Laura, but as Lynch told me, "her presence is in every scene." A few years before Preminger's *Laura*, Daphne du Maurier's novel *Rebecca*, later adapted into a film by Alfred Hitchcock, introduced the story of a dead woman whose "being" haunts the living. The film *Laura* was based on Vera Caspary's novel, which came out after the book and film of *Rebecca*. "Becky" is short for "Rebecca."

What does all this add up to? The idea that Lynch's work fosters a psychic climate that stimulates speculations, reveries, the perception of correspondences, mirrors, and echoes. In the mind of the beholder, as they say.

In the early innings of *The Return*, it's clear that the tales of the various Coopers will be foremost, with Laura coming on strong later. In the 1990-91 *Twin Peaks*, Lynch and Frost created one of popular culture's most compelling murder mysteries, so we assume they'll do it again. Will Becky be in the vulnerable, threatened Laura Palmer position of yore? Will Tom—that is, Steven—kill Becky?

Just as the tragic loss of Laura stained *Twin Peaks* forever, that nocturnal red traffic light marked the town as a permanent danger zone. In the scenes that introduce Becky, Lynch subtly ignites little sparks of concern around the young beauty. Norma in her booth workspace shifts all her attention to the diner's entrance when Becky comes in and stands by the cash register talking to her mom, Shelly. Lynch, a master orchestrator of sound, sometimes turns down the volume to focus our attention, and he sonically keeps us at Norma's distance from Shelly and Becky. All we can make out is that there's tension in the air: mother and daughter are angry, and Becky seems to be asking for money. From Norma's distance, we see the diner counter, Shelly and Becky, the entrance door, the big front windows, and, almost beyond notice, the street outside. The action between Becky and Shelly is the dramatic foreground, but in the background, soft-focus behind Becky, we see that the don't-cross-the-street sign, the raised palm of a hand, is burning red. And in the street traffic flow, a red fire truck goes by (not at emergency speed), then a red aid car. After Becky gets the money she asked for, she goes out and gets in a white convertible—with a big red firebird painted on its hood.

Lynch has spoken to me about the power of love at first sight ("The elevator experience: you get on, some woman you've never seen before is in there, and you're a goner") and the danger of "walking with the wrong person," having a detrimental romantic partner. It's Steve's car that's marked with red, and Becky eagerly climbs in. Watching from inside the café, Norma, the voice of experience, says to Shelly, "If you don't help her now, it's going to be worse later," implying that Becky needs money for some kind of frequent habit and that the emotional cost of living with Steve is high.

Shifting from the wise point of view of the concerned adults, Lynch puts us in the car with the young people, concerned with breaking free from being observed and supervised by authority figures. Becky's cross, sullen, and worried. She can see that Steve was coked up for his job interview, which he says went well, but we've seen that it was a disaster. Even if she knows that he's a liar, his sweet talk and kisses are winning. And the car's moving; there's music on the radio, "I Love How You Love Me" from the 1950s, and Becky's wafting on love and the magic powder she's just inhaled like a breath of blue sky. In one of the most ecstatic shots Lynch has ever created, we see, for an unedited, unbroken minute, Becky's smiling, exultant face filling the frame, her wind-blown golden hair and sky-reflecting eyes. She's looking up, heavenward, where the camera's positioned. A second before Lynch has us stare at Becky's full face for a minute, he adds an almost subliminal note of wariness. For her face comes downward into the frame as the car starts to move forward, Kinaesthetically, from our position as viewers, the car, Bad Steve's little world that includes Becky, is sinking down. Becky's level of risky living doesn't compare to Laura's, yet, but she's on a treacherous road.

Aesthetically, *The Return*, like Lynch's *Dune*, has a water planet (Twin Peaks and its lush environs) and a desert planet (the Rancho Rosa housing development outside Las Vegas). Will Kyle MacLachlan, as the "sleeping" Cooper-as-Dougie, "awaken," as he did as Paul Atreides in *Dune*? And in both *The Return* and *Dune*, some unusual (for us) transportation got MacLachlan to the desert; in *Dune*, it was called "folding space" and did not involve a giant electrical outlet.

The rows of carbon-copy Rancho Rosa houses, many unoccupied, are sand colored, like the landscape, as if they're half erased, ghosts of the economic downturn, returning to mineral dust. The fading painted happy-family faces on the Rancho Rosa billboard are pale, Caucasian; the only person of color we see in this place is the prostitute Jade: a subtle sociopolitical statement on Lynch and Frost's part. Dougie's white car is still parked in front of the empty house where she had her tryst with Dougie, who became impaired Cooper. Like hungry sharks swimming in beige waters, two predatory cars cruise the street.

Lynch can make powerful use of close-ups. Actor Bill Pullman said that in *Lost Highway*, Lynch got his camera closer to Pullman's face, his emotional insides, than any other director he had worked with. But in his paintings, Lynch shows figures and objects from a medium distance, sometimes even from far away. In his domestic life, the artist likes to live in uncluttered spaces (his painting/workspace is an exception):

there's plenty of air around people and things. And in Lynch's film and TV work, his painterly sense of compositional space allows the elements within a shot room to breathe, to fully emit their specific energy. In Rancho Rosa, in warm daylight, on a beige street with its rows of beige houses, Lynch, in a single, spacious, unbroken shot, creates a potent tableau of menace.

For whatever reason (gambling debts?), some guys are out to kill Dougie. Gene of the bad crew has put a bomb under Dougie's white car, which sits where he left it when Jade took him to Vegas and dropped him at the casino. We see a wide shot of the street and the houses, and Gene's car, the ruddy color of congealed blood, cruises right to left along the row of houses, cool and slow. Dougie's car's still there, so Gene keeps rolling left, out to the street's vanishing point. The action of the shot seems over, but Lynch's camera senses something and pans back to the center position as we perceive a screaming buzz saw sound on the right, and the camera turns to find a big, wicked black car floating slowly in from the right. The windows are open, and shredded-metal music blasts out, assaulting the quiet street. The car stops, centered in front of one of the tract houses. Whoever's in the car is looking over at Dougie's car (and, threateningly, at us/the camera). Gene and his crew were sinister enough, but this car is some unknown darkness, just sitting there, a black spot of evil energy in a beige world: an abstraction that echoes the dark shape on Mr. C's ace playing card, the black stain of Mr C's fingerprint on a prison booking form, the black bomb like a leech beneath Dougie's pale car. I once told Lynch that a friend of nineteenth-century English visionary poet-painter William Blake wrote that Blake could "stare at the dark knot in a piece of wood until he was afraid of it." Lynch knew the feeling, said, "Yeah." Lynch holds on the black car until we fully feel its dark vibration, then longer, into sublime uncanniness, before it throbs off down the street in the red car's direction. Big deal. A black car in the desert. Is it really a metaphysical omen, the dark Mark of the Beast, W. B. Yeats's "rough beast, its hour come round at last/ Slouches towards Bethlehem to be born?" Lynch and Frost will make that happen in Part Eight, but Lynch's emphasis on the black car in Part Five is a prefiguration of desert fire and brimstone to come. Lynch was once so disturbed by seeing 666, the biblical mark of the beast, on a car license plate that he had to drive around until he spotted his personal lucky number seven on some other car.

Elsewhere in the desert, the casino-owning Mitchum brothers (Bradley: Jim Belushi, Rodney: Robert Knepper) are punching and kicking the unlucky manager who was on duty when Cooper/Dougie, following supernatural prompts, just about broke their bank. Leaning against the wall watching the beating with unsurprised expressions are three blonde beauties dressed in identical gleaming, thigh-length pink dresses and high heels, like 1950s cocktail waitresses. These three, Candie (Amy Shiels), Mandie (Andrea Leal), and Sandie (Giselle DaMier), are the Mitchums' constant companions and providers, the Pink Ladies, like Las Vegas geishas. Candie's a bit more active than the other two. She's got her own neural music playing in her head, or she feels some intangible harmonies in the air. As the two fist-happy brothers in their dark Italian suits rain punishment on the poor manager, Candie's extended hand moves in graceful waves. Who says there's no surrealism left in the world? Oh, right, Donald Trump is president.

The characters whom Naomi Watts plays have suffered a lot on-screen (Lynch's *Mulholland Drive* is a prime example), and her Janey-E in *The Return* has her trials and tribulations—but she also gets to be the boss. Sonny Jim is easy to handle; he's quiet and does what Mom says (at what point do we notice that we haven't heard the boy speak a word, though his silence exudes a wise innocence?). But her husband, Dougie is a grown-up; he shouldn't have to be prompted moment-to-moment to "Get in the car, Dougie," "Get out of the car, Dougie," and "Go to work, Dougie" when she stops in front of his office building. Her treatment of Dougie is harsh; she's angry. As Lynch and I once discussed, fear can be expressed as anger, and the physical-mental-emotional state of Janey-E's husband is deeply disturbing.

If your partner started acting like Dougie, you'd drive them to the doctor's office. But we're in the realm of artistic expression here, where Janey-E's heightened emotions and her attempt to believe that her near-catatonic husband is simply having a bad day communicate Lynch's sense of the world as a scary and absurd place. We rely on people looking and sounding and behaving within the interactive parameters we've established for them. Both bad Mr. C, by running from the Black Lodge rather than going back in, and good Dale Cooper, through metaphysical processes beyond his control, have become outliers. We viewers know how severely not himself Cooper is as Dougie, but even by the standards of the community familiar with Dougie's quirks, he's now at a new level of strangeness and incapacity.

For Lynch and Frost, Dougie's disabled state is a perfect dramatic status quo that they can occasionally violate with something stunning and surprising, like Dougie's thirty casino jackpot wins. Lynch identifies with "fringeland people" and often shows that they have extraordinary abilities. In the screenplay of *Mulholland Drive* (not the film), there's a "boy who has something wrong with him" who's dazzlingly brilliant, and in the film, the protagonist is a downtrodden bit-part actress who dreams her life as the toast of Hollywood. *The Grandmother*'s abused Boy grows himself a loving companion, *Eraserhead*'s downtrodden Henry can envision, and eventually embrace, a heavenly woman, and in *The Elephant Man*, the shunned, hideous-looking John Merrick is embraced and celebrated by class-conscious Victorian society for his refined soul, exquisite manners, and artistic talent.

In Special Agent Dale Cooper, Lynch and Frost and Kyle MacLachlan created a unique, resonant icon of 1990s popular culture. And decades later in *The Return*, with the addition of Mr. C and Dougie, the Cooper creators have the ability to craft three rich Cooper themes and voices, which, as in a musical/cinematic fugue, will present separately and build toward a complex, interactive climactic form. It's interesting to note how three creative men who were born in the mid-1940s (the Beatles' Paul McCartney, the Who's Pete Townshend, and David Lynch) and came of artistic age in the 1960s all embraced Indian spirituality (the Maharishi and Transcendental Meditation for McCartney and Lynch, the guru Meher Baba for Townshend) and the idea of humble, simple wisdom. Each man also created a subnormal, impaired, shunned character with extraordinary capacities: McCartney's solitary, visionary Fool on the Hill; Townshend's "deaf, dumb and blind kid," *Tommy* the pinball wizard; and Dougie the slot machine king, with more talents to come.

The sage Meher Baba, who didn't speak from 1924 to his 1969 death, wrote the resonant words "Don't worry, be happy." Whenever Baba's assistant Adi encountered Townshend, he would say, "Where are you, what are you, who are you?" The last question inspired one of the Who's anthems ("Who Are You"), but the full Where? What? Who? are Dougie's themes. Dougie bears a resemblance to Tommy, the hero of Townshend's Tony award-winning rock opera. Tommy was traumatized into his impaired state as a boy. His normal human capacities, like Dougie's, are harshly impaired. And Townshend echoes Lynch's "The sleeper must awaken" idea when he says, "Tommy's deaf, dumb blindness is a metaphor for the spiritual veils we carry" (*Behind Blue Eyes: The Life of Pete Townshend*).

Forget veils; Dougie's lost in a fog of incomprehension. Janey-E's shoved him out of the car and pushed him toward "work," whatever that is. (Like Lynch, Dougie would probably rather stay home.) There's a plaza, a big building, and people are going into it, but Dougie's transfixed by the giant bronze man rising from the concrete. The face and clothing (pants and shirt) of the male statue look rather modern, and the medium-brim hat looks more Western contemporary than frontiersman. The man's arm is at a sharp horizontal angle from his body, and he's pointing a pistol. He's not wearing a badge or insignia; he has the aura of a universal peacekeeper, and he's got Dougie's full attention. We've seen Dougie respond to badges and male lawmen even in his traumatized state, with a dim, speechless spark of recognition, some tribal, almost animal fellow feeling.

What's with the gun? Having Cooper-as-Dougie deeply stirred by a monumental artistic/socio political statement that men and guns go together like fish and water strikes a dissonant, disturbing note. Yes, Cooper has upheld the law with a gun in the past, but Lynch and Frost have always emphasized Cooper's magnificent rational/intuitive mind as his primal crime-fighting tool. If there was a statue of Cooper at his best, he'd be pointing but without a gun, pointing to where some inner impulse has told him he should look for the next clue, pointing beyond the horizon: crime fighter as spiritual explorer. And this Cooper, as Dougie, imprisoned in confusion and frailty, does point. Dougie's arm and hand rise up in response to the gun-wielding statue, but Lynch carefully angles his shot (our point of view is from behind Dougie) so that his hand is pointing between the gun on the left and the building on the right, pointing to a small section of blue sky. This shot, the TV show we're watching, is a manifestation of Lynch-Frost's mind, and it's a complex place. Dougie seems to be pointing above and beyond the reptile-brain of physical aggression and gun violence (somewhere over the rainbow?).

During the run of *The Return*, a number of commentators saw Cooper as a rescuing knight and Laura as his lady in need. Albert Camus, in his pre-existentialist youth, wrote a fairy tale titled "Melusina's Book," in which he called his archetypal female fairy She, which recalls *Twin Peaks*'s designation of Laura as the One. She is a protectress who wants to help human beings and grant wishes, but she's vulnerable, echoing Laura's character. A knight enters Camus's tale. He must choose between a path to the sky and one leading into the dark woods, where She dances. He chooses the sky way, and devouring night claims the fairy. "But the miracle of her death ceaselessly being born again lives in the perfume of the hour." Inarticulate Dougie points to the sky, the blue, the pull of the unknown, some transcendent destiny. As the *Twin Peaks* saga evolves, Cooper will understand that his proper high path is in the dark forest, with Laura in need, her spirit in motion, death . . . rebirth.

In *The Return*'s shot of Dougie pointing skyward, there's another element that's a spiritual sign: on the plaza, in the background behind the gun statue, there's an asymmetrical sculpture of a white mountain with three lower peaks that rise to sharp summit points. The lesser peaks and the top point have those cheery, French-film-referencing red balloons of positivity attached to them, like key points on a map, stations of the cross, stairsteps to heaven. Cooper/Dougie has a big mountain to climb, but a fulfillment that's ruby red, or maybe pink (reflecting pre-Dougie Cooper's time with Naido, glowing pink), is worth striving for.

But for now, he's earthbound. All he can do is look upward, at the feet of the man with the gun. Are Lynch and Frost making a statement about America's gun culture? As we've noted, the figure doesn't display the markers of a policeman, soldier, or FBI agent. If anything, his attire suggests one of Teddy Roosevelt's Rough Riders, who fought in the Spanish-American War (1898) and would be resonant exemplars of stalwart American masculinity for *The Return*'s creators. But web searches of Rough Rider statues and all statues with guns show men holding rifles at waist level. Amusingly, or disgustingly, depending on your point of view, there's a pistol-pointing figure that's a dead ringer for *The Return*'s statue. It's a four-inch-tall figure on a cork, a bottle stopper referenced by the gun culture buzzwords "NRA," "tactical," "open carry." And in synch with Lynch's find-the-light-within-darkness worldview, on my computer screen, amid all the pictures of men pointing guns are serene Asian images of the Buddha pointing ahead to the path of wisdom and enlightenment: the power of pointing, directing our attention, to dark and light.

Growing up in rural settings and being a conscientious Eagle Scout, Lynch knew that you don't point guns at something unless there's a good reason. By current standards of legal nomenclature, corporations are classified as people so they can donate to political campaigns. Dougie is pointing to the sky, but from another angle the statue's gun is aimed at the corporate building, a foreshadowing of, back in Twin Peaks, Doctor Jacoby's broadcast rants against the blood-sucking, mind-warping, soul-killing, environment-poisoning, satanic American corporate complex.

By the time this book is published, who knows how many more killing and wounding and malaise-expanding shootings there will be in the land of the free? The evening Lynch spoke in Seattle was Valentine's Day, February 14, 2018. That morning in Parkland, Florida a high school student had killed seventeen of his classmates with an automatic rifle. By evening on the West Coast, some of the shooting survivors were passionately speaking out against the NRA gun lobby and citing statistics showing that most Americans favor tighter gun control measures. That night in the Seattle synagogue, over a thousand of us were euphoric about getting to see and hear Lynch, but we were equally stunned, shell-shocked, grief-stricken. Over the years I've seen Lynch speak publicly six times, never before with a noticeable police presence. Tonight armed officers ushered our cars into the parking lot and others patrolled the sidewalks.

Standing in a beautiful, high-ceilinged spiritual space, having just been introduced, Lynch spoke reverently of growing up in the Northwest and how "the forest was like being in a cathedral." Then, with classic Lynchian deadpan wit, he said, "Thank you very much," as if he was finished and ready to leave. Everyone laughed, and I'm sure we all expected him to say something about today's school shooting. The printed program for the evening billed Lynch as an international peace ambassador as well as an artistic genius. After acknowledging "the terrible tragedy," he stressed his (and the Maharishi's) usual theme of the individual's inner, personal harmony, expanded by practicing Transcendental Meditation, being a bulwark against toxic anger and violence and a building block of a peaceable kingdom. As the Beatles sang after their meetings with the Maharishi, instead of fomenting anarchic revolution, "You better free your mind instead" and "change your head." Some years ago Lynch said that "kids bringing guns to school" motivated him to start the David Lynch Foundation to enable kids to learn the calming, anger-reducing practice of meditation. The Valentine's Day massacre of 2018 was one more horrific reminder of the need for a behavioral technique that would help foster emotional and social stability.

Twin Peaks is a multiverse; its symbols can be interpreted many ways. That's how Lynch and Frost like it. Still, it's disturbing that online research shows that the only sculptural figure that's a dead ringer for their bronze gunman is that bottle stopper being marketed to America's gun worshippers. I'm sure *The Return*'s statue, especially as it's linked to Cooper, is meant to signify the peacekeeping spirit, ever ready to take physical action to uphold noble values, to protect and serve. But if Lynch and Frost had been writing their *Return* script on February 14, 2018, and talking about the gun statue idea, would they have proceeded with it?

They say that all politics is personal, and the statue was actually born from Lynch's spiritual practice of honoring his father. During production, a crew member noticed that Lynch said to the statue, "Hi, Dad," and he has, uncharacteristically, recently divulged that the figure was modeled on an old photograph of his father, Donald (1915-2007), the woodsman, aiming a pistol. From Lynch's heart to our questioning minds.

In Los Angeles, homes like Lynch's that can afford a security system often have a discreet "Armed Response" sign in the front yard. In the spring of 2000, I asked Lynch about the Million Moms March against gun violence, which drew hundreds of thousands of marchers in Washington, DC, and nationwide. The march's slogans were "Enough Is Enough" and "We Need Sensible Gun Laws." Lynch was noncommittal about the idea of gun control, and regarding the march: "I don't know about that." These days, when Hollywood is devoted to remaking and franchising movies and

TV shows, someone asked Lynch how he'd feel if some filmmaker wanted to remake *Eraserhead*: "I'd shoot them. If I had a gun."

With *The Return*'s gun-pointing statue, Lynch is honoring his biological and spiritual father, Donald, who introduced toddler David to the wondrous "cathedral of the forest," taught him to revere wood and choose the right tools to make things with it. And Donald, a forestry scientist and a religious man, was a living example of how two often opposed ways of thinking can be transcended by a third way, for Donald believed in both God and Charles Darwin, heaven and the heavens.

The Return also honors Lynch's artistic-creative spiritual father, Bushnell Keeler (1925-2012). Growing up in the 1950s, young David thought that only adults in foreign countries got to be artists. As a kid, he loved to draw (often gangster-style machine guns) and knew that creating images was his greatest joy, but how could he make a living that way? Lynch told me that his friend Toby Keeler's father, Bushnell, was a "real painter, not a house painter," and "it thrilled my soul." Bushnell had paints, easels, models, a whole studio to work in whenever he wanted to. Keeler taught Lynch and had him read artist-educator Robert Henri's *The Art Spirit*, which became the fledgling artist's bible and crystalized some of his deepest intuitions. One of Henri's dictums virtually sums up Lynch's approach to art and life: "There is an undercurrent, the real life, beneath all appearances everywhere. I do not say that any master has fully comprehended it at any time, but the value of his work is in that he has sensed it and his work reports the measure of his experience." When there was tension at the Lynch house because of David's art obsession, the Keelers let him stay with them for most of a school year. In a couple of years, Bushnell used a tough love strategy to kick Lynch out of his familiar, cozy neighborhood art-making nest and get him admitted to Philadelphia's august Pennsylvania Academy of the Fine Arts. The academy, and Philadelphia, would be a portal to love (Peggy Lentz), family (add Jennifer Lynch), and aroused emotional-artistic energies that would be realized as *Eraserhead.* Lynch tends to credit Transcendental Meditation for being the key to his charmed life, the light that illuminated his path of personal and professional advancement. But clearly his unique visionary and technical skills, his passion for art, were enlivened before he heard of the Maharishi. As Bushnell Keeler told me, "David's approach was very creative, very interesting. I was tickled to be working with a young guy who was so talented, so dedicated; it made me feel kind of important."

It was likely Lynch who decided to name Dougie's boss at the Lucky 7 Insurance company Bushnell, so that both of Lynch's fathers could be near in physical/emotional/poetic space. Will Bushnell Mullins fill an important, mentoring/surrogate-father role in Cooper-as-Dougie's life, as Bushnell Keeler did in Lynch's? Time will tell.

Who would wear the proud name of Bushnell in Lynch and Frost's production? Of course, someone who'd kissed Marilyn Monroe, many times. The pop culture icons of Lynch's beloved 1950s were Marilyn Monroe and Elvis Presley (both of whom he reflected in *Wild at Heart*'s Lula and Sailor). As Mark Frost says in *Conversations with Mark Frost*, Monroe "plugged into his [Lynch's] interest in the archetype of the fallen, or wounded, woman, which has been a constant theme in his work." Lynch and Frost's first joint, pre-*Twin Peaks* project was *Venus Descending*, a fictionalization of Monroe's rise and fall, from stardom to liaisons with the Kennedy brothers to her suicide/accidental overdose/possible murder. The film never got made, but it's possible to discern the ghost of an iconic blonde in the falling lifeline of Laura Palmer. Regarding his frequent theme of women in deep trouble, as Lynch says in *Room to Dream*, "Everything is about Marilyn Monroe." David Lynch's fictional lodestar, his dream, is to restore a semblance of mythic midcentury warm and safe and wondrous community, light and love triumphing over darkness. Cooper's working on it, but it may take him forever. Jeffrey and Sandy in *Blue Velvet* and *Wild at Heart*'s Sailor and Lula came close. To build the ideal, to generate energy for the task, Lynch includes resonant guideposts, touchstones, objects, mindsets, and actors from the midcentury peaceable kingdom. Such a one is actor Don Murray (born 1929), who, in *Bus Stop* (1956), plays a naive, no-nonsense 1950s cowboy who decides to marry a singer (Monroe), without asking her permission. Even in the twenty-first century, Lynch can, as he told me, "feel an air of old Hollywood" in the atmosphere of Los Angeles, and in making *The Return*, he would interact with the man who hoisted Marilyn Monroe's character on his right shoulder and carried her off to a brighter future. Don Murray would be Bushnell Mullins.

Forthright, gentlemanly, and handsome at age eighty-six in his gray suit and blue shirt (deliver us from men in black!). It's meeting time for the insurance agents (even as Dougie, Cooper remains an investigating agent), and in this pleasant office full of tasteful men and women chitchatting Dougie stands out like a surrealist performance piece. In a sartorial world of tailored gray, beige, and charcoal, Dougie's wearing his chartreuse sack of a blazer. He doesn't talk, he grabs and slurps down someone else's coffee, and he presses hard on his crotch when he has to pee. As the meeting begins, agent Tony Sinclair (Tom Sizemore) says some ingratiating, manipulative pleasantries to out-of-it Dougie. A bit later, Tony reports that the company should pay on a suspicious fire claim, and Dougie stuns everyone, us included, by suddenly, crisply, decisively saying, "He's lying." Tony fires back some flustered, angry, defensive words, and Bushnell tells Dougie to meet him privately in his office. For viewers of the full *Twin Peaks* saga, Dougie's Zen-flash accusation of Tony is thrilling, a momentary breakthrough of a fully functioning Cooper, since that Coop could determine someone's guilt, or relationship status, in the blink of an eye. How he did it was evocatively unexplained. Cooper has existed in the Red Room for twenty-five years, breathing paranormal air; maybe his inherent, already super strength intuition has been visually augmented, so he can see "signs" delineating winning slot machines and a green flicker on Tony's lying face. Maybe because Cooper-as-Dougie's powers of action, thought, and speech have been so drastically reduced, the moment-to-moment noise of social interaction muffled, he/we can more easily perceive currents of consciousness forming signs.

The vibe at the Lucky 7 Insurance company indicates that the pre-Cooper Dougie was known for boozy high living and trying to kiss the office women. In the boss's office, we get the feeling that Bushnell, like Lynch's mentor Bushnell, cares and is personally concerned about Dougie's waywardness, but he needs him to pull himself together, now. He sends Dougie home with bulging file folders to tackle; maybe this task will jolt him back to excellence (wake him up), orient him back to his proper path. Of course, we know that Dougie's faculties are so impaired that the rectangular tan things (the files) Bushnell hands him might as well be chunks of wood or cereal boxes, whatever those things might be. Bushnell Mullins radiates Bushnell Keeler's humane, gruff honesty, and behind Mullins's desk is a big poster showing boxer "Battling Bud " Mullins in fighting trim back in the 1950s. When I asked Bushnell Keeler's son, Toby, one of Lynch's oldest friends, if his dad ("Bush" to Toby) was ever a boxer, he said, "No, he was a water man. He loved to sail his boat and took David out sometimes."

Mark Frost's *The Secret History of Twin Peaks*, the show itself, and Lynch's personal philosophy encourage us to plunge into mysteries, to quest for knowledge, which can be both a rewarding and a dangerous pursuit. Both Lynch and Frost have young children at this time in their lives, so the idea of imparting lessons about the value of adventurous exploration is on their minds. And *Wild at Heart* counseled us about the trouble that can result from "a lack of parental supervision." Outside of Las Vegas, the little Rancho Rosa boy's mother is conked out at her card table. Earlier, the kid saw a man doing something to the white car, and now he goes out to investigate. The boy is very skinny, and as he crosses the street he oddly holds his spindly arms straight down at his sides rather than swinging them naturally. Diane Arbus is one of Lynch's favorite photographers, and his image of the boy with the straight-down arms may be an homage to Arbus's 1962 photo of a stiff-armed boy who's holding a hand grenade in his right hand. The grenade was a toy, but the Rancho Rosa boy's right hand is reaching out to touch a live bomb.

With a screech of tires, that predatory black abstraction of a car is suddenly back, with a concrete, worldly purpose: steal Dougie's car. Men from the car throw rocks at the boy to get him to "fuck off!" As he hops away, he hears a blast and turns: Dougie's vehicle is now a jagged car shape, torn open to let the fire out. The black-car guys were angels of death—for themselves—and the boy's saviors. Like a talisman, a piece of the car landed on the roof of the boy's house. Bodies bubble and crisp on a neighborhood street. Once again, with his intuitive, poetic curation of elements, Lynch paints with cinema.

Northeast of Nevada, Mr. C reclines in his South Dakota prison cell. Does he wonder if he convinced Gordon and Albert that he was their good old familiar Cooper? Both Mr. C and Cooper have been recently buffeted by electromagnetic storms: Mr. C when he didn't enter the Red Room as he was supposed to and Cooper when he endured a far more punishing interdimensional journey. Dougie exercised his Cooperesque intuition when he detected and called out a lying business colleague, and now Mr. C, in his cell, just knows that his meal will be delivered in a minute, and it is. Mr. C checks to see if he's functioning fully by seeing Bob melded with his own mirror reflection. When Dougie sees Dougie in the mirror he's at a loss; his road to full Cooperness is of indeterminate length.

Mr. C flexes his powers by showing that he has manipulative knowledge about the prison warden that makes the man tremble and by making the walls and the air shake with flashing light and electrical noise. This chaotic maelstrom of dark energy that comes and goes at Mr. C's bidding is linked to his legally mandated phone call. He intones into the receiver, "The cow jumped over the moon." We don't know whom he called, but he could be referring to Mr. C jumping right out of prison, and a plan to make that happen. And we remember that L. Frank Baum, who wrote *The Wizard of Oz,* lived in South Dakota, believed in mystical realities coexisting with our own and in travel between dimensions, wrote a tale of an "electrical demon," and adapted Mother Goose rhymes into short stories, one of which was "How the Cow Jumped Over the Moon."

Lynch and Frost emphasize the brainy, Cooperish aspect of Mr. C over the more animalistic supernatural muscle of Bob that he possesses. We get the sense that Mr. C is an international man of malevolence, a master of strategies with a global reach. In Part Five we see that there's a link between a woman named Lorraine and Gene, the Las Vegas guy who wired Dougie's car to explode. We know that Mr. C has seen Dougie vanish from Vegas, meaning Cooper has arrived and must be eliminated through some process involving Lorraine and Gene. The first thing we see in Part Five is Lorraine sending a message to the name ARGENT, which, we see at the end of Five, references Argentina (Buenos Aires). When Mr. C made his phone call in prison, he dialed many numbers, as he would for an international connection, and the chaotic prison disruption of flashing light and sound ended when he hung up the phone. In Argentina, we saw some technological device vanish. Super science? Magic? Everything linked in some master plan? Mr. C is a force to be reckoned with. Argentina reminds us of "long gone" Special Agent Phillip Jeffries, who vanished from Buenos Aires and immediately appeared in Philadelphia, much to the astonishment of Gordon Cole, Cooper, and Albert Rosenfield. At FBI headquarters, Jeffries, traumatized and distraught, told of time spent with Bob and otherworldly denizens, then vanished, leaving no technological trace of ever having been there. As *The Return* proceeds, we'll gather that Jeffries was in Argentina seeking the presence of Judy. As Franck Boulègue notes in *The Return of Twin Peaks: Squaring the Circle*, science shows us that the world's electromagnetic field is weakest in this part of the globe, least able to repel dark invaders, like notorious World War II Nazi aeronautical scientists. Earlier in *The Return*, Mr. C spoke on the phone to Jeffries, or someone pretending to be him. Even in prison Mr. C is an energetic swirl of strategies in motion. Poor Dougie is like a fallen leaf in a side eddy of a slow-moving stream, directionless, circling and bobbing at the feet of the gun-pointing statue as night falls.

Northwest of Las Vegas, in Twin Peaks, Dr. Jacoby, a hyperactive contrast to Dougie, is broadcasting his screed against all that's wrong with America, and there's plenty. Like a Paul Revere of the north woods, via his podcast and his charismatic persona of Dr. Amp, he gives warning that the US corporate-capitalist-materialist empire is poisoning our air, water, food, values, minds, and souls. In sum: we're sunk in shit—but there's a way out. Doctor Jacoby was the first person we recognized in *The Return*, accepting a shipment of boxes at his modest abode in the woods. We're now in the fifth hour of *The Return*, and between Part One and Five we've checked in to see him unpack shovels and, using a very steampunk, low-tech, gears/wheels/belts assembly line system, suspend the shovels and spray paint them golden. Now, on his podcast, he's selling the shovels for $29.99 each: get your own golden symbol of rebellion against the villains ruining everything and, ironically, help support Doctor Jacoby's capitalist enterprise. But a guy's gotta eat, and a funky local cottage industry is spiritually preferable to faceless, greedy, power-mad schemers in their corporate fortress towers.

Lynch once told me that in his work he likes "to put people in hell, deeper and deeper down. Then they stop somehow and start to rise: there's a way out." He creates an escape door using story elements, but in his life his way out of the mess is Transcendental Meditation. Lynch has characterized the world's darkness and negativity as "sludge," which, in the world's current state of amped-up anxiety, confusion, and chaos, has become Dr. Amp's "shit." Metaphorically, the good doctor's golden shovel is meditation: as the Maharishi said in *Science of Being and Art of Living*, "Individual meditates—Individual life improves—Society as a whole improves." Before *The Return* hit the airwaves, I thought Lynch might convey his meditation beliefs in the story and actually mention the word. But metaphors are more poetic: something hard and metal called a shovel representing an invisible path to expanded consciousness, an idea that Mark Frost may well have come up with. After all it's a Lynch-Frost production.

For the first time in *The Return*, we see Nadine (Wendy Robie), with her striking red hair and black eye patch, somewhere in Twin Peaks, avidly absorbing Dr. Amp's passionate rant and shovel pitch. Is her last name still Hurley? Is she still married to Big Ed (Everett McGill), the man who accidentally shot out her eye and has been in love with Double R's Norma (Peggy Lipton) for years? In the original *Twin Peaks*, Ed, a decent, salt-of-the-earth man, stays with Nadine out of guilt and his sense of dutiful, proper behavior, but his heart beats for Norma. Nadine, well aware of Ed's love for Norma, has been through a lot: obsession with perfecting silent drape runners, amnesia, surviving a suicide attempt, mental regression to high school age, the acquisition of superstrength. Her emotions are intense, and she impulsively acts them out, which can be funny and poignant all at once. Essentially, she's a woman in torment, but tonight, alone, she's enthralled by Dr. Amp's broadcast. She's got a calm, beneficent smile on her face, and the small space (office?) she's in is very, very neat.

In Twin Peaks tonight, there are also harsher vibes in the air. At the Roadhouse, the guitar group Trouble is laying down some throbbing, raunchy lines, with David Lynch's son Riley playing lead ax. The lights are dim, the air smoky, the dance floor's jammed, and gossiping high school girls fill the booths. The tune Trouble's playing is called "Snake Eyes," and Richard Horne (Eamon Farren), with his reptile eyes and high, aristocratic forehead, sits alone in a booth near the cuties. In his shadow-colored clothes and with his urge for sexualized violence, he's like a younger Frank Booth (*Blue Velvet*) or Bobby Peru (*Wild at Heart*). Richard has a moment with something new to *Twin Peaks*, a corrupt, bad-apple Sheriff's Department officer, Chad (John Pirruccello), and slips him a wad of money. Then Richard lures a timid girl to his booth and—as Riley Lynch shreds the air with tortured metal sounds—suddenly grabs her, jerks her terrified face up to his, and snarls, "You want to fuck me?" Lynch cuts the shot with Richard's hand in a strangle grip on her throat.

Richard Horne. The name Horne is a major one in *Twin Peaks*. Can he be the son of Benjamin Horne (Richard Beymer), owner of the Great Northern, reformed reprobate once suspected of killing Laura Palmer, now in his upper seventies? Or the child of Benjamin's daughter Audrey Horne (Sherilyn Fenn), contemporary of Laura Palmer, mischievous, rebellious temptress of Dale Cooper, conscientious sociopolitical activist who, we last saw, had chained herself to a bank vault to make a statement—just in time for the building to explode? Mark Frost's pre-*The Return* book *The Secret History of Twin Peaks* tells us that Audrey was protesting her father's plan to sell the town lumber mill and surrounding forests for suburban development and that she survived the blast. Lynch didn't read that book. At the end of the 1991 *Twin Peaks*, the bank blew up, leaving Audrey's fate a question mark.

Before *The Return* debuted, Lynch clamped down as much as he could on storyline and character leaks, but Sherilyn Fenn was clearly part of cast group photos in magazine spreads. So if she survived and gave birth to monstrous Richard, who's the father?

Thirty years earlier, in *Blue Velvet*, Lynch's alter ego, Jeffrey Beaumont (Kyle MacLachlan), wondered, "Why are there such bad people; why is there so much trouble in the world?" In 2016, things are not well and good in Twin Peaks tonight, nor, as Dr. Amp reminds us, in the big, wide world. Trouble, pain, sorrow.

A melancholy saxophone tune ("Windswept") haunts the dark Las Vegas plaza with the gun-pointing statue. Everyone went home hours ago, but Dougie stands, like a little lost boy, swaying slightly in the breeze at the statue's base. The big bronze man with no name is Dougie's totem. Dougie/Cooper is miles from grasping his true self; he doesn't know how to get home, frozen near the image of a hero.

–CHAPTER TWELVE–

CHUTES AND LADDERS
(PART SIX)

Lynch opens Part Six with a shot of the gun-pointing statue at the Las Vegas business plaza outside the building where Dougie works. It's night, the light's dim, but we see that Lynch has framed the pointing arm and the red balloon atop that white sculpture together in a single image. Everyone's gone home except for Dougie, lost and impotent at the statue's base. Does he have a faint memory that he's Cooper, that in his normal, empowered state he could have posed for the heroic statue's sculptor and been represented by the happy vitality of a red balloon? (Does Dougie's state of loss represent Lynch's and Frost's sense of their own aging, an acknowledgement of the gap between then and now, in all the ways that can be measured?) Cooper can't measure up now, and far from being able to point a righteous gun, he hides his hand inside the sloppy, too-big sleeve of his gaudy chartreuse blazer.

Bob Dylan once sang, "With no direction home." But no matter where Dougie's head is at, he knows enough to seek redness, and a business plaza security guard delivers him home to Janey-E's red front door. So tonight it's a different set of cops bringing him home, and this time his arms are full of file folders, not casino money bags. He's way late again. Sonny Jim's already gone to bed. Janey-E's understandably worried about her husband's worsening bizarre behavior, or lack of normal behavior, like conversing and exhibiting more than frozen-in-place motor skills. But her fear for him makes her angry, and sound designer Lynch punctuates the tense silence of their very, very late sandwich dinner with Janey-E's aggressive lettuce-crunching bites and Dougie's crackling potato chips.

Dougie's stock falls further when Janey-E looks at a photo someone left on their doorstep: Dougie and Jade the prostitute looking very chummy. Dougie doesn't help matters by saying, "Jade gives two rides," meaning one on/in her body and one in her Jeep going to town. Janey-E, picturing two sex sessions, humiliated and pissed off, says, "I'll bet she did!" She gets torqued still further when the bad guys Dougie owes money to phone in, and she has to alter her plans and commit to meeting them with the money the next day. Exasperated by all her troubles, she orders Dougie to go upstairs and say goodnight to Sonny Jim, adding, "He's been waiting up for you."

Dougie's verbalizations consist of a few isolated words that float in space. They're not part of a sentence flow: they're like epigrams that break his usual silence. We never know when he's going to say one, so they have an aura of specialness. After Janey-E says, "He's been waiting up for you," Dougie says, "Up for you." He slowly fumbles his way to the foot of the stairs and pauses. Janey-E is steaming: "Upstairs!" Like a child new to stairs, he secures both feet on the bottom stair before climbing higher. In his literal-minded way, he's going up because she told him to. This is a deep Cooper resonance: Cooper the nonmacho detective in touch with his feminine side (intuition, tender empathy), whose journey is to help and be helped by women and female energies. And remembering that red balloon high atop the white business plaza sculpture, he must strive upward to regain himself and find fulfillment.

Upstairs with Sonny Jim is certainly a golden place. Just when we're starting to think that the palpable bond between the impaired Cooper-as-Dougie and the boy is partly based on, in addition to common DNA, a shared social differentness (we've never heard Sonny Jim speak), the boy announces, "I brushed my teeth." The boy has to show Dougie how to come sit on his bed. Then he shows off his bedside lamp with its "Cowboy" shade; it's on, then off, then on. Dougie has never encountered a light fixture activated by hand claps, and father and son, two kids, delightedly trade claps, controlling light and darkness. If only it was that easy, but then we wouldn't be in *Twin Peaks*.

Back downstairs at the dinner table, Janey-E sums up her annoyance and anger: "What a mess you've made of our lives, Dougie." But looking at the man she loves in his sad, sorry state, tenderness sweeps her, and she kisses the top of his head. He's sitting, she's standing, and she bends down to kiss him. She leaves to go upstairs, and Lynch gives us a shot of Dougie reacting to the kiss bestowed from above by tipping his head back and looking up. In the original *Twin Peaks*, Cooper exhibited this head-back-face-upward gesture/attitude, sunken in mysteries, looking upward for answers, or blessings.

Earlier, Dougie followed Janey-E's female guidance by going "Upstairs!" to see Sonny Jim, and now, before she goes up, she says, "Get to work!" Bushnell Mullins's case files are a jumble on the table—can Dougie even tell if they're upside down or backward?

We hear the Red Room electromagnetic sound of some metaphysical mechanism, and see the Room's plane of existence misting into Dougie's field of vision. The One-Armed Man is desperate, entreating, "You must wake up; do not die." The cosmic balance must depend on Cooper regaining his fighting form, but Dougie just stares as the Red Room vision fades away. Recalling the way the One-Armed Man helped Dougie win big at the casino by materializing a Red Room symbol above certain slot machines, Dougie now sees a small dot of white light gleam on one of the case file claim forms.

Lynch's metaphor of "We're all detectives confronting the mysteries of life" is ever active. Cooper may be virtually incapacitated, but he knows to follow female and paranormal guidance. He takes a pencil in his fist like a little child would, the lead barely peeking out below, and makes a heavy rubbing motion on the dot of light. As Dougie connects the dots and moves beyond them, Lynch does a mesmerizing job of capturing that late-night domestic feeling of when everyone else has gone to bed, and you're in a little timeless space, lost in some task. As Dougie works, we hear the melancholy saxophone music that accompanied Dougie lost and alone after hours at the business plaza, but the melody now seems to have an air of hope.

File after file, page after page, Dougie keeps working. His expression is blank as he makes marks, often without the light-dot cues. Since Dougie received the One-Armed Man's "You must wake up" message before he opened the files, we assume that Cooper's Red Room helper sent the dots. As the One-Armed Man spoke to Cooper, he made an out-thrusting/fanning arm motion as if he were sending out some invisible mojo to him. It's as if the dots got him going and enlivened some of his Cooperish intuition; he makes his most prominent marks without the dots. Twice we see Dougie make two parallel vertical lines, then small vertical strokes between them: a ladder. Then, next to the ladder, stairs going up. From the highest stairstep a line falls far down to a tangled dark splat mark at the page bottom. A high climb, a far fall.

Thirty years ago, David Lynch made a pastel drawing showing a male figure in a black suit falling against a gray background, his body almost horizontal as he plummets, leaving a painful dark-smudged wound-streak trail. He's in a bad way, and six little ladder forms, like the ones Dougie's drawing, are falling with him. The man in black seems to be a goner. He's traumatized, has suffered violence, has nothing to cling to; the ladders for climbing are tossed to the wind. Discernible in the gray background are some huge blocklike forms, and below the falling man are the waves of a dark sea. Did this image, born in Lynch's psyche in 1986, become *The Return*'s traumatized Cooper falling from the Red Room toward the blocklike mansion above the dark purple sea? And does Dougie's insurance files drawing of the ladder leading to the stairs leading to the far-falling arc line way down to the tangled splat form represent something hugely important to Cooper? In the Mansion, we sensed a warm bond quickly established, then broken, when Cooper and Naido glowed pink together and climbed a ladder and Naido fell away in an arc like the one Dougie's drawn. Did she go splat somewhere beyond time and space, or is that arc one of *The Return*'s major ones, to be rejoined way later?

Dougie's fallen, he's battered, but he knows enough to climb toward human warmth and family, toward coffee and the dim, fragmented perceptions that we hope will coalesce into a luminous, restored Dale Cooper.

Lynch believes in the dynamic of "action and reaction," "behavior has consequences," "what we do today influences our tomorrow; our actions in this lifetime shape our future lifetimes": good karma, bad karma, reincarnation.

Do all roads lead to *The Wizard of Oz*, the movie that Lynch has treasured from childhood on? When author Salman Rushdie (*The Satanic Verses*) was ten years old in

Bombay, India, he saw the film and was inspired to write his first short story, "Over the Rainbow." A young boy finds "a rainbow's beginning, like a grand staircase," and "naturally, begins to climb." Rushdie has climbed high in the literary world, but he suffered a fall when *The Satanic Verses* so enraged Islamic extremists that they marked him for death, and he had to go into hiding for years. While giving a lecture in October 2022, Rushdie was stabbed by an Islamic extremist, and he has lost one eye and the use of one hand. Such a price to pay for the power of one's art. The central metaphor of young Rushdie's book *The Midnight Child* is the ancient Hindu game Snakes and Ladders, which illuminates "the eternal truth that for every ladder that we climb, a snake is waiting just around the corner, and for every snake a ladder will compensate." Moreover, very much in the Lynchian vein, "implicit in the game is the unchanging twoness of things, the duality of all conceivable oppositions."

On a board is arranged a grid work of numbered squares, overlaid by snake forms and ladders. Taking turns, you and a fellow player roll the dice and, starting at the bottom of the board, advance your game piece the number of squares indicated on the dice. As you proceed, you're boosted ahead (ladder) or dropped down (snake), the winner being the one who reaches the topmost square first. A roll of the dice, a game of chance. Or is Snakes and Ladders, like Lynch's Red Room, which reflects the spiritual state of the one experiencing it, a map of the player's karma, which influences whether each dice roll advances or impedes one's progress? The game illustrates the philosophy that good actions move us forward, but bad actions set us back. Karma is based on the body taking action, but while we're playing Snakes and Ladders, there's no mental strategy, power of will, or physical action that will help us win. So the same two people can play on different days and alternate winning. Does fate, destiny, call the tune? Or did the player who won yesterday do something negative in the last twenty-three hours that karmically influenced their loss today?

For the ancient Greeks and their gods, fate was the first and last word. One's life path was predetermined; it couldn't be changed no matter how you tried. If divinely decreed disasters were your lot in life, so be it, as Greek tragic literature shows. Likewise, if your existence was determined to be a sweet bowl of cherries, a bed of roses, you couldn't ruin it no matter how hard you tried. Fate is set in stone; karma is fluid, in motion, capable of change and improvement over a lifetime or influenced by accumulated actions over many lifetimes. The tragic form of literature does not exist in India.

The game of Snakes and Ladders has resonated with the human psyche in many cultures. The English Victorians played it, and the American version, Chutes and Ladders, came out in 1943 and has been going strong ever since, with variations for fans of *Sesame Street* and *Dora the Explorer*.

Ladders and chutes, climbing and falling. Dougie makes his pencil-line marks on a printed insurance form, like an artist with his canvas, outlining a deeper structure he can see beneath the surface. He's doing this for Bushnell Mullins. When David Lynch was a fledgling artist, Bushnell Keeler gave him Robert Henri's book The Art Spirit (Lynch's "bible"), which says, "You are using the line for a deeper impression, the reality, not the surface. Do not copy the surface, see through it." The unique visions that Lynch saw and expressed on canvas or paper pleased Bushnell Keeler. And when Dougie (for the first time wearing his crisp black suit at work) presents the files to Bushnell Mullins, there are suspenseful moments as the boss looks at Dougie's childlike scribbles in dismay. Dougie's work is certainly "outside the lines," as Lynch has said of his own child-age art, but Las Vegas Bushnell begins to see a meaningful pattern in the seemingly chaotic pencil marks. He finally looks at Dougie as if he's witnessed a miracle and says a heartfelt "Thank you, Dougie. What you've found is disturbing. I'll take it from here. You certainly are an interesting fellow," validating the contribution of someone who's way, way out beyond corporate-office norms. While Bushnell was poring over Dougie's work, Dougie stared up at the poster of "Battling Bud" Mullins, the youthful boxing champ, and slowly reflected Mullins's stance by making fists, as if to say, "Dougie be like Bushnell"; David Lynch be like Bushnell Keeler.

So in the game of life, Cooper has fallen down the chute out of the Red Room and suffered the setback of being Dougie, but he knows to move in the upward direction as best he can, whereas Richard Horne, of the Twin Peaks Hornes, seems born to choose the downward slide. We last saw him verbally and physically assaulting a terrified young woman. That was on his after-hours downtime, but even on a workday, he's bad medicine.

As in the original *Twin Peaks*, the town has a drug problem: maybe people need to zone out to cope with a depressed economy and that dreadful strangeness in the air, the darkness that never fades away, the black hole where Laura used to be. Richard's happy to fill the townsfolk's desperate need, and get rich doing it. He's got a deep mean streak, supercharged by his own drug use, and thinks he's a big-time player, but when he has to deal with Red (Balthazar Getty, that new guy in town who exchanged glances with Shelly in Part One), we see Richard's just a wannabe. When he shows up for his job interview, he's wearing a brown jacket, while Red and his henchmen, each holding an automatic rifle, are in black. They're in a large garage/small warehouse that Lynch has textured to his satisfaction. (While watching Lynch film *Fire Walk With Me*, I saw him drift dust onto an old car and then spatter it with waterdrops, making it look long-neglected and rained on). The walls of Red's meeting space are black metal, scarred and pockmarked, torn, as if to suggest what Red will do to flesh that doesn't behave. He bristles with barely contained aggression, making sudden karate thrusts at Richard, peppered with two-finger gun-pointing gestures, like Frank Booth (Dennis Hopper) did in *Blue Velvet*.

The space is galvanized with fierce male energy: tough guys taking their stances. Richard will be distributing the heavy drugs that Red brings to Twin Peaks, and there's no question who the underling will be. When Red sees that Richard hates being called kid, he keeps doing it, rubbing it in as Richard's blood boils. If Richard tries to cheat him, Red, making a very Lynchian head-centric declaration, will "saw your head open and eat your brains." And Red has powers beyond the physical. He flips a dime into the air, where it hangs with a high singing sound, then vanishes, only to appear in Richard's mouth. The message is the message of all Lynch's malefactors: "I can get inside you." Richard clearly has powers and skills from some other place.

Richard thinks he's climbing the ladder, but he's rolling down the chute, and he's going to take someone with him. Red blasts off in his sleek, black speed machine, while Richard chugs away in his beat-up truck. He's driving on a rural back road outside of town, an everyday, nothing special road. Lynch doesn't compose images that are splashy picture postcard views; he knows that the commonplace contains dark depths and luminous heights.

Red humiliated Richard ("Called me kid!"), made him feel emasculated, and he's pissed-off. His truck, old and heavy and big (he has to climb up into the driver's seat), rolls faster and faster as, over the engine's ever-louder roar, Richard yells and curses, "Kid! Fuck you, man." In *Mulholland Drive,* a character says, "A man's attitude goes a long way towards determining how his life will be," just as physical actions in this life determine the shape of future lives. The Red Room reflects the spiritual state of the person experiencing it. Lynch once told me, "If you're in a good mood while driving, you're happy to let someone in in front of you, but if you're in a bad mood, and they cut in, you want to kill them." Red makes Richard see red. As he approaches the first intersection at the edge of town, furious at Red and the world, he sees that traffic's stopped, so he veers over into the left and blasts ahead.

Twin Peaks interweaves reality and meta reality, and Lynch and Frost brilliantly bring two story streams together on a pleasant fall day in the town. Seeing red, Richard drives in a rage; Carl Rodd (Harry Dean Stanton, at age ninety) sees blue sky and sits serenely in a park. Harry Dean, as Lynch calls him: gaunt, with eyes both haunted and kind, and the sweetest smile on earth, a dear friend of Lynch's and one of the greatest character actors ever. Twenty-five years ago in *Fire Walk With Me*, Carl ran the rundown, low-rent Fat Trout Trailer Park, where we glimpsed the Owl Cave Ring just before FBI agent Chet Desmond (Chris Isaak) disappeared forever. The empty-trailer-stall number six had a telephone pole and tangle of wires that seemed part of some metaphysical grid. At one point, looking dazed, Carl said, out of context with the conversation, "I've already gone places. I just want to stay where I am." Lynch and Stanton improvised this mysterious line, not in the script, and let it hang in the air, and our minds. Perhaps not surprisingly, Mark Frost got literal and, in his *The Secret History of Twin Peaks*, explained in detail that Carl Rodd (and Margaret Lanterman, the Log Lady) had been abducted by aliens as children, lost time that was vague at best in their memories. Lynch's poetic-aesthetic sense chooses to have Stanton's weathered face convey the imprint of some *unspecified* past trauma. He's an old man near the end of his life, "waiting for the hammer to come down," but he's looking up at the blue sky.

From contemplating what comes after this life, Carl is pulled back down to earth by a young mother and her little boy walking by, playing a simple game of their own devising. She stands still, he runs ahead and stops, she catches up to him, he runs ahead, she catches up, on across the park. The eternal dance: love tested and affirmed; independence sampled, but I still need Mom. Carl Rodd, the old man sitting still, smiles at the vibrant motion of youth, the cycle of play and love.

We've all seen countless movies and TV shows: certain editing rhythms telegraph certain story outcomes. The moment Lynch cuts from the mother and boy to raging Richard speeding in his truck, we're on danger alert. Lynch conveys details quickly; like Mr. C refusing to go back in the Red Room and speeding down the highway, Richard is going to defiantly blow right past a stop sign. A trucker stopped at the intersection doesn't see Richard flying up from behind, so he waves the mother and boy to cross. They're still playing their fun game. The boy runs ahead and stops midcrossing, waiting for Mom to catch up. From her viewing angle, left to right, the truck enters the frame, strikes her boy, keeps going. Lynch knows the power of simplicity. There's no need for gory close-ups. The running boy is now still, his mother kneels on the asphalt, cradles him, and weeps. A few townsfolk gasp, stare solemnly, weep. The trucker who waved them to cross covers his face with his hand. Richard, now with more reason to be furious, speeding away, yells, "I told you to get out of the fucking way!" (we didn't hear him say this). Thirty years ago, in Lynch's opening montage tour of the town of Lumberton (*Blue Velvet*), a crosswalk was safe for children to cross; not so today in Twin Peaks.

A moment earlier, Carl Rodd sat on his bench (red for the life force) with the image of the happy mother and boy lingering in his mind. Now he hears her scream and comes upon the terrible scene. Lynch, after making *Fire Walk With Me*, which delves deeply into Laura Palmer's life, murder, and afterlife, spoke of the relative ease with which an old person living a natural lifespan "pulls themselves out of their earthly existence." Old Carl Rodd dwells with thoughts of mortality; his departure time is near. Death is a familiar presence, so when he stands with the aghast onlookers witnessing the mother and her dead child, he can see a golden light like a blossoming flame ascend from the body and disappear in the blue sky. Carl feels other people's pain and responds to it. He's the one who steps forward, kneels with the mother, and silently pours his love into her searching eyes.

Decades earlier, in *Fire Walk With Me*, Carl was younger and more ornery. After the death of Teresa Banks, what felt like an endless parade of local police and invasive FBI personnel disrupted his trailer park routines, and he shouted in frustration, "GOD!" Now, in *The Return*, he sees the dead boy's essence, or soul, ascend, and softly mutters, "God."

God, beyond knowing or understanding, working in mysterious ways, letting bad things happen to good people—why? After every catastrophic fire, flood, drought, hurricane, tsunami, famine, racial genocide, school shooting, people ask, How could a loving, forgiving God allow this to happen? Is he reminding us that we're all fallen sinners who've fallen even farther behind, and need to work harder to gain his favor? After all, the Great Shepherd, the Ultimate Author, above Lynch and Frost, sacrificed his son Jesus to redeem us all ("I am the death of death. I am called a lamb.") It seems like we owe Him something; let's try harder to please the father figure in the sky.

An accident. It's sad; it simply just happened. Richard was raging; he chose to speed through a stop sign intersection. The truck driver waved the boy to cross; the mother nudged her son forward, still playing their you-go-I-catch-up game. Chutes and ladders. Definitely a drop for Richard, the trucker, the mother; a fall from this world for the boy, but also a ladder into heaven? A predestined occurrence? A transaction activated by the karmic debt of the participants, which certainly boosted Richard's bad karma? Some Hindus believe that there's a specific spiritual ratio between the effects of destiny, karma, and free will. A Chinese Taoist sage might watch a flowing stream and look up to see an airplane in flames and say, "It's the nature of things." C'est la vie. As Doris Day sang, "Que será, será."

We know that Lynch and Frost are deeply interested in Asian/Hindu/Tibetan spirituality, so prominent in *Twin Peaks*: mystical visions, altered states of consciousness, prophecy, karma, reincarnation, the Red Room as a way station between reincarnations for Laura and Leland Palmer. (It's a measure of Laura's compelling magnitude—"Laura is the One"—that Leland, the other "dead mortal" in the Red Room, is a fringe narrative element in *The Return*.) Young Lynch and Frost were raised as Christians (Lynch's early artworks had Christian themes and motifs), so their *Twin Peaks* mythology encompasses traditional angels and demons, ideas of heaven and liberated states beyond multiple reincarnations, prayer, and sacraments of secular spirituality (pie and coffee), all flashing and humming with electricity.

Carl Rodd kneels with the weeping mother and her dead child, his hand on her shoulder, his sad, kind eyes meeting hers: a human angel bearing witness. To end the sequence, Lynch cuts from Carl's face to *Twin Peaks*'s all-unifying electricity: telephone pole number six, with its crowning tangle of wires vectoring out beyond the frame into mystery. In the original *Twin Peaks*, electricity seemed to have an abnormal, unruly life of its own, making light flash on and off above Laura Palmer's gray-blue dead body in an examining room. Lynch called the effect "magical," and it was not planned: a happy accident that was meant to be. Electricity powers the artistic grid of many Lynch projects, but it really became prominent in *Fire Walk With Me*, which the director considers "required viewing" for fully experiencing *The Return*.

In *Fire Walk With Me*, telephone pole number six became a totem pole of human disappearance and death, extradimensional, otherworldly denizens' desire and transport, its wires twittering with bad vibrations. The pole and the wires, wood and electricity: an abstraction of *Twin Peaks*. The pole was in the trailer park of Carl Rodd, who had been places and seen things he didn't want to see again. The pole was a stone's throw from the intersection where, in *The Return*, Carl comforts the grieving mother, the intersection that was, in *Fire Walk With Me*, a narrative focal point for Laura, Leland, and the One-Armed Man in his earthly form. In *The Return*'s crosswalk, a boy is killed; in *Fire Walk With Me*, an old man using a walker takes forever to cross, suspending time for one of Lynch's archetypal scenes in which daily life is eerily invaded by otherness.

Leland and Laura, in the family convertible, "going to meet Mom for breakfast." Stopped at the crosswalk as the old man labors across, they're accosted by a strange man (the One-Armed Man). He roars up in his little truck, in the lane next to driver

Leland, the lane in which *The Return*'s speeding Richard struck the boy. Leland doesn't know the man, who babbles furiously, "The thread will be torn, Mr. Palmer," and to Laura, "It's your father"; the man is wearing the jade Owl Cave ring. The stranger is Bob's former dark familiar, who's "gone straight" on the side of good. He knows that Bob possesses Leland (Leland doesn't know this) and that Bob, through the vehicle of Leland, wants to devour Laura, body and soul. The thread that will be torn is the line of Laura's life if she doesn't somehow escape Bob's domination—but this is all beyond Leland's and Laura's comprehension, so the tragedy will play out. "It's your father" is a final, blunt attempt to make Laura see the horrific, sad web she's trapped in, but she must use her own inner resources, and take more time, to discover the truth. Leland and Laura can't decipher the One-Armed Man's coded presentation; they must keep falling down the chute.

Just as Lynch hopes we'll watch *The Return* wearing headphones to fully appreciate his layered sound design, he knows that having had the *Fire Walk With Me* intersection/crosswalk experience will heighten the place's narrative/spiritual resonance when we return there in 2017. Laura Palmer's life line was stretched thin; the boy's life line was severed. God's will, the will of the gods, destiny, karma happenstance, falling down a chute, or ascending to heaven—beneath a humming telephone pole.

Janey-E is playing life's Chutes and Ladders to win. She's a homemaker and a family defender, and if Dougie can't cope with life's tribulations, she bloody well can (as Brit/Aussie Naomi Watts would say). She strides up to the two thugs Dougie owes gambling money to and says, "You get this straight." They're trying to extort more dollars than Dougie owes, and she talks them into accepting a lower figure. We have to assume they didn't hear about Dougie/Mr. Jackpots winning a king's ransom at the casino: she's giving them just one-eighteenth of those winnings. What does the karmic balance sheet say about not disclosing to bad people that she's got a bundle of cash she could draw on? All for the good cause of her family's financial welfare? Maybe the baddies received a karmic boost by accepting Janey-E's terms.

Las Vegas Lorraine's hold on the good life seems tenuous at best. Her path is plummeting. Working for some evil agent who wants Dougie killed, she deals with bomb-planting Gene and his crew. Nervous is her middle name; she knows she's supping with devils. And further downtown in his baronial office, Todd knows that he's made a deal with the Devil by "working for someone like him." The "him" has sent Todd a white envelope with a black spot on it. Though the spot is symmetrical and smooth, it recalls the roundish black smudge form with little horns/ears on Mr. C's ace of spades playing card, the mysterious representation of his ultimate object of desire. The black marks in two locations link Mr. C to Lorraine, Gene, Todd, and dark Las Vegas doings.

Todd's spotted envelope contains two photographs, of Lorraine and Dougie, and when four-foot-tall Ike the Spike (Christophe Zajac-Denek) receives them, he gets out his ice pick. Since Mr. C knows that pre-Cooper Dougie dematerialized in the Red Room and that Las Vegas Dougie is now occupied by good Cooper, it seems that the black spot trail leads to the conclusion that Mr. C is the overlord pulling Lorraine, Gene, Todd, and Ike's strings.

Ike is a lethal little beast, an unstoppable Energizer Bunny of doom, his ice pick festooned with leather strips like a ritualistic sacrificial blade. Lorraine stands in alarm by her desk, hearing sounds of commotion and screams from the outer office. Ike scurries down the hall, through her doorway, and he's on her like a rabid dog, stabbing, stabbing, their faces sprayed with her blood, rotating the pick in her chest like stirring a stew pot. A touch of grisly comedy: Ike says, "Oh, no!"—striking her breast bone has bent his pick. As for Ike's pursuit of Dougie? All in good time.

Native American Sheriff's Deputy Hawk (Michael Horse) has been on the upward spiritual climb from way back; it's hard to imagine what could ever roll him down the chute. With the steady, calming presence of an old soul cedar tree, Hawk is a compendium of wise street smarts, ancient tribal knowledge, and mystical visionary intuition. For the first few parts of *The Return*, he's been on alert: the frail, ailing Log Lady told him, "Something's missing regarding Dale Cooper and the Laura Palmer case, something to do with your heritage." After some deadpan, low-key comic scenes with Andy and Lucy, and the wrenching moment when Bobby weeps seeing Laura's picture again, all the old evidence has supplied no answers. But Lynch's gospel says Pay Attention to Everything: the mundane can yield wonders.

After washing his hands in the office restroom and checking his long silver hair in the mirror, Hawk pulls his comb out, and a coin falls from his pocket, a nickel, an Indian head nickel. Hawk opens himself to the field of information around him. The toilet stall door was made by the Nez Perce steel company (Mark Frost referenced the tribe in his book), and Hawk notices that the door's top edge is a hair irregular. This is *The Return*, so he proceeds slowly: a step stool, some tools, gets rid of irritating intruder Officer Chad, and finally Hawk separates the door's steel sheets like an envelope, yielding some handwritten pieces of paper. Thank you for the alert, Log Lady: the missing thing has been found; these papers are big news.

The Cooper that Gordon Cole and Albert experienced in the South Dakota prison (only we knew that this was Mr. C, the Bob-possessed Cooper) was cold and creepy, distinctly different from their old colleague and friend. They need someone who knows Cooper even better than they do to evaluate him, someone we never saw in the 1990-91 *Twin Peaks*, someone who was bound to him in a stream of tape-recorded thoughts and feelings, tied to him with a lifeline of electronic intimacy.

On a film noir night of dark streets and pouring rain, Albert steps into a bar. He burrows into the dim, smoky, crowded space and approaches the slim, elegant back of a tall woman at the bar. Her perfect, smooth, silver-blonde hair bob feathers the nape of her tall neck. He says, "Diane." All poise, she turns; they lock eyes, neither smiling. A suspenseful moment of gravitas, communion between two old warriors. She (Laura Dern) says, "Hello, Albert," perhaps with a faint breath of weary disdain.

So after twenty-five years, we finally see Diane, Cooper's secretary, who received his musings and hard evidence from the field, his closest confidant and perhaps more. She's the perfect person to size up Cooper, with prison bars between them, and their meeting and its aftermath will be dramatic high points of *The Return*. Diane will emerge as one of the show's most enigmatic characters.

Lynch is fascinated by opposites, and combined opposites. Falling, rising; up, down; above, below. As above, so below. Head in the stars, feet in the dust. We approach wholeness, enlightenment, by plumbing our subconscious; when Lynch meditates, he "transcends" by "diving down." Can a person be climbing a ladder and falling down a chute at the same time; playing a game, landing on a ladder and a snake all at once?

–CHAPTER THIRTEEN–

TWO BLONDES
(PART SEVEN)

No disrespect intended, love and bon voyage to you all: actor Michael Ontkean, who played *Twin Peaks*'s original sheriff, Harry Truman, was in a retiring mode and chose not to be in *The Return*.

In the annals of crime fiction, it's traditional that when the FBI gets involved, there's tension between the incoming feds and "local law enforcement": males and their testosterone-driven territoriality. Down-to-earth Sheriff Harry Truman and the more head-trippy Special Agent Dale Cooper quickly became almost brotherly crime fighters, combining their talents to plumb the depths of Laura Palmer's murder and confront the intrigues and enigmas that rippled through the town. Both men were stalwart, loyal, and true, and Harry readily adopted Cooper's "every day, give yourself a present" philosophy, which opened a portal to *Twin Peaks*'s signature treats of doughnuts, pie, and coffee. Harry was a key component of *Twin Peaks*'s love-and-mysteries-in-the-air theme, and his romance with sawmill owner Josie Packard (Joan Chen, as a clandestine femme fatale) linked up with further appealing plotlines.

Harry was such a pleasant, comforting presence that the prospect of him not being in *The Return* sounded tragic. But Lynch and Frost astutely made his physical absence tragic in story terms: he's very ill and getting worse, but he's a resonant emotional presence via his connection with his brother Frank, who's now the acting sheriff. There's no actor who could better represent the Truman clan than Robert Forster. His Frank is a man of fewer words than Harry, but his lived-in face, which has ridden out many storms, is eloquent. As we watch Frank's side of his phone talks with Harry, we feel their warm, loving bond, conveyed with true, understated emotion, not sentimentality. Having lost my beloved Linda six months earlier, I knew the poignance of two people, closer than close, carrying on with simple human things like talking to each other, both knowing without saying it that the medical interventions probably aren't going to work and that one will be leaving soon, alone.

Deputy Chief Hawk shows Frank Truman the pages he found, lost pages of Laura

Palmer's diary: Hawk, the keeper of Native American legends interwoven with the saga of *Twin Peaks*, of which Frank's brother is a never-to-be-forgotten part. Dale Cooper comes to town to investigate Laura's death. He never met her, yet she had written in her diary that someone in a dream told her that "Dale's in the Lodge and he can't leave." But Hawk emphasizes that after Laura was dead and Cooper was investigating, the FBI man went into the Black Lodge, and "Harry saw Cooper come out." So the "one who came out was not the good Cooper."

"Cooper" looked like Cooper to his colleagues and friends, and Harry, with Doc Hayward, took him to the hospital to be examined. Sheriff Frank Truman wasn't part of these scenes twenty-five years ago; he's being brought up to speed. Doc's now retired, but Frank checks in with him via Skype. Since doubleness is the name of *Twin Peaks*'s game, these days the Sheriff's Department has two sections: old school with wood paneling, Frank, Bobby, Andy, and Lucy; and new school with a twenty-first-century high-tech center, Maggie (Jodee Thelen, a gray-haired woman in a power position!), bad-apple Chad, and a few minor newbie officers.

Lynch and Frost give us a last, warm and homey look at Doc Hayward, played by Frost's father, Warren: an old man's face and strained voice, outdoorsman's cap, white mustache and goatee, wire-rimmed spectacles with which he's observed and diagnosed countless grateful town residents. He says he remembers that time at the hospital and "Cooper with a strange face" leaving intensive care after visiting high schooler Audrey Horne, in a coma from the bank bomb blast. (Good Cooper had evaded Audrey's romantic advances, feeling she was too young for him, but maybe Bad Cooper found her comatose body ripe for raping; hence, Richard Horne would be his son). In a very *Twin Peaks* way, Doc closes with a description of his brown trout and English-muffin-with-huckleberry-jam breakfast and wishes ailing Harry and Sheriff Frank well; Frank says, "Keep working the sunny side of the river." A tantalizing taste of a world watched over by men of loving grace.

Such a man was Major Garland Briggs, tried-and-true military hero, loving husband, and father of cantankerous son Bobby and a frontiersman where paranormal forces interface with the north woods. He has worked on the UFO/extraterrestrials-investigating Project Bluebook and maintained the secret Listening Post Alpha in the woods above Twin Peaks. He knew that it was his, and the town's, fate to confront great darkness. He'd been whisked away to an alternative dimension and kidnapped, drugged, and questioned by Windom Earle, Cooper's crazed former partner and seeker of the Black Lodge's mystical power. Briggs escaped Earle's clutches, and Earle made it into the Lodge, where he learned he shouldn't play with fire as Bob destroyed him. While Earle was still alive in the Lodge, he communicated with Major Briggs via the medium of Laura's mother, Sarah, saying, "I'm in the Black Lodge with Dale Cooper," so Briggs knew Cooper was in the Red Room. The male voice that issued from Sarah's mouth could also have been that of her husband Leland, Laura's killer, now dead and an occupant of the Red Room. But Leland's voice would have been mournful; the one that Sarah spews out is demonic, in the tonal range of Bob.

We saw no more of Major Briggs in the final episode of the original *Twin Peaks*, but Mark Frost's book chronicles how Briggs, knowing that something's wrong on a cosmic scale, says he'll meet with the pseudo-Cooper, then, before he arrives, hastily strategizes to fake his own death and disappear. As we've said, Lynch didn't read Frost's book, so Frost's final narrative detail about Briggs is missing from *The Return*. In Lynch and Frost's *Return* saga, we arc decades from a voice within Sarah Palmer telling Briggs that Cooper's in the Black Lodge to Briggs being the headless corpse found in a South Dakota apartment bed, topped with the severed head of Ruth, the town librarian. As Dorothy says in *The Wizard of Oz*, "Oh my!"

What does it all add up to? The burly headless torso looks like Briggs's physiognomy; it has his fingerprints. But forensics say that he died a few days ago, and his body's that of a man in his forties, rather than the seventy-two Briggs would be. He has Janey-E's wedding ring in his stomach. His fingerprints have shown up sixteen times over the years he's been gone, and his disembodied head has manifested to Cooper, saying "Blue Rose," indicating he has an advanced understanding of powerful, ineffable forces in play.

At this point in *The Return*, Briggs is a locus of mystery, and since his military work has been top secret, Lieutenant Cynthia Knox (Adele René) has flown to South Dakota to investigate the situation regarding his body. Reporting by phone to her superior, we see her face in close up, a soft-focus hallway behind her. As she confirms that it is Briggs's corpse that's been found, a pulsing black blur, way down the hall behind her but visually near her head in the frame, materializes like an abstraction of fear and evil. She goes back into the examining room, rejoining local law enforcement and the forensic team, and we see what they don't: a creepy, charcoal-blackened man like the one earlier near Bill Hastings's cell, who passes by outside the room. Will law enforcers and the military be any match for this walking horror that radiates the power of shadows and makes that otherworldly electromagnetic clicking sound?

It's a sunny morning in Philadelphia, and Gordon Cole and Albert are going to visit Diane, unannounced. Before they leave FBI headquarters, we get a privileged moment with Gordon alone in his office. Tipping back in his desk chair, eyes closed, he's not saying his mantra; he's whistling the sweet melody of composer Nino Rota's theme for Federico Fellini's 1973 film *Amarcord* ("I remember" in Italian). Fellini is one of Lynch's favorite directors, and *Amarcord* a special film. It was Lynch's art mentor Bushnell Keeler's favorite, and I was proud to give Bushnell a video of it when it was otherwise unavailable. But in Lynch's multi-valenced world, his whistled notes also evoke the whistling opening of Rammstein's *Engel* (*Angel*). Rammstein's heavy, sledge-hammering rock is a structural element in Lynch's *Lost Highway*. In *Engel* Rammstein's angels are afraid and alone, in need of protection and help, like *Twin Peaks'* vulnerable souls. Cole's whistled notes also match the synthesizer notes of rapper Warren G's "Do You See," especially the way the last note is warbled/trilled by Lynch's mouth/Warren G's synthesizer. As Cole whistles, we notice a photo of an ear of corn counterbalancing the photo mural of the atom bomb blast. Sustenance and destruction, the life force and death, existence and nonexistence: the tension between opposing forces that keeps everything spinning, manifesting the All. At the moment of electrical space-time turbulence when the defiant Mr. C stayed in our world and Cooper became Dougie, both vomited bile-like creamed corn, Mr. C in gushing quantities, perhaps because of Bob's presence within him. In *Fire Walk With Me*, Phillip Jeffries described a meeting of otherworldly denizens, including Bob, above a convenience store, where we saw bowls of creamed corn. And near the film's end, Leland (having just killed Laura), the One-Armed Man (formerly Mike), the Man From Another Place (formerly Mike's arm), and Bob are together in the Red Room. The otherworldly ones speak of the corn as "garmonbozia," a sacramental nutrient of great value. Bob has a bottomless appetite for others' torment. He takes what he wants, which includes the convenience store corn, and he must atone to his cohorts.

In the universe of *Fire Walk With Me*, "garmonbozia" translates as "pain and suffering," and Leland's murderous crime and his anguish over victimizing his daughter is visualized as a chest wound that bloodies his white shirt. Bob, with his hand, converts the wound to corn sustenance for Mike and the Man From Another Place. We see a close-up of the golden goop entering the Man from Another Place's (Michael J. Anderson) mouth. If the corn is sacred to the entities of darkness, so is getting the shot just right for Lynch. Anderson recalls that "Lynch got quite upset when I spilled some of the corn. He squatted down and talked to me, and he goes, 'Now, you don't want to spill it at all. Not even a little bit. It's like gold.' And he just stood there like, 'Do you get it? Can you grasp what I am telling you?' He was very serious. It wasn't a joke." Perhaps we can be allowed a discrete chuckle: Mark Frost told me that the creamed idea came from Lynch having eaten some for lunch one day and being inspired to put it in the show. The corn made a small appearance in the original *Twin Peaks*, but gained its new name and full resonance in *Fire Walk With Me*.

So David Lynch knows all about the corn/garmonbozia, but does Gordon Cole? The answer is no if we go by the evidence of his appearances in the TV *Twin Peaks* and *Fire Walk With Me*. Maybe, as Cole whistles in his chair, he likes being positioned between negative (bomb) and positive (nutritious corn) poles, that vibrant energy zone between opposing forces that generates his sense of purpose, his balance-keeping life mission. But *The Return* shows us that Cole sometimes knows more than he lets on, so maybe he's thinking about some way the dark ones and their food relate to nuclear fission.

We've always seen Dale Cooper as a visitor, not a householder, in the town of Twin Peaks and in the Red Room. In the original series he spoke of settling in town, and Twin Peaks's woodsy, homey, 1950s ambience seems a natural fit for him. And by extension, we picture the unseen Diane, who, via Cooper's tape-recorded messages to her, was intimately linked to his thoughts and feelings, as a sweet, nurturing helpmate: Cooper-like. But no, Lynch and Frost live to jolt us with the unexpected.

Diane's abode is Contemporary Asian Cool. Her boyfriend/hookup's just leaving, dressed in un-Cooper-like hip black shirt and pants, with a sleek gray blazer. Diane's floors are gleaming bare hardwood, the furniture and fixtures midcentury modern, the artwork Asian screens, vases, and figurines; she's wrapped in a kimono-like red robe. She's got major attitude that you couldn't cut with a knife, because she'd cut you first. Compared with the other women Laura Dern has played for Lynch (warmhearted, with flowing golden hair in *Blue Velvet* and *Wild at Heart*), Diane is almost an alien with her sour spirit and severe, skull-pressing helmet of frost-hued hair. Frost-hued and "Fuck You!"—Diane's favorite expression, always said with feeling.

Gordon, Albert,and Diane stand in her living room. She's chilly and hostile, but Gordon won't be deterred. *Twin Peaks* rituals and sacraments are in order: a sit-down over coffee. Does she have any? "No!" But she goes around the corner to fix some. And when she brings it, Gordon, characteristically an unironic speaker, says a supersweet "Thank you, Diane" with a note of playful sarcasm—thanks so much for your arduous effort. Maybe this biting-edged banter is their familiar way of relating to each other.

In Diane's living room, while Gordon and Albert were waiting for her to come back around the corner (with coffee?), both men having received their "Fuck you," Gordon summed up Diane for Albert: "Tough cookie." Does this ring a bell, *Return* watchers? When Janey-E paid the two gambling-debt-collecting thugs, they summed her up as a "tough dame." Both Diane Evans and Janey-E have E in their names; both become identified with the color red (as was the ruby-dressed Naido in the purple sea Mansion); all three women speak/communicate with ardent emotion and have been close to Cooper in one way or another. I certainly didn't make these connections while first watching Part Seven, but on reflection, we'll see that it's a meaningful triangulation.

Diane, a tough cookie by any measure, but Gordon Cole has dealt with many a hair-triggered, acid-tongued person with minimal impulse control in his time, and Albert used to be one of them. In the original *Twin Peaks*, Albert was a triple threat: snide, sarcastic, snarky, and impatient. People couldn't keep up with his brilliant, speeding mind, and he loved to point that out. But just as hotel owner Ben Horne pulled himself out of a downward spiral of shady business and personal dealings, Albert became more attuned to interpersonal harmony and the wisdom traditions of Gandhi and Martin Luther King, Jr. These days he's older, still brilliant, still adept with an occasional stinging wisecrack, but he listens before he speaks. He and Cole seem able to read each other deeply, and others as well.

On the private jet taking Cole, Albert, Diane, and Tammy to their South Dakota rendezvous with "Cooper," Albert can feel Diane's nervous tension, and he brings her a small mini bar bottle of vodka. Her response: "Fuck you, Albert!" And she makes sure to include the new, female member of Cole's professional family in her scorn: "Fuck you, Tammy!" It's easy to imagine the gentle, receptive, thoughtful Tammy being the one Dale Cooper sent his tape messages to in 1990-91, but not Diane the combative, aggressive hellion of 2016. We get the sense that Diane's bark and bite are defensive armor protecting a wounded heart and soul and that Mr. C well could have been the perpetrator.

As *The Return* rolls along, we see that Gordon Cole possesses esoteric knowledge and perceptions above and beyond those of his colleagues, and he chooses when and where to share them (David Lynch exercising his essential final cut). Cole had clearly been disturbed by his prison encounter with "Cooper," and now he details a troubling metaphysical connection between the black smudge of "Cooper's" ring-finger fingerprint (the spiritual finger)—recalls to us the black-smudge form on Mr. C's ace of spades card—which is reversed, and the way "Cooper" had said "yrev" instead of "very" when Cole and "Cooper" were "very glad to see each other" again. A coded FBI greeting that had twisted into darkness. Albert shares a more earthbound puzzle piece, a photo of "Cooper" (Mr. C to us) standing in front of his palatial white villa in Rio, wearing a south-of-the-equator white linen jacket. So it seems his criminal empire actually extends way beyond South Dakota, into a part of the world *The Return* links with Las Vegas Lorraine's communiques and Phillip Jeffries and that Columbian FBI agent who was killed, probably by Mr. C. Twin Peaks, a man of two hemispheres: Dale Cooper and Bob in one. And there are two hemispheres of the human brain, which Dr. Jacoby feels can be beneficially stimulated by wearing eyeglasses with a blue lens for the left eye, a red lens for the right. Blue and red meld into purple, like the vast sea by the Mansion somewhere beyond.

At the prison, Diane is nervous, scared, energized, in Let's do this thing mode. She enters the dim control room alone, presses the button, and the metal curtain goes up, revealing "Cooper" behind thick glass. He's sitting facing her, and even in repose his presence is so powerful that she stands up, making herself as formidable as she can. Neither even approaches a smile; his voice has that thick, stretched, low-tone slowness. She asks if he remembers the last night they saw each other; he says he'll never forget it—and she can't hold back: "Who are you?" Like Gordon Cole, Diane is shaken and repulsed by "Cooper's" sepulchral otherness; her breath is ragged, almost sobbing as she brings down the curtain.

Diane's few moments with "Cooper" have been a wounding experience, like a bone-deep betrayal. She and Gordon Cole have spent a good share of their professional lives together, and out on the pavement, beyond her attitude and his need to know, they hold each other for comfort, an embrace of something stable and sane. "That (she doesn't say "he") isn't the Dale Cooper I knew. Something isn't right here (she touches her heart)." Gordon's in personal and professional mode: "That's good enough for me, Diane; we'll have to talk more." No need for extra words now. As Diane regains her emotional footing, she finishes off that vodka bottle with a cynical "Cheers to the FBI."

After they leave, Mr. C plays his blackmail trump card with whatever information he's holding over Warden Murphy's head, and Murphy agrees to let him and Ray Monroe (Mr. C's local partner in crime) go free, with a car with a gun in its glove compartment.

Southwest in Las Vegas at Lucky 7 Insurance, Sinclair seems overly curious and concerned about Dougie's presentation of his homework files (which reference Sinclair's cases) to Bushnell Mullins, indicating (to us) that Dougie's earlier intuition about Sinclair ("He's lying") had been spot on.

Next, Lynch and Frost give us a long (five minutes) ensemble (six characters) scene that illustrates the human comedy of conveying a simple message (Dougie's blown-up car has been found). In Dougie's office are Dougie, Janey-E, Bushnell Mullins, and the Detectives Fusco (three hulking Las Vegas police detectives). As so often in life, communication is hard to achieve, but a mutual understanding is finally reached. It's after business hours; Janey-E came in the building only because Dougie didn't come out after five p.m. This is just a few hours after she paid, and told off, the gambling-debt thugs, and in Dougie's office, she's again shown her gift for expressing common sense, with passionate sarcasm.

We're lulled by the familiar rhythm: Janey-E chattering about something ("Don't you ever gamble again!"), Dougie silent, blank-faced as she guides him out onto the business plaza, slowly heading for her car. Then a Lynchian occurrence out of nowhere, thrilling. As Janey-E and Dougie walk toward us, Dougie tilts his head up: there's an ominous low vibration in the psychic air. From behind some strolling people, little Ike the Spike leaps forward, firing a handgun. Dougie isn't hit and, now miraculously limber, quick, and loose, joins his sudden forcefulness with Ike's oncoming momentum and pivots the assassin down onto the concrete, where the Red Room's electric tree bursts forth, its blob head entreating, "Squeeze his hand off!" Ike's hand is on the gun; Dougie's hand covers it, pressing hard. They tussle for a moment, then Ike wriggles free and runs off, leaving some of the palm of his hand mashed into the pistol's grip. Stunning.

Janey-E had jumped into the melee and landed a few blows, and she and Dougie stood together, her head on his chest. She's panting for breath, clinging to him, repeating, "Oh, Dougie, are you alright?" as if they have just had sex. His attention to that invisible warning signal fades with the low sound, and he tilts his head back down to earth. Drinking coffee for the first time as Dougie did not return Cooper to self-realization. But this threat of lethal danger triggered a motor memory of Cooper's strength and coordination (a witness says he "moved like a cobra; he was just a blur"). He isn't Cooper, and Janey-E isn't Laura Palmer, but he's enacted the archetype of chivalry and saved his blonde, blue-eyed lady. In the midst of the action, we caught a couple of glimpses of not the gun-pointing statue, but life-affirming daubes of red, on the other plaza sculpture's red balloon forms and on Janey-E's scarlet purse. This incident is an apotheosis for Cooper's true self that foreshadows his future full awakening and triumph, and it deepens the bond between this man (whatever we call him) and Janey-E.

I once delighted David Lynch by trying to describe the sound of Betty Elms's (Naomi Watts) apartment kitchen, its room presence, in *Mulholland Drive.* There wasn't anything overt, like a dripping faucet or something heating on the stove. It was the sound of nothing specific, but beyond the way the room looked, I could feel the space in my head. Lynch must love the science of hearing, which transmutes invisible sound waves into fluid waves in an inner spiral chamber, then into electrical impulses in the brain.

In 1998, the year that Lynch pitched *Mulholland Drive* as a TV pilot, he produced a CD of the music of twelfth-century female Christian mystic Hildegard von Bingen, who said, "What the ear hears will shake a person's insides." Medieval Christians believed that Christ, the word of God incarnated, was conceived in the Virgin Mary's womb after a dove, the fertile wind of the Holy Spirit, entered her ear. And what a saga resulted! In Lynch's *Blue Velvet* (1986), Kyle MacLachlan's character finds a severed ear that leads him into the mysteries of his street, his town, good and evil, love and death. MacLachlan's deep journey of discovery commences when Lynch's camera descends into the dark inner passage of the ear, accompanied by an unclassifiable sound that's perhaps a near duplicate of the base sound of the universe (you can Google it). Lynch said, "It had to be an ear. You can go down into it, and it goes somewhere vast." In India, the land of Lynch's spiritual beliefs, legends say that a sound created the universe. A drone, a hum, repeating and repeating like a mantra, the blood singing in your ears. Evocative musical melodies abound in Lynch's work, but he's especially adept at conjuring soundscapes of mood and atmosphere, noises, found sounds as soundtrack.

As *The Return* transitions realms, from Las Vegas to Twin Peaks, sound master Lynch blends inorganic and organic as the sound of a helicopter hovering above Dougie's triumph over Ike becomes the whooshing cascade of White Tail Falls next to the Great Northern Hotel. Inside, Lynch gives us an enchanting few minutes that no one else would ever dream up. It's well after the dinner hour; the concierge stands alone at the front desk. We hear the just-perceptible clack of a computer keyboard and far-off voices, but the atmosphere is hushed, cocooned in an inner world. Lynch's persistent, fervent wish is to float us into a dream, and his camera gently glides along warm, amber-gold wood paneling, and as it progresses, we hear a ringing/humming sound that rises, falls, rises, never quite goes away. We've floated into the hotel's inner sanctum, Ben Horne's office, where he and his assistant Beverly (Ashley Judd) stand silently, listening. The sound isn't overwhelming; it seems to emanate from the room, but what's the source? A mysterious occurrence; the human impulse to solve it.

A courtly older gentleman, an attractive middle-aged woman. We have history with Ben from the original *Twin Peaks*: a hubris-driven, shady, predatory businessman with appetites and vices who was even accused of killing Laura Palmer and did have sex with her. But as though trying to reform himself and pay karmic debts in this lifetime, he works at being a better man, and deals with a parade of problems, often family related, with as much grace as he can muster (I'm friends with Ben Horne actor Richard Beymer, who recently told me that he's also "working at being a better human being"). And we'll soon learn that Beverly is burdened with infuriating, guilt-inducing family complications. Lynch has given them a dalliance, a haven (a taste of heaven?) with a roaming room tone that prompts a sort of dance as they follow the shifting sound, trying to find its heart: here, there, pause, commence, in a space of glowing amber light. They can't solve it, so they say goodnight, for the first time on a first-name basis.

Is the sound the music of love? The Sanctus bell of Christian ritual, the Hindu OM of supreme reality? Does it relate to the Native American objects in Ben's office or *Twin Peaks*'s history (years ago, Agent Cooper was shot in the hotel; Josie Packard is paranormally imprisoned in its woodwork). Enough of speculation; we'll return to the sound later. Quiet the mind; enjoy the poetry, Lynch's "room to dream."

Across the way at the Roadhouse, it's much later: no band, no crowd, no drinks. It's closed, but we're inside. Lynch the painter loves the work of twentieth-century American master Edward Hopper (1882-1967), famous for his late-night cafés, diners, bars, movie houses. Inside the Roadhouse, there's a Hopper-like feel to Lynch's composition, with the long bar angling into the frame on the left and the bar stools neatly aligned along the counter's face. The lighting's soft, the barkeep is wrapping up some business behind the bar, and in the foreground a guy is sweeping the floor with a broom. Lynch's camera is planted, it doesn't move, for the length of time it takes the recording of Booker T & the MGs' instrumental "Green Onions" to play. So we're watching an uncut tableau, like a moving painting. Sweeping, sweeping, it engages our kinesthetic senses. Would we start a small pile of peanut shells, paper bits, etc. on the left, leave it and go over to the right and start another pile, and then go back for the rest or would we try to move it all forward at once? Like Dougie's way-slow activities, this shot makes some viewers angrily impatient. Lynch believes that most humble tasks can be meditative, and he has a reverence for the ethos of work. Himself an artist and a wood craftsman who works at home, Lynch personally likes sweeping up; it's a proper part of the art life. The Roadhouse sweeper is like a Zen monk sweeping the sand in a rock garden. There, imperfection is part of the scene's beauty, so a leaf or some little irregularity is left as is. When Lynch leaves the Roadhouse sweeper, every last bit of refuse has not been picked up.

Part Seven ends at the Double R diner. It seems odd that the café's open and filled with so many people even after the Roadhouse is closed. The diner's interior is bisected by a long counter, with stools on both sides and booths along the outer-left and-right walls. "Sleepwalk," like "Green Onions" a midcentury instrumental Lynch loves, is playing. Lots of folks at the counter and in the booths, enjoying their food and drink, with owner Norma presiding at her booth/office workstation. "Sleepwalk" plays uninterrupted, and a kid (Riley Lynch) enters for a second, urgently asks, "Hey, has anybody seen Billy?" He leaves; Lynch cuts from one side of the counter to the other, always looking toward the entrance where the kid questioned the room. Very straightforward, with the music and kid constant, but after the camera cuts to the left and returns to the right, something's very strange. In the split second it takes to shift from one side to the other, some of the patrons are different, or wearing different clothes, or have the same clothes but are in different positions. Dreamlike.

Sleepwalk. Being in motion without being aware of it, maybe dreaming of a familiar place at different times, but both times needing to find Billy. Further down *The Return* road, we'll encounter someone obsessed with a Billy, a dreamy dancer linked with the diner twenty-five years ago, who's not sure where, when, or who she is.

–CHAPTER FOURTEEN–

SEASON OF THE WITCH
(PART EIGHT)

Like a hunter stalking his prey, Sherlock Holmes said "The game is afoot" as he tested his mettle against the complex turnings of good and evil. And back at the beginning of *The Return*, Mark Frost, Holmes fan and detective novel author, has Mr. C say, "The game begins" as he enacts his plan to evade going back into the Black Lodge and keep from being killed by his criminal associates Ray and Darya, hired for the job by Phillip Jeffries, who's "nowhere." A pillow over Darya's face, and bullets into the pillow, eliminated her. And now Ray and Mr. C, let out of prison, are driving through the night, each man's head brimming with plans that include the other being dead. Mr. C needs esoteric information from Ray that will get him closer to the paranormal source of dark power, perhaps the black-hole being of Judy herself—then Mr. C can let the night air into Ray's head.

Lynch titled singer Julee Cruise's 1989 album, for which he wrote the lyrics, *Floating Into the Night*, and again and again in Lynch's films and TV work, he floats his camera's eye, our subjective point of view, down roads at night. Ray's driving, Mr. C's riding, and he electronically nullifies the tracking device Warden Murphy had attached to their car. It's the two of them on their own, and the nocturnal point of view out the windshield glides from state highway to side road to dirt track in the wilderness.

Things are getting primal now. Mr. C wants what Ray has, the information Ray has memorized, and he'll reveal it in exchange for a big financial payoff. It's high-tension standoff time, but Ray steps away from the car. Mr. C opens the glove box. Yes—the warden came through. He grabs the loaded pistol, steps out of the car, and speaks to Ray's back, thirty feet away. One last time: "I want that information." What calculation is Mr. C making? If Ray won't tell him, Mr. C won't pay. Mr. C could overpower and torture him, but Ray's tough. Besides, there are others who have the information, and Ray's betrayed him, wants him dead, and he sees that Ray's got a gun. Fuck all this strategic rationality. Bob's animal ferocity, his base hunger for pain and suffering, grips Mr. C, and he fires three times. But he hears the sound of three clicks—no powder in the bullets. Ray answers with two perfect shots to the kill zone of Mr. C's middle: "Tricked you, fucker." A jolting moment. This can't be the end of Mr. C, though, approaching the halfway point of *The Return*, we've learned that Lynch and Frost are devoted to throwing our expectations out the window. Remember the way Alfred Hitchcock killed off *Psycho*'s leading lady in the first third of the film? Lynch does.

The place where Ray executes Mr. C is one of Lynch's dark-on-dark compositions. Faintly lit, as though by emaciated moonlight, we make out a field with pale, tall dead grass and the black shapes of deciduous trees. Ray stands over Mr. C. As he raises his gun to trigger more shots, there's a silent, cloudy flash of electric blue light, heralding one of Lynch's most uncanny sequences. We hear soft, muffled, ominous tones as from a piano drowned in the River Styx and perceive the dark forms of men, like large, black fallen leaves from the trees, fluttering in the pale grass, moving forward into our reality from somewhere godforsaken. Ancient, dirt-caked faces and bodies, long greasy hair and beards, draped in grimy rags. They seem both extradimensional and of the earth, dust devils.

Ray is our surrogate; he does what we would do. Knees won't hold, falling onto the dirt, sitting, watching in awe and fear as seven or eight of the beings (which Lynch calls the Woodsmen) enact a ritual of death and life. In *Fire Walk With Me*, Phillip Jeffries appeared in Gordon Cole's FBI office, interacted with Cole, Cooper and Albert, and yet "was never here." In Lynch's Woodsmen sequence, the director's ability to make us experience different planes of reality melding has taken a quantum leap. Or is it a cubist leap, as Lynch collages light flickers, crisp images, images superimposed and multiplied, so sometimes the Woodsmen's repetitive motions are layered over Ray sitting, watching with his mouth open: places, spatial positions, moments, all at this moment.

If, on the Las Vegas business plaza, full-fledged Cooper becoming activated to deal with Ike the Spike was part of some White Lodge Emergency Response System, then the Woodsmen bending over Mr. C are the Black Lodge version. A few of the dark, grubby men kneel and put their hands on Mr. C's destroyed chest as others bob and sway around the periphery. They push and push on Mr. C's torn flesh, smearing his blood on his torso and face. When Bob's head, encased in a gray, glistening membrane orb, starts to emerge from Mr. C's chest, the men push it back in. In Lynch's beloved *The Wizard of Oz* film, when the straw-filled Scarecrow is roughed up, his friends, including the Tin Woodsman, push and prod and put him back together. *The Return*'s Woodsmen look like they're made of man-shaped primeval ooze, not hard, shiny tin, but having done their best, they slip away in a fading, electricity-flashing mist.

Ray, who moaned in horror as the Woodsmen worked, leaped in his car and took off. He called Phillip Jeffries to say, "I think he's dead." But if not, Ray knows he can find Mr. C at the Farm, a bad-guy gathering place.

When Trent Reznor, composer and lead singer of Nine Inch Nails, produced drone sounds and songs for Lynch's *Lost Highway* (1997), Lynch said in *Rolling Stone*, "Trent's got a great mind for sound and music." It's the witching hour at the Roadhouse, and if the performers we've seen and heard so far have been warm to hot, this one's nuclear fission. Trent Reznor screams, and Nine Inch Nails play an unrelenting, pounding-factory beat whipsawed with guitar distortion; Reznor's in such a dark place he needs his shades to see. His heart bleeds a message, over and over: "She's gone away," wailing all the loss we've all ever felt. Roadhouse patrons usually chatter and dance to the beat, but tonight they're silent and still, entranced by the convulsion of sound, a drone that seeps over into the next shot, as Mr. C, lying prone on the dirt, sits up, alive.

Ray would be happy to kill Mr. C for money, but he doesn't have the Bob-destroying sense of mission that motivates Gordon Cole, Albert, and Cooper and that, we trust, will propel a restored Cooper into *The Return*'s climactic confrontation. In dramatic terms, Mr. C has to stay alive for Cooper: the two opponents who are worthy of each other, who *are* each other.

So Mr. C didn't give up the ghost, and Lynch and Frost will now reveal the ghost in their fiction machine.

A ghost-colored landscape in the dimmest morning light, July 16, 1945, 5:29 a.m., White Sands, New Mexico. Dark in the foreground, like earth we could step out onto, with pale gray-white features beyond: ridges, sand dunes? Then, as Lynch's camera moves forward onto the dark part, toward the dim paleness, a jaw-dropping scale shift in image and meaning. As if midnight was instantly illuminated by white-hot light, we see that the dark foreground was the rim above a vast valley, with mountains on the far background horizon, and central in the bright white of the frame is the light source, a product of humankind's Promethean search for knowledge and the primal working of matter and energy. An awestruck quote from the Bhagavad Gita ("the light of a thousand suns") was uttered by physicist Robert J. Oppenheimer, director of the Manhattan Project, which developed the first atomic bomb and performed its first test, called Trinity, at White Sands. Then, as the world's first mushroom-shaped nuclear cloud bloomed, Oppenheimer added another Hindu phrase, "Now I am become Death, the destroyer of worlds."

In the world of seventeenth-century English physicist Isaac Newton (1642-1727), time and space were "absolute": a minute on earth was a minute on Mars; a yardstick was thirty-six inches on both planets. By the early twentieth century, science had constructed an impregnable fortress of universal laws concerning the nature of light, matter, gravity, electrical and magnetic fields. In 1905, German physicist Albert Einstein (1879-1955) advanced theories that exploded the fortress: time and space are relative, light is both wave and particle, matter can become energy, and energy matter, the smallest bit of matter might be able to release a transcendent amount of energy. Ironically, with shades of Dougie, when Einstein was a little boy it took him so long to learn to talk that the family maid called him the "dopey one."

The Atomic Age was born, the baby boomer age that Lynch, Frost, and I grew up in. When science showed us that solid objects were made of invisible energy systems (was energy spirit?), when science fiction time-traveled us, rocketed us to other planets, showed us the imminent advent of flying cars. When, in spite of the beneficent, protective, golden glow generated by Elvis, Marilyn Monroe, and Natalie Wood, Cokes and shakes and burgers, our parents and teachers telling us "It's a big, beautiful world," we lived in the shadow of a mushroom-shaped cloud. For America had dropped the bomb on Japan, precipitating the end of World War II. But now our enemy Russia had the bomb too, so the whole world could become a fireball this afternoon, or tomorrow. We could feel this all the time.

It was fun to be scared by made-up stories at the movies, but the threat of nuclear annihilation was real, haunting our waking and sleeping hours. There were neighborhood Civil Defense officers ready to go into action when the blasts came, radiation fallout shelters in backyards, duck-and-cover exercises at school, where we saw nuclear bomb test footage of ranch houses blowing away and images of the wastelands of Hiroshima and Nagasaki, where the ground temperature had been four-thousand degrees Celsius for a moment and the shadows of vaporized human beings stained concrete. Tens of thousands dead, survivors with their skin falling off, their "brains coming out," radiation sickness, cancers, people's genetic lines tainted and mutated. And we Americans, God-fearing and God endorsed, had dropped the bombs. A horrendous calculation had had to be made: word was that the Germans were working on a nuclear weapon, the Soviets were also interested, but if we bombed the Japanese (who'd struck us first at Pearl Harbor, but with conventional weapons), it would end World War II. It did, but at what a price. The nuclear mushroom cloud joined the Holocaust death camps as a symbol, a reminder, of the evil that men do.

While the war was raging, before the Manhattan Project, Einstein (a Jew whose house was raided by the Nazis in the 1930s) feared for civilization's survival and wrote to President Roosevelt, urging atomic bomb research. A few years later, after he'd become a US citizen, he heard that the bomb had been dropped on Hiroshima and said, "Oh, weh" ("Oh, my God"). For the remaining ten years of Einstein's life, he hated being called the godfather of the bomb, and he was a tireless advocate of "world government," a global authority to help prevent nuclear war.

When the pre-bomb Manhattan Project was beginning, Oppenheimer answered yes to two questions: Will we manufacture a bomb?, Will we use it? After the bomb was dropped on Japan, he said, "The physicists have known sin" and, to President Truman, "I have blood on my hands."

Ultimately, dropping the bomb was a military and political decision. There was talk that Truman would be impeached if he didn't use the weapon that was sure to win the war for our side and might scare the world into ending war forever. The Japanese surrendered; the bombing stopped, Truman having "hated the idea of killing all those kids" (*The Atlantic*). The scientific and engineering expertise of Oppenheimer and his Manhattan Project collaborators had worked wonders, but any euphoric sense of triumph quickly turned to revulsion, "an intensely personal experience of the reality of evil," as Alice Kimball Smith, wife of a Los Alamos scientist put it. The monster of nuclear destruction bit the hand of one of its creators. In 1946, New

Mexico, a year after the war ended, physicist Louis Slotin, who helped assemble the first atomic weapon, was experimenting with the fissionable core of a third weapon, which was not used after the Nagasaki bomb. Slotin's hand slipped; the room was flooded with blue light, and five times the amount of radiation that would kill a man saturated his body. He vomited, his hand was numb, he suffered "mental confusion" and died in a few days. The incident was a physical, scientific reality, but those who wrote about it alluded to metaphysics, the supernatural, saying Slotin had been "teasing the dragon's tail" as he worked on the "demon core." After the accident, a government memo advised "more liberal application of the inverse-square law": use remote control devices when handling fissionable material. If you've created a monster, keep your distance. Be ready to run, but where can you hide in this new, nuclear age? In the realm of correspondences, Slotin's accident happened at 3pm, and 2:53 pm will be a significant number throughout *The Return*. Also, flashing blue light, vomiting, and a limb that's numb have prominence in the *Twin Peaks* universe.

As the world contemplated the discovery, manipulation, and unleashing of the secret power of the cosmos, it felt a new, invasive, existential unease. As philosophical journalist Edward R. Morrow said, "Seldom, if ever, has a war ended leaving the victors with such a sense of uncertainty and fear, with such a realization that the future is obscure and that survival is not assured." As the great noir novelist Raymond Chandler once wrote, "It is not a fragrant world, but it is the world you live in."

In *The Return*, the atom bomb mushroom cloud is like a film noir femme fatale, beautiful, alluring, dangerous beyond measure: both Eros and Thanatos, irresistible. Mesmerized, we are carried forward in a point of view that travels down into and across the nocturnal New Mexico valley, its crisp features etched blinding silver-white, closer, closer to the expanding mottled mushroom cloud with vapor waves and electrical storms at its base: sublime, terrible beauty. Monstrous, obscene, gorgeous, like a toadstool on the ground where giant witches dance. We feel Pandora's box opening, the release of ur-energy, hidden in nature till now. On the contemporary 1945 scale of awe, it's comparable to black-and-white still photographs of exploding stars.

With the nervous, atonal sounds of screaming violins quivering like fissioning Uranium-235, Lynch's camera floats toward the bulbous, expanding blast cloud. True to the key dynamic of Lynch's art and life, we're penetrating the surface, going deep inside, from scientific/historical reality to the heart of the *Twin Peaks* legend.

True to the accounts of Trinity test witnesses like Manhattan Project physicist Richard Feynman, Lynch initially blasts us with huge fiery waves of red, yellow, orange, then gives us a privileged interior microview of swimming white-on-black gamma and X-ray particles, the kind that make Geiger counters buzz in 1950s sci-fi movies. To accompany his bomb-explosion imagery (which many feel eclipses Christopher Nolan's *Oppenheimer*'s [2023] Trinity blast), Lynch appropriately chose the symphonic composition "Threnody for the Victims of Hiroshima" (1960) by Polish composer Krysztotf Penderecki. Using fifty-two stringed instruments, Penderecki created a stunning expression of the anguish of the first atomic victims and the bomb's unholy power. He used tone clusters and textural counterpoint to form a sonic abstraction, just as Lynch creates visual abstractions for emotions and states of mind.

Inside the blast, on and on, Lynch rocks and buffets us with fire clouds—swarming particles, dark clouds spiked with spectral sparks of color, flying into our faces. Matter and energy come at us, but we also penetrate space, roaring down dark tunnels of clockwise-rotating smoke-fire-light, again and again, toward a central bright spot, as though we're inside the contractions of a cosmic birth canal. This image mirrors *Eraserhead*'s subjective point-of-view "birth" shot, which travels in a dark tunnel toward a spot of light. Characteristically, Lynch uses the rhythms of his presentation to give us a surreal jolt. The mesmerizing motion of the tunnels, color, and music drop away, and we're looking at a still, stark black-and-white image that's like a previously undiscovered Edward Hopper painting. It's night, the ground is dirt; in the foreground are two 1940s gas pumps, behind them an empty convenience store. Everything's dusty, weathered. It all feels deserted, left behind by civilization. Lynch lets us absorb the tableau's beauty and stillness, then a white smoke manifests at the base of the right gas pump. We can feel another reality trying to penetrate the tableau; it's a site where powerful forces are warping space-time millisecond to millisecond. Faster than you can blink, the white smoke cloud is small, huge, medium-sized, and a bustling crew of those sooty Woodsmen are scampering around the frame in cubistically shifting positions, in and out of the store, where jump-cutting, strobing light flashes indicate that the store is being prepared for new use.

All this pixilated, supernatural activity is prelude to overarching waves of meaning. For a moment, a light-on-dark background circular form is superimposed on the store window, becoming a white crescent moonlike shape that lingers as the store fades out. In artistic representations of the Virgin Mary, the Madonna, the vessel of divine birth who gives the world the fruit of the Holy Ghost, rests her feet on a crescent moon that represents a lower realm of being; her orientation is upward toward heaven, sun and stars. Throughout art history, the crescent's sharp edge also connotes the sickle of death, the Luna of alchemy, harvester of souls, "witchlike and terrible." And the crescent moon suggests the "horned gateway" of time's cycling. Lynch's crescent fades to the right into some dark medium that fills the frame. Is this the starless realm of eternal night? Are we deep in the diabolical brew of a witch's cauldron?

In the darkness a pale naked female form floats upper right. She's kin to the New York glass box demon but is distinguished by little sprig horns or ears on her smooth head, and her left arm and hand sprout from her shoulder backward. Like the glass box demon, her head is mainly mouth, and she spews a pale gooey river down across the frame into our faces. In the stream we see Bob's head in a circular bubble, and countless small eggs with mottled shells. So is this the birth of Bob, the medium of his entry into our world? To hell with virgin birth; maybe the naked female creature is vomiting the Devil's semen. The long, pale stream, studded with eggs of malevolent potential, suggest the chain necklace of skulls that Kali the Hindu goddess of death and destruction, an entity in Lynch's spiritual studies, wears. And Kali is sometimes portrayed with a supernaturally long, protruding tongue, like the vomit stream.

With the feeling that inside the mushroom cloud we're immersed in a single forward-moving flow that has various side aspects and dimensions, we're now out of the black-and-white vomit stream and back into the churning red-orange fire cloud corridors—no crescent shapes, but a central, slightly asymmetrical translucent golden bubble that grows to fill the frame. We're now seeing through the filter of the bubble, and the roiling flames seem honeyed, less harsh. The bubble evokes the iconic Part One opening credits image of Laura Palmer's face in a golden orb. We're still inside the bomb blast, Penderecki's disturbing music is still a torment, but Lynch is subtly shifting the tone in a more positive direction. Lynch has declared to me and others, "My films are about finding love in hell."

The fiery, fissioning material is still coming at us, but it's waning. Its color is a rhubarb red, grading away from fire orange toward pink. The music stops, and the last of the rhubarb embers fade. We're still moving forward, over a dark purple-black sea, the sea that Dale Cooper, having dropped/fallen from the Red Room, had contemplated from the Mansion's balcony. Cooper had passed through a pink cloud to get there, and he glowed pink, as did Naido, a woman with a face somehow altered from normal. There'd been a short-lived yearning bond between Cooper and this woman, who couldn't speak words and sacrificed herself to further his journey, thus making the pink glow depart. In early black-and-white silent films, scenes of love and human warmth were often hand-tinted pink, and sometimes pink-glowing women floated in heavenly star fields. For Lynch, the positive aura of pink could partly be a projection of his warm feelings for his Hollywood Hills Lloyd Wright house, which he calls the Pink House and has happily occupied for decades. In one of his online daily weather reports, he said, "This morning the sky is a strange pink—zowie!"

And in the summer of 2023 the world's moviegoers figuratively said zowie as they embraced the feminized pinker than pink utopia of Greta Gerrwig's film *Barbie*. The online *Twin Peaks* community equated Barbieland, radiant with empowered positive femininity, with the White Lodge; a Reddit.com artwork showed Cooper in *Barbie*'s pink realm. Maybe in Part Three when Cooper glowed pink for a short time, Lynch was visually coding a taste of transcnedence/ heaven/ nirvana, the elusive full illumination we strive for in this fallen world, the Hindu Dark Age he feels we're in. In *The Return*'s writing period, before filming started, Lynch did a short commercial for his David Lynch Signature Cup Coffee that features a blonde, blue-eyed woman who's a venerated "the One" in world culture, a Barbie doll. Wearing pink lipstick, her head's cradled in Lynch's pinkish palm, very close-up. His voice and her's (also his, made tiny and tender) have a simple conversation. He says he'll fix her a coffee; this gives her "dreamy" thoughts. Lynch is talking to himself/ honoring the goddess of female divinity/ maybe having pink thoughts for *The Return*.

Emerging from the bomb-blast passages, the camera swoops up from the purple sea and climbs high up a tower-like rock that's topped by silver metallic structures like streamlined art moderne silos with curved tops. They don't glow pink, but we see that it's a benevolent place when the camera enters the single, vertical slit opening in the compound's fortresslike façade (as his camera penetrated the slit in the hood covering *The Elephant Man*'s head). The interior is like a homey retro-future-steampunk mash-up in which a sweet-faced woman wearing an early-twentieth-century gown sits on that era's padded furniture, surrounded by wrought iron curlicues and a vintage gramophone horn playing pleasant 1920s music. Filling the left side of the tableau is a huge black metal bell shape, electrified like the one atop the Mansion's box in space, where Naido threw a switch and then plunged into the void. The bell shape is a powerful machine and starts sounding some kind of alert. Around the corner to investigate comes the Fireman, wearing a dark smoking jacket over his familiar white shirt and bow tie. So this is his place, and Senorita Dido (Joy Nash) is his lady. Have we seen any location that's more qualified to be the White Lodge? Mark Frost doesn't think so (*Conversations With Mark Frost*).

In *The Return*, the supernatural is often presented in black and white: the glass box demon and the one spewing Bob and the eggs, the convenience store being readied by the Woodsmen, and, on the good side, the Fireman and his abode, which, judging by the furniture and the gramophone, is where we saw Cooper and the Fireman in Part One's first image. Since that was during Cooper's twenty-five-year imprisonment in the Red Room, the Fireman must have had the ability to import Cooper for a short briefing, then send him back. The Fireman possesses formidable power, but not enough to straightforwardly wrap up the narrative as a championship-winning score for the good team. Part of *Twin Peaks*'s tantalizing allure is its mysteriously shifting power balance, psychically and physically, the physics, mindsets, and spiritual states that enable, or prohibit, action.

Action and reaction: a monumental occurrence requires a prodigious response. The Fireman's alert system machine is making a cycling electrified pounding sound and flashing a light. He stands next to it and silently looks at Dido in a pregnant pause that communicates their deep psychic-emotional bond. Then, standing still, he looks forward into "space," where we are, his sight line angling over our left shoulders, so to speak. Moments of deep gravitas pass as the machine blinks and the Fireman reads the air, ponders, maybe communes with some higher power for guidance. On the sides of both good and evil, we sense unseen, ineffable intelligences with force and intent.

All of the spaces of the Fireman's place are vast and dark, any discernible details fading into shadow at the edges. We see him slowly climb black carpeted stairs and turn to the right. Every move the Fireman makes has an aura of serious consequence, ritual, and ceremony. On the karmic balance sheet of chutes and ladders, he's always climbing; his consciousness may be so enlightened that he's beyond the karmic wheel of death and rebirth, but he chooses to incarnate as a righteous yogi of beneficence. As nineteenth-century American transcendentalist Ralph Waldo Emerson said, "not virtuous, but Virtue."

When the artistic strength of Lynch's first short films enabled him to attend the Beverly Hills location of the American Film Institute in the 1970s, situated in the vast Greystone Mansion and park built by Edmund Doheney in 1927, the class screenings were held in the mansion's former grand ballroom. And in *The Return*, the Fireman crosses a large floor that could accommodate dancers and stares up at the proscenium arch and movie screen at the room's far end. The black beeping machine has alerted him to begin a process. He raises his hand and images (black and white, like everything in his realm) appear on the screen: the Trinity test atom bomb blast and, inside it, the spewed stream of evil life (Bob, all those eggs), plus the Woodsmen readying the convenience store; a bad moon is rising. The Fireman is so spiritually evolved, so firmly on the heavenward path, that he can levitate, and he floats up to the right of the screen. (Lynch's spiritual master, the Maharishi Mahesh Yogi, who founded Transcendental Meditation, wrote about the reality of "yogic flying.") The Fireman may be the manifestation of cosmic goodness, but he's personified in this world of dualities, where a being who's a counterforce to Bob needs to be created. As the floating Fireman concentrates on his inner, metaphysical work, Senorita Dido enters the room, a white circle of light illuminating her approach. She sees Bob on the screen and looks up in awe and devotion at the Fireman. This sequence is accompanied by the reverent vibrations of organ chords, and the air is alive with harmonics, the consonance of unspoken inner knowing. The Fireman understands the situation. Senorita Dido understands, and in some poetic way, we at least feel a little breeze of anticipatory comprehension.

As a youth, when Lynch was discovering and pursuing his personal art-making mission, most of the school-taught classes he signed up for were in science, leaning toward physics: always the fascination for inner workings, the deep questions the world keeps posing, the drive to look for clues. The rational, scientific method of addressing the world that Lynch studied in the twentieth century can be traced back to the alchemy of the early centuries after Christ's death. Alchemy was a multivalenced process encompassing a quest to produce a health elixir, then to synthesize gold from combined base materials. The gold-making process had seven (Lynch's favorite number) stages and involved the element mercury, symbolized by a crescent atop a circle, like the little horns on the demon head that spewed out Bob and the eggs, like the horned circle on Mr. C's playing card, the thing he wants (does the Bob part of Mr. C have a subconscious urge to merge with his Dark Mother?). But ultimately, alchemy is about transfiguration, converting spiritual darkness into the light of salvation, like the golden orb aura surrounding Laura Palmer's face at the beginning of every episode of *The Return*.

The Fireman floats; Senorita Dido watches him lovingly, and there's a further shift toward positivity. The screen image of Bob is gone; there's a fresh canvas to work with, a field of stars, slightly in motion: change, volatility are possible. And from the Fireman's head emanates a protoplasmic stream of swarming gold particles that forms a cloud of beneficent golden warmth in answer to the chilling, deathly mushroom cloud of evil. Reflecting the honeyed bubble within the bomb's cloud that presaged a tonal shift before we came to the Fireman's stronghold, a golden orb shape separates from the Fireman's glittering head flow. It floats down to Senorita Dido, who's in black and white, but whose face warmly reflects the orb's gold as she gives it a blessing kiss. Within the perfect circle is Laura Palmer's luminous smiling face. In the spirit world, she is "the One," the best hope to challenge, counterbalance, perhaps defeat evil forces, which is Cooper's role in the mortal, temporal world. But this is 1945; Laura won't be born until 1971, and we know she will be victimized and overpowered. Still, in the long view of reincarnation evolution, she is the Fireman's—or the forces he's a conduit for—champion to be, perhaps the embryonic form of a future goddess. Like Jor-El in the *Superman* legend, the Fireman and Senorita Dido are parent figures sending their very special child to earth. Via Lynch's charmingly factory-style process, Laura's orb floats up and passes through a huge golden, saxophone-shaped horn that floats it toward the map of America that now occupies the Fireman's movie screen. Lynch fades the shot before we can determine exactly where the golden being will touch down.

The monumental space-time-bridging saxophone transportation device can be seen as Lynch's homage to the Dave Brubeck Quartet's sax man Paul Desmond. Desmond's cool sounds are elsewhere on *The Return*'s soundtrack and are the on-hold music on Lynch's business phone. And since the golden materials from the Fireman's head go in the large end of the horn, then out the small end before heading to the USA, there's the sense that we're moving back to the generating breath, the source of things. But Lynch and Frost have established a universe in which many moments seem pregnant with past, present, and future. *The Return*'s creators are both keen on the Bible's Book of Revelations, where a being can exist "who is, and who was, and who will be." Laura Palmer saying to Cooper in Part One, "I am dead, and yet I live," echoes Christ declaring, "I died, and behold I am alive for evermore."

The New Testament's Revelation to John is a phantasmagoric panorama of prophecies chronicling the ongoing battle between forces of darkness and evil and the powers of goodness and light. The saga is presented in seven visions full of symbols and allegories that have spawned countless interpretations. Sounds like *Twin Peaks*. And like *The Return*, Revelations abounds in sevens: seven churches, lampstands, stars, angels, trumpets, spirits of God. God and Satan are the ultimate combatants, but their contending wills and energies are embodied and enacted by surrogate mortals and supernatural beings in earthly and cosmic environs. The stories foretell the coming of Christ, the final defeat of evil, and the formation of a radiant new Earth and heaven. In *Blue Velvet*, Lynch transmuted this story arc into Sandy's (Laura Dern) dream of a darkened world struggling in misery until "the robins come," bringing the light of peace and love. For Lynch personally and in his work, bad times, death itself, are not the end of the road; they're passages to glory, even if it takes multiple lifetimes to achieve the goal. The potential for illumination is always present, though sometimes, as in *Lost Highway*, the movie ends before the protagonist gets there, but Lynch feels that in the long view, he can. Lynch may be a Happy Endings believer, but he makes the dark, predatory opposing forces terrifyingly potent, sometimes insurmountable. And strange.

In 1956, eleven years after the Trinity test opened a portal into our world for Bob and that flow of eggs, we see a single egg in the desert sand. Something's stirring inside as the night winds blow. Slowly, the egg cracks, and a frog with insect wings folded on its back emerges and crawls off across the sand. Clouds obscure the moon, and we see something Lynch has shown us before: a soft nocturnal scene of young people on the verge of love. In *Blue Velvet*, teenage Jeffrey and Sandy, having just met, stroll beneath gently rustling trees and feel a budding warmth between them. In *The Return*, a younger pair, barely pubescent, stroll in rural New Mexico past a barn with two gas pumps (a shivery reminder of the Bob-related convenience store gas pumps and skittering Woodsmen). The boy (Xolo Mariduena) sports the classic Lynchian ensemble of black jacket and white shirt; the girl's (Tikaeni Faircrest) black dress shows a fringe of white petticoat, and she has Lynch's childlike sense of wonder, of magic in the dust: "Oh, look, I found a penny, and it's heads up; that means good luck." As she beams at the gleaming circle of Abraham Lincoln's profile, the boy says, "I hope that it brings you good luck." It's a heartwarming moment, but Lynch loves to sow subtle, sometimes subliminal, disquietude: the chief, most malevolent Woodsman is played by actor Robert Broski, who's portrayed Abraham Lincoln on stage, and looks like him.

This scene, and the rest of Part Eight, is in black and white, a supernatural signifier in *The Return*. With his care for the nuanced tonalities of his images, Lynch renders the dim desert night in a softened dark and light that grades toward gray; the images have the look/feel of Lynch's black-and-white still photographs. In the desert night, landscape and sky are almost the same color, but we perceive a darker form drop from the sky: a sooty man shape like the one in imprisoned Bill Hastings's cellblock and the ones that pushed and prodded gut-shot Mr. C back to life. The desert shape is joined by another. They drift in like black leaves on the wind, but they have heft and purpose and crunch the ground as they move forward.

Compared with some other countries, America is a land of anxious insecurity. We don't save money; we spend it. We can fall through the social services safety net like water through a sieve. Over the years, it's intrigued me how many women I know, some executive directors of major cultural institutions, who have a genuine, deep fear that their seemingly secure world will fall apart and they'll become homeless "bag ladies." It's easy to project our there-but-for-the-grace-of-this-month's-paycheck-go-I fears onto those grubby, derelict wraiths who haunt our cities like walking dead, seemingly closer kin to feral animals. They're the shadows we might easily become, which is why, in Lynch's *Mulholland Drive*, the filth-encrusted Bum (an unrecognizable Bonnie Aarons) behind the cheery café, whose sheer presence causes a man to drop dead, is such a powerful visual-emotional concept, one of Lynch's major abstractions. The Woodsmen, with their dirty faces, hair, beards, and ragged clothes, embody that chilling sense of human as other, or the inhuman in human form.

On a night road through the desert, the dark a saturated black, not a touch of gray, a middle-aged couple are driving home, the man at the wheel. We're in the car with them, looking at the road ahead. The headlights of a car coming in the opposite direction get weird, blinking as though something passed in front of them. That car stops, and "our" car stops. We're suspended in terrifying, apprehensive moments; something's so wrong—but what? Then there's a Woodsman on the roadside, one by our car, outside the woman passenger's window, and the most prominent one, with a blazing-white cigarette in his mouth, keeps asking the driver, "Got a light?" as electricity flashes and the woman's moan of horror garbles in the somehow distorted air. It's a norm of horror movies that the characters find themselves in a situation that will soon turn splatteringly lethal, and the audience silently urges them to "Get Out Now!" but they don't. Lynch and Frost avoid this cliché and let the couple speed away, no doubt shaken and traumatized. Lynch is fluent in the poetry of linkages, associations, correspondences, the way something here, something there can join to conjure Baudelaire's "strange expansion of things." For those strolling youngsters falling in love, the visage of Abraham Lincoln on a penny was a symbol of good luck and the best of America, but the scary Woodsman, pulsing with evil intent, who waylaid the older couple's car and asked for a light has the face of Lincoln, in unclean, unholy, ghoulish mode.

The Woodsmen, what do they want? In our time period we've seen them save evil Mr. C's life. And seventy-two years earlier, they'd arrived on earth via a Bob-harboring dimensional delivery system blast-powered by nuclear fission and then prepared the convenience store for Bob and other malefic denizens. If this is an earth-takeover mission, it's going to be a slow process, proceeding via one person here, one person there. If the man in the New Mexico car had given the Woodsman the light he asked for, what then? In the world of *Twin Peaks*, fire, as in *Fire Walk With Me*, is the supremely dark and dominating power, symbiotically bonded with electricity: the grail sought by the wicked. But there are rituals, protocols, proper ways to proceed, prohibitions, and permissions. In *Lost Highway*, the evil Mystery Man, who has invaded Fred Madison's house and psyche, says, "I don't go where I'm not invited." And Bob couldn't just metaphysically swallow Laura in a gulp; worming his way into her, steering her toward darkness, was an insidious process. The couple in the car weren't about to offer their necks to the soul-sucking vampire with Lincoln's face. Just as Bob feeds on our pain, fear, suffering, he and the invading Evil Ones, at all levels of their powers, even above Judy, can't resist our Earth. They're sharks smelling blood in the water; our Fallen, Dark Age is irresistible, already wounded and trembling, at least halfway to "Non-ex-is-tence."

In Lynch's *Blue Velvet* (1986), Kyle MacLachlan's character, Jeffrey, asks, "Why are there men like Frank? (Dennis Hopper's monstrous Frank Booth). "Why is there so much trouble in the world?" At one point, Frank says to Jeffrey, "You're just like me," and the youth does act out his own impulses to have sadistic sex, but he ultimately chooses the path of virtuous behavior. Still, the mystery of evil in the world, of dark urges within us, remains. Is it the vestigial, primitive reptile brain, the primal biological imperatives of biting and eating and spurting our genetic code into future generations that can cause us to do the damnedest things? Is it a spiritual situation? Do we breathe the foul air of a fallen world, swayed by Satanic forces, entranced by the Whore of Babylon, a form of the Antichrist; attacked by the Woodsmen, Bob, Judy? Forces that cloud our minds with a fog of deception, forgetting, fear, a contracting, dwindling consciousness of our divine nature, our proper place in the Garden, our memory of the Garden's very existence? As a youth, Lynch sensed a "force of wild pain and decay" at work in the world. And his Forest Service scientist father showed that a speck of contagion could eventually blight an entire forest. Through his meditation practice, Lynch knows that the righteous path, the garden of golden thoughts and actions, can be found, reclaimed, restored; we can be undeceived. Through the enlivening power of Lynch's imagination, the poetic and the prosaic, the miraculous and the mundane, the symbolic and the literal can be unified: a reflection of his and our best selves. But it's easy to be put to sleep, hard to awaken.

When the Woodsman's around, we hear that electromechanical clicking sound, like wicked circuits linking up down the line. In the late 1970s, between *Eraserhead* and *The Elephant Man*, Lynch, in his screenplay *Ronnie Rocket*, wrote about his concept of bad electricity, with which an archvillain plagued innocent populations. The film never got made, but the bad electricity couldn't be contained and zapped into *Fire Walk With Me* and *The Return*. In terms of electricity being a key narrative-artistic element of *Twin Peaks*, it's Lynch's hand that's on the voltage control. For as Mark Frost says in *Conversations With Mark Frost* regarding Lynch and electricity, "He's always had a fear and fascination of it that frankly I don't share."

This is the Woodsman's lucky night, or maybe he's following the scent of activated electrons, for far off in the horizontal desert landscape he sees an isolated radio station, its tall electromagnetic, wave-receiving-and-sending tower like a vertical beacon. Lynch and I grew up in the 1950s, and we've talked about how in the era when the rectilinear modernist architecture and design we love was coming in, there were still traces of curvilinear art deco and art moderne in the built landscape, like the interior of my neighborhood Bellevue Theatre, where Lynch's *The Grandmother* won a Bellevue Film Festival prize in 1970. *The Return*'s desert radio station KPJK is a brilliantly art-directed 1940s moderne creation, from its streamlined stucco and glass brick exterior to its blond wood interior and period broadcasting equipment. On Lynch's fifteenth birthday, January 20, 1961, he proudly wore his Eagle Scout uniform "seating VIPs" for the inauguration parade of optimistic young President John Fitzgetald Kennedy (*Room to Dream*). Kennedy's assassination was especially traumatic to Lynch and Frost's baby boom generation, and when the two became creative partners, well before *Twin Peaks*, they considered, but rejected, the idea of making a film that tackled the mystery surrounding Kennedy's death. Could *The Return*'s radio station, KPJK, be code for Keep John Kennedy, keep his ideals and positive spirit alive?

Mood master Lynch has established the desert as a cold place barely touched by human existence. It's late, the station is isolated, and there's a woman alone in the office, dressed and posed to echo Edward Hopper's 1940 painting *Office at Night*. The Woodsman enters the space, says, "Got a light?" The woman, as though pulled by a force field, silently approaches him against her will, her face horrified. He places his hand on top of her head; we hear her skull cracking and brain scrambling, and streaming bloody dark matter shrouds her face.

The station's other occupant is the disc jockey, at work in his booth playing the Platters' "My Prayer" ("is to linger with you/at the end of the day/in a dream that's divine"). This song, wafting on the broadcast airwaves of night, links a montage of three people who are alone: a guy working on his car, a woman cleaning up a café after closing time, and the young "lucky penny" girl who'd walked home with the boy. Sitting on her bed (like Sandy in *Blue Velvet*), wearing a white-with-flower-sprigs nightgown, she is in a smiling, dreamy mood. The boy kissed her, and shy, embarrassed, and happy, she gave him a little wave as she entered her house. (She bears a dark-haired-beauty resemblance to Lynch's wife, Emily, who, Lynch says, stole his heart when she gave him a goodbye wave the day they met.)

Suddenly, the little community of radio listeners is jolted midsong by a low rumble/scratching sound—no more sweet harmonies and sentiments. At the station, the Woodsman's hand is on the disc jockey's head, somehow slowly shredding its contents. The Woodsman's face is dark, as though scorched by nuclear-electrical fires, the cigarette bright white between his lips as he repeats an incantation into the microphone: "This is the water, and this is the well/Drink full and descend/The horse is the white of the eyes/And dark within." His voice has the deep tones and cadence of John Huston in *Chinatown*, portraying a powerful, black-hearted predator who speaks to a detective (Jack Nicholson) about pervasive human evil. There will be further echoes of *Chinatown*, one of Lynch's and Frost's favorite films, as *The Return* plays out.

The Woodsman's lulling words, the electricity: a circuit is formed between him and the radio listeners. In Lynch's *Ronnie Rocket* screenplay, the bad electricity, wielded by another talkative villain, holds a big city in its sway, and its effects are proportionally large: light is sucked away; people are unable to think, talk, and remember; some eat their own hands and feet or burst into flames. The Woodsman's small rural community hears just one speech, and it makes the car guy and the café woman collapse. Asleep? Dead? In some suspended state? Or just receptive, entranced by the bad?

It's amazing how just a few short images and words of well-crafted cinema can grab us. We've quickly come to feel tenderly protective of the shy country girl sitting on her bed with her legs tucked under her. The dial on her radio glows at the 70 . . . 90 position, which adds up to seven in Lynch's magical addition—not always lucky, as we remember the penny she found and the voice she's now hearing, an entity who looks like Lincoln, intoning, "The horse is the white of the eyes and dark within." Unlike the two adults who collapsed, the conscious girl lies down in a horizontal position and closes her eyes as the "horse" part of the incantation comes around again; she's meant for something special. The phrase repeats again as the egg-hatched winged frog comes crawling from the desert, flies up to the windowsill and into her bedroom. And after the god-awful thing has crawled into her mouth, we again hear, "The horse is the white of the eyes and dark within." As Part Eight concludes, the girl's mouth and eyes are closed, and we hear that grating biological-mechanical-electrical sound working within her. Outside the radio station, the Woodsman walks off into the dark, and we hear an unseen horse whinnying.

Conceptually and aesthetically stunning, Part Eight was immediately hailed as one of the most extraordinary hours of television ever produced. And it made good on *The Return*'s opening-credits hint that we were going to explore further horizons this time around. Macrocosm, microcosm, above and below, before and after, all together now. Lynch has always had an expansive creative view, and when he was driving from Philadelphia to a bountiful new life in Los Angeles, he saw, from a high ridge above a vast valley, four different weather systems happening at once. And sleeping among some roadside New Mexico bushes on a moonless night, he heard mysterious sounds that turned out to be a horse.

Lynch's late-1970s *Ronnie Rocket* screenplay introduced both his concept of bad electricity and the detective's credo that would form Agent Cooper's foundation decades later: "Stay alert. Concentrate. Stay clean." *Ronnie Rocket*'s Detective character, like Lynch, is drawn to the boundary line where knowledge and mystery meet, and he has a sense of balance: "I know some things but not everything." Another character voices a key Lynchian attitude: "I don't go around explainin' the unexplainable, Buddy." How many different ways has Lynch said that over the years? But the human need to have bits and pieces of information add up to form a collage of understanding is strong (Lynch's Hindu oneness, the secret heart inside multiplicity). As a *Ronnie Rocket* character says, "Look . . . two needles working . . . See? Look . . . yarn . . . a continuum . . . the fabric . . . the form." So what has Part Eight added to our sense of *The Return*'s continuum, its form?

In his life, Lynch has experienced the sound of an unseen horse at night; Part Eight ends with that sound. The words "horse" and "white" are linked with the Woodsman's chant in 1956, and that part of the chant is linked to the girl going to sleep, the frog-moth entering her room and climbing inside her. Three decades later, in the original *Twin Peaks*, Sarah, Laura Palmer's mother, has visions of a white horse when Bob's evil energy is motivating her husband to rape and eventually murder Laura. Sarah is clairvoyant, and when the New Mexico girl walks home with the boy she says she "just knew" where he lived. Would this information be enough for Agent Cooper to conclude that this girl will grow up to be Sarah Palmer? What would Jake Gittes, the detective in *Chinatown*, conclude? Jake, who misinterprets evidence and, as he did in the past, brings harm to someone he's trying to save right now, in the present.

When the white horse appears *Twin Peaks* and *Fire Walk With Me*, it is massive, filling the Palmer living room. The Woodsman says, "The horse is the white of the eyes," the eyes of what larger cosmic horror beyond imagining? In Revelations, Satan is characterized as "the beast," and issuing from its mouth are "foul spirits like frogs, demonic spirits." Associated with magic and witches in ancient lore, frogs became a staple of fables and fairy tales, most notably the Grimm Brothers' "The Frog Prince." There's a beautiful princess, a dark forest, a deep well, a golden ball she loses down the well. The frog will fetch the ball if the princess "wouldst love me"and let him "sleep in thy little bed." She promises she will, but breaks her word once she gets her ball. She's back at her castle home, and the frog follows her. She tells her father, the king, that the frog "is outside the door, and he wants to come in to me." The king orders her to keep her promise. The frog says, "Make ready your silken bed, and we will lie down together." Disgusted, she throws the frog against the wall, and he becomes a handsome prince, who tells her "a wicked witch had bound him by her spells." He and the princess will marry and depart in a carriage pulled by white horses. Most fairy tales were written by adults, so it's not surprising that some, like "The Frog Prince," project a veiled eroticism. And *The Return* may be presenting a veiled, New Mexico echo of this Old World tale, both with their beautiful girl, a frog seeking to be her bed partner, a deep well and white horse (the Woodsman's chant), and golden ball (the golden orb in which Laura Palmer comes to Earth).

In *The Secret History of Twin Peaks*, Mark Frost references the real-life efforts of occultist rocket scientist Jack Parsons and sci-fi author L. Ron Hubbard to open a portal for Revelations's Whore of Babylon to enter our world. She's called Babylon in the Bible and is the "mother of abominations," an apt name for *The Return*'s female demon spewing Bob and the eggs. But Babylon isn't the whole dark show. In Revelations she rides on the back of the beast, the Adversary itself, the serpent in the garden, a personification of deepest fear, of the horror that would have gripped a defenseless, early human faced with a saber-toothed tiger. The capacity for evil is part of the human psyche; the atom bomb didn't introduce it to the world, though it amplified its power stupendously.

Lynch and Frost are fascinated by dark power, within and without, and by those who dabble in it. *The Secret History*'s theme of two people seeking to open a paranormal portal will appear far from the desert in *The Return*, but David Lynch is desert haunted. Once, in a desert, he violated his no-red-meat food rule, and he had a horrible dream that night. It was "diabolical" and spawned an inner crisis so significant that the next day, "I couldn't talk to anybody and had to be alone to fight it mentally. That ended the desert for me." (*Room to Dream*). And Lynch took years of his life making *Dune* in the Mexican desert, a tale of a desert planet that was a double death for the writer-director: a creative and a commercial failure. The film's complex plot centers on a man striving to learn his fate and live it, in opposition to the powerful machinations of a Bene Gesserit Witch (not named Judy). The man triumphs, but Lynch, in a position where he had to be influenced by others, betrayed his artistic soul, and, as he told me, "I sold out and suffered a huge sadness. It killed me."

In 1966, ten years after *The Return*'s frog-moth entered the New Mexico girl, Lynch's friend singer-songwriter Donovan, fellow meditator and acolyte of Hindu spirituality, wrote a popular song. And he wrote this about that song: "And the sorceress, she is dancing her Kali dance into the numina" (the spirits of places). Kali, the Hindu goddess sowing death and destruction in the play of time. Likewise *The Return*'s female desert demon, spewing Bob and seed eggs of doom in our direction. Donovan and Lynch believe in the coming of a bright new morning, but the weather changed in the New Mexico desert of 1945. The time changed too. The Doomsday Clock that indicates how close we are to worldwide nuclear destruction now says only two minutes left to midnight. The letters of Donovan's song add up to lucky seven, but it's still the "Season of the Witch."

–CHAPTER FIFTEEN–

LA VIE EN ROSE
(PART NINE)

Scary as the idea of Bob (introduced in 1990) is, the real-life fear of nuclear annihilation invaded our psyches and never left. Thirty-eight years after the first atom bomb test, the ABC-TV network (which would greenlight *Twin Peaks* in six years) aired *The Day After*, a telemovie chronicling the aftermath of enemy-sent nuclear bombs exploding in America's heartland. Even the show's prescreening promotional images were traumatizing, giving people sleepless nights. In the program, following the first bomb blasts, the creeping doom of radiation sickness is graphically depicted. For individuals, families, the whole country, there is no escape, no hope. *The Day After* remains the most-watched TV movie in history, according to Nielsen ratings.

The season of the witch is a long one. Lynch believes that there's a field of unity and peace for everyone, but these days there also seems to be an expanding force field of lies, mistrust, anxiety, anger, hatred, fear. In Hindu terms, we're in a cycle of increasing negativity, the Kali Yuga, when the dark goddess dances. Lynch believes there's a two thouand–year golden age coming: "Nobody knows when it kicks in, but it's something to look forward to." Until then, we sweep the floor, sharpen our tools, do our work, and keep moving in the right direction.

Forces of darkness and light will always be warring. Maybe the best we can do is to keep the balance tipped toward the positive, but that's no small task. Kyle MacLachlan says that he summed up his evil character Mr. C for himself with one word, "Dominate." With the help of the Woodsmen's hands-on triage, he's survived being shot by Ray and is walking toward us on a country road to the Farm in South Dakota. As he advances, getting larger in the frame, we see a flutter of red on the right, a bandana marking the Farm's entrance. So far in *The Return*, the color red has usually been associated with good people and deeds, an abstraction of the beneficent life force. The iconic Red Room curtains seem more neutral. Some years ago, sitting in Lynch's ruddy-curtain-walled sound/music/movie-watching studio, I asked, "Is there a place behind those curtains?" He deadpanned, "No, there is not." In *Room to Dream* (2018) Lynch said he loves curtains because they "hide something; you don't know if it's good or bad." This time, with the Mr. C-welcoming bandana, the color red heralds a gathering of bad people, just as the red associated with Becky's guy Steve marked him as a potential danger to her in Part Ten.

We first met Chantal (Jennifer Jason Leigh) in Part Two, she of the booze, handgun, and spreading thighs. After Mr. C killed disloyal Darya, who, with Ray, was plotting to rub out their boss, he checked in with Chantal to set up a rendezvous with her and her husband, Hutch (Tim Roth), after Mr. C goes AWOL from returning to the Red Room.

Now Mr. C, free of the Red Room, has survived Ray's assassination attempt, and Hutch and Chantal welcome him to the Farm, which isn't theirs: the old-couple owners are cold and stacked like wood against a shed. Unlike Las Vegas's Mr. Todd, who quakes in fear of the dominant Mr. C, Hutch and Chantal (with the usual flavorful juice Roth and Jason Leigh bring to their roles), have a hang-loose, amiable relationship with their boss. They're as loyal to Bad Cooper as the Twin Peaks Sheriff's Office is to good Cooper, if they're ever going to see him again. Mr. C's crew is quick with grins, but they're stone killers: Chantal has a fondness for Cheetos, and for sadistically "messing with" victims before they're shot. Lynch is also a Cheetos fan, and he wanted some close at hand while performing his delightful cameo in Steven Speilberg's *The Fabelmans* (2022), portraying crusty old pantheon director John Ford.

Whatever the shape and scope of Mr. C's criminal empire and dark-power seeking, he hasn't gotten this far without being good at cleaning up loose ends. He tells Hutch to take out Warden Murphy, then "do a doubleheader" in Vegas (Dougie? And?). Hutch and Chantal have a big black pickup truck and provisions prepared for Mr. C's road trip, but before he heads out (to where?), Hutch tells Chantal, "Give the boss man a big wet one," and he watches as they deep kiss. When Mr. C and Chantal were alone before, it was a different kind of wet one, but now Mr. C will "take a rain check" on further carnal sharing. Hutch is clearly a lenient, easygoing husband; maybe he got the message early that he'd better be cheerful about it.

As black-clad Mr. C entered the Farm property he jammed that vibrant red bandana into his pocket, snuffing it in shadow. Now Lynch proceeds to restore red's more positive, life-affirming associations. After the dramatic incident where Ike the Spike attacked Dougie with a gun and the Cooper part of Dougie, under mortal threat, disarmed Ike like a champion, he reverted to slow, suppressed Dougie as Ike fled. At the Las Vegas Police Station, Dougie and Janey-E wait to be interviewed about the incident. Full-of-life Janey-E wears her red shoes (magical, like Dorothy's in *The Wizard of Oz*?), and Dougie drinks deep from his red mug of coffee. How does Lynch know to take a few moments of silent screen time and link them in a haiku of stillness that resonates an essence that can't be described? What do an American flag, red high heels, and an electrical wall outlet have in common? To us, maybe not much, but they're in the vision field of Dougie/Cooper's pale face: a blank-eyed witness or a mind trying to work? Maybe he just senses the emotional temperature of things. Former Eagle Scout Lynch, who, like other baby boomer school kids, used to put his hand on his heart and recite the Pledge of Allegiance, links the American flag Dougie sees with musical strains of "America the Beautiful," like a whiff of Cooper's patriotic dedication to virtue. Then a woman walking past the flag left to right catches Dougie's eyes with her red high heels. The woman he's sitting with (Janey-E), whom he lives with, has red shoes. Or . . . what else? Some woman who wore red (Naido) or had red hair? The ruddy atmosphere of female warmth? The motion of the red high heels swings Dougie's eyes to an electrical wall socket. It hums: power; don't know; go places?

At the Twin Peaks Sheriff's Office, Andy and Lucy get in on *The Return*'s red action. They want to buy a new easy chair for their living room: he wants a red chair; she wants a beige one. Once again, duality and balance in *Twin Peaks*: Andy, who wears beige and brown, wants red, and Lucy, who wears red skirts and sweaters, wants beige. They want each other. These two are sometimes so cute with each other, so prone to baby-talk hyperempathy and mutual consideration, that it drives some viewers crazy. After they go back and forth about the prospective chair ("Red," "No, beige") in a low-key manner (no yelling, no red faces), Andy apologizes ("I'm sorry, Punky") and says Lucy can get the beige chair. They're on the same website, each on their own computer. Lucy smiles to herself and presses the red chair button. True love.

Big, strong, tall Andy Brennan in his sheriff's deputy uniform breaks down in protracted sobs in the primal 1990s *Twin Peaks* scene in which Laura Palmer's corpse is discovered. This unexpected, deeply human moment strikes a chord of anguished loss and emotional depth that resonates throughout the series. Andy cries again, into his portable phone, when they discover Laura's murder scene, trying, failing to put the horror into words. Hearing him, feeling his pain and sadness over the phone line, is Sheriff's Department receptionist Lucy Moran. Her sweet, little-girl voice is consoling; her fingers touch the phone receiver like she's tenderly caressing Andy's face. Humorously slow on the uptake and long on explanations, Lucy can be moody and peevish. Over *Twin Peaks*' first thirty episodes, she and Andy battle and reconcile, split up and reunite, but their ultimate good-heartedness prevails, and they emerge as *The Return*'s single solid romantic, and married, couple from the original show.

The sensibilities of Lynch and Frost and actors Harry Goaz (Andy) and Kimmy Robertson (Lucy) have created a crime-fighting, law-enforcing couple like no other. A world away from macho swagger and paramilitary fire power, they can be slow, simple, gentle, innocent, and whimsical, like children. They are in tune with *The Wizard of Oz*'s Dorothy, who, in that film Lynch loves, says in response to the Wizard's "I am Oz, the great and powerful," "I am Dorothy, the small and meek." The Bible says that "the meek shall inherit the earth," and in Lynch and Frost's unique universe, Andy and Lucy could well rise to heights of heroism.

Gordon Cole's (and David Lynch's) red wine, Naido's red dress, Diane's red robe, red balloons in Vegas, the red front door of Dougie's house, Janey-E's purse and shoes, Becky and Steve's red-upholstered Firebird, the red for valor of the American flag, Mr. C's red bandana, the Red Room, Andy and Lucy's red chair. A few bad-connoting reds, but mostly good. This is *Twin Peaks*, so one red chair leads to another.

Major Garland Briggs (Don Davis), like Laura Palmer dead but not gone, could see farther than anyone in *Twin Peaks*. A "retired" Air Force man, a man of science, he had a grasp of the natural and supernatural laws of Earth and the cosmos, a love of family and community, and a soul-chilling understanding of devouring dark forces creeping ever nearer. There was a war in the air that couldn't be seen but was being enacted in the minds and bodies of people he knew. Cooper/some other Cooper was/were involved, Gordon Cole, extradimensional entities and places. Briggs gathered data, strategized, left information to be found, was killed, appears to Cooper, knows the Blue Rose.

I'm looking at Don Davis's business card, "Blue Productions, Ltd." Don (1942-2008) was a warm and friendly man and an accomplished artist as well as a wonderful actor. Over the years, I chatted with him a number of times at Seattle Art Museum *Twin Peaks*/Lynch-film screenings. He departed before *The Return* was filmed, and Mark Frost in *The Secret History of Twin Peaks* and Frost and Lynch in *The Return* do a masterful job of making Major Briggs an emotional and narrative touchstone. Briggs not only knew who would be playing the high-stakes grand game over the years, but also what their moves would likely be. When Garland and Betty's now-adult son Bobby, Sheriff Frank Truman, and Deputy Hawk show up at the Briggs house in the present, years after Garland's death, Betty's not surprised. Briggs said they would—decades earlier. Back when Bobby was known for his insolent attitude and bad behavior (whatever happened about the guy he killed in *Fire Walk With Me*?) and for being Laura Palmer's boyfriend and drug provider, his father had a dream about Bobby turning his life around and becoming golden. Yes, Bobby killed a man, who was going to kill him, but now he's devoted to protecting and serving his community; he's climbing the ladder, not falling. Today Bobby's face glows with reverent love for his father as his mother speaks of "the faith your father had in you," and Bobby's fellow peacekeepers, who are also his friends, listen in loving, respectful silence.

And there's the red chair, more elegant and refined than those blocky art deco chairs at the Fireman's and the Red Room. Is this where Major Briggs sat and pondered the fate of his town, and maybe the world, and planned his next moves? The wooden trim surrounding the red upholstery, where Briggs's head must have rested, contains the sum of his knowledge and the seed of *The Return*'s future. We can imagine Lynch's enjoyment in crafting a little mechanism that springs a section of the wood open to reveal a small metal cylinder with no visible way to open it. The motto of Lynch's Forest Service scientist father could have been "Look to the wood for answers." Back at the sheriff's office, Frank and Hawk puzzle over the tantalizing piece of metal. Bobby watches them, amused, and chuckles, "We need to go outside." Lynch, the proponent of wide-open artistic freedom, who likes to paint and make his artworks outdoors, has said he prefers to be outside while he explores deep inner regions.

Bobby knows to throw the cylinder hard, twice (this is *Twin Peaks*), against the concrete. The impact makes the metal ring and sing with a sound similar to the phantom tone in Ben Horne's office, but a bit different; we live in a world of vibrations. Inside the capsule: what looks like a white cigarette (a little joke from zealous smoker Lynch?). Unrolled, it's a white piece of paper with Major Briggs's markings. Most prominent: twin peaks in black, and above the left one, a big red spot (the sun, the force of goodness?). Over the right peak, a smaller black spot with little horns/ears like Mr. C's ace of spades: what he's seeking. Above the black spot, a small red crescent that echoes the black-and-white crescent form within the bomb blast that ushered in the demon spewing out Bob and the eggs. So, twin peaks, the forces of light (the big red spot) and darkness (the black spot), and the smaller touch of red (the crescent) on the dark spot side. If the black spot is linked with Mr. C, maybe the red crescent is the Cooper part of him, and the opposing full red spot is the radiance of Cooper at full force, awakened and restored. Or is it the radiant power of Laura, "the One," the future goddess who will restore universal order? Perhaps it's the beaming energy of Cooper and Laura, partnered to battle the cosmic darkness. There's a second strip of paper in the cylinder, a printout from Briggs's cosmic listening post. Some intelligence from beyond was telling him something: "COOPER/COOPER." Hawk underscores the point: "Two Coopers." Lynch, who grew up exploring Northwest forest paths and as a kid fell in love with *The Wizard of Oz*'s yellow brick road, is tracing a red-marked trail through *The Return*. As poet Sylvia Plath said, "The world is blood-hot."

What path is Diane Evans on? Why does it need to be questioned? Decades ago, she was introduced to the Laura Palmer case, and us (though never seen), as FBI Special Agent Dale Cooper's Philadelphia-based assistant, to whom he, while out investigating in the field, sent audiotapes of his everyday thoughts and feelings. They were apart, but so close. Then, sometime after Cooper's departure from Twin Peaks (we know he was actually trapped in the Red Room), he (we know it was Bad Cooper, Mr. C) came to her "that night" and pierced her emotions like a knife. Now her heart's an angry wound, and she masks her pain with brusque, antagonistic cynicism. But her sobbing true heart gushed out in Gordon Cole's consoling embrace after seeing "Cooper" (Mr. C) incarcerated at the South Dakota prison. Like Cole and Albert before her, she could tell that today's Cooper was different, something wasn't right in a deeply disturbing way. At one time, before Cooper left town, in a way she'd been the woman in his life; they'd shared a connection that was a kind of love. I mean, he was Special Agent Dale Cooper! But now, weeping in Gordon Cole's arms, she puts her hand to her breast: this South Dakota "Cooper's" heart and soul are black, or not there at all.

Lynch and Frost and Laura Dern have made Diane a fascinating character, and her relationship with Cooper—in his various forms—is a key dynamic of *The Return*. In many ways the creators of *Twin Peaks* make the unseen visible, and Diane in the flesh, who was previously always off camera, rivets our attention.

Off the earth, up in the air over South Dakota after Diane interviewed "Cooper," things are in flux in the private FBI jet plane. Albert and Diane are asleep, Diane holding her iPhone. Gordon Cole gets a phone call from the Pentagon and speaks to Tammy about a police lieutenant in Buckhorn, South Dakota. Diane's eyes are open and shifting as she overhears Cole. A moment later, he approaches her, and her eyes are closed. She "wakes up" to hear him asking if she would mind a short detour to Buckhorn regarding an old case that involved Cooper. She gives a response that shows how deeply she'd been embedded in the FBI's inner circle: "A Blue Rose Case?" "Yes." During this short exchange, Cole's hand is on Diane's shoulder, kneading her jacket fabric like a cat with a soft blanket. The jacket is faux leopard skin. We're learning that there's more to Diane than was originally evident, and experiencing this passage of feline abstraction, we wonder, Is she a leopard who changes her spots, a predator hiding her claws, a witch's wicked cat familiar?

This scene precedes the one in which Bobby, Frank, and Hawk examine the paper pictograph Major Briggs left for them, which showed two peaks, a big red spot on the left and a small red crescent linked with a horned black spot on the right. Diane wears, in addition to her leopard skin, a bracelet on her right arm, which reads as a red crescent, since part of its circle is hidden by her arm. A subliminal indicator that she's on the dark side, in part or completely? Ambiguity is *The Return*'s default setting.

How about an overt indicator? When Mr. C's at the rural retreat with Hutch and Chantal, after setting things in motion for Hutch to kill Warden Murphy, and later Dougie, the boss man sends a text: "Around the dinner table conversation is lively." The wheels of William Blake's "Satanic mills" are turning. In Lynch's screenplay for *Dune*, he has one of the villains repeat the incantation "It is by will alone I set my mind in motion." Mr. C is abuzz, in the flow state of making bad thoughts become bad deeds; the conversation is lively, firing neurons chattering away. Stunningly, it is Diane who receives the text.

Cognitive dissonance. This does not compute. Back in the day, Diane and Cooper were joined at the hip—or at least the tape recorder—fighting for truth, justice, and the American way. Then, years ago, after the Laura Palmer case, they had a personal, we assume sexual, encounter that left Diane emotionally wounded, devastated. And we just saw them encounter each other for the first time in decades at the prison, where just talking about "that night" whipsawed Diane's heart and mind. Was she acting, pretending to be traumatized, trembling in Gordon Cole's comforting arms?

Diane reads the text off by herself and is now smoking a cigarette, while Gordon, Albert, and Tammy are in the morgue absorbing cold facts about Major Brigg's headless body. The corpse is forty-five years old, but Briggs would be seventy-two in 2016. Buckhorn Police Detective Mackley introduces new information. School principal Bill Hastings, who'd been having an affair with librarian Ruth, whose head is positioned on Briggs's body, is a seeker of powerful esoteric knowledge. He and Ruth had located the "Zone," an extradimensional plane, and "met the major."

Clearly, the FBI needs to speak to Hastings directly.

But first, a couple of those special, telling moments that Lynch can convey so well. Quirky forensics expert Constance Talbot (Jane Adams), who performs stand-up comedy when she's not delving into crime scenes, mentions that Bill Hastings was once marbles champion of the sixth grade. Deadpan Albert instantly responds, "When did he lose his marbles?" Constance deadpans back, "When the dog ate his cat's eyes" (a type of marble). In a wide tableau shot containing Constance, Albert, and Gordon Cole, we can make out the slightest grin on Cole's face; like Cooper twenty-five years ago, he can read the signs of two people being on the same wavelength.

What can the mystery that is Diane tell Cole? On the back steps of the police office, she's smoking alone. Cole and Tammy join her, and the two old friends regard each other. Is he giving Diane that deep-truth scanning like he did to Albert after they'd seen "Cooper" at the prison? Or is his head full of fond memories of his and Diane's good old days? Maybe he's just craving her cigarette. He holds out two fingers (like a peace sign), and Diane hands him her smoke. Throughout decades of film history, sharing a cigarette is a talisman of deep bonding. After one puff ("whoa!"), Gordon hands it back and mentions their days of smoking together. Diane, smiling for the first time, her voice tenderly soft, says, "We sure did, Gordon, we sure did." Very sweet, with the full power of stillness and quiet: a perfect rendering of a just-hangin'-out moment. So Diane texts with the enemy, and now this. Maybe, unbeknownst to Gordon, she's playing on the FBI team, pretending to help Mr. C so she can get close to him and help bring him down.

Lynch devised this unscripted smoking scene on the spot, and it has in intertextural resonance. Tammy and Gordon are on the top step, officially in league. Gordon is on the right, and a few steps down, so is Diane. He's "together" with each woman, but we feel his linkage to Diane most strongly. They have their history (as do Lynch and Laura Dern: three big films together), they're smoking, and they're at ease, with just a few subdued movements, whereas Tammy (Chrysta Bell in her first big acting job) is self-conscious, feeling like a third wheel, nervously shifting her positions like she's modeling her dark blue suit.

Lynch has faith in Chrysta Bell the actress (he already knows she's an ace moody-dream singer and songwriter) and in her Tammy character. As Cole told Denise Bryson, "Tammy's got the stuff," and he sends her into the Buckhorn Police Department interrogation room for one of *The Return*'s big scenes. As Cole, Albert, and Diane watch through a one-way window/mirror, Tammy sits down to interview Bill Hastings. Impeccably professional, showing no emotion but not uncaring, Tammy gets the moaning, sobbing, permanently dazed man's story.

Bill, though married to Phyllis, found his soulmate in librarian Ruth, and in addition to their shared physical passion, they pursued the romance of seeking and sharing knowledge. Like Lynch and Frost, and various people in the *Twin Peaks* universe, Bill and Ruth were fascinated by the idea of other spaces and times coexisting with our own. And in *The Return*'s exploration of that idea, Bill declares, "It's real, it's all real," as though Lynch and Frost are emphasizing, everything's at stake here; these eighteen hours of *Twin Peaks* will not turn out to be a dream! Hastings's declaration brings to mind a key moment in Lynch's film *Mulholland Drive* (2001). Aspiring actress Betty (Naomi Watts) is about to begin her big audition scene at Paramount Pictures, which produced *Sunset Boulevard* (1950), which contained the character Gordon Cole, which Lynch took for his *Twin Peaks* character's name. Betty's in a nerve-racking situation. The room's jammed with agents, PR people, various assistants, the mature, established star Jimmy Katz (Chad Everett) whom Betty's going to play the scene with, and the prospective film's director. All eyes will be on Betty, sizing her up, moment to moment. Before they begin, the director makes a statement that sounds like cryptic Hollywood-insider jargon, or a Zen koan: "Don't play it for real until it gets real." Jimmy responds, "Acting is reacting; I just play off them." As someone once said, acting is playing pretend, using your voice, face, gestures, your whole body to portray attitudes, thoughts, emotions. It's mimicry; you can be thinking about your shopping list while convincingly pretending to be seduced by your fellow actor's character. Or you can truly be your character, really feel it in the moment, not a performance but an expression from your gut, your senses and thoughts one with those of your character. Betty's home rehearsal of the scene was tentative, tepid, but now, under high-pressure scrutiny, in front of the pros, some alchemy happens, she's white-hot. She goes beyond herself, loses and surprises herself; it gets real, and Jimmy responds in kind. The audition ends with a unanimous ovation for Betty. Actor Matthew Lillard's self-involvement in being Bill Hastings helps make *The Return* "all real."

Ruth's studies and calculations convinced her that if she and Bill were at a certain place at a certain time they would enter the Zone and meet "a certain person." They did this, and it was Major Briggs. He was hiding there, "hibernating," as he said. Sounds like he was hiding from Mr. C/the Woodsmen and hibernating outside of our temporal reality for twenty-five years, like Cooper imprisoned in the Red Room, the two bonded as ever, working the big Blue Rose case the long way around, via the scenic route. Worried that "others" were going to find him, the major asked for help, and Ruth hacked a "secure" government database to get the coordinates Briggs needed to go into deeper hiding in some further-out pocket of space-time. The secret database idea reinforces *The Return*'s sense of layers of knowledge, on the sides of good and evil and in between. Briggs got the information he needed, but Hastings tells Tammy that "others came in" and killed Ruth and Major Briggs. Briggs's head floated up, saying, "Cooper, Cooper" (two Coopers), then disappearing. As with Laura Palmer, Briggs's body is dead, but his spirit self lives on, floating in space to reassure Cooper on his journey from the Red Room to being Dougie. So who killed Ruth and the major? The glass box demon is an animalistic body shredder, and the "Got a light?" Woodsman is a messy head cruncher. But Ruth was shot, and her and Briggs' "surgeries" took time and care; the resulting body parts were transported and staged: the work of a thinker, a master strategist. Mr. C is the sort of potent presence that Hastings would remember seeing, but "others" had pushed Hastings face down onto the ground, so he didn't view the killing acts and who did them. Ruth's eye was shot out (perhaps Lynch's homage to the ending of the 1974 film *Chinatown,* which he calls "perfect"), with the blood-splash pattern indicating a bullet entering the back of her head and exiting the front, which is exactly the way Hastings's wife, Phyllis, looked after Mr. C executed her in Part Two. But if the coordinates Ruth gave Briggs enabled him, even without his body, to float off into realms beyond and Ruth had written those numbers on her hand, why didn't Bad Cooper write them down, if he'd just killed her in the Zone? We're hearing a very disturbed Bill Hastings's verbal account, so maybe Mr. C was there and did note the coordinates. But in Part Two Mr. C was badgering Ray about needing the information before Mr. C shot Phyllis, with Bill Hastings already in jail, after Ruth's and Briggs's bodies were found posed in Ruth's apartment.

So maybe the "many others" that were with Hastings, Ruth, and the major in the Zone were the Woodsmen. We remember the Woodsman near Hastings's holding cell, who dematerialized into the air. And what looked like the same Woodsman haunting the morgue hallway outside the room where Briggs's torso was being examined. We've seen the Woodsmen flicker in and out of existence beginning in 1945 in the New Mexico desert, helping to get the convenience store ready for Bob and the invaders, and later when Bob's occupying Cooper, putting the wounded Mr. C back together with some effective hands-on-body surgery. So if they segmented the major and Ruth, why didn't they convey her body's coordinates information to Mr. C? Again, we sense vertical hierarchies of power. Bob is not the uberevil, the Dark Mother, symbolized by the dark horned spot on Mr. C's playing card and the drawing Major Briggs left for Bobby and the good guys to find. Bob/Mr. C may want her power, but they can't have it—let them grope in the dark for traces of her. Maybe the Ruth-and-Briggs-killing Woodsmen are keepers/guardians of their zone, their portal, with a strong feeling of territorial imperative; they can't abide trespassers at their secret address.

Minutes before Tammy interrogated Hastings, the FBI team learned that a wedding ring inscribed "To Janey-E with love from Dougie" was found in Major Briggs's stomach. We know who Janey-E and Dougie are; the FBI does not. Did Briggs swallow the ring knowing it would point Cole and company, after doing research, in the direction of Las Vegas and Dougie/Cooper? But how did Briggs obtain the ring? Does this mean he had something to do with Dougie's creation, manufacture? Or did the Fireman make Dougie and get the ring to the major in the Zone? Or did Mr. C, playing the long game, manufacture Dougie decades ago, in the period when Mr. C met Briggs before Briggs faked his death and hid out in the Zone? When Mr. C and Briggs met, did Bad Cooper have the ring on him? Did Briggs steal it for possible future use, eventually swallowing it before being killed so it could be a signpost for the FBI? In the original *Twin Peaks*, the Giant (*The Return*'s Fireman) made a ring of Cooper's (not the Owl Cave jade ring) go away and come back. And we've seen the Fireman manufacture Laura's spirit and seed the earth with it. Maybe the Fireman and Judy are playing the longest competitive game of all, eternally, in American neighborhoods.

In *Blue Velvet*, young Jeffrey says to Sandy's policeman father, "It must be wonderful being a detective." The man replies, "Horrible too." Wonder and fear: the sublime state. Bill Hastings witnessed, with his face turned away, the murders of Ruth and Major Briggs, but he also saw the moment ("It was so beautiful") when Briggs' head "floated up," becoming spirit. As Tammy concludes her interrogation, she shows Hastings photos of six males and asks him to mark the one that's the major. He takes the pen, red for beneficent energy, and circumscribes Briggs's head in a smooth circle that's symmetrically kin to Laura in her golden orb.

Warmed by amber light, the air in Ben Horne's office still makes that ringing sound. Ben and Beverly move here and there with hushed motions, seeking the sound's elusive source, murmuring softly, "Mesmerizing, otherworldly." They speak of the sound, but they seem to be seeking love in a realm of enchantment. But Ben, his hand gently touching her cheek, says, "I can't do this." And Beverly says, "You're a good man." Ben, a morally reformed, unhappily married man; Beverly an unhappily married woman. They mention simple facts: it's late, he's her boss. Their spell is broken. But the sounds keep ringing.

To state the obvious, in the original *Twin Peaks*, everyone was younger. Laura and her classmates and friends were teenagers, and their doings and intrigues, and those of their parents' generation, were gripping and vitally important. There was a symmetrical balance between the kids' and the grown-ups' stories. In *The Return*, the original characters are decades older, and most of the new ones are grown-ups, so there's less time devoted to high schoolers or fledgling adults. But like the Roadhouse's singers and patrons, young folks are part of the *Twin Peaks* texture, its ethos, its collage of stories, layer upon layer of places and lives. Lives vulnerable, open to adventures, rebellion, pushing limits, so many choices to make.

As in 1989, some young lives seem old before their time: jaded, bored, ambitions not even dreamed, let alone pursued, stuck in a loop of same old, same old. But Lynch and Frost have the ability to make this all quirky and fresh and to empathize with young people the age of some of their own children.

A blonde (Ella: Sky Ferreira), a brunette (Chole: Karolina Wydra), each with a beer in a booth at the Roadhouse. Looking pretty slutty, they're not on the fast track to bright futures. Ella got fired, can't remember why. Was she high, late again? She got another job, same job, across the street, flipping burgers. Someone they know, Zebra, is out of jail again. They cackle: good times ahead. They regard each other with empty looks, then sigh and laugh, reminding us of wastrels Laura Palmer and Ronette Pulaski in one of their *Fire Walk With Me* nights of debauchery. Things are fucked, we're fucked, so it goes. Life can be a wicked rash, like the one festering in Ella's armpit. Her fingernails keep tearing at it. Beneath her pale flesh, the raw red.

–CHAPTER SIXTEEN–

VISTA VISION

(PART TEN)

Twin Peaks's mountains, in morning light. At the mountains' base, a green field, in the foreground, a little white house trailer with a small angel statue near the door. A car drives up; a story's in motion. Richard Horne, parentage unknown, the punk who killed the little boy when he blasted his truck through the crosswalk, angry and high. A voice from inside the trailer: Miriam (Sarah Jean Long), the woman who recognized Richard as the hit-and-run driver. Miriam the smart woman, still safe inside her trailer, who tells Richard she's told all to the police and sent a letter to Sheriff Truman: If anything happens to me, Richard's to blame. She's spoken, incriminated him, written about it—he's got to silence her big mouth. Richard charges forward, breaks the trailer's glass door, enters.

For a long twenty-five seconds we gaze at the serene tableau of trailer, field, mountain base in sunlight, just like before Richard arrived, but now the door frame is a black void, an abstraction of the "force of wild pain and decay" that Lynch has sensed since boyhood. Riveted by the beauty of the scene, the blackness, we hear screams and ugly thumps. The blackness, the angel figure. As Laura Palmer said in *Fire Walk With Me*, "The angels wouldn't help you. Because they've all gone away."

The long pause with the trailer and the field made an artist/teacher/arts administrator friend of mine think of photographer Gregory Crewdson's (born 1962) imagery. As an artist watching *Blue Velvet* for the first time, Crewdson "realized that my perception of things would never be the same." The film shaped his vision of "the complexities of American life," and today he's renowned for his gorgeous large color photos of nocturnal neighborhood scenes pregnant with stillness, mystery, traces of some story in progress, people suspended in tableaus of strangeness. Lynch loves his work. Crewdson's still-photo scenes, composed of many elements, are staged like movie shoots (his crews are often as extensive as those for feature films), and the results are beautiful and evocative, like stills from a longer narrative. Both Crewdson and Lynch are observing "the neighborhood," but Lynch's images are more dense and powerful in their simplicity: with their visceral thrust, they strike closer to the heart of our emotions. We feel distanced from Crewdson's impeccable images because part of our brain is marveling at all the thinking, preplanning, construction, and coordination that went into them. We're hyperaware of the images' posed, artificial nature. Lynch, without even knowing how he got there, can show us a severed ear in a golden field; backyard barbeque flames leaping too high, tended by a woman in a pale blue party dress; a house trailer with an entryway that's a black space, with an angel statue in front—"still" images outside of story that feel like our own dreams. Crewdson seems like a cerebral connoisseur and curator of strangeness. Lynch feels a yelp in his subconscious, hits us in the eye, in the gut.

Lynch, after letting us become mesmerized by an image that could be titled "Trailer With Black Void, Field," breaks the tension by letting us see inside. Richard's left, Miriam's large body is face down in her dim kitchen, her head in a pool of black-red blood. A candle burns on the counter a few feet from the angel figure outside. Perhaps for Lynch this is a devotional flame honoring Miriam and her spiritually inclined do-the-right-thing ways. But it's also part of Richard's dark process: the gas hissing from the open oven door will soon ignite the traces of his deed.

The 2017 *Twin Peaks* is presented in a far more fragmented form than the original show and *Fire Walk With Me*, with bits of various stories sometimes jaggedly butting up against each other, but some extended passages have a smooth thematic flow. From Richard confronting Miriam, who witnessed his hit-and-run killing of the boy, Lynch cuts to trailer park manager-resident Carl Rodd, who had comforted the boy's mother at the accident scene. We keep waiting to hear the sound of Miriam's trailer exploding in the distance. The blast doesn't come, but Lynch and Frost give us another kind of explosion. Carl sits with his guitar, singing the dear old song "Red River Valley" ("Come and sit by my side little darling"), his beverage cooler nearby (it's life-affirming red, with red roses arching above). Carl's sweet performance is interrupted by a crash sound as a red coffee mug shatters a trailer window and thuds on the ground. The red of a loving heart has been ejected. Carl can read this code: "It's a fuckin' nightmare." Through the broken window (another black void in a white trailer) we hear Steven screaming at Shelley's daughter, Becky. Furious, paranoid, probably high, he looms huge above her as she cowers, flinching, expecting to be hit any second. He threatens her ("I know what you did"—we have no idea what it was), and, with snot dribbling from his coke-red nose, berates her for not bringing in more money, when he's the one who can't get a job.

Following this path of domestic violence, we move on to Las Vegas and see where the Mitchum brothers live. *The Return* has a number of blood-kin male groupings: Frank and Harry Truman, Ben and Jerry Horne, the Vegas police detective Fusco brothers, and the Mitchum boys (Bradley: Jim Belushi, Rodney: Robert Knepper), with whom we spend the most time. The brothers have a boyish zest for life and fun, even with their dark Italian suits and million-dollar bank accounts. Best friends growing up, they now occupy themselves with high-stakes, perhaps shady business deals, running a casino, and getting tough, even lethal, with those who would impede their forward momentum (a trait of Mr. C's). They live together like when they were kids, and their friends the three Pink Ladies are always around. Blonde, long-legged in their short gleaming cocktail waitress dresses. In Greek mythology, the three graces, Brilliance, Bloom, and Joy illuminated beauty and charm in nature and humanity. The pink Vegas graces may share their loving aura with casino customers, but we see them as a mostly silent, glowing presence in the Mitchum brothers' lives, at work and at home. It feels good to have them around, a euphoric dose of adoring, succoring beauty and fun always at the ready: Vegas geishas. The relationship almost feels like adults playing prepubescent kids; do any of these people go to bed together? The brothers and the ladies live in their own eccentric, enchanted bubble; it's almost as if the Mitchums dreamed up these radiant companions. But a harsh reality intrudes, and a sense of the brothers' humanity is expressed when Bradley says that Candie (Amy Shiels) would have no place to go if they didn't shelter and take care of her.

The women often stand together, quietly, in a rosy grouping. But Candie stands out, or her hands do: My hands reach out, feel the air, therefore I am. Her hands make gentle wave motions—or they get violent, snapping the air with a red napkin (*The Return* can't get enough of the light rays with the spectrum's longest wavelength), trying to kill an elusive fly (it may buzz like electricity, but it's got to go). The irritating fly is coursing around the Mitchum brothers' house, *The Return*'s only modernist abode besides Diane's apartment. Bradley and Rodney's expansive, horizontal house is masculine elegant, a composition in black, white, dark brown, and gold, with gold-and-black abstract paintings. Throughout *The Return*, the wall art, save for the brothers' abstract paint splashes and Diane's Asian accents, features realistic representations of Americana and nature: cowboys, noble forests, waterfalls, Native American motifs, mostly from the mid-twentieth century, a golden time and place for Lynch.

The three Pink Ladies are kin to the three Ranch Gals who serve up food and beer in Lynch's *The Cowboy and the Frenchman* (1987), which includes three other cosmic women in the sky, who sing about "the cheerful sound of the meadowlark." Angel-women who serve and comfort the souls of Lynch's men include *The Grandmother*'s Grandmother, *Eraserhead*'s The Lady in the Radiator, *The Elephant Man*'s spirit of Merrick's mother and Mrs. Kendall, *Blue Velvet*'s Sandy, and *Wild at Heart*'s Good Witch.

Just because we can see a punch line coming doesn't mean it isn't funny. Candie can't catch the fly. She's frustrated, Rodney's reading some papers. The fly lands on his cheek for a second. Candie's hand in the air grabs the TV remote and whops Rodney and, we hope, the fly. As though suddenly focusing on the reality of what she's done, Candie screams and sobs and holds Rodney tight, her face distorted in grief. Rodney's got a bleeding gash in his face, but he cares more about comforting Candie and calming her down ("I'm fine, I'm okay"). She wonders, "Will you ever love me after what I did?" Lynch is a master of complex tonal mixtures: humor/emotional anguish, repulsive horror/humor, awe/fear. As he says, "artistic contrast," but also the way life is.

It's evening at the Mitchum house and Candie's still devastated, hiccup sobbing like a child who cries and cries. Like a pink teardrop, she is in the corner of the frame as the brothers watch the TV news. They see that Ike the Spike's been arrested. Good, they don't have to spend money having him rubbed out for their own reasons; the Mitchums are breezy and casual about the business of liquidation. Then there's coverage of Dougie ("Mr. Jones") and Janey-E being interviewed after Dougie thwarted Ike's attack, and the brothers recognize the Mr. Jackpots who took home so much of their casino money the other night. With classic Lynchian doubling, Bradley says, "Mr. Jones is Mr. Jones" (two are one), and we know that Dougie is a being further multiplied. Lynch and Frost are introducing Dougie to the Mitchums as a prelude to future mutual stories.

Janey-E took Dougie to the doctor today. In the span of a few days, almost magically, she's seen her garishly clothed, bloated husband become a svelte man in a trim black suit, but still acting bizarrely, more sluggish and slow-witted than ever before, yet able, in a flash, to subdue an attacker like a prime warrior, but then revert.

She needs a medical opinion of her man, The doctor's impressed. Dougie's lost weight, his vital signs are robust, "remarkable." "Remarkable," Janey-E repeats with a dreamy look as she drinks in the sight of Cooper's muscle-defined bare chest. In the background as Dougie gets dressed is a soft-focus red box or container (not heart shaped, like in Kurt Cobain's song, but still).

Back home, Janey-E's wearing her red shoes and pink sweater, sitting on a red chair watching Dougie silently enjoying a big piece of chocolate cake. She's got a come-hither gleam in her eye and subtly shifts her position in the chair as she asks, "Do you find me attractive?" as though (and actually with Cooper) for the first time. He looks at her, then back to his cake.

The next shot, in their darkened bedroom, shows that she's persisted, as we watch her slender naked back undulating as she straddles Dougie while he flaps his arms like a bird in flight in unison with her rhythm. She repeats "Dougie" with each deep breath, finally climaxing with "Dougieeeeeee!" Her ecstatic cry wakes Sonny Jim down the hall, and he sits up in bed, and Dougie has a blissed-out grin like he's in cherry pie heaven. Decades earlier, at the start of *Twin Peaks*'s second season, Cooper had been shot and felt he was dying. He regretted never having found a good woman and a house full of love. Now, in *The Return*, nestled under a red coverlet with Janey-E, their faces warmly glowing, with Sonny Jim next door, he has found it. Janey-E says, "Dougie, I love you." He says it his way, "Love you." Janey-E's husband has become wonderful, her newly handsome protector and lover. Next morning she pulls him aside and kisses him on the mouth (first time we've seen this), like a newlywed.

How's Candie doing today? She's back in the Pink Lady triad, standing against the wall in the Mitchum brothers' casino nerve center with the guys. On the monitors, which previously showed them Dougie winning so damn much of their money, they see insurance man Tony Sinclair (whom Dougie accused of lying at that meeting) down on the gaming floor. Rodney, his cheek scarred from Candie's earlier blow, tells her to go down, get Sinclair, and bring him up. A simple task, but she's embedded in that surreal, dissociated Lynchian stasis. She doesn't move or acknowledge the request. Last time we saw her she'd wept for hours over hurting Rodney, so what's up now? Is she being smug, feeling secure again (Of course they still love me), zoned out, or just being her own strange self? Blank faced, with no affect, she restates Rodney's request and then makes her way to the door, slowly, incrementally, finally touching the door and closing it behind her like she's never done it before. Who but Lynch can make such extended moments mesmerizing? She's a Dougie-like discoverer of the world.

The Mitchums, and we, are focused on the monitor showing Sinclair waiting one floor below. Candie enters the frame, and her hands can't resist the air. She makes flowing, wavy gestures and extends her arms here and there in various directions. Even the kindly Mitchums are losing patience, anxious to hear why Sinclair's here and having to endure one more of no doubt many Candie situations. Lynch and Frost choose to rob Candie of her fairy tale aura by having her explain, when she comes back with Sinclair, that she'd been talking to him about Las Vegas's climatic inversion layer and pointing out the casino's air conditioning outlets. Funny, yes; we misread the evidence. Less magical, but more character for Candie. *The Return*'s creators decided to emphasize Candie's humanity, and the brothers' empathy. They say to each other that, yes, she can be a handful, but if we turned her out she'd have no place to go.

Sinclair finally delivers his message. He thinks that Dougie knows the details of the shady dealings he's been up to, which involve the Mitchums. We know that Dougie's "He's lying" declaration regarding Sinclair at the meeting was intuitive and that the "analysis" of case files for Bushnell consists of pencil marks on paper that formed a meaningful pattern in Bushnell's eyes. Does this mean that Dougie is capable of standing up and making a verbal case against Sinclair? No. But Sinclair thinks Dougie's got his number, so he tells the Mitchums that Dougie "conspired to deny them" a massive insurance claim payment. Sinclair's summary message: "Douglas Jones seems to have a personal vendetta against you. . . . You have an enemy in Douglas Jones." Now Sinclair can relax, knowing the brothers will get Dougie off his back, maybe forever. So in the Mitchums' eyes, Dougie's robbed them two times. And they voice this reflection by putting a personal spin on a familiar aphorism: "You fuck us once, shame on you. You fuck us twice, shame on you. You're dead!" This sinister declaration emphasizes their relatively lighthearted, unintentionally funny villainy.

There are more layers of darkness motivating Sinclair's visit. Mr. Todd, who commands a palatial Las Vegas office, quakes in fear of his ultimate boss, Mr. C. Mr. C wants Dougie/Cooper dead, and since Ike the Spike failed that mission and is now behind bars, Mr. C needs to inflame the Mitchums enough to kill Dougie. Sinclair, without knowing about all the complex machinations, can be the messenger to poke the hornets' nest. The scope of Mr. C's shadowy network is extensive, and growing.

Cooper's brain plus Bob's black metaphysical fire equals one hell of a combination.

Gordon Cole reveals a hidden layer of his own when he tells Albert that when he comforted Diane after her ordeal talking to "Cooper" (Mr. C) at the prison, he felt something was amiss with her, something suspicious. And Albert, who's been monitoring Diane's texts, says that she's sent messages to Mr. C after he left the prison: the police/FBI "have Hastings, and they're going to take him to the site," presumably the Zone, where he and Ruth had met the major and where Briggs and Ruth were killed. That's an exciting prospect, and Gordon and Albert will keep her under close observation.

Tammy provides a key puzzle piece when she shows her colleagues a New York photo of Mr. C in the glass box room. So he's the "anonymous billionaire" funding the experiment, the scientific/metaphysical setup that's a conduit for demonic forces, a transportive passage that Cooper falling from the Red Room momentarily entered and was quickly rerouted from. It's a technological expression of Mr. C's quest for a place outside of time, like the major hibernating in the Zone, where he can hide and desire and feed forever with the Dark Mother or even kill her and become supreme. In a scene cut from *Fire Walk With Me*, the little Red Room denizen the Man from Another Place tells Cooper, now trapped there, "You're here now, so all you can do is go HOME!" So many of Lynch's characters, even lone wolf Mr. C, want to go home to somewhere Beyond.

Richard Horne's on his way to Grandma's house—but this ain't no Hallmark card nursery rhyme. In the life game of chutes and ladders, he just keeps dropping lower. Every detail of *The Return* generates waves of online analysis and speculation. The consensus wisdom is that Richard is the offspring of a comatose Audrey Horne, who'd been raped by Mr. C. Richard certainly behaves like Mr. C's son, but without his father's dark elegance and self-possession. Richard's a hothead, and he storms into Sylvia Horne's (Jan D'Arcy, playing Ben Horne's estranged wife) lodge-sized Northwest country house like a terrorist. In Lynch's short film *The Grandmother*, a parentally abused boy's grandmother was a loving angel figure, but in *Mulholland Drive* Diane was menaced by an elderly grandparent-like couple. This time around the grandmother is the target of a hellion. Sylvia is prim and proper in her café au lait cashmere sweater and string of pearls, but she's got a backbone of steel, and she orders Richard to get out. Not a chance; he slams her to the floor, calling her a "cock-sucking bitch" and "cunt" for good measure ("bad language" was not tolerated in the house Lynch grew up in). With a stranglehold on her windpipe, Richard sadistically mocks her for not speaking louder as she wheezes out the combination to her safe. Then he feeds and feeds, grabbing up her money, treasured jewelry, silverware. Lynch presents this home invasion/violation with his expected gut-punch intensity, and he amplifies the scene's physical and emotional violence by having someone else in the room.

Johnny Horne (Erik Rondell), firstborn child of Ben and Sylvia, is a tall, strapping man in his fifties, but his mental level never developed beyond early childhood. That's somewhat the way Dougie is presented, but we know that he contains super

Cooper, who will (?) fully burst forth someday. Johnny's just pathetic. Years ago, Laura Palmer tried to tutor him, but he preferred to bash his head against hard surfaces. He still does this as a grown up, and he recently put a head-shaped crater, with blood smear, into one of Sylvia's walls. Can we ever count up all the people wounded, marked by pain in Lynch's work? Before Richard shows up, Sylvia's gotten Johnny set up at the mahogany dining table, his limbs trussed to his chair so he can't slam into the wall again. There's sweet, soothing Montovani classical music filling the room, and on the table, filling Johnny's attention, is a strange Lynch-created object. Johnny stares at the fuzzy brown teddy bear with a round plastic head (eye spots, O-shaped mouth) with a light bulb inside that blinks on in unison with a recorded voice soothingly saying, "Hello, Johnny, how are you today?" over and over.

When Richard bursts in and attacks his grandmother, Johnny's alarmed emotions fire his muscles, but he's constrained by the chair straps, and his spasmodic motion tips the chair over, so all he can do is grovel and moan on the floor. In our ears: the din of syrupy violins and "Hello, Johnny" screams, groans, gutter curses, sobbing. In our eyes: a young man's face, inflamed with fury and greed, a dignified older woman's face terrified, the woman assaulted, her money and treasures stolen, her impaired son on the floor, trying to help, hobbled. In our minds: the sanctuary and sanctity of a family violated, virtually raped by one of their own, the terrible power of unrestrained desire. Assuming Mr. C is Richard's father, there's a similarity and a difference. Mr. C owns all his darkness: it is me and I am it. But Richard indulges in the more human trait of blaming others, projecting his guilt onto them. After he ran over the little boy he yelled, "I told you not to step out" (we never heard him say this), and as he leaves Sylvia's devastated home he says, "Why did you make something so simple so difficult?" In the classic film noir *On Dangerous Ground* (1951), Robert Ryan plays a cop who breaks all the rules, beating suspects to a pulp while saying, "Why do you punks make me do this?"

Richard certainly seems to carry the spiritual mark of the beast, and he's a cunning one. We never heard Miriam's trailer explode, but we assume that went as planned. She's beyond talking now, and Richard's taken care of that Richard-incriminating letter she sent to Sheriff Truman. He never got it, thanks to Deputy Chad, who's in cahoots with Richard and is the one bad apple in *Twin Peaks*' local law enforcement. In order to intercept the letter, Chad had to maneuver in front of receptionist Lucy's watchful eyes. He pulled it off, but the scene reinforced the idea that Lucy is an alert agent of the law, without a badge.

In the Buckhorn Hotel where the FBI agents are staying, there are four badges in proximity, none visible. It's evening in the dining room, and Gordon Cole and Tammy are grinning as they peek around a corner at Albert having dinner and chatting away with police pathologist Constance. That spark Gordon sensed between the two is sweetly hotter now. And—*mais oui*—they're sitting on red chairs, and a woman carrying a small French flag walks across the shot.

Back in Twin Peaks, in Ben Horne's Great Northern hotel office, that invisible warm, ringing sound that had enveloped Ben and Beverly is gone; the light is more neutral than golden. The sound that Ben, on the phone, hears is poor victimized Sylvia telling him about Richard's attack and robbery. Ben asks if Johnny is okay before he asks about Sylvia; she's offended, importunes him for more money, says she's calling her lawyer. In 1991, the Bravo TV network was the first to rebroadcast the original *Twin Peaks* episodes, and Lynch wrote prologues that the Log Lady (Catherine Coulson) delivered before each one. (Catherine sent me colored-paper Xeroxes of Lynch's original typed pages). In reference to the amoral Ben's efforts to become a better man, the Log Lady said, "You know in your heart if you have hurt someone; don't wait another day before making things right." In *INLAND EMPIRE* (2006), karma believer Lynch has a character speak of a spiritual "unpaid bill that needs paying," and for decades Ben's been paying materially, emotionally, and heroically. In Lynch's films, men with heads full of woe (*Lost Highway*'s Fred Madison, *The Return*'s Bill Hastings) tip their heads down and cover their crowns with their hands, and Ben, after the call with Sylvia, joins the club. The humming, ringing sound that had accompanied Ben and Beverly's tête-à-tête in this room is gone. Both unhappily married, they'd been on the verge of kissing, but Ben chose for both of them: "Beverly, I can't do this." Now he's slammed the phone down on Sylvia's haranguing voice. She's been victimized, she's in need, she's furious. There's a ten-ton wrecking ball pounding Ben's head. He calls out, "Beverly, do you want to have dinner with me?" Her choice.

Horrors on our screens: The first atomic bomb mushroom cloud, the Woodsmen, the glass box demon, Bob. Bob the sly, the insidious, maybe inside us, whether we know it or not. Both Miguel Ferrer (Albert Rosenfield) and Catherine Coulson (the Log Lady) knew that cancer was at work inside them, thriving, when they shot their scenes for *The Return*. Ferrer lived for months after the production wrapped, but died before the series aired. Coulson died a few days after she did her scenes.

Coulson and Lynch had been dear friends for over forty years, since the *Eraserhead* days, when she was married to Jack Nance (Henry) and was a vital assistant to the production. Lynch had saved her life once when she had a gastric seizure and vomited up part of her stomach lining, but there was nothing he could do this time. In recent decades, Coulson had been a beloved member of Ashland, Oregon's Shakespeare Festival repertory company, performing many classic and contemporary roles. *Twin Peaks* is imbued with Lynch's belief in mysteries and clues manifested in realms of materiality and spirit, and Coulson's Log Lady embodies and communicates the poetry of this essence. Coulson just had to be part of *The Return*, and she kept the extent of her illness hidden from Lynch when she signed on. But her cancer was so advanced, she was so frail, that she couldn't fly to Seattle to shoot her scenes. So Lynch had an Oregon crew prepare a Log Lady Cabin Interior set at Coulson's hospice care facility and light it with a warm glowing lamp prominent. Then, in an emotional experience for both of them, he directed her by Skype.

Nestled in her log cabin, cradling her cosmic/metaphysical message-receiving log to her heart, she talks to Hawk deep in the Twin Peaks night. She's in a red chair, and the frame of her large glasses is red. Her head has a halo sheen of short silver hair;

her expression is concerned, loving, tender. A tube helps her breath, oxygenating her receptive and wise mind. She voices Lynch's poetics of the electricity that makes mountains and rivers and seas and stars hum and glow: good electricity, the vital force of life. "But in these days the glow is dying," the black fire, the bad electricity are ascendant: "the darkness that remains." Lynch's humming doughnut is his primal dual focus on the battle between good and evil, and on womankind in general. He's said that "everything is about Marilyn Monroe," his abstract way of communicating his sensitivity to, and obsession with, "women in trouble" and women who are "real mysterious," Laura Palmer being a prime example. He feels "women know much more than men," that they're "more advanced in many ways because they're mothers, and the mothering thing is so important. If women ran the world, I think peace would be way closer" (*Room to Dream*). Margaret Lanterman, the Log Lady, is the spiritual mother of *Twin Peaks*.

Lynch's moving-image artworks, his paintings, and his drawings often present women as victims, but also as perpetrators, as helpers and bewitchers, demons and embodiments of heaven. Colossal writer-producer-director-actor Orson Welles once said that the most perceptive male artists have feminine souls. Lynch's Hindu and Tibetan beliefs say that though the world teems with male and female beings, animals and objects, the indivisible essence manifesting all this is female. As Lynch quotes the Upanishads, "The Great Mother is the master magician, and this whole world is peopled by her many parts." (*Catching the Big Fish*). The ultimate female reality, the One, can even appear to be a male God who creates the world or as a Good Mother and a Terrible Mother warring. Laura versus Judy? Laura didn't have a child, but throughout the ages and in many cultures, the psyche's female principle, Jung's anima, is represented in a spectrum from carnal desire to spiritual beatification, the pure light within Laura in the Red Room. In 1993, when Lynch wrote his intros for the Bravo TV rebroadcasts of *Twin Peaks*, which the Log Lady narrated, he echoed the Great Mother Upanishad: "The One leading to the many is Laura Palmer. Laura is the One." Now, in *The Return*, it's a darker time. There are good men who will fight the gathering evil, but the Log Lady emphasizes, "Hawk, Laura is the One." But where is she? Though she was full of powerful light in the Red Room, she was torn away to who knows where. She may be on a journey to ultimately confront Judy, but her path to that end is mysterious and long, as is that of her fellow *Twin Peaks* icon, Dale Cooper. In Lynch's terms, she may be the doughnut, but at this point she's an empty space. She is, as she was twenty-five years ago, lost. In addition to having the Log Lady call Laura "the One," Lynch reminds us of her primacy by having Laura appear, in wrenching anguish, as a momentary vision to Gordon Cole, in an image from *Fire Walk With Me*.

Lynch transitions to the Roadhouse with a shot of the moon, throughout history a feminine principle, associated with both the Virgin Mary and soul-stealing witches, an orb with a womanly gaze that pulls the seas this way and that, in harmony with the ebb and flow of menstrual blood. Lynch's moon shows the dark aspect ascendant; it's light a pale crescent like the crescent form that led to the A-bomb mushroom blast demon spewing her eggs, the curved scythe that harvests souls, the crescent form of the bracelet on duplicitous Diane's wrist. In *Fire Walk With Me*, Lynch showed us the moon just before Leland killed Laura; here it's a gateway to a mournful mood.

The Roadhouse stage is lit like midnight; singer Rebekah Del Rio caresses the microphone like it's a lost love. The world discovered her rich, full voice in *Mulholland Drive* when she sang Roy Orbison's lament "Crying" in Spanish ("Llorando") and, midsong on some otherworldly theater stage, her head tipped away from the microphone, she dropped to the floor. Life left her, and she was carried off, but her voice, the song, kept filling the air, and our hearts. In this abstraction of death and reincarnation, Lynch showed that the body dies but the spirit essence moves forward.

Tonight at the Roadhouse, Rebekah is again lamenting a love lost. The Log Lady just spoke of the world's positive, good electricity fading ("the glow is dying") and darkness enveloping all. Rebekah's song, written by her, Lynch, and Lynch's sound engineer and musician John Neff, is, again, in a softer tonality, the cry of a broken heart. The song's woman wants to return to "that place where it all began, you know the one." Where their love was born, blessed by the stars above. There were needs ("Hold me") and promises ("Don't be afraid") and stars ("I saw them in your eyes"), the stars that "we're with." But now: devastation and pain. This was all long ago; now it's just a dream, and there are "No stars/No stars/No stars," forever and ever. Love is gone, but there's the dream, the memory of love.

Marcel Proust (1871-1922), the romantic novelist of memories that live and time that's regained, wrote the seven volumes of his *In Search of Lost Time* after the scent and taste of a madeleine biscuit dipped in lime tea transported him back into his childhood. It wasn't the memories he wracked his brain methodically trying to retrieve that were magical; it was those that came involuntarily, unwilled, unbidden, like a sudden trilling of bird song outside a shuttered window.

Watching the last minutes of Part Ten, hearing the first chords of "No Stars," seeing Rebekah before she even sings a word spreads a warm, melting feeling in my chest; my throat constricts; I've got tears in my eyes. My love Linda died six months ago, but I'm back seventeen years with her to June 23, 2000, and she and David Lynch and I are sitting in the dark. Linda's on my right, Lynch, scented with coffee and cigarettes, is on my left. The lights are off in his sound studio/movie watching room, but by the faint glow of the sound-mixing console I can see John Neff press a button, and Rebekah's voice, singing "No Stars," fills our heads and hearts, loudly, as Lynch likes it. As the "No stars" repetitions faded into the air, John brought up the lights. The song was beautiful and so sad, but I felt plugged into the universe. Lynch's sensibility, mind, and art had entered my life thirty summers earlier when I'd seen *The Grandmother* at the Bellevue Film Festival. Some twenty-three-year-old kid from Philadelphia had made this unique film about a parentally abused boy who grows a loving grandmother from a seed. The idea was so psychologically resonant, and given form in live action and animation, it floated into my head like a dream. I was hooked, and over the decades, after reading about Lynch and his work, seeing his films and TV ventures, and showing his moving-image work and still photographs at the Seattle Art Museum, I embarked on the project of exploring his life and art in a book.

Because there were yearslong gaps between Lynch's films and projects, the book was always waiting for his next big thing. I had plenty of time to interview Lynch's personal and professional associates, and from his earliest school friends to his current assistants, I got the strong impression that he was a friendly, lovable guy who wanted to be left alone to do his work. People around Lynch were enthusiastically helpful to my book project, and Lynch gave me hours of his time on the phone, but sometimes, instead of keeping a phone appointment, he was "over in the studio messing with his guitar" or painting. Frustrating, but it goes with the David Lynch territory.

Lynch never asked to read a word of what I was writing, and those close to him said, "He must really trust you." Our phone relationship was—as we said in the 1950s that Lynch and I grew up in—solid, Jack. Right off the bat we bonded over being raised in the Northwest and the fact that our fathers were woodsmen, my dad a youthful lumberjack in the forest around "Twin Peaks," Lynch's father a Forest Service research scientist. It got so he'd call me "Bud" or "Ace" and sign off saying "Cool, swingin'."

When Linda Bowers and I met at the Seattle Art Museum in 1982 and started falling for each other, she tended toward high culture and I was more pop, but she read the stars clearly: "We're going to have so much fun together!" That's the overflowing truth. We spent half our lifetimes together, intimate in every way, feeling closer to each other than anyone else in our lives, sharing all the changes, hard work, and blessings of love.

Before I started writing *David Lynch: Beautiful Dark*, there must have been moments when Linda wondered, "Who is David Lynch, and how has he captured Greg's brain?" But over time and dinner discussions, this woman who venerated African tribal art, the Italian Renaissance, Picasso, Gene Roddenberry's humane, optimistic sensibility (*Star Trek*), *The Wire*, *Angels in America*, *My Neighbor Totoro*, Lance Armstrong, Kurt Cobain, and Patti Smith, became a Lynch appreciator. She entered my typed manuscript pages onto discs, and the deeper she got into Lynch's life and art and spirituality, the deeper he became to her. She was especially moved by his love of women and understanding of their psychosexual complexity.

That day almost didn't happen. Linda and I had a few days left in Los Angeles before we had to fly home to Seattle, and I kept trying to get him by phone. He'd been late in getting started on an art project he was doing for a friend, and it was "pedal to the metal time"; he had his assistant relay to me that "I'm up to my neck in foam!" I understood; Lynch has to make his art, but still. This trip had another Lynch-related storyline. When he moved to LA from Philadelphia in 1970, he spent time driving around trying to find a driveway that was in one of his favorite movies, Billy Wilder's *Sunset Boulevard* (1950). In this classic film noir, screenwriter Joe Gillis (William Holden), speeding on Sunset Boulevard, being chased by two men, has a blowout and swerves his car into an old shrub-shrouded driveway. He discovers that the drive leads to the decrepit mansion of aging has-been movie star

Norma Desmond (Gloria Swanson), where he will become ensnared in her web of warped, needy love and dream factory madness. Lynch knew that the Doheny Mansion (now the headquarters of Getty Oil) doubled as Norma's house, but where was that driveway? Lynch likes to create and perpetuate mysteries, but this was one he personally wanted to solve.

It's Hollywood's way to combine disparate locations into a whole, a realm, that's both "real" and illusory. In the weeks before Linda and I flew to LA, I imagined that Lynch might join us on a driveway-hunting expedition, so I did some research. Amazingly, the name Judy Garland popped up, Dorothy in *The Wizard of Oz* herself. She and her husband director Vincente Minnelli had lived in a house on Evanview Drive that seemed to be part of the equation. When I told Lynch this over the phone, his voice had a reverent hush: "Judy Garland." The man who laser focuses when two things happen together was thrilled. I had provided a link between two of his beloved films, *Sunset Boulevard* and *The Wizard of Oz*—maybe. Field research would have to occur, to which he said, "Yeah, maybe we could do that." In a classic Lynchian doubling, I further discovered that from 1948 to 1951, Garland and Minnelli had another address, on Sunset Boulevard, and the film was made in 1950. Two houses.

On the ground in LA, while Lynch worked toward meeting his art project deadline, Linda and I found the Evanview house, a boxy modernist structure on a narrow hillside, streets away from Sunset. On Sunset, we did find the Garland-Minnelli place, or at least the palatial gate and lush landscaping that obscured it from the street. The approach was too grand to be the film's driveway. One of the world's most storied roads, Sunset Boulevard snakes for twenty-some miles from Hollywood to a final straight stretch into a burnt-orange sunset over the Pacific. You can't park on Sunset Boulevard; there are no sidewalks, and any driver with an ounce of sporting blood leaves the speed limit far behind, as witness Jeff Bridges and James Woods racing in *Against All Odds* (1984) and Jan and Dean's song "Dead Man's Curve" (1963). The thing was, just west of the current entrance to the former Garland-Minnelli estate, at curb marker 10060 (adds to seven), there was an old driveway, overgrown with shrubs and shortened by a wall added after 1950, and this section of Sunset looked like the patch where William Holden was driving. Pay dirt! Now I had to snap a photo to give to Lynch. The boulevard had midday traffic and was four lanes wide on this stretch. In order to get any kind of angle for a proper image, I had to be out on the road. Convincing myself that my life's journey was not going to end here, I set the camera on autofocus, jumped out, turned, snapped, and got a couple of shots.

Linda was relieved that she'd heard no screeching brakes and that I was still around to get back in the car. By this point in our relationship, she was an integral part of the Lynch-pursuit team, but she had a moment of fear-based anger over my risking myself. Pissed, but a little proud too.

Sunset Boulevard was definitively in the air on this LA trip. Lynch loves the modernism of Los Angeles, the heady sense of progressive thinkers and artists making new things right now. But he treasures "the air of Old Hollywood" in the sultry breeze, the past that's present. In Billy Wilder's film, William Holden's character lives in the Alto Nido Apartments, a six-story café-au-lait stucco 1930s structure that's still there. Linda and I stood next to the building and looked down Ivar Avenue, which slopes to the distant bright stripe of Hollywood Boulevard below, the exact shot that Wilder had composed fifty years earlier.

Amazingly, and somehow almost expectedly, *Sunset Boulevard* was on TV that night. The next day was our last before flying home, so no in-person Lynch this trip. I knew he was engulfed in his art-project obligation, but I wanted to try to get him on the phone to tell him about finding and photographing the elusive driveway. I was surprised and happy to hear his twangy loud voice come on the line sounding like a thrilled little boy: "*Sunset Boulevard* was on TV last night!" I said, "Yeah, someone could have been sitting in William Holden's old room watching the movie." When I told him he'd been on the right track in his driveway search thirty years earlier, Lynch chuckled and said, "I'll be darned." That's the way the world is, things connected, if we can just see it. He said, "Why don't you guys come over for coffee?" Am I leading a charmed life? Is my karmic balance in good shape? These are the good old days.

Sitting in Lynch's cluttered art studio sipping coffee, Linda and I watched clouds of his American Spirit cigarette smoke form an indoor micro climate. We all seemed at ease with each other, and he excitedly told us about his desire "to dig for treasure on my property—I don't care if it's water, gold, or oil." I think of Lynch's Forest Service father, and Lynch in his work and spiritual philosophy, seeking what's beneath the surface of things. He rhapsodizes about the concrete pilings and hidden superstructure sunken into the hillside that anchor his compound to the slope's substrata and will withstand earthquakes (he knocks on his old wooden desk). Lynch realizes that his residential neighborhood treasure digging might come afoul of environmental laws and authorities, and he bursts out with one of his key principles: "I won't have other people telling me what to do." When I was on the phone with him before we came over, he said, "The neighbors hate my guts," and he gave me detailed instructions on where and how to park. Lynch knows that rock-solid appearances can be deceiving, and he talks about the ground actually being "light and loose" and how once a rainstorm freed a huge boulder that "thundered down the hill like an earthquake," missing his three houses and landing in his neighbor's pool. He was on a roll, and he went beneath the surface, telling us about wood excavated from the bottom of Lake Superior that he bought and sent to his eighty-four-year-old father to make into a violin. The verbal flow in Lynch's films and TV shows is known for sudden nonsequitur shifts, as when *Blue Velvet*'s Jeffrey, on a quiet nocturnal stroll with Sandy, out of nowhere says, "Do you know the chicken walk?" When Lynch was talking about a property owner's rights to whatever's under their ground, I jokingly said, "What about the air rights above your property?" And he said, "You look just like my cousin—his name is Mike—are you a runner?" I said, "No, but I like to take walks at night."

Lynch had always told me how vital "having a good setup"was to him, and he proudly, in a casual, low-key way, showed off his smooth, "organic" concrete walls and floors, orange-amber Douglas Fir woodwork (Agent Dale Cooper's favorite tree), and gleaming chrome coffee makers. As we strolled around, art historian Linda and Lynch kept up a dialogue about his work. A number of his large paintings, bristling with thick surface texture, were propped against various walls, and Linda suggested he might like to try an ancient painting technique that involves warm wax. I heard them chatting about a five-by-seven-foot painting, *Bob Loves Sally Until She Is Blue in the Face,* that is probably Lynch's most overtly sexual canvas. Looking at Linda's face, Lynch said, "I know why you're smiling." He listened carefully to Linda's riff on how his love of women is so evident in his work, and she wondered how he creates such psychologically complex female characters. Lynch's face lit up, and he burst out with, "I love the female psyche!"

Lynch leads us across the steep, landscaped hillside above and behind his dwellings to various parts of his compound, and he points out a constructed outdoor living room tableau that he's set up, hoping to lure in a coyote with meat so he can film it. Come on in, coyotes, art's more important than neighborhood rules and regulations.

Lynch has designed as much of his compound as he can, and we enter his stunning sound and music studio/projection room. Two tiers of seven seats are at one end, mixing console center, movie screen at the far end, above a selection of guitars and a drum kit. The black-carpeted space is hushed, with soft sunken ceiling lights and dark hues. I once asked Lynch what artistic medium most readily produces the "floating into a dream" sensation he likes to produce for his audience, and he instantly said, "Sound." As in *Blue Velvet,* have we entered an ear found in a field, a passage into Lynch's dream? He explains that the room we're in "floats" within a hidden space, inside outer walls, so that absolutely no sound from outside can penetrate. With a grin I ask him if "there's a strange room behind those curtains," alluding to the Red Room. A slight smile breaks through his deadpan response, "No, there isn't." "Have any weird people come through those curtains?" "No, they have not."

He explains that the shape of the studio makes sounds recorded here sonically neutral, conveying no intrusive room presence. I ask him if he ever comes in here alone and sits in the rarified hush. He does, but "It can be eerie." Eighteen years later, in the era of *The Return,* he told *The Guardian* that if he was alone too much he might get "funny, and not in a humorous way." Maybe, sitting here by himself, he communes with the spirit of Alan Splet, his late friend and sound-creating wizard, some of whose ashes are mixed into the sound console base in front of us.

Whether due to chance or karma, Lynch says, "I get these happy accidents." During the production of *Mulholland Drive,* he met singer Rebekah Del Rio when she came by the studio for coffee. Before she took a sip she sang a stunning rendition of Roy Orbison's song "Crying" in Spanish, and sound engineer and musician John Neff got it on tape, the exact tape we hear in *Mulholland Drive* when Rebekah's on stage at Club Silencio. The tape of "No Stars" (written by Lynch, Rebekah and John Neff) that Lynch played for Linda and me is the one we hear in *The Return,* for the first time in public. It's approximately seven minutes long. In Lynch's studio in 2000, after we all sink deep into the beautiful pain of the song and Rebekah's performance, Lynch slowly raises the lights and we compose ourselves. Lynch breaks the silence, "I think the ending is a hair too long." I softly respond, "I've only heard it once, but it seemed dreamy and wonderful at this length," to which John Neff, down at console, says in Lynch's direction, "*See*," indicating that this is a point of artistic contention between the collaborators.

Lynch led Linda and me to a door and opened it on his inner sanctum. In one of Lynch and my earliest phone conversations, I spoke about the psychological effect of being confined to a small space, "living in an eight-foot-by-eight-foot world," and Lynch completed the thought: "But your mind can soar." His office is a bit larger than eight-by-eight, but very intimate. The soft, slightly sweet scent of Indian incense permeates the room; with every breath, Lynch is reminded of the Unified Field of being. In this space he delves into his deepest thoughts and feelings. A small, high window admits light as Light, not a distracting pictorial view; in this concrete cell he sees the inner world. There's a niche in the wall where he can light a small fire, and a black 1950s modern lounge chair where he sits meditating, and where he mentally recomposed his planned TV show *Mulholland Drive* into one of his feature film masterpieces. In this space he manifests his mind: Rebekah's "No Stars" words and, for *The Return*, the Log Lady's electric-glowing stars.

Lynch had been Linda's and my star this day, and it was hard to break away from the warm flow of his intimacy, but there was some place we had to be: up Crescent Heights and into the LA dream. We'd invited David to come with us, but he had to tend to his art making.

In 1960, when Linda, David, and I were teenagers, an iconic photograph of a modern house, called "the house heard around the world," cantilevered out in the night air over the Los Angeles light scape, grabbed the hearts and minds of millions. Julius Shulman's black-and-white photograph of pioneering modernist architect Pierre Koenig's Stahl House shows a rectangular glass box with a steel-beam roof thrusting into the frame at a thirty-degree angle from left to center, the lines of the foreground house merging with the lines of the dark background carpet of street-grid lights far below—all in sharp focus. In the living room, sitting on rectilinear midcentury modern furniture, are two women in pale, puffy midcentury dresses. They're at ease, smiling; the transparent glass walls let them meld with the magic carpet of lights out ahead, the promise of new possibilities, life refreshed. For some of us born in the mid-1940s, like Lynch, Linda, and I, the Stahl House *Life* magazine cover photograph evoked the fresh breeze of modernism, the utopian aspirations of West Coast America. Lynch had built himself a new life in LA, and Linda and I were thinking of doing the same. Lynch laughed when I said, "Up in Seattle you get tired of moss and mold after a while."

Being a good detective, Linda, who had many connections in the worlds of art, architecture, and design, found the email address of Stahl House creator Pierre Koenig, then seventy-four years old. Those "happy accidents" Lynch talks about were pelting Linda and me like Seattle rain: Koenig got the impression that Linda knew the lady of the Stahl House, Carlotta Stahl, and gave her her phone number. Carlotta's three-digit prefix was my prefix at the Seattle Art Museum, and the four digits of the rest of Carlotta's number were the four digits of Linda's work phone.

The view Julius Shulman photographed can't be seen from where we parked, but we go through a gate, around the turquoise pool, and there it is, sparkling white-silver against the crystalline blue sky. Even without the aura of lit-up night, the house and the city of dreams beyond are magical. Parts of the house have opaque walls where pictures are hung, but its major, revolutionary space, encompassing the kitchen and living room, is glass walled, so from all angles it feels like you're living in the sky. Carlotta and Linda obligingly posed for me out at the cantilevered end of the living room, the view before them and beneath them forty years after Julius Shulman composed what an international panel of photography experts and archivists have called "one of the most important images of all time."

We can sit in our chairs pondering the idea that all things are connected, but sometimes life shows us that they truly are. Koenig's email address contained the star name Mizar. When, after dinner on this day, Linda and I visited the Griffith Park Planetarium, the iconic white, triple-domed art deco masterwork where *Rebel Without a Cause* climaxed, we lined up to look through the giant telescope and saw that it was focused—amazingly—on Mizar. Mizar is the center, fulcrum star in the Big Dipper's curved handle, the best place to grip to scoop a big dip; the sort of thing an architect like Koenig, his mind attuned to physics, astronomy, and aesthetics, would notice. Linda said, "Wow, so many connected things in the same day!"

In Lynch's *Lost Highway*, Patricia Arquette's character gives directions to two police detectives: "We're near the observatory." Painter-photographer Man Ray (1890-1976), like Lynch a onetime Philadelphia resident and also one of the Surrealist artists Lynch reveres, painted an iconic image, *Observatory Time—The Lovers*, which shows giant, disembodied sunset-red female lips floating above the Griffith Park Observatory dome. In *The Misfits* (1960), Marilyn Monroe's last film (David Lynch: "Everything is about Marilyn Monroe"), she asks Clark Gable, "How do you find your way back in the dark?" He says, "Just head for that big star straight on." Our mothers gave birth to us, but we're all star stuff. As boys, Lynch and his brother, John, used to look up at the stars together, and at the end of *The Straight Story*, two previously estranged brothers, rejoined at the end of their lives, repeat a childhood ritual, looking up into a somehow warm star field that comes forward to welcome them, like *Eraserhead* Henry's heavenly angel woman coming forward to embrace him. At the end of Lynch's *The Elephant Man*, as John Merrick's sublime soul departs the torment of his twisted, misshapen body, his loving mother's face appears in the stars, saying, "Never, no never; nothing will die; nothing dies," reflecting Lynch's Hindu beliefs. Merrick's mother's words echo the coda of Jean Renoir's film *The River*, a tale of life and death along India's sacred Ganges River: "Sun follows day, night, stars, and moon; the day ends, the end begins."

These are all good, consoling words. But Linda and I, both only children, had been together for over half our lives. When she died, Lynch/Rebekah Del Rio/John

Neff's "No Stars" said it all. Gone. She'd been connected to every part of my life, every place, season, meal, movie, book, song, shirt, and sweater. There was no escape from the pain. So, as many wise people have said, the hurt has to be embraced, not avoided. Trial by fire. A box of Kleenex wouldn't last a week. But Linda's love reached out to me, in words in books that she'd marked for me to find, like Louise Gluck's poem "The Evening Star," which has "cast enough light to make my thought visible again."

Linda would have loved the full solar eclipse of August 21, 2017, She and I had once observed the summer solstice with hundreds of Los Angelenos at the Griffith Park Observatory, we'd lost ourselves in pulsing star fields far from civilization in the Northwest wilderness, seen stars reflected in the night beach wash of the Pacific Ocean. As the eclipse got rolling I was out on the lawn wearing my viewing glasses. I came into the house to see what things looked like there, and peered out my familiar window view at a strange mid-morning twilight landscape. I could feel Linda close to me, and I went into my work room, where I keep my favorite picture of her, and got a warm surge from her smile. Something on the floor drew my attention. The room's east-facing window has a bushy hedge outside it, but shafts of light from the sun that took eight minutes to get here were randomly piercing through the hedge and falling on the wood floor in a sprinkling of separate little eclipses. I've always known that I can sometimes laugh and cry at the same time. When I was little, and crying, my mother would hold a paper cup to my cheek and say, "Here, let me catch those tears," and I'd always laugh. Wow, yes, Linda, so many things today.

–CHAPTER SEVENTEEN–

FRIEND GOOD
(PART ELEVEN)

Deep in the American grain, Norman Rockwell (1894-1978) and Andrew Wyeth (1917-2009) are the country's most famously representative painters.

In Rockwell's *Thanksgiving* (1941-1943), we look, from foreground to background, along a table lined with smiling faces, young and old, and pristine dinner table settings and overflowing bowls of fruit as, center frame, patriarch grandpa watches proudly while grandma sets the gigantic, succulent turkey before the assembled family. Behind the grandparents we see white wainscoting, pale floral wallpaper, a white-framed curtained window. Safety, bounty, and happy family sharing reign.

In Wyeth's *Groundhog Day* (1959), we also look from front to back along a table with a white cloth. The table setting consists of just a single plate, a cup, and a knife. No food, no chair to sit in, no people. Behind the table, as in Rockwell's room, we see almost identical pale floral wallpaper, white wainscoting, white-framed window, no curtain. Right outside, as vivid as the table inside, is a big log with a jaggedly cut end that for Wyeth is "the fangs of the dog. That dog is nasty, you have to watch her." (*Two Worlds of Andrew Wyeth*). Safety, bounty, joy, and family sharing? No. Something lonely, disquieting, disturbing, even dangerous? Yes.

Akin to young David Lynch discerning a "sense of wild pain and decay" at work in the world, young Norman Rockwell "found the world wasn't always the pleasant place I thought it would be" (*Norman Rockwell: The Underside of Innocence*). He decided that "If it wasn't an ideal world, it should be and I painted only the ideal aspects of it." Rockwell cheered us up with the hope that Hometown, USA, was a safe place brimming with common sense, gentle humor, and folksy tolerance, where people enjoying life worked to nurture and perpetuate a common good. He knew there was a worm in the bright red apple, and in rare occurrences his conscience moved him to show it, as in *The Problem We All Live With* (1964), in which US marshals have to keep a little African American girl safe from racist violence as she enters a white school in the segregated mid century South.

Rockwell lived and worked in picture-postcard New England, a region that Wyeth called too perfect and "pretty." His domain was the hardscrabble farm country of rural Pennsylvania, where Rockwell's homey, cluttered coziness was an unknown quantity: vast stretches of bleak winter-brown ground, dilapidated houses, people using newspaper stacks as furniture, barely scraping by. Rockwell's images brim with familiar narrative details that tell a story. Wyeth's images are comparatively sparse, with an elusive hint of meaning, an evocation of secret connections. Sounding like Lynch, Wyeth seeks to "find the abstract in the everyday" (*Two Worlds of Andrew Wyeth*). He believes in "dream-like associations," and that "it's what's not there that's important." Wyeth's recognizable rural places and people can be shadowed with an air that the artist characterizes with words like "strange," "looming," "weird and off balance," "frighteningly deep," "the power and the horror."

Rockwell, Wyeth, and Lynch portray the sunshine and the noir of America, and Eagle Scout Lynch intuitively seeks Wyeth's amalgamated "mystery and incongruity" (*Two Worlds of Andrew Wyeth*): a boy in a golden field, a severed ear swarming with ants in the grass (*Blue Velvet*). The first scene of *The Return*'s Part Eleven: did Norman Rockwell paint this? In morning light, three young brothers of varying heights play catch with a baseball. If they make a catch, they congratulate each other ("Nice"); if they miss, they're not mocked ("Oh, almost"). Sounds like a happy family. One boy misses; the ball rolls away; the oldest boy chases it. He steps out onto the rural road—no cars in sight—and freezes in his tracks. There's something moving, on the ground in the tall grass, horrible, a large woman, dark hair, blood-streaked face, moaning, crying. We feel the chilling horror, but the saving connection the boy needs to make is close at hand: "Go tell Mom." Lynch's sensibility: the balance of darkness and light.

We recognize the woman as Miriam, who survived Richard Horne's pummeling and must have extinguished the candle and turned off the gas, so her trailer didn't explode. She's a survivor and can point a bloody, accusing finger at Richard.

In *The Return*, we've seen a car and an atomic bomb explode, and Lynch's penchant for boiling emotions reaching volcanic heights has been on full display. Hot steam is almost pouring out of Becky's ears. She's in her ne'er-do-well boyfriend/husband Steven's trailer. She's on the phone; someone's telling her things. She bursts out with an intense "Where? What?" and screams in fury. She pulls a gun out from under the couch. Steve's got the car, and she needs to travel, fast. Her mom, Shelly, leaves the Double R and brings her car over. Becky grabs the keys (red), but before she can floor the accelerator, Shelly frantically spread-eagles herself on the car's hood to stop her. Becky won't be stopped. She hits the gas; the car spins a doughnut; Shelly flies off the hood onto the grass as her high heels sail through the air. Becky's gone, and Shelly's in one piece. Maybe her red shoes are as lucky as Dorothy's in *The Wizard of Oz*.

Becky stands before the door of apartment 208. She's been told, "They're not there." She screams, "Fuck you, Steven!" and pumps eight slugs into the wood at

Steven's height. Seems there's been some two-timing going on, and Lynch roars his camera down hallways, down stairs to a lower stairwell, where Steven and a young woman hold each other, quivering, listening for further blasting sounds. We may not recognize this woman, Gersten Hayward (Alicia Witt), Donna Hayward's sister, for we last saw her in the original *Twin Peaks* decades ago, costumed as a pink princess for a school event. Maybe in *Twin Peaks* idealized female royalty is bound for trouble: Gersten, Laura Palmer (homecoming queen), Annie Blackburn (Miss Twin Peaks).

A shot of the sheriff's office, with gray-haired Maggie (Jodee Thelen) at the communications control board, shows that there's plenty of trouble to go around. One on top of the other, calls of distress and alarm come in. Again and again Maggie repeats, "Location?" "Someone's on the way." The office offers help, and heart, from Frank Truman's by-the-book policing to Hawk's mystical insights to Bobby's empathy, and Lucy can play quirky angles when you least expect it. The walls at Maggie's communications station are heartbeat red.

Old Fat Trout Trailer Park Manager Carl Rodd seemed burned out and near the end of his years twenty-five years ago in *Fire Walk With Me*, but in *The Return* he's actively engaged in the community, almost like an unofficial, honorary deputy. He doesn't have a patrol car or a Batmobile always at the ready, but when he blows a note on his flute, his buddy/driver Bill (unnamed performer) appears in his vintage VW bus, at Carl's service. After Shelly was flung onto the ground trying to stop Becky from fleeing with Shelly's car, Carl helped her up and into the VW. He comforts her ("I feel for you and your girl, okay, Shelly?") and, on his back seat landline phone, has Maggie patch through so Shelly can talk to Bobby about her troubles with Becky.

How many times has Double R owner-manager Norma Jennings watched personal dramas and conflicts get aired, if not solved? She's not a kibitzer, but tonight, at a respectful distance, she pays attention to the gathering of her dear, longtime friends Bobby, Shelly, and Becky. Lynch and Frost establish that Becky is married to Steven, and that she's the daughter of the divorced Bobby and Shelley. They want to respect Becky as an adult, and they ask her what she wants to do about troublesome Steve, but her answers are all over the place: "I hate him; I love him; I want out." She makes excuses for Steve: "He's just going through a bad time right now. He's been looking for work every day; at least that's what I thought he did." Becky's face is puffy and red with her passionate emotions, and we remember her father's intensity twenty-five years ago, denying any kind of generalized wrongdoing on his part and, at Laura Palmer's funeral, lambasting the community, and himself, for not realizing how much she'd needed help. With Becky, Bobby is calm and firm: "You've got to make this right," meaning pay for the damage to Gersten's shot-up door and apartment. But Bobby's toughness is tender; he'll loan her the money, which she must pay back.

Shelly and Becky are sitting opposite Bobby, and she hugs their child and weeps, "We don't want to lose you." It's a sweet family moment, which Norma blesses with a warm, caring look, but in Lynch's world, there's always a shadow at the window. Red the black-jacketed criminal Shelly made eyes with in Part One, who's Richard

Horne's shady boss, appears out of the night, and Shelly breaks her hug with Becky to get up and go to him. Bobby and Becky look at each other in embarrassed silence as Shelly scoots outside, where she and Red kiss passionately and arrange a rendezvous for later. In a few minutes, Shelly slides back into the booth next to Becky, a big sexed-up grin on her face. Norma, wise without speaking, is probably thinking about the propensity of both mother and daughter to be crazy about bad men.

Bobby's maturity is stunning. This is the guy who used to rant and rave at Laura or whomever over the slightest perceived offense. Now, here's his ex-wife, while they're in the middle of a tense encounter session with their daughter, ducking out for a make out break with a nasty punk. When she comes back, Bobby and Becky just stare at her in silence. They don't have to act out their hurt or displeasure, or maybe they're weighing whether to say something—when a bullet does the talking. Right through the window above Bobby. Shattered glass rains down; people scream, Bobby takes control: "Everyone on the floor; turn the lights out." Is this that jerk Red, playing kiss-kiss, then bang-bang? Bobby leaves his family matters and jumps into those of others. He's looking 1990 *Twin Peaks* cool: black leather jacket, dark T-shirt, unbuttoned plaid flannel shirt—but his hair is white and he's flashing his sheriff's deputy badge. In *Twin Peaks*, the past is always present.

When Lynch was a boy, families drove in curvaceous, beautifully designed sedans. Now the standard American family vehicle is a box shaped van or some big, dumb, militaristic, aggressive-looking truck or SUV. Outside the Double R, the commotion centers on a van. A mother is screaming at her husband for having a pistol in the vehicle, a gun their little boy found and fired, accidentally or on purpose. Far from *The Andy Griffith Show*'s Mayberry, where Andy and Opie strolled country roads with their fishing poles, segments of American society think it's fine for kids to wear camouflage gear and play with guns. *The Return*'s scolding Mom sees the wrong of it, and Bobby, with a silent what-have-we-come-to? look on his face, regards the father, then the son, who's striking a defiant, little-hand-on-his-hip stance.

Bobby's having a stressful night, dealing with Becky's troubles, witnessing Shelly's misguided romance, and now here's a kid playing with a deadly weapon, terrifying folks enjoying the diner, the homiest place in town. The chaos isn't through with Bobby yet. The gun owner's van is stopped in the middle of the street, and right behind it a woman driver keeps honking, over seventy separate blasts in a maximally irritating intermittent rhythm. Bobby tries to keep cool, goes to her window, and is buffeted by her rage: "Why is this happening? We have to get home!" From Bobby's point of view, looking in at the apoplectic woman, there's a void on the passenger side. But then two stiff, jerky arms rise out of the darkness: a sick girl silently starts vomiting gray-green liquid and moves towards the driver, who yells-screams louder still. Bobby's close-up face is silent, at a loss for words. Is this supremely messy evening karmic payback for some of Bobby's past misdeeds and shortcomings? If so, he's committed to doing his spiritual due diligence. When we met him decades ago, he masked his sensitivity and vulnerability with bravado and anger. Now he's climbing the spiritual ladder, dealing with misbehaving, suffering people day and night. Bobby's face, looking in at the horn-honking, screaming woman and the seizure-gripped girl, is careworn and full of compassion.

The night in the sheriff's office conference room is hushed, and the faces of Frank Truman and Hawk are open and receptive as Hawk unrolls an old Native American map painted on animal hide (actor Michael Horse did this art piece). Hawk says it is "very old, but it is always current, a living thing." The map shows the town's twin mountains and other landmarks, but it's essentially a spiritual narrative with signs representing the age-old "always current" battle between good and evil. The map is alive because it's symbiotically linked with benign and malignant forces, and people, that we know right now: the battle this time. A fire symbol signifies a powerful force "like modern electricity" that can be used by people with either good or evil intentions: Lynch's *Ronnie Rocket* bad or helpful electricity, used by villains and heroes. Over the decades of *Twin Peaks*, creamed corn (garmonbozia) has been linked with the wicked, otherworldly denizens like Bob and the Man From Another Place; it's the human pain and suffering they feed on. There's a crop of black corn on Hawk's map that augments that dark meaning ("It's black. Diseased or unnatural. Death"). And when evilly intended fire ignites black corn, the resulting black fire can consume the stars. Did Native American shamans foresee the advent of nuclear fission enabling the coming of Bob and his kind? The map echoes the space-time coordinates on that little piece of paper Major Briggs left for the lawmen to follow. Clearly, the major studied and understood energies and entities almost beyond human comprehension and, through awe-inspiring advance planning, has enabled a handful of brave people to fight the ancient/current good fight. Just as Las Vegas's Mr. Todd told an underling, "You don't want to get involved with someone like him!" (meaning Mr. C), Hawk, referring to a round black smudge with ears/horns like on Mr. C's playing card, says, "You don't ever want to know about that. Really." And next to the black abstraction on the map: the sickle blade of the crescent moon, sharp for harvesting souls.

The map existed before the town, though probably not before the Owl Cave petroglyphs. Maybe the map's aliveness, its "current" quality, means it's an I Ching-like book of changes that reads and pictorializes the forces and spiritual states active right now. It seems the region's moral/cosmic battle has been in a steady state for ages. Perhaps, fifty years after *The Return*'s climax, the map will paint a different, more positive picture. Or maybe it will be the same, like that Magic 8 Ball toy from the 1950s, the black plastic ball you rotate, then read how the oracle sees the moment: "Not now, try again later." The battle's still on. Are earlier and later the same?

Bill Hastings, out of his jail cell and in the back seat of Detective Macklay's Buckhorn Police Department sedan, is returning somewhere he's been. The monumental place where he and his love, Ruth, met Major Briggs the space/time traveler and were helping further his strategic journey when Briggs and Ruth were killed, presumably by Woodsmen. Gordon Cole, Albert, Tammy, and Diane are all here to check the place out. It's on Sycamore Street, which emanates an otherworldly fragrance, since *Twin Peaks*'s Glastonbury Grove sycamore trees stand at the Red Room's entrance. But to see this Sycamore Street, you wouldn't even think the place had a name. It's one of Lynch's perfectly realized "nowhere places" that put your mind in the "room to dream" state that he loves to conjure. Lynch's perceptive eye made *The Straight Story*'s minimalist, "empty" landscapes and roads evocative. The place of Bill Hastings's drama has more elements, but it's got a bleak, midday-gray-light, abandoned-habitation atmosphere where creepiness dwells. Lynch's sense of place and space, influenced by his art history and painting experience, prompts him to begin many sequences with a panoramic view of the far distance. A police car and the FBI car, small in the frame, enter a landscape. There are green deciduous trees in the background, but the foreground is in a desolate, pale palette of dusty earth, overgrown weeds, and dead tall grass, spiked with a few dark telephone poles. As wan as the earth, and falling to earth, are a couple of decaying, empty houses with flaking paint and broken windows, situated at odd, random angles in the tableau: no logical grid pattern in this unplanned community. Lynch must have thanked his lucky stars when he saw that this out-of-the-way wasteland had a heavy, galvanized chain link fence around it, emphasizing the place's forbidden-zone feeling.

The cars and people are outside the fence, but Lynch, as always, needs to penetrate surface appearances and seek hidden truths. Bill Hastings and Ruth began the process with their desire for knowledge and their actions; there's an opening slit in the thick-wire fence. In the 1950s sci-fi movies of Lynch's youth, intrepid Americans stepped onto the surface of alien worlds. Pistols in hand, Gordon Cole and Albert slip through the fence into a shunned, haunted realm. Here the ghosts are filthy black, encrusted; Hastings, Diane, Gordon, and Albert have seen a Woodsman flicker at the edge of their vision. Only the FBI men mention it, in terse, military-mission style: "I see it," as it vanishes.

It's often said that in *Dune*, *Blue Velvet*, and *Twin Peaks*, Kyle MacLachlan's characters are surrogates, alter egos representing Lynch's attitudes and beliefs. Since both appear in *The Return*, it's only fitting that they each have a heavy electricity experience. Gordon isn't sucked into a giant wall socket like Cooper, but a sucking maelstrom of electrified air wants to take him away.

Inside the fence, with Hastings, Detective Macklay, Diane, and Tammy outside, Gordon says, "Think there's one in there, Albert?" Albert says, "We'll soon find out." One what—another Woodsman? Once again we sense that Gordon and Albert have depths of esoteric, beneath-the-surface knowledge that's a bonding agent for their professional, life's-mission pursuits and friendship. There are one or two electrical wires in the air above the desolate ground and ramshackle structures, and as Gordon steps forward, we hear an intensifying crackling. Like many of the figures in Lynch's work who want to know more, Gordon lifts his face skyward. This sky is unstable, in flux, beginning to whirl clockwise from a circular center point outward, curving phone poles and trees at the outer edges, sucking everything normal, familiar, into a gray-white vortex tunnel, with inner lightning flashes that make the curved corridor of air form that wicked, sharp-edged crescent shape that signifies cosmic evil. Within the vortex, for a flashing moment, Gordon sees a rickety staircase with three dark Woodsmen huddled on it. In Part Eight, we saw the Woodsmen enter our world, hustling around, preparing a rundown convenience store for Bob's coming, stacking cans of creamed corn in the window. The staircase (and Woodsmen) must lead up to the area "above a convenience store" that Phillip Jeffries (in *Fire Walk With Me*) tells Cole he visited, through some twist of space and time. At "one of their meetings," Jeffries saw Bob, the Man From Another Place, a Woodsman, and other occult denizens. When Jeffries entered Cole's FBI office in February 1989, Cooper was there, and Jeffries pointed at him and said, "Who do you think that is there?" Why did he say that about our rock-solid hero? Why would Jeffries question Cooper's identity and, by implication, what he's up to? Unless Jeffries has a broader space-time overview than anyone in the room—or maybe he's just really mixed up. He does come across as extremely distraught, scattered, semicoherent. But he makes a firm, succinct declaration: there will be no talk about the dark-matter subject Judy. Jeffries vanishes in a flash of static-crackling light, and he is said to be missing, "nowhere," in *The Return*. We will eventually see that going up those stairs above the convenience store leads to where Jeffries is now.

In Part Two, Mr. C speaks with Jeffries, or someone pretending to be Jeffries, on an electronic device and gets the feeling that Jeffries wants him out of the way. Jeffries says he wants to "be with Bob again," which is the position Mr. C now occupies. And in Part Eight, after Ray Monroe has shot Mr. C, Ray calls Jeffries and says, "I think I got him." It seems like veteran FBI ace Jeffries is now a free/rogue agent and perhaps, like the original *Twin Peaks*'s FBI man Windom Earle, has become a seeker/purveyor of dark, esoteric knowledge. In the DVD "Missing Pieces" from *Fire Walk With Me*, Jeffries says, regarding his interaction with the otherworldly invaders above the convenience store, "And I followed." Earle was killed by Bob for trying to amass/usurp dark power for himself. It sounds like Jeffries still lives, but perhaps consorting with devils has transformed him, bringing on some wicked punishment for his hubris. Or maybe he's gained powerful knowledge and has evolved/been transformed in the process, becoming a slippery agent of both darkness and light, like the Man from Another Place and the One-Armed Man.

Even steadfast lawman Gordon Cole, awestruck, gazing up into the flashing vortex tunnel, seeing the stairs, the Woodsmen, the whirlwind of electricity tugging at him, his arms raised high (in supplication?), feels the allure of seeing and knowing everything, being reborn at the far end of this roaring passageway. But not while Albert is watching his back. Cole's form is blurring and flickering out of being, so Albert says, "That's enough," and he pulls his friend back to firmer material and psychic ground.

In *The Return*, Jeffries, Major Briggs, and the Fireman seem to have the deepest view of the shifting, coexistent planes of space and time. Briggs's and the Fireman's perceptions generate understanding and effective action, but Jeffries's situation is more ambiguous. He and his doings radiate uncertainty, confusion, slipperiness. In 1992, David Bowie straightforwardly said this of Jeffries: "My character is an intensely over-traveled upholder of the law. He has seen too much and has little ability to do much about it." It seems his creators are responsible for his mysterious aura. Jeffries first appeared in *Fire Walk With Me*, which Lynch cowrote with Robert Engels. Engels, speaking of the scene in Gordon Cole's office where Jeffries describes his convenience store experiences, then vanishes, said, "It was like photographing these realities converging. He is there when he is not there. They are looking at another time." (*The Blue Rose* magazine). Scrambled time will turn out to be at the core of *The Return*, and *Fire Walk With Me*, which Lynch called "required homework" for viewing the new show, strongly established the concept.

In addition to Cooper being in the Red Room while Laura's still alive, and before he's come to *Twin Peaks*, there's a major When Is It? question attached to Jeffries's appearance/disappearance in Cole's office. The scene has a time stamp (February 16, 1989) because Cooper saw that date in a dream (good and bad dreams come true in Lynch's world). In script-based footage shot but not included in *Fire Walk With Me*'s final cut, Jeffries, just before he vanishes, is surprised to see that Cole's wall calendar says May 1989. As *The Return* plays out, Jeffries and confusion over dates will be linked in a major way: the idea that "separate" times can be happening in the same moment.

In a moment, the South Dakota vortex vanishes. The sky, and Gordon Cole, is back to normal. He and Albert agree: they "found out" Bill Hastings was one-hundred-percent right about this site accessing a conduit to other places that coexist with our familiar, visible world. Cole doesn't know that the Woodsmen he saw were "above a convenience store," as Jeffries said in *Fire Walk With Me*, but we do. So if Major Briggs's head floated up from this vacant South Dakota lot via the vortex, and Cooper, on his fall/journey from the Red Room toward being Dougie, saw Briggs's head floating in the star field outside the Mansion by the Purple Sea, whose exterior resembles the Fireman's fortress, also on a rocky pinnacle, above that sea, are the environments of the convenience store (the forces of darkness) and the Fireman's place (the forces of light) on a common dimensional plane? Or maybe just as the Red Room reflects the nature of the person experiencing it, the South Dakota vortex takes the "traveler" to the place that synchronizes with their intentional and spiritual state. Or maybe, like Laura and eons of questers, you have to first engage with the darkness and understand it to get to the light.

Back down to South Dakota earth, there's a body in the pale, dry grass. Ruth Davenport, naked, a raw, severed edge where her head should be, her right arm pointing skyward: the perpetrators went that way.

For Lynch, this tableau may have a French connection. During the years (1966–1971) he lived in Philadelphia, he studied at the Pennsylvania Academy of the Fine Arts, and he and Peggy Lentz had their daughter, Jennifer They got married, and Lynch made his short films *The Alphabet* and *The Grandmother*. They lived near the Philadelphia Museum of Art, which has the world's largest collection of works by French Surrealist pioneer Marcel Duchamp (1887-1968). Duchamp's milestone painting, *Nude Descending a Staircase*, No. 2 (1912), shows a female figure multiplied, strobing, composed of many bits of slightly separated time perceived at once as she comes down the stairs: a painting of cinema, you might say. Duchamp also made short films and was among the early-twentieth-century experimental filmmakers who fascinated Lynch because "they could start altering time," a key concept of *The Return*.

In 1969, before Lynch left Philadelphia, the Museum of Art debuted, and it became the permanent home for, a mysterious installation tableau that Duchamp had been working on in secret for twenty years. Those coming to see *Étant donnés*: 1. la chute d'eau, 2. le gaz d'éclairage (*Given*: 1. The Waterfall, 2. The Illuminating Gas) were met with a heavy wooden door in a wall. The door had no knob—it couldn't be opened—but there was a little hole to peek through, one person at a time. Through the aperture one saw a naked woman, lying on the ground, in twigs and grass, her legs spread, her body angled so that her head wasn't visible. The first impression is that the woman is headless, but a tiny tendril of blonde hair peeking around the edge of the frame, visible only in large photographs shot through the door-hole view, shows that that's a misperception. No blood stains the woman's pale flesh, but it feels like she's a victim, that she's been violated, perhaps in many ways.

The hand of the woman's raised left arm holds a small glowing gas lamp. In the distance are woods and a waterfall. Would the lamp illuminate the efforts of viewers/investigators to find meaning here? *Étant donnés* caused an instant sensation. At the heart of the Surrealist movement that Duchamp embraced is the idea that when we're presented with things that don't go together, that are in categories that don't normally associate with each other in a familiar, predictable way, our minds are enlivened, frustrated, and challenged, stimulated to read the combined elements, to have them fit into some narrative and tell us something we understand. Lynch's paintings and short films were driven by this dynamic well before he ever saw Duchamp's *Étant donnés*, if he ever did; sometimes he thinks so, other times not.

Young Lynch's instinct for surreal, mysterious linkages melded with his spiritual beliefs as he matured. When he was making *INLAND EMPIRE* (2006), his intuitive choice making led him to film a shot composed of disparate elements. Thinking about what he just did, he concluded, "If there is a Unified field, there must be a unity between a red Christmas tree bulb and this man from Poland who came in wearing these strange glasses. It's interesting to see how these unrelated things live together. How do they relate when they seem so far apart? It conjures up a third thing that almost unifies those first two. There's an ocean of unity and all the separate things float on it" (*Catching the Big Fish*). Duchamp's *Étant donnés*, and Lynch's art in general, lives in the realm of "almost unified," leaving us "room to dream," with our imaginations, our minds, tantalized, energized, activated. Of course, when Lynch envisions and crafts forms that for him are "almost unified," viewers often perceive the results as being confusing and chaotic. They may feel more secure when mysteries are completely tied up in neat, order-restoring bows by the likes of Sherlock Holmes, Agatha Christie, and Perry Mason.

Whether or not Lynch experienced *Étant donnés* in person, he was familiar with it, for his 2012 lithograph *E.D.* (*Tomorrow Started*) shows Duchamp's naked woman splayed across a weedy strip of ground. But Lynch, true to his fascination with contrast and doubling/doppelgänger has mirror-reversed the woman's position in the frame, and it's her right arm that extends the little lamp skyward, like Ruth's raised right arm in *The Return*.

In 1990, on ABC network TV, Laura Palmer's naked body was found wrapped in an obscuring veil of plastic. There was no way that Laura's splayed legs, vagina, and breasts could be exposed to America's living rooms. But in 2017, on Showtime cable TV, Lynch could expose Ruth's naked corpse in the spirit and physicality of Duchamp's work.

For decades, people have been haunted by Los Angeles's still unsolved 1947 Black Dahlia murder case, which has inspired commentators, historians, fiction and nonfiction authors, artists, and filmmakers. Elizabeth Short, called the Black Dahlia for her ebony hair and favorite outfits, was a pretty twenty-two-year-old dreaming of breaking into movies. Her body was found in the overgrown grass of a vacant lot, naked, drained of blood, washed clean of stains, and cut in two at the waist, with an obscene negative space swatch of ground between her pale lower and upper body, and a grotesque wide smile carved into her face. Looking down at the body, her arms are raised above her head.

Elizabeth Short was found by a little girl on her way to school, who, before screaming, thought she was looking at a segmented clothing store mannequin. These days, someone might mistake it for a conceptual art piece tableau. Elizabeth Short's corpse probably launched the fictional book/movies/TV trope, almost a cliché, of killers "posing" their dead victims, making a statement with dead flesh. In the 1940s, the American art world discovered the disquieting, mysterious enchantments of European Surrealism, which sometimes featured dislocated mannequins in noncommercial, transgressive poses. The desecration of Short's body took a lot of hard, careful work, and some wondered if the never-caught perpetrator was a surgeon with an artistic bent.

American Surrealist photographer-artist Man Ray, who dwelled at the intersection of reality and dream, was a lifelong friend and collaborator of Marcel Duchamp, beginning in the 1920s. Duchamp worked on *Étant donnés* for twenty years before its 1969 Philadelphia debut. Commentators note that Man Ray was fascinated by the 1947 photos of Elizabeth Short/the Black Dahlia's corpse-in-nature and most probably showed them to Duchamp in the period that he was conceptualizing and constructing *Étant donnés*.

Lynch is one of the artists fascinated by the Black Dahlia. He once looked at the Elizabeth Short photos over dinner with John St. John, the second detective on the unsolved homicide case. A *Lost Highway* image of Renee's (Patricia Arquette) segmented corpse appears to be Lynch's homage to Elizabeth Short, as is Ruth's headless body in *The Return*, both images also reflecting *Étant donnés*. A Lynch lithograph from the series that includes his print *E.D.* also evokes the Black Dahlia. It's a naked female torso, not segmented, but incised with the words "I Write on Your

Skin How Much I Love You," a familiar Lynchworld expression of Eros/Thanatos, love twisted into violence, death's abiding claim on the living, its signature.

The Return's Ruth wrote the extradimensional coordinates on her arm, not on her hand, as Bill had remembered when Tammy interviewed him. Is this an echo of *Lost Highway*'s Fred Madison, who likes "to remember things my way, not necessarily the way they happened"? Maybe Bill just loved his lover Ruth's hands.

Since at the height of Gordon Cole's vortex experience, when his hands were raised to the roaring, spiraling electrified air, director Lynch cut to a peaceful, silent, distant panoramic shot of cars, people, vacant lot, with no vortex, we assume that only Gordon, and maybe Albert, saw the whirling maelstrom. Throughout the vacant lot scenes, Bill has sat in the police car, stunned, quiet, swaying slightly, maybe reliving his tragic time here with Ruth—but now his time is up. One of the sooty, dust-faced Woodsmen comes up to the car from behind, bent forward at the waist, creeping forward like an animal, the way Bob invaded living rooms and bedrooms in the original *Twin Peaks*. The Woodsman vanishes as he reaches the car, and we see Bill in the back seat, unaware. In the past when we've seen a Woodsman kill, he's been visible, putting his hands on a victim's head and somehow scrambling its contents. Going for variety, Lynch shows us unaccosted Bill, no Woodsman, but with a crackling sound starting in the air, then Detective Macklay startled, horrified, then Bill's torso and neck topped by what looks like an exploded flesh melon filled with blood and brains. Lynch orchestrates the moment's tone like a maestro, letting us gasp-laugh as Gordon Cole says, deadpan, "He's dead."

So Bill and Ruth, explorers of the *mysterium*, searching the sky, and beyond, for secret esoteric knowledge, have paid with their heads. The Woodsmen, the dark powers, have avenged this invasion of their territory. Surely Gordon Cole is on their hit list, if he wasn't already.

We saw Gordon Cole emotionally shaken after his encounter with long-lost Cooper (now evil Mr. C), and now, after being pulled toward the raw, dark energy of the vortex, seeing the Woodsmen within it and witnessing Bill Hastings's uncanny death, he can't stop his hand from trembling. (Citizen Lynch often flutters his hand to emphasize a point he's passionate about.)

Back at Buckhorn police headquarters, everyone calms down with coffee (a cigarette for Diane), and Gordon, with the loud intensity of a David Lynch sound bite, characterizes the Woodsmen as "dirty, bearded men in a room." Maybe eagle-eyed Cole connects the vortex space the Woodsmen were in with Phillip Jeffries's distraught account of an extradimensional room above a convenience store where he witnessed fearsome things. Albert shows Gordon the photo of the coordinates on Ruth's arm and notices that Diane, from an oblique angle, is laser-focused on them. We assume she'll communicate the numbers to Mr. C, which confirms that he wasn't at the scene of Ruth and Major Briggs's killings. If he'd been there, he could have gotten the coordinates himself. But maybe he was rushed. Earlier, Diane had texted Mr. C that the FBI and local police were going to "the site," as if both Mr. C and Diane knew the significance of that term, that place. Lynch and Frost are adept at maintaining an atmosphere of ambiguity. The final numbers in the long string of coordinates are smudged, so the journeys of both bad Mr. C and good Cooper (now Dougie) are far from over. But Albert says the existing numbers point toward "a small town in the North . . . ," a negative space that sounds like Twin Peaks.

At this moment, Dougie's in his boss's Las Vegas office, holding his tall coffee cup in both hands and sucking on the lid straw like an infant with their bottle. Dougie's coffee brother/boss Bushnell sips his joe the usual way. It's a big day for him and Dougie. He's puffed up, triumphant: with absurdist logic, Lynch and Frost pay off the childlike pencil scrawls Dougie made on those insurance file papers without knowing what he was doing. He moved his pencil to where a little light appeared. Was this divine inspiration, the guiding luminous intelligence that author Philip K. Dick experienced, or helpful pointers from the One-Armed Man, the Fireman, *The Wizard of Oz*'s Good Witch of the North? Dougie's seemingly meaningless pencil marks were inspirational for Bushnell, helping him conclude that a ring of organized crime and police corruption was somehow linked to the Lucky 7 Insurance company, and that the dark forces aware of Dougie's investigative potency have tried to kill him (Ike the Spike's attack, Dougie's bomb-blasted car).

Bushnell calls the Mitchum brothers "alleged gangsters," but the criminal mastermind is "somebody else" (we know it's Mr. C, through his linkage with Las Vegas's Mr. Todd). Tony Sinclair is also tied to Mr. Todd, and Sinclair casts a nervous gaze at Bushnell's office as Dougie goes in for his meeting. The Mitchums may perennially arouse suspicion, but this time they're owed $30 million. Wise Bushnell had taken out a secondary policy, so his company will profit from the Mitchum situation. Praise for Dougie, a big payoff for the Mitchums and Bushnell, it's a red letter day that will climax with Dougie personally giving the brothers their check. The meeting's set for 5:30 p.m. The Mitchums don't know about the money coming their way. Dougie's their enemy. They're going to kill him before dinner.

Running their casino, or other nocturnal pursuits, keeps the Mitchums up late; they're having breakfast at 2:30 in the afternoon. Rodney's calmly reading the paper, but Bradley's so wound up he can't even eat his cereal and milk. He "can't wait to kill this Dougie Jones fuck," who, combining his Mr. Jackpot winnings with the $30 million of insurance money Dougie's denying them, has absconded with $30.425 million of their money. Unacceptable! Plus, Tony Sinclair told them Dougie's out to get them. It's cut-and-dried: Dougie will die today. But something's making Bradley unsure, conflicted. In Lynch's world, ethereal factors have at least as much weight as concrete ones: Bradley had a dream. Can Bradley, in defiance of all the "incriminating" evidence against Dougie, subconsciously sense the Copperesque righteous goodwill within Dougie, his drive to "uncover wrong and right it" that Bushnell mentions as he gives Dougie the $30 million check for the Mitchums? In *The Return*, many objects are coded red for love, the heart, optimism, the life force. Before Bradley dons his black Vegas tough guy suit, he's wearing red.

At the downtown business plaza, with the gun-pointing statue and the white mountain sculpture punctuated with red balloon forms, Dougie and Bushnell wait for the Mitchums's limousine. The Red Room's One-Armed Man sent Dougie signs that helped him win many jackpots and pointers of light that guided his marking on the insurance files. Now the One-Armed Man beckons Dougie into the mall bakery, and he emerges clutching a big square cardboard box to his chest. He's got the check in his pocket, and Bushnell wishes him well as the limo pulls out.

Even in daylight, the Vegas strip glitters, and the limo glides along to the sound of Shawn Colvin's punky version of the song "Viva Las Vegas," made famous by Elvis in 1964. The lyrics manage to echo *The Return*'s theme of time's fluid nature, as Colvin sings of a day being forty hours long, as well as twenty-four.

Bradley may have had some kind of troubling dream, but Rodney's maintaining his killing-mood edge. Still, a wave of beneficence is starting to build. Bradley tells Rodney that in the dream, the facial scar that Candie gave him was gone, and in real life it is. In Lynch's world, ethereal information transmissions can be powerfully meaningful, but subject to metaphysical static, stuttering wavelengths. Now that Rodney's intrigued, Bradley can't remember the rest of his dream—shades of the original *Twin Peaks*, in which Cooper couldn't remember who killed Laura Palmer after she told him in a dream. However, the gap between forgetting and remembering will be far shorter for Bradley than Cooper.

We're far from civilization, out in the desert wildlands, a place of wicked connotations for Lynch: his personal dislike of deserts, Fred Madison on his *Lost Highway*, Sherilyn Fenn portraying a mutilated accident victim in *Wild at Heart*, *The Return*'s atom bomb of historical and paranormal evil. Lynch's painterly eye is always evident: amber late-afternoon light, off the paved road, golden earth, endless horizon, the Mitchums's black car, their monumental vertical forms standing in their black suits, casting long shadows. A white car approaches; Dougie in his black suit climbs out. The Mitchums tell Dougie's driver to go back to town. Dougie won't be needing him. Sounds like the killing's going to happen. Dougie's silent, open expression is quietly stirring, and Bradley recalls the rest of his dream. It hinges on what's inside that box Dougie's holding.

Lynch believes we all have the capacity for light and darkness within us, and the balance in his work often tips toward the shadow zone of pain, confusion, despair—but the possibility of breaking through into the light is always there. Rodney and Bradley are Vegas bad guys, but the angels of their better nature are hovering near, and *The Return*'s angelic grace has the form of a *Twin Peaks* sacrament. Rodney is quivering with adrenalin. He's the trigger man. His gun's out and aimed at Dougie, but Bradley pulls him close in a brotherly embrace. Bradley's dream is clear: if "a certain thing" is in Dougie's box, "we can't kill him; it proves he's not our enemy." The power of dreams, the word of his brother; Rodney will pause so Bradley can look in the box. And yes! Sweet hallelujah! Bradley looks down on the golden circle crust of a cherry pie. He jubilantly proclaims, "Cherry pie!" So it is, and so it shall be. Rodney uncocks his gun, but still wants Dougie frisked for weapons. Bradley obliges and finds the check to pay the Mitchums's claim. Bradley shakes Dougie's hands and shouts, "I love this guy!" Through some kind of alchemy, their enemy has been converted into their friend.

Lynch knows death is a fact of life. And he knows that "the mind wants to go to fields of greater happiness." It envisions states beyond the death of the "I" thinking these thoughts: being reborn into another I, each successive birth ascending to a point where all accumulated karma has been played out, a point of ultimate release from materiality, from multiplicity, into the oneness.

Lynch gives us foretastes of the great culmination, the attainment of our heart and soul's desire. In *Eraserhead*, a strangely beautiful woman promises Henry that "in heaven, everything is fine," and in *Twin Peaks* cherry pie has the blissful savor of heaven. In popular culture, cherry pie, gooey and gushy and red inside, is metaphorically linked to female genitalia. In *American Pie* (1999), Jason Biggs sexually pleasures himself with a cherry pie, and in *Lolita* (1962), a film Lynch loves, James Mason drools over nymphet Sue Lyon as he tells her landlord mother that he'll stay because of the household's cherry pies. And pies connote the typically female art and craft of baking.

Dougie got the pie he gave the Mitchums from a woman at a Las Vegas mall store. In the original *Twin Peaks*, pies came from Norma Jennings's female realm of the Double R diner. And North Bend, Washington's earth mother Pat Cokewell (born 1931), owned, managed, and made pies at the town's Mar-T Café before the show came along. When the program became a fast hit, Pat had to double her staff to meet the pie demand, and sweet-smelling, carefully wrapped packages were being air-shipped around the country. In print and on TV news, Pat became a celebrity, but she never lost her personal, motherly touch. One chilly late night during the outdoor *Fire Walk With Me* filming, I saw her arrive on set with a big smile and a steaming bowl of special-recipe chili for Harry Dean Stanton, just the way he liked it. Tough, wise, empathetic, tender, kindly, helpful, loving female energy is a priceless asset in *Twin Peaks*, and everywhere. In the years after *Fire Walk With Me*, Pat's café was recognizable as the Double R. But when new owner Carl Twede barged in, he restyled the place with a sports theme, put his name on the marquee, and complained in interviews that it cost way more to make cherry pies than the other varieties. During preplanning for *The Return*, Lynch sat down with Twede and said he wanted to restore the café to its original, *Twin Peaks* self. And so it is today.

In addition to remaking a building in North Bend, Lynch believes in the human capacity for transformation and transcendence. After the Mitchum brothers arrived in the desert and waited for Dougie to show up so they could kill him, they stepped away from their black car. Bradley, who'd had a dream that made him doubt their violent mission, walked forward. Rodney, the angry, determined one who will pull the trigger, walks backward, looking at the view, the horizon. But he takes seven steps, a sign of positive change. Rodney listens to the dream wisdom of his dear brother, he doesn't shoot, and both men gain the privilege of experiencing Dougie's sweet soul. As the desert sequence concludes, Bradley shakes Dougie's hand and says, "What a pleasure it is to meet you, Dougie." The brothers' previous experience of Dougie was painful; he'd won so much of their casino money, and Tony Sinclair said

Dougie had a "personal vendetta" against them. Now they'll experience the real man, free of preconceptions.

We're in a cozy "fine dining" room right out of midcentury America, the kind of place baby boomers like Lynch and I as kids would have gone with our families, dressed up for a special-occasion dinner. Nestled in an intimate space: embracing soft, warm lighting, red leather booth, red lampshades, dark ruddy mahogany paneling. A black grand piano, a tuxedoed player with white Burt Bacharach hair, a Euro-waltz melody, the gentle murmur of people enjoying themselves. Heavenly, and it gets better.

The scene glows with an aura of amity that recalls Quaker artist Edward Hicks's (1780-1849) idealistic Arcadian painting *Peaceable Kingdom*, in which women, men, children, farm animals, lions, and lambs crowd close to one another in sweet harmony. Dougie the gentle lamb is supping with the lion-like Mitchum brothers tonight, but in Lynch's world of fluid identities and dualities, the brothers have turned out to be lambs. We learn that they were orphans, suffering and struggling as children; hence their sensitivity to the childlike Candie and the impaired-in-some-way Dougie, whom they raise their champagne-filled glasses to, after putting a glass in his hand so he can join in.

Dougie tastes the golden effervescent nectar and responds appropriately: "Mmmm." At this warm, lulling moment, Lynch shifts the mood almost shockingly. The piano player's cheery waltz-of-life melody slips into minor-key melancholy, a graveyard shiver tune, and Lynch moves in closer on Dougie's face as he turns toward the music. Is this a half-remembered melody, meaningful to Cooper, impaired and befuddled within Dougie? Or is it that sinking feeling we get sometimes? In the midst of the happiest moments, the subconscious knowledge that the moment is fleeting, like life; the grave awaits. Lynch was raised in Christian America, with its Puritan heritage that says we fallen sinners must pay for our pleasures; make hay while the sun shines because the tornado, the flood, the yawning abyss is beneath you. Lynch has said that "death is the number one fear," but over the years he's evolved into the Hindu belief that deaths become births, endings become beginnings, a karmic wheel generating increasing bliss and release—for the virtuous.

While Dougie is transfixed by the sad song, a dignified white-haired elderly lady approaches him. It's the grizzled, shrunken woman with the wild white hair who had witnessed his casino run of slot machine jackpots. A little Red Room symbol, sent by the One-Armed Man, had shown Dougie which machines to play. But after winning thirty jackpots, he let the old woman make a winning pull. Now we see that she's been transformed. As the somber music plays, we see that her hair is neatly styled, and she's wearing a sparkling green gown and a beautiful necklace. Dougie's good heartedness, like that of Jimmy Stewart in *It's a Wonderful Life*, has radiated out into the world. The money enabled the woman to revitalize herself. She's kicked her gambling addiction, has a house and a dog, and has been reunited with her son, who's standing proudly at her side. Dougie is indeed her Mr. Jackpots, as she named him.

It's a complex moment. The woman is thanking Dougie and kissing his cheek, but he still seems sidetracked by the song, and we feel the sad mood of Cooper the lost. Thanks to Kyle MacLachlan's beautifully subtle performance, we see the slight shift of Dougie's attention to the woman. She tells the Mitchum brothers how special a person Dougie is, and we can tell that they agree. As the woman and her son leave the table, the piano music swings upbeat again, and the Mitchums' Pink Ladies arrive with the cherry pie. Dark feelings and thoughts can transport us away from a happy occasion, but they make our return to the beauty and beneficence of being right here right now that much sweeter.

Dougie is cradled in feminine warmth, the vertical folds of the red leather banquette, the midriffs of the Pink Ladies hovering behind his head, Candie's pink-gloved hand near his head like a blessing as he digs into his pie. As with the champagne, his response to the pie's juicy delights is eloquent: "Mmmm." Cherry pie is emblematic of the original *Twin Peaks*, in which Dale Cooper was fully himself and powerful. Dougie's first jolt of coffee didn't wake up his inner Cooper, but maybe the pie will.

No, he's still Dougie, Dougie in secular heaven, bathed in happy music, the Ladies' ministrations, the goodwill of his former enemies. This being *Twin Peaks*, there's a second toast, as the Mitchums salute the "pie that saved Dougie's life, and our money." Bradley says, "Candie, get another piece of pie for our friend." In one of *The Return*'s most joyful moments, Dougie smiles as much as he can with his mouth full of sugary goodness and says Part Eleven's last word, "Friend."

This high moment of *The Return* radiates the positivity Lynch believes we can realize in ourselves and generate in the world, and it recalls a glowing moment in James Whale's *The Bride of Frankenstein* (1935). Dr. Frankenstein's monster (Boris Karloff), an ultimate misfit/outsider, shunned, alone and hounded by an angry mob, takes refuge in the cabin of a blind hermit, who can't see his horrific appearance. Thanks to the hermit, the monster discovers the joys of food, music, and fellowship. The creature, like Dougie, is a being of very few words. But he sums up the new, warm feeling in his chest: "Friend g-o-o-d."

–CHAPTER EIGHTEEN–

TWO BY TWO, AGAIN AND AGAIN (PART TWELVE)

We left Part Eleven as an ebullient bond of fresh understanding and emotional warmth was forged between the Mitchum brothers and Dougie, the three sipping champagne over a Las Vegas table of sharing, in a room burnished with Old World elegance. The first scene of Part Twelve finds Gordon Cole, Albert, and Tammy in a South Dakota hotel room similarly well-appointed, with dark wood, warm lighting, and leather seating, sitting around a table, sharing a glass of French red wine (Lynch's favorite). Like the Mitchum brothers and Dougie, these three have an understanding and a warm feeling for each other, but a new chapter is opening: Tammy is being christened as a new member of the Blue Rose Task Force. (Albert says the wine comes from Cole's wine cellar, alluding to Francophile Lynch's connoisseurship of red wine—maybe he even provided the libations for the *The Return* shoot.)

The Blue Rose. An image, an idea as evocative as the Red Room. In *Fire Walk With Me*, Lynch, as Gordon Cole, enacted the artist-to-audience relationship he has with us with two FBI agents. He presented seasoned Chet Desmond (Chris Isaak) and less-experienced Sam Stanley (Kiefer Sutherland) with a performance-art piece for them to decipher, coded clues about the new case they will be working on. Lil (Kimberly Ann Cole), a woman in a red dress, makes odd, dance-like gestures, which Desmond interprets for Stanley. There's a fabric blue rose pinned to the dress, which Desmond doesn't explain. He says, "I can't tell you about that." Lynch is a born seeker, obsessed with Mystery. He's looked at the world and meditated and made his art for over seven decades, functioning as a grown-up but maintaining his sense of the world as a place of wonder and magic. He doesn't study electrical engineering textbooks; he likes to think of electricity as a strange, powerful force within the walls around him. He doesn't want to put Latin name tags on every tree in the forest; he wants it to be a dark, murmuring place that can take the shape of an owl, an owl like a man form. He can experience a sudden spark of love, or something dark, behind a smiling face, and understand coffee and chocolate milkshakes to be powerful elixirs.

Scientists, artists, poets, and detectives will never solve all the mysteries, answer all the questions, and that's the way Lynch likes it: a universe buzzing with enlivened possibility, room to dream. He knows that not having all the answers gives life its savor, keeps us all adventuring, doing our work, seeking our balance and inner peace. Lynch's talisman of the ineffable, the Great Whatsit, the thing always beyond our grasp, is the blue rose, which lives in the imagination, not botanical reality.

When Lil the human message was presenting her dance for the agents, Lynch gave us a huge close-up of the blue rose (a vibrant blue-white, as though charged with electricity) against the red background of her dress. Lil is gently swaying, the shot is in slow motion, so the words "blue rose" conjure that floating, dreamy image in our mindscape. An image of mystery and secrets with a feminine scent, like the Sphinx or the Mona Lisa's half-smile.

Lynch sees *The Return* as a unified artistic composition, like a painting presented in weekly segments over fifteen weeks. As though balancing the subject elements, colors, and textures on a canvas, Lynch shapes *The Return*'s balance of mysteries perpetuated or explained. He can make mundane objects glow with eerie otherness and strange power, but sadly, for some viewers, he and Frost bring the blue rose, the floating, expansive inscrutability of life and death, clunking to earth. Poetry becomes prose. Mystical enchantment is reduced to a police procedural.

Albert relates the history of the Blue Rose Task Force to Tammy. In 1970, the Air Force shut down the UFO-investigating Project Blue Book, which Major Briggs had been part of, saying there was no UFO threat to America, but actually covering up its knowledge of extraterrestrial visitors and paranormal happenings. The FBI and the military made a secret liaison to investigate unresolved cases that had a mystical aura, that had to be approached on alternative paths to knowledge. Gordon Cole suggested his fellow FBI high achiever Phillip Jeffries to head up a task force consisting of agent Chet Desmond, Albert, and Dale Cooper, Albert being the only one available for comment these days. We viewers know Cooper's in Dougie; the FBI does not. None of us have a clue about Desmond's whereabouts, and Jeffries's situation is elusive at best. The term "blue rose" was a phrase uttered by a woman enmeshed in a strange case involving occurrences not found in nature or physics as we know them. As *The Return* proceeds, Lynch and Frost drag the enchanted blue rose of our imaginations into the harsh light of typical, everyday work.

When you're confronting unknown forces that can shred your body and soul, it's important to have close comrades with a commitment to a shared mission, trustworthy people who know what you know, who've got your back. Albert reveals that the Blue Rose group has had their eye on Tammy from her stellar high school career onward; as Cole told Denise Bryson, "She's got the stuff." When Lynch was young, he thought benign, efficient grown-ups, the country's institutions and agencies, "had some sort of control over what happened in my neighborhood, but now we know that's not true. Dark things used to be in proper balance with good." Lynch is a serious-minded evangelist for the ability of positive spiritual light to banish the negativity of darkness, and it's touching to see him, in *The Return*, make the Blue Rose Task Force a homegrown group striving to make it safe for kids to sleep at night. Lynch stages Tammy's induction into the group with due gravitas: simple, spare dialogue; warm, somber music chords; serious, dignified facial close-ups of Cole, Albert and Tammy; and a group toast "to the Blue Rose." Chrysta Bell as Tammy projects a perfect mixed tone of professional, even feminist, pride, and sweet flustered emotion.

The room the trio occupies is a compendium of what these good people are fighting to maintain in the world, a calm zone of safety and civilization, with beautiful furnishings, shelves of books, and paintings on the walls, where those with fine minds and beneficent intentions make plans. There's also something odd about the room. The back wall is all red curtains. We know it's nighttime, so maybe the curtains cover windows. But a moment after Tammy's induction, with a camera angle shift, we see that the wall behind what had been our point of view is also red curtains. So dislocation is always imminent within stability.

As the scene in this room began, before Tammy is inducted, Gordon Cole scanned the room with an electronic device to detect hidden microphones/surveillance—the bug man, as *Blue Velvet*'s Dorothy Vallens once called Jeffrey Beaumont, who was pretending to be an insect exterminator. (Lynch also employs insects as signs of maleficence in his paintings, drawings, and prints). Cole's turning movement, device in hand, suggests a shaman laying down a circle of protection against uninvited evil. In *Lost Highway*, the wicked Mystery Man tells Fred Madison, "I don't go where I'm not invited." After Tammy's induction, Cole presses a signal button on his phone, and Diane parts the red curtains and enters. He invites her in, to sit at the table, and to be deputized to help with the big Blue Rose case involving "two Coopers." She's skeptical, resistant, but Albert stresses that she may get to learn more about the permutations of the most significant man in her life.

Albert and Cole know Diane's been in electronic contact with the sinister Cooper, and having her near may provide them with vital information that can help them formulate a game plan. Diane is untrustworthy, and there's something cloudy, perturbed, ill at ease in her aura. The Blue Rose trio looks to her for her answer: will she join them? In a cloud of her cigarette smoke, she puts two fingers together, like Frank Booth's gun-shooting gesture in *Blue Velvet*, and declares, "Let's rock," a phrase linked with the Man From Another Place, a paranormal being sometimes helpful, sometimes maleficent, who dwelled within red curtains. A split second after Diane's "Let's rock," Cole raps his knuckles on the table as a punctuation beat that ends the scene. Maybe he's knocking on wood for good luck; it could be dangerous to have Diane in their circle.

Is Diane at war with herself, helping Mr. C but, driven by her long association with the FBI and its people, wanting to help them too? Does she subconsciously want to confess her double-agent status with that two-finger gesture? Director Lynch telegraphs Diane's doubleness as she sits at the bar later. The color red most often signifies life-affirming, positive energy in *The Return*, but the blouse Diane wears is hellfire, *Fire Walk With Me* red. And over it she wears her leopard skin jacket, connoting bestial, predatory forces. Sure enough, she receives a text from Mr. C, asking if Las Vegas is part of the FBI investigation. Las Vegas, where Mr. C is trying, via his agents, to get Cooper-in-Dougie killed.

We're in a convenience store, not the spooky one. The colorfully stocked shelves of the *Twin Peaks* minimart are brightly lit, but down the aisle comes a haunted figure: Sarah Palmer. We're used to seeing her at home, sunken in the dark cave of her living room, marinated in alcohol and nicotine, tortured by the mystery of how, two decades ago, the golden life of her and her husband Leland and their daughter, Laura, could become a horror: Leland the rapist and killer of Laura, then his suicide in a jail cell. All these years without them both, lost in grief, and as long as we've known her, subject to visions of Laura's lost necklace, a white horse (prefiguring the Woodsman's menacing "The horse is the white of the eyes" chant?), Bob's face, and, in a voice not her own, telling Major Briggs that Agent Cooper is in the Black Lodge.

The Palmer living room is one of *Twin Peaks*'s iconic spaces, and Sarah rarely leaves it, but she needs provisions to keep body and soul together as well as she can. In the store, with her long gray hair and staring eyes, she looks more like a witchy crone than ever, and she fills her cart with spirits (the bottled kind) and Salem cigarettes (Salem, the site of seventeenth-century witchcraft trials).

Two high school kids are at the checkout cash register, and there's a stand with two kinds of jerky, the familiar beef and the new turkey. This doubleness disturbs Sarah. In a tense voice she asks about the turkey, and the girl says, "It's the same as the beef, except it's turkey." The same, and different, at the same time. The way Laura had been the model golden girl while leading a secret life of dissipation, just as community pillar Leland had been secretly raping her and eventually killed her.

Sarah herself seems split, saying aloud to herself, "Leave this place, find car key, find car." Standing at the cash register, she's beset by a metaphysical turbulence, a raw storm of memory and prophecy, a hyperawareness of otherness hiding within the familiar. She's disturbed: "The room is different." How did the turkey slip inside this place of beef, Bob inside her Leland? And a subconscious awareness that she's been invaded. Lynch and Frost's metaphors of doubling and personal psychic invasion further the idea that Sarah was the New Mexico girl who had the frog-moth enter her mouth and go to work. Lynch accompanies Sarah's convenience store existential-metaphysical panic attack with the weird emotional-electrical falling/sliding sounds, high to low, that in *Fire Walk With Me* filled the air when Leland and Laura, both unaware of their unholy couplings with Bob, were confronted by the One-Armed Man, who knew everything.

Two thirds of the way through *The Return*, we see the iconic exterior view of the Palmer house for the first time. The pleasant symmetrical white face of a two-story Dutch Colonial, the central door balanced by windows left and right, downstairs and upstairs. The sort of place that welcomed trick-or-treaters and Girl Scouts selling cookies, while inside was a zone of human dread and pain, spawned by inhuman invasion. The dark forces' most fearsome manifestation, when Bob-as-Leland violated

Laura, was linked to the circling ceiling fan outside Laura's bedroom, cycling like a generator of bad electricity. In *The Return*, after establishing the house's front image, Lynch cuts inside to the fan blades turning slowly, in altered time, accompanied by a rhythmic whooshing-beating sound like the flapping wings of a demonic bird of prey. Leland and Laura are long gone, but the blades still turn, for Sarah.

Deputy Hawk, having heard about Sarah's strange behavior at the store, stops by to check on her. After experiencing *Twin Peaks* for so many years, we feel the communal warmth of people who care about each other's welfare. In the previous years of the *Twin Peaks* saga, there'd been a welcoming heart-shaped wreath on the Palmer front door, but it's gone now. Hawk and Sarah stand at her threshold. He says people have been worried about her, and she momentarily puts on an expression of normal social engagement. She says she didn't know what came over her in the store—and there's a sudden sound of bottles clinking somewhere behind her. He asks if someone's in the house. She says, "No, just something in the kitchen." Maybe some booze bottles fell over (she no doubt has plenty of empties), but more likely it's the store kid delivering the provisions she abandoned when she fled the store. Maybe she said no so Hawk would hurry up and leave. Or maybe it's a reflexive denial of a hidden reality, out-of-sight, like the dark selves of Leland and Laura, and herself, that she has habitually tried, and tries, to keep out of her consciousness. Hawk and Sarah are metaphysically sensitive, attuned to other planes of existence, forces working beyond mortal and temporal reality. She breaks through the façade of social nicety with a tense grimace: "It's a goddamn bad story, isn't it, Hawk?" He, steadfastly on the side of goodness, leaves saying, "I'm always here to help." But something in her knows that help would get in her way. Grace Zabriskie's complex performance makes Sarah a sympathetic, tortured soul—and someone to fear.

Out in that South Dakota field where Gordon Cole saw the vortex and Albert found Ruth's corpse, Albert photographed the coordinates Ruth wrote on her arm, which helped Major Briggs chart a space-time course to a more secure hiding place. When Albert showed the photo to Cole, Diane spied the coordinates, and Albert noticed her line of sight. Now Diane, days after her FBI deputization, enters the coordinates in her phone's GPS. The final numbers had been smudged on Ruth's arm, so Diane adds "plus two" at the end, another sign of doubleness. Through technology that is like magic, Diane's phone hones in on a town in Washington State: Twin Peaks. So that was to have been Major Briggs's arc, to leave home, then return, to know it anew? All the while enacting a strategy to fight evil? But his journey was violently interrupted by the Woodsmen, who separated Briggs' head from his body, the head now floating in another plane of existence, where Cooper saw it on his journey from the Red Room. But all of *The Return*'s metaphoric roads still lead to Twin Peaks, as Gordon Cole, Mr. C, Cooper, and Laura Palmer will discover.

Upstairs in the South Dakota hotel, Albert intercepts a text from Mr. C to Diane and goes to Cole's room to tell him about it. But the boss is occupied, delightfully. Before Albert arrives we're in the room with Cole and a chic and sexy French woman

(Bérénice Marlohe). The space is a warm, dimly lit cocoon: dark brown colors, an inviting couch symmetrically centered, Cole on the left telling a rousing tale of his FBI exploits, the woman nuzzled up to him, her face filling the curve of his neck, an open wine bottle and two half-filled glasses handy. Lynch is a wide-ranging traveler in his mind and imagination, but in the concrete reality of daily life, he seeks the comfort and security of an habitual "good setup," with everything he needs close at hand, and the hotel room tableau is Cole's perfect setup: Lynch/Cole the artist telling his stories to an adoring audience. But Lynch the artist knows that privileged moments are more potent when limited, transient, and the climax of Cole's narration to the woman is cut short by Albert's knock at the door.

Albert? At this hour? Right now? Not only is he disrupting Cole's verbal foreplay tête-à-tête, he's also asking Cole's "friend" to leave. Cole may be pissed off, but he tamps it down, doesn't show it. Cole's wedded to the bureau; he and Albert are brothers on a soul-deep lifetime mission, so Albert must be here for a good reason. Cole has to delay gratification; he tells the woman to wait for him in the hotel bar. And in this world of balanced doubleness, Albert experiences disruption and the frustrating delay in imparting his information. He stands to the left of the couch-centered composition as the woman pulls herself together to leave. Lynch is a past master of stretching cinematic time, and for over three minutes of screentime, Albert stands silently as the woman straightens her short dress (red, of course), puts on her high heels (red-bottomed Louboutins, *mais oui*), her black sweater, sips a little wine, puts on a little more red lipstick, pouts a little sweet talk in French, and exits. We can feel the heat of Albert's unexpressed irritation at having to wait so long, but by 2016 he's mellowed from the anger-and-scorn-spitting cynic of twenty-five years ago. If patience is a virtue, Albert is almost a saint.

For the aging Cole, the French woman is a life-affirming fire-red gush of desire personified, a promise who will wait for him at the bar. He bids her adieu, closes the door, and walks back into the room, his footsteps silent, hushed by the soft carpeting. I once pleased Lynch by mentioning the somehow strange clicking sound of Dale Cooper's steps in the Red Room. We can't hear footfalls in Cole's room, but it's another of Lynch's unique, uncanny spaces, like the room in Lynch and Barry Gifford's 1993 HBO teleplay, *Hotel Room*: "The space for the hotel room existed, undefined. Mankind captured it, gave it shape, and passed through." In *The Return*'s room, things are slowed almost to stasis, a feeling Lynch will echo at the end of Part Twelve. Cole and Albert seem suspended in time, intensely focused on each other, speaking only essential words. Cole tells Albert that the French woman is "visiting a friend of her mother, whose daughter's gone missing. The mother owns a turnip farm, and I said, 'The daughter will turn up eventually.'" A silent stare from Albert. Cole says, "She didn't get it either; being French, it doesn't translate." Okay, "turnip"/"turn up": it's a joke, but no one's laughing. In *Fire Walk With Me* (1992), Cole imparted information on a Blue Rose case to two FBI agents using a verbal code involving "my mother's sister's girl." Granted, here in *The Return* Cole is lit up with red wine (Bordeaux suggests the Tibetan Bardo state, the Red Room-like zone between death and rebirth, and Cole's coming rendezvous with director Lynch's dream of a desirable French woman), but Albert is not amused. For Cole to use the FBI verbal code format in a joke is virtually sacreligious.

Finally, five minutes after Albert urgently entered Cole's room, Cole says, "What is it, Albert?" Dramatist Lynch, after suspending Albert in containment, gives him release, at 11:05 pm (adds to seven) by Cole's watch. Albert tells him about the intercepted tweet from Mr. C to Diane asking how much the FBI knows about Las Vegas (we understand that Mr. C knows Dougie/Cooper's in Vegas, and Mr. C's agents are trying to kill him, plus Mr. C's general criminal network has the town ensnared). Cole, less in the know, wonders to Albert, "What do we know that we haven't asked Diane about?" They instantly agree to table it, think about it. Albert's message is a small thing; his time in this space is really about the emotions in the room: Cole and the woman, Albert's repression of his impatience with Cole and the woman, and, most deeply, Cole and Albert's relationship.

For the second time in *The Return*, Lynch and Frost create a moving tableau of the two men standing together looking into each other's faces without speaking, first one face, then the other, back and forth, so we can feel the gravity of how long these two have known each other and how our knowledge of others is always limited, incomplete: we trust on faith. (Maybe we can picture Mark Frost and David Lynch instead of Albert and Cole: some observers who've been close to *Twin Peaks* productions over the years feel Lynch and Frost have grounds for mutual creative trust issues.)

At the end of Part Four, the other time that Cole and Albert stood facing each other in an extended period of silent communion, it was a matter of Cole detecting if he could trust Albert again after learning that his colleague had kept a grave professional secret from him. Trust was restored and the partners moved on, bonded as ever. Their Part Twelve silent, deep perusal of each other raises the unspoken question "How are you leading your life, old friend?" In the original *Twin Peaks*, one of Cooper's mottos was "Every day, once a day, give yourself a present," like pie, coffee, a refreshing walk in the woods, a phone call to a friend—you decide. Cooper taught Sheriff Truman this life lesson, and he may have learned it from Gordon Cole, who, as more fully characterized in *The Return*, clearly indulges in coffee, fine wine, young women, and, in younger days, many cigarettes. If you keep the smokes, these are some of David Lynch's favorite things. He believes we're pleasure-seekers, in the sensory-temporal world and in our spiritual consciousness, which, through meditation, can expand and connect everything in a unified field of bliss, "electric gold" (recalling Laura's glowing golden globe). Lynch/Cole, through his perceptiveness, seeker's mindset, talents, karma, fate has found his blissful way through life. Maybe Cole looks into Albert's eyes and wants to say, "Lighten up, old buddy, relax a little, enjoy life." Maybe the never-smiling Albert wants to say to Cole, "Straighten up, we're professionals, we've got work to do." They don't say anything, until Cole reaches out, puts his hand on Albert's shoulder and gently kneads it: "Sometimes I worry about you, Albert." Albert's eyes seem to say, "Right back at you." The artist-intuitive/the rule-following researcher. Gordon Cole/Albert Rosenfield, David Lynch/Mark Frost? It takes both to make *Twin Peaks*.

Up in the country of the double mountains and the whispering fir trees, *The Return* gives us a number of two-person scenes. Sheriff Frank Truman tells Ben Horne that his grandson Richard killed the boy at the crosswalk and tried to kill witness Miriam, who has massive hospital bills that need paying. Dr. Jacoby, as Dr. Amp, broadcasts his obsessive, passionate diatribe against corporate corruption and environmental apocalypse, and across town Nadine, his only audience that we see, drinks it in adoringly (it feels like Jacoby and Nadine share a common emotional space). And, at last, two-thirds of the way through *The Return*, we see Audrey (Sherilyn Fenn), and her husband, Charlie (Clark Middleton), arguing away into the night.

Over the years since the original *Twin Peaks*, Audrey has grown from a mischievous rich girl/high school vixen to a feisty fighter and survivor. She's lived through a bomb blast, was comatose in a hospital, where she was raped by Mr. C. This violent mating spawned Richard Horne, *The Return*'s terrifying young hit-and-run child killer and grandmother assaulter and robber. The information about his parentage comes to us indirectly, through the words of others and our deductions as viewers. Now we see Audrey for the first time since she was chained in protest to a pre-explosion bank vault. She's here because actress Sherilyn Fenn fought to be here. She was to be a more peripheral presence in Lynch and Frost's original conception, but as Lynch says, "She's a hellcat" (*The Return* DVD special features), and she insisted on more substantial material to work with, which Lynch, more than Frost, provided.

The room she's standing in is new to the *Twin Peaks* locations canon. It looks like the library of a fine old house: warm, wood paneling, glowing marble fireplace, shelves overflowing with old books, all surfaces covered with homey clutter. It feels like it's from an earlier decade: there's a black rotary phone, a rolodex, an hourglass half full/half empty. One of the books on the shelf is poet T. S. Eliot's (1888-1965) *Four Quartets*, which emphasizes that time past, present, and future are one, which echoes the One-Armed Man's recurring question, "Is it past or is it future?" This room could have come out of a 1940s movie, but Audrey is clearly a grown-up, mature woman, an angry and frustrated one. She's glaring at Charlie, who sits in front of her, his desk strewn with papers. (When Part Twelve was broadcast, the internet lit up with angry *Twin Peaks* fans who'd hoped Audrey would end up with Cooper in *The Return*, since decades ago actor Kyle MacLachlan had nixed having a romantic relationship with high school student Audrey. With no disrespect to Clark Middleton, Charlie is no Cooper. He's short and squat, his pudgy, large bald head sits atop small shoulders. Audrey sums him up: "You're a loser with no balls." Ouch!

In one of *The Return*'s standout sequences, they parry and thrust, back and forth for many minutes. We've come right into the middle of their ongoing relationship, and the air's electrified with their power struggle and the work of two actors in top form. In Lynch's own life, and from 1974's short film *The Amputee* on through his career, his knowledge of tangled relationships, temptations, betrayals, clashes of will, the human propensity to make an emotional mess has been on display. There are three points of contention between Audrey and Charlie. There are papers (divorce?) she wants him to sign; he won't. She wants him to go out to the Roadhouse; he won't. She wants him to help find Billy, the young man she's been "fucking" and who's missing; Charlie won't.

Charlie won't sign her papers, but his desk is covered with papers. They are his "allotted duty in life"; he's "got a deadline." Having one's mobility constrained by imposed drudgery evokes the fictional worlds of writer Franz Kafka, one of Lynch's artistic heroes. In the original *Twin Peaks*, where Audrey was a willful, headstrong teenager, she was always in forward motion, but here and now there's an almost surreal, bad-dream sense that she and Charlie can't get out of this room, a feeling that the great cinematic surrealist Luis Buñuel (1900–1983) conjured in *The Exterminating Angel* (worshippers can't seem to leave a church) and *The Discreet Charm of the Bourgeoisie* (people are stuck in a dinner party). Lynch has always treasured surrealist thought and imagery, and his personal freedom is of the highest value.

Audrey loves Billy. She wants out of this house. She's got her red (life-affirming) jacket on, ready to go. But there sits Charlie, infuriatingly patient and manipulative. He says he will go with Audrey to the Roadhouse—but then says wait, maybe he'll make the phone call Audrey's been bugging him about, to Tina, the last one to have seen Billy. The phone call pause is a lightning rod for all of Audrey's animosity and a stunning, bravura exhibition of Sherilyn Fenn's acting talent. Charlie's conversation with Tina is a pause-filled, drawn-out agony for Audrey, who quivers in suspense. She, and we, hear only Charlie's side of the conversation, just out-of-context fragments. She's in the position Lynch feels we're all in in our lives, including as his audience members, trying to form bits of information into a meaningful whole. It's Lynch's way, and Charlie's, to make it a challenging process. As Charlie's phone call drones on, Sherilyn Fenn gives us a condensation of Audrey's frustration, impatience, and anger in over twenty separate reaction shots, each different from the other. At one point, Charlie says to Tina, "Unbelievable, what you're telling me." After concluding the call, Lynch ends the scene with Audrey: "You're not going to tell me what she said? Charlie!" So many questions, so few answers—welcome to *Twin Peaks*, and life in general.

It's easy to get stuck in unfulfilling work and personal relationships, to practice behaviors that harm us, get trapped in situations that stifle our deep, essential selves, our souls, and not realize our plight. Or to come to our senses late in the game and not be able to find a way out. In Samuel Beckett's play *Waiting for Godot* (1947-48), a masterpiece of human entrapment, a representative Everyperson "wastes and pines wastes and pines." We humans aren't standing tall, we're "on our hands and knees." Beckett's characters say, "Yes, let's go" and remain motionless. In 1929, English novelist and poet D. H. Lawrence (1885-1930) spoke of "the putrid little space in which we are cribbed." Even *Psycho*'s (1959) killer, Norman Bates, realizes "We're all caught in our private traps," slaves to repetition and inertia, cocooned in what Lynch calls the "Suffocating Rubber Clown Suit of Negativity" (*Catching the Big*

Fish: Meditation, Consciousness, and Creativity).

Lynch's meditation practice expands his view of life and creativity, provides a bigger picture of factors he can evaluate and maybe act on, for or against. Englishman D. H. Lawrence, like America's Walt Whitman (1819-1892), was a poet-prophet who sang the sanctity of the Individual Soul, the deep-body blood wisdom in the dark beneath the intellect, which could be at odds with social and moralistic dictates. Lawrence would have whispered in Ben Horne's ear, when he and Beverly were in his office listening to that sweet invisible ringing sound, "Kiss her, touch her." But what would the collective community say? Ben is a sinner of many stripes and is trying to shape himself into a community-approved "good man." But is this self-imposed task feeding his innermost being? The interplay between actor and character is fascinating. Richard Beymer told me that Ben's example is making him "work on being a better person."

Dr. Jacoby's inner being is a hot furnace of fiery anger and bitter bile. This conspiracy hound is terrified of an abstraction: the military-industrial-capitalist complex that's poisoning our institutions, food, water, and air. He's on alert; his alarm is always ringing. Jacoby's a brilliant, creative man, but his energies are devoted to paranoia and pessimism. His mindset is stuck on negativity, but it has produced art, his broadcast, which sparks something in Nadine. Does she share his dark socio-political-environmental obsessive vision, or is she moved by his vibrant, plucky spirit? She's a spunky person herself; maybe she can alter his course. In D. H. Lawrence's *Women in Love* (1920), one woman speaks to another about a man: "He's got go, anyhow." The other woman says, "The unfortunate thing is, where does his go go to, what becomes of it?"

Audrey wants to change; she is changing. She wants Charlie to sign those papers; she wants to go to the Roadhouse; she wants to find her lover, Billy. She saw him in a dream, bleeding. Dreamers sometimes sleepwalk. In Part Seven, the 1950s instrumental "Sleepwalk" was playing and we saw the Double R diner interior and a kid came to the door seeking a Billy, and the people in the café changed/switched positions in the scene, as though we were seeing someone's dream, someone worried, in love with Bill. Audrey.

Charlie is thwarting Audrey's forward motion at every turn, like in a nightmare. In the scene with Audrey and Charlie, before we realized he was her husband, it seemed he might be her psychiatrist, and this library his office. He spoke of offering her "compassion and protection." Maybe the papers she wants signed are the release forms of a mental institution. Maybe that earlier, strange diner scene with shifting people, and this long Audrey-Charlie dialogue scene, is her inner psychic drama of entrapment and a dreamed-for release, at the Roadhouse, with Billy, dancing to the cool jazz in her head.

Some commentators feel that all eighteen hours of *The Return* are Cooper's dream, while he's trapped in the Red Room. But Lynch and Frost don't want the full, serious force of their thoughts and feelings diluted, diminished in a corrosive fog of Didn't-Really-Happen. Yet Audrey, damaged by a bomb blast twenty five years ago, concussed and traumatized, raped, made a mother against her will, deserves to get lost in a dream.

A future episode will reveal that Audrey's interactions with Charlie are a psychic narrative. Her inner drama, not happening in the temporal world, but real as can be to her. For all his life, two of Lynch's favorite films have been *The Wizard of Oz* and *Sunset Boulevard*, both of which teach the artistic lesson that screen stories can reshape our familiar sense of how the world works to compelling, powerful effect: the unreal as hyperreal. It doesn't matter that Dorothy's adventures in *Oz* turn out to be a dream; they speak meaningfully to her and our thoughts and deep feelings. And *Sunset Boulevard* is a tale told by a dead man, the film's main character, but this fact only intensifies the unfolding drama, like putting a frame on a painting. Films, like dreams, create their own reality, shifting here and there, backward and forward in time: worlds that resonate with our worlds. Lynch, with his sensitivity to the objective world outside him and the subjective one within, shows us the dreaminess of reality and the psychic realism of dreams and the interpenetration of the two. Lynch's moving-image works are driven by his serious, unironic intent and their hyper-charged emotional through-lines, whether he's telling the true story of Alvin Straight (*The Straight Story*) or the dream-laced Hollywood story of actress Diane Selwyn (*Mulholland Drive*) as it flows through her dying mind.

Lynch can transition between worlds like a magician, but every project is different, with its own sense of correct proportion. *The Return* can be seen as a window view of a cosmic battle between invisible forces, enacted by characters, people we know. The paranormal is part of the show's narrative reality: a vortex in the sky, a Red Room somewhere, a humming-ringing sound in a hotel owner's office. As Bill Hastings says, "It's all real." The idea held by some that the whole of *The Return* is Cooper's (or some other character's) dream violates the *Twin Peaks* schema, its modus operandi as Lynch and Frost established it in 1990. In the original *Twin Peaks* and *Fire Walk With Me*, dreams were delineated as dreams, the "mind revealing itself to itself," as Major Briggs once said. Dreams were significant, discrete bits of subjective information that occurred within the hours and hours of the basic objective, omniscient narrative, like raisins in raisin bread. In the last moments of *Mulholland Drive*, Lynch can reveal that the preceding narrative of the film has been Diane Selwyn's subjective point of view, but the overall flow of *Twin Peaks* doesn't move like that. Realizing we've been inhabiting Audrey's disturbed consciousness fits with her character and situation. Concluding that all eighteen hours of *The Return* is some character's dream or vision does not fit Lynch and Frost's modus operandi.

We seek what makes us feel better. Little kids have to watch a favorite video or hear a favorite song, again and again. But they broaden their interests and desires as they grow, as their consciousness awakens and expands. Still, the security of the familiar exerts a strong pull. Just look at how offended some *Twin Peaks* fans were when they realized *The Return* was vectoring off far beyond the show's "good old days." The universe is flowing all around us and within us, but as D. H. Lawrence says, we're myopic, mechanistically repeating ourselves: "The living, wakeful soul is so flexible and sensitive, it has a horror of automatism. While the soul really lives, its deepest dread is perhaps the dread of automatism" (*Fantasia of the Unconscious*). Open to change, creatively thriving on it, Lynch and Frost reevaluated *Twin Peaks* and gave us *The Return*. The theme of evolution is always in the air.

The universe is composed of atoms, atoms composed of particle polarities in balance, yin and yang. Lynch and Frost, in their personal spiritual studies and practices, seek to see within temporal reality and beyond, the moon reflected in the gutter. This is the inclination, and mission, of Gordon Cole, Albert Rosenfield, Tamara Preston, the Blue Rose Task Force, and Dale Cooper, wherever he may be.

–CHAPTER NINETEEN–

WALK THE LAND, PLAY THE MUSIC (PART THIRTEEN)

A filmmaker unsure of himself, puzzling over what to put on screen, the shape and content of his next film. This is the problem facing Guido (Marcello Mastroianni) in Federico Fellini's *8 ½* (1963), one of Lynch's favorite films. Lynch has struggled with the elusiveness of artistic inspiration, slumping with depression in the middle of making *INLAND EMPIRE* (2006), saying, in the *Lynch (one)* documentary, "I have no idea what I'm doing." Guido needs time and space in which to be quiet, to let his creative juices flow. But he's beset by a babble of voices and problems: his wife, his mistress, his producer and screenwriter, want-to-be actors, dreams of his dead parents and his boyhood. Guido's life and art are in chaos; he's at the pinnacle of crisis.

Fellini has said that ever since boyhood, he's had a sense of suspension, of "waiting for something to happen," and in his art he can make it so. In one of the cinema's most perfect images of self-acceptance, and the acceptance of life's unruly messiness, Guido, in the persona of a circus ringmaster, directs a single-file procession, a parade, of all the people who have bedeviled and blessed is life. On and on they come, now directed by Guido the boy, who, like Lynch, awed by the wonder of the world, shaped it into art. Lynch, who seeks a mindset of a singleness that integrates opposites, was so moved by Guido's procession of personal polarities transcended that he made twelve lithographs (*The 8 ½ Suite*) that are like impressionistic sketches of Guido's heart-driven parade.

As Guido, boy and man, leads his life's journey parade, he declares, "Life is a festival. Let us live it!" And Lynch's first image in Part Thirteen is an homage to the spirit and picture of Guido/Fellini's parade. It's the morning after the Mitchum brothers and Dougie enjoyed the warm glow of harmonious rapprochement, their points of contention and misunderstanding having vanished as they were served cherry pie and champagne by the Pink Ladies in a beautiful room. Now in a six-person, woman-man-woman-man-woman-man line, they come sashaying/dancing into the Lucky 7 Insurance company, swaying to their own inner music, a sweet echo of Fellini's carnival. Jubilation rules. The ripple effect of Lynch and the Maharishi's belief in transformative high positivity illuminates Bushnell Mullins's office. The Mitchum brothers may be guilty of past dubious practices, but not this time. Dougie's unconscious/intuitive "research" uncovered the fact that Mullins's company owed the Mitchums $30 million, and Mullins's business savvy made it possible for the brothers to get the giant payment and for Lucky 7 to make a profit in the process. Bradley Mitchum brims with joy: "A wrong has been righted, and the sun is shining bright." (David Lynch to me: "Turn on the light and the darkness goes.") The Mitchums and the Pink Ladies have presents for Bushnell, and people take turns praising each other.

The wave of the Mitchums' beneficence surges out to the suburbs, where Janey-E is surprised and bliss besotted as a new outdoor gym set is delivered for Sonny Jim (the orphaned Mitchums didn't have one as kids), plus a red-ribbon-wrapped new BMW for her and Dougie. Following Lynch's dynamic of disjointed information fragments coalescing to form a collage of understanding, Janey-E sees that all of Dougie's disturbing, worrying, exasperating behaviors have formed a transcendent, golden portrait of her slow but gentle, loving, riches-providing husband.

That night, in warm light, husband and wife stand watching Sonny Jim joyfully romp around the new backyard gym set. The tableau of Sonny Jim playing has a Felliniesque carnival feel. The forms of the gym, like metal tree branches, twinkle with hundreds of little lights, like Rome's illuminated Via Veneto Boulevard in Fellini's 1960 *La Dolce Vita* (*The Sweet Life*). And as Sonny Jim cavorts around, a white-circle spot light plays across the scene, echoing the spotlight on *8 1/2*'s Guido-as-boy self at the parade-of-life ending. Perhaps Lynch's composition of the warm, glowing Jones family backyard evoked one of his own fond memories. At the time of the original *Twin Peaks*, Lynch was in Italy with his love Isabella Rossellini (daughter of renowned director Roberto Rossellini), who is treated like royalty in her home country. In a backyard outdoor restaurant, with lights twinkling in the trees, Lynch and Isabella had dinner with *8½*'s Guido himself, Marcello Mastroianni. The iconic actor made it possible for Lynch to meet Fellini, and a couple of years later Lynch visited Maestro Fellini on his deathbed. Lynch held Fellini's hand, and they shared their love of cinema, its blending of dream and reality, and the creative value of intuitively following one's imagination. After Fellini's death, Lynch was told that after he left the room that day, Fellini said, "That's a good boy." As I write this, Lynch is four years older (seventy-seven) than Fellini's age at passing.

Dougie-Cooper Jones is a "good boy" and a good man, a prince of peace in the desert who emanates right living and banishes shadows. He's a spiritual-moral battery charger whose contact powers up the angels of our better natures. Living with Dougie has made Janey-E more tolerant and kind, and unlocked her loving heart. Dougie's behavior and aura have awakened the Mitchum brothers' latent sense of gratitude and generosity. Now Dougie, unconsciously in a state of beneficent grace, goes to work on Tony Sinclair, and his dandruff.

Young David Lynch grew up Christian, enveloped by the Golden Rule, "Do unto others as you would have them do unto you," which dovetails nicely with his belief in karma, the conviction that good and bad actions in this life shape our spiritual progress through future incarnations. As Lynch says, "When you do something to someone else, you might as well be doing it to yourself." Sometimes you don't have to wait for your next life to get your comeuppance. As John Lennon's song says, "Instant karma's going to get you, going to knock you right on the head."

As we've noted, Mr. C's Bob-nurtured dark side ultimately wants to tap into the mysterious wellspring of evil cosmic power. He couldn't pursue that quest trapped back in the Red Room, so he defied the metaphysical order to report for duty, and he remains a rogue actor in our world. He has amassed a rewarding criminal empire, but he can't rest until he's eliminated his nemesis, the good Cooper, who's incapacitated within Dougie, who lives in Las Vegas. Mr. C's man in Vegas, Duncan Todd, has failed, via his agents, to get Dougie killed. Todd knows about Tony Sinclair's shady financial/business dealings, so Sinclair's vulnerable to Todd's manipulations. Todd figures he can come out golden with Mr. C if he can get Sinclair to inflame the casino-owning Mitchum brothers' animosity towards casino-money-winning Dougie enough to kill him. All the wheels are turning toward that conclusion.

But then, one morning in his office, Sinclair sees the Mitchums and their Pink Ladies come dancing into the Lucky 7 offices with their new best friend, the very alive Dougie Jones. We read Sinclair's lips through a glass partition: "Holy shit!" Instant karma indeed—his goose is cooked; he can't understand what's happened. Maybe the "someone terrible" (Mr. C) Duncan Todd's so afraid of will come for Sinclair now. It's time for desperate measures. He'll have to kill Dougie himself. Dougie, who's called him a liar in front of their boss and has been analyzing Sinclair's past insurance work and talking about it with Bushnell.

True to the history and folklore of Las Vegas, and the tenets of noir film and literary fiction, there's a network of corruption beneath the city's glittering surface. Not surprisingly, Sinclair's in league with some bad cops, one of whom provides him with a little bottle of poisonous white powder, "undetectable."

For maximum dramatic and emotional impact, Lynch and Frost make a steaming black cup of coffee, the sacred elixir of *Twin Peaks* culture, the lethal delivery system. Sinclair has come on all palsy with Dougie and said he'll buy him a cup of joe. Dougie and Sinclair are seated at the outdoor business plaza. Their coffee arrives, and Dougie stares unsmiling at Sinclair without a word. Nervous, Sinclair probably thinks Dougie has read his wicked, murderous mind. Lynch has staged the shot so that Dougie seems to be studying Sinclair's face, but he's actually gazing beyond him, at a pastry case featuring cherry pie. Maybe Dougie's pie for the Mitchum brothers came from this store. Dougie's coffee can wait; he goes straight to the pastry display and presses his nose against the glass like a kid.

What luck for Sinclair. While Dougie's gone, Sinclair quickly slips the white powder into Dougie's coffee, which remains black as midnight. The store waitress says she'll bring Dougie a big slice of pie, so he heads back to Sinclair, slowly coming up on him from the rear. Lynch pulls off a visual rhyme scheme with two elements: white powder into black coffee, and a dusting of white dandruff on the back of Sinclair's black suit collar. The first element is lethal; the second is the key to Sinclair's redemption.

Sinclair looks toward us, his face twisted in emotional turmoil and existential fear. Dougie stands behind him, his fingers lightly touching the pale sprinkle of white specks by the back of Sinclair's neck. It's the softest, gentlest gesture, a little moment of Dougie discovering something new in the world, but it's also profound, releasing a basic goodness in Sinclair that's been buried under a sludge of money-grubbing corruption. Dougie's touch is a nudge into contrition, giving him permission to unburden himself, sobbing, "I never meant to hurt anyone." Lynch knows that things can be deeply serious and funny at the same time. Dougie has no idea why Sinclair stands up, grabs Dougie's coffee, and runs away with it. If that's the way it is, Dougie will take Sinclair's coffee, and he's enjoying it and his pie when Sinclair returns, having dumped the deadly brew in the men's room. In there a man standing peeing at a urinal saw the sobbing Sinclair pour away the coffee and said, "That bad, huh?" Bad coffee and bad behavior. Back outside in the public space, Sinclair, small in the frame, like a little boy caught misbehaving, shouts at Dougie from twenty feet away, "Oh my God, I never wanted to hurt you; I'm *so*, so sorry."

There is no Bob within Sinclair. He knows better than to be devilish, but he's weak; he's been seduced by a value system that craves the things money can buy. In the eight-minute screen arc that flows from Sinclair's murder attempt to his confession and apology to Dougie and Bushnell in Bushnell's office, he says "God" three times. He details his misdeeds: potential murder, being in league with Duncan Todd and corrupt cops, cheating his boss out of big money. Sinclair has reaped physical, emotional and spiritual anguish, rather than pleasure and fulfillment. It's simple, and hard as hell: "I have to change or die." Lynch and Frost are stressing the need to find and nurture a better self within. We recall Lynch as Gordon Cole recounting having lectured coworkers to "Fix your hearts or die" regarding accepting a transgendered colleague with compassion. Moral choices have profound consequences. Lynch once said to me, "Let's pump some coherence into the world and get on with a beautiful life." He wants us to lessen the suffering we bring on ourselves and others, to, like Saint Hildegard of Bingen (1098-1179), "see the light in my soul, much brighter than the clouds which bear the sun," the light that shines forth from Laura Palmer's face early in *The Return* when she's in the Red Room with Cooper.

We've noted that Lynch and Frost's multifarious adult spiritual and philosophical beliefs have evolved from Christian boyhoods. Sinclair's sobbing confession has an aura of Christian redemption. He isn't spilling his heart just because he got caught, but because he chose to, having been touched literally and figuratively by the gentle lamb Dougie. Sinclair's progress toward spiritual liberation has the feeling of Apostle Paul recognizing and acknowledging the fundamental truth that "Christ liveth in me" (*Galatians*, 2:20).

When Sinclair was sitting at the table staring at the coffee cup he'd poisoned and was unexpectedly touched from behind by his intended victim, he had what Zen Buddhists call a satori experience, as a profound illumination of reality flooded into his consciousness. When visionary author-philosopher Philip K. Dick was eight years old in 1936, he had a similar experience while he was in the midst of harming a fellow creature, a beetle. Young Dick was poised to smash it with a rock when an empathetic love swept over him: "This beetle was just like I was." In his adult journals, Dick wrote that he'd realized that the beetle "was as holy as Christ," that he'd felt the creature's vulnerability and suffering "by the sudden grace of God" (*The Divine Madness of Philip K. Dick*).

The Christian aspect of Lynch's spirituality can allude to God and Christ and gentle Jesus and angels, while his Hindu beliefs can see Sinclair as having a sudden realization of the underlying connection, the oneness of everything, such that what he does to Dougie he does to himself. A joke about someone seeking a mate says, "I'm looking for a me-based life form." Maybe the ultimate joke is that plants, people, Toyotas, atoms, galaxies exploding and being born, the living and the dead, past, present and future are all me forms, the single suchness. But a multiplicity of different, "separate" people, actions, polarities, conflicts, aspirations, and sufferings makes for more and better stories, like a big dream someone's dreaming. Like David Lynch's dreamlike stories, or the David Lynch that's dreamed. By whom?

Mr. C has a dream of acquiring power. Although he has the personal style of a back roads bad boy, he controls an international crime operation. On our earthly plane he can manipulate people to do his will, but Bob, who has spanned dimensions, is part of Mr. C's inner self, so he senses that there are vast forces to be discovered and tapped into, a hierarchy of puppet masters somewhere beyond. He wants to find them, to learn darker arts, and overthrow the overlords. It's not easy when you're dealing with paranormal physics. He's learned of the powerful Judy from Phillip Jeffries and tried to tap some aspect of her in the New York glass box, but she broke out and is in the wind.

Then there's that damned Dale Cooper to worry about, who's as good as Mr. C is bad. But Cooper's superlative skills are diminished, confined within the being Dougie Jones, whom Mr.C "manufactured" metaphysically. Cooper-in-Dougie is still dangerous. He may awaken to his full warrior powers, so he should be killed immediately. But he seems shielded by grace: lethal attempts by Mr. C's agents (desert sharpshooters, bomb planters, Ike the Spike's gun, Tony Sinclair's poison) have failed, while Dougie has thrived. Mr. C will have to take on Cooper one-on-one, and we assume he's on the road to that eventual outcome.

Mr. C's Las Vegas cohorts may not have been able to rub out Dougie, but his associates Hutch and Chantal are bloody good at eliminating some of his dangling entanglements. When Mr. C was in the South Dakota prison, he'd been able to leverage his knowledge of Warden Murphy's shady past into an immediate release for him and Ray Monroe. Now that Mr. C's out in the world making the moves he wants to make, he has Hutch and Chantal welcome Warden Murphy home with a quick, crisp scope-rifle shot. Before Murphy can reach his front door, he's lifeless, face down, a blood mist puff staining the night air. Lynch and Frost, both fathers of sons, want us to feel the pain: Murphy's little boy opens the front door, his torn voice screams, "Daddy!"

Before Mr. C defied the cosmic summons to return to the Red Room, crashed his car and was imprisoned, his own hands had done his dirty work, shooting Darya, blasting Phyllis Hastings, and mushing a man's face like it was wet clay. Now, having survived being shot by Ray Monroe, and being put back together, body and dark spirit, by the Woodsmen, Mr. C is back in direct action, rolling in a big, honking black pickup truck on a Northwestern vector, from South Dakota to Montana, where Lynch was born and his father's father had been a wheat farmer. Not to jump ahead, but if you follow Mr. C's direction of travel, you end up in Twin Peaks, Washington.

After shooting Mr. C and seeing the eerie Woodsmen working on him, Ray panicked and sped away. He immediately reported in to Phillip Jeffries, who, we clearly now know, is the one who recruited Ray to get close to Mr. C and kill him. In Part Four, after Gordon Cole and Albert first encountered Mr. C in the South Dakota prison, Albert confessed to Cole that in the past he'd authorized Phillip Jeffries to give "Cooper" (who they now realize is pseudo-Cooper) information about an FBI agent who was subsequently murdered. So Jeffries knew of the Bad Cooper? Did he figure the good Dale had gone wrong, yielded to dark temptation? Or, having witnessed a gathering of Bob and the paranormal invaders and personally experienced the slipperiness of time, space, and identity, did Jeffries realize this "Cooper" being was Dale occupied by an otherness that must be destroyed? Since, as Gordon Cole says, Phillip Jeffries is "nowhere," off the map, Ray could be on an assassination job for Jeffries. Ray tried, but Mr. C lives on. Bad Cooper knows Ray's bound for a Montana place called the Farm, and he's hot on his trail.

In Lynch's thoughts and emotions, the words Montana and farm evoke his birth state and the place where his father's father farmed wheat as a homesteader. But *The Return*'s Farm cultivates evil schemes and boiling-testosterone violence. Out in wild country, it is a weathered two-story wooden warehouse full of backwoods criminal men, from middle-age on up, well armed, smoking, and swigging whisky, with comparatively svelte Ray Monroe among them. On the second floor, watching a giant TV screen, they see Mr. C pull his truck into the lower level, a locking gate closing behind him. Two levels, in-person reality and two-dimensional reality, framed on a screen: Lynch's constant, overarching awareness of multiple levels of existence in a space.

Ray shot, but didn't kill, Mr. C five episodes ago, so there's high dramatic tension built up for their confrontation. Ray's trembling, eager to get at "that fuck." But Lynch and Frost, being good storytellers, make him, and us, wait. Lynch likes to dream up particular places with their own look and way of being, culture, rules of engagement: the Red Room, the Fireman's realm, Phillip Jeffries' abode, when we finally get there. A tall, bald powerhouse of a man, Renzo (Derek Mears), rules the Farm. He says Ray can have Mr. C, but first things first. For ten years Renzo's arm wrestled newcomers, and always won. The losers are then Renzo's to command; if they disobey, they're killed. Early in *The Return*, Mr. C said, "The game begins," so of course he will play this one.

Facing each other across a table top, elbows on its surface, Mr. C and Renzo begin, as the male animals surrounding them grunt and shout. With his unsmiling, unblinking black marble eyes drilling into Renzo, Mr. C toys with him, letting Renzo seem to be winning, then snapping his arm at the shoulder and punching his face almost through the back of his head, sloshing blood and brains onto the floor. Previously we've seen Mr. C seek to end others' lives by proxy or kill them directly with a gun. This demonstration of his invincible empty-handed power makes us fear all the more for Cooper: even if he awakens from being Dougie and regains his only-human mortal force, Mr. C is Bob supercharged.

Now, at last, it's go time with Ray. The Farm men immediately accept Mr. C as their boss and clear the room so that he and Ray can get down to business. Mr. C is holding his black pistol; Ray has no gun, but he makes a quick move to flee around the corner to the armed Farm denizens. Mr. C stops him with a flesh wound to the back of his leg, so Ray lies prone and groaning with pain for their talk. Young painter David Lynch became a filmmaker after imagining that a figure in one of his canvases had moved slightly. And as a director he creates motion picture frames that at moments are barely moving, tableaus of reality evocatively suspended, timeless, pressurized spaces sometimes spiked with absurdity. In the Farm's big, barren gray-washed space, Ray is horizontal, Mr. C is vertical. They're silent, and they both notice a man standing still against a wall. He wears a businessman's suit and studious glasses. He says, "Do you need any money?" Mr. C says, "No." In *The Return* the path to knowledge is often fragmented, disrupted, the expected rhythms of narration subverted. Now Ray and Mr. C's mano-a-mano showdown can commence. And also typical of *The Return*, their confrontation is about dueling minds more than bodies.

In Part Two, Darya told Mr. C that her and Ray's directive to kill him came through Phillip Jeffries. Ray confirms this to Mr. C, saying that Jeffries arranged with Warden Murphy to get Ray and Mr. C in prison together and release them together so Ray could proceed to kill Mr. C. In Part Two, there was the alternative plan to have Darya shoot Mr. C, but he discovered that scheme and took her out. Ray emphasized that he talked to Jeffries only on the phone and never met him. So Jeffries was a conveyor of information, an arranger of action. But why? Ray reveals a major key: "You've got something inside that they want." Does Gordon Cole have overview knowledge and a master plan? Does he know Bob is inside Mr. C and is using Cole's Blue Rose cohort Jeffries, who's off somewhere, to facilitate Mr. C/Bob's death? Back in 1992's *Fire Walk With Me*, Lynch and cowriter Robert Engels embedded Phillip Jeffries in a fog of ambiguity, having him instantaneously appear in Buenos Aires/Philadelphia/Buenos Aires, be unstuck in time, and be an intellectually and emotionally engaged witness of the convenience store extradimensional invaders, fascinated and inspired by them: "I followed."

In Part Two, when Mr. C talked to phone-voice Phillip Jeffries, Jeffries referred to Mr. C going back in the Black Lodge tomorrow (this is before Mr. C's rogue defiance of the cosmic plan), saying when Mr. C goes in "I will be with Bob again." The logical person to say this line is the One-Armed Man, who used to be Bob's partner in evil action before switching to the path of goodness. We've never heard the One-Armed Man put on another voice, let alone the southern gentleman drawl of Phillip Jeffries. Since David Bowie, who played Jeffries in *Fire Walk With Me*, had died and would have to be voiced by another actor, did Lynch and Frost decide to go meta and make Jeffries noncorporeal, of the air, in a removed atmosphere such that those communicating with him weren't sure if it was him? No matter what medium Jeffries's essence is in, is he on the side of good or bad? Ray Monroe has things in his pockets. On a small piece of paper: the space-time coordinates Bill Hastings and Ruth gave Major Briggs in the Zone, which Ray got from Hastings's secretary, who was clearly a weak link in Hastings's secret mission. In the other denim-fabric cave of Ray's jeans: the Owl Cave jade ring, an otherworldly power object. A prison guard gave it to Ray before he and Mr. C were released. Phillip Jeffries had told Ray to put the ring on Mr. C after he'd killed him. Mr. C has Ray slip the ring on the third finger of *his* left hand. Mr. C shoots him dead, and the ring vanishes from Ray's hand, then lands tinkling on the zigzag floor of the Red Room. Ray's body remains in the Farm warehouse, but also appears prone and bleeding on the Red Room floor. In close-up, the One-Armed Man reverently returns the ring to the black marble surface we first saw in *Fire Walk With Me*: the sacred object's ritual resting place.

It seems that Phillip Jeffries is still a righteous, if mysterious, agent for good. Over the years his metaphysical travels have familiarized him with Bob, Mr. C, the Red Room, the ring, and he seems dedicated to counteracting threats that are beyond measure. Maybe it was Jeffries on the phone with Mr. C in Part Two, talking about rejoining Bob to confuse and disorient the bad man. Maybe Jeffries is enacting a master plan engineered with Major Briggs/the Fireman.

Cooper is a master detective, and so is his dark side, Mr. C, who wants to find Jeffries, to tap into his powerful knowledge, to learn more about the high darkness that is Judy. Before Mr. C shoots Ray, Ray says Jeffries is "at a place called the Dutchman's," a term that could be Lynch's homage to the legend of African American Mississippi blues genius Robert Johnson (1911-1938). Johnson, who could barely play his guitar and sing, left town for who knows where and returned a year later with a deep and dazzling talent that eclipsed all other bluesmen. In this black Delta culture intimately familiar with devils and angels, it was said that Johnson's new gift did not come from above. In Alan Greenberg's 1983 screenplay *Love in Vain: A Vison of Robert Johnson*, which Lynch has been obsessed with for three decades, the "devilman" who bestows Johnson's genius is called Dutch Boy.

Lynch has always been fascinated by films that "take you to another world"—places like Federico Fellini's Italy, Billy Wilder's *Sunset Boulevard* Hollywood, *The Wizard of Oz*'s over the rainbow—and Lynch's own films are mesmerizingly transportive. *Love in Vain* immersed Lynch, raised middle class in the pretty much lily-white Northwest, in a pungently enchanting world of dirt-poor black sharecroppers who toil in misery by day and cut loose in a glory of music, drink, and sex when the sun goes down. Deeply respectful of Delta culture, Greenberg's screenplay centers on the legend/myth that the Devil tuned up Johnson's guitar at a midnight crossroads called Charlie's Trace (in *The Return*, Audrey's nemesis is named Charlie) and Johnson later had to pay for the gift with his life. Over the years the myth and reality of Robert Johnson have entranced creative people like a voodoo spell. Eric Clapton, the greatest of the British electric-guitar bluesmen, references the Johnson legend in his song "Crossroads" (1966), and in his masterpiece "Layla" (1972), a cry of his own personal pain contains the line "all my love's in vain" in homage to Johnson's "Love in Vain." Greenberg's screenplay has captivated everyone from Bob Dylan and Keith Richards to music scholars and critics Stanley Crouch and Greil Marcus and directors Werner Herzog and Martin Scorsese.

Lynch first contacted Greenberg in 1983, the year the screenplay was completed. Over the years, the two talked on and off about making the film, but Greenberg died in 2015, so time will tell if Lynch will be the one to bring *Love in Vain* to further light; it's already glowing.

Since the mid-1980s, when Lynch was writing, directing, and suffering making *Dune*, before *Blue Velvet* and *Twin Peaks* and all the rest, *Love in Vain* has been on his conscious/subconscious mind. Are there correspondences, echoes, and reflections of Greenberg's poetic fantasia about a historical man's life to be found in Lynch's work, especially *Twin Peaks*?

The 1990–1991 *Twin Peaks* was a lamentation for Laura Palmer being gone, not here, torn from her beloved town by an act of murder. But Lynch, with his fluid sense that all-time-is-now and his heart's need for her, returned to her in 1992's *Fire Walk With Me*. In *The Return*'s Part Two, Laura was whisked away from the Red Room, but fifteen parts later, she'll be back. The "I" in Greenberg's *Love in Vain* preface could be Laura and/or Lynch: "When I leave this town I'm gonna bid you fair farewell. And when I return again you'll have a great long story to tell."

Early in *Love in Vain*, an old blues man's guitar plays by itself at bedtime, and he sees this as a manifestation of his dead wife's spirit checking up on him, a reminder of how "fearful an' lonesome things is." In a footnote to this page, Greenberg says, "Abstract spiritual systems find manifold ways to work on a human being's naked soul." Lynch's amalgamated Christian/Hindu/artistic spiritual system underpins *The Return* and relates to Greenberg's fascination with the African American cultural concept of "conjure." "Like Christianity, Conjure is a system of belief, a way of perceiving the world so that people are placed in the context of another world no less 'real' than the ordinary one. Both attempt to locate the cause of suffering. Conjure is a theory for experiencing the mystery of evil and a practice for doing something about it, to locate the source of misfortune and do something about it."

Love in Vain's Mississippi's Delta land, like the world of *Twin Peaks*, is a place where "there's miracles all around," where "these Piney Woods eat meat" and someone is advised to connect his soul to the spirit "telephone in the central skies" (via *Fire Walk With Me* and *The Return*'s telephone pole number six?). Spirits of good and evil hover close, swirling in the humid air, and "people hear things there, fearful things, like angels moanin' an' bells tollin' where there ain't none, and see lost souls flyin' to an island of light." *Twin Peaks*'s the Man From Another Place's words about his home dimension, where "there's always music in the air," apply to *Love in Vain*'s Delta, where glory shouts and heavenly choruses compete with tempting, alluring lowdown devil music. Like Leland Palmer at Laura's burial, an emotion-gripped character at a public burial lunges toward the grave. As Bob sought to occupy Laura's body and soul ("I want to taste with your mouth"), "A man, like a god I mean, hisself, through her mouth he got her speech." Greenberg could be describing *Twin Peaks* when he says, "People are half seen, acts are half followed, as in dreams." Early in *Love in Vain*, before Robert Johnson's career takes off, a conjurer gives him advice that would fit and describe David Lynch: "You see what no one sees an' feel what no one feels, an' less you get what's inside you out, it'll kill you. You got the power of the hidden way—so you need a good strong hand."

In real life, and in *Love in Vain*, Robert Johnson was/is poisoned by the jealous husband of a woman who was flirting with him at a house party where he was playing and singing. As Lynch has done so often since reading *Love in Vain* in the mid-1980s, Greenberg makes the juncture of near death/death/the beyond a passage of extraordinary happenings. Johnson sees a woman who's always been lame jumping high on two good legs. In the enclosed space of not a Red Room but a one-room shack, the Devilman, the Satanic Tempter who gave Johnson his genius talent at the crossroads, attends Johnson's last moments alive. The dark one who'd earlier told Robert his name was the Dutch Boy asks the dying man what his name is now. Robert writes on a slip of paper: "Jesus Christ my saver an' redeemer." Is this poor expiring Robert's delirium talking, his fevered mind confusing the Devil with Christ? Or is Greenberg presenting a profound spiritual paradox? Johnson was a boozer, a breaker of Commandments who mistreated his women and considered himself a sinner. Jonson's historical family insisted that he gave his soul to Christ at the end. Greenberg may be making a fictional point that an entity of darkness, the Devilman, can inspire a journey to grace and salvation. Just as Lynch, years after first experiencing *Love in Vain* made evil Bob, through Laura Palmer's resistance to him, the catalyst of her ultimate angel-attended beatification. Throughout centuries of life and art, the shadow side of the human psyche has been represented by the rebellious fallen Christian angel with a dual aspect: Satan the wicked tempting serpent, and Lucifer, the God-defying, but ultimately resplendent, bringer of light. Robert Johnson and Laura Palmer live sinfully, but they choose to change course: their downward paths lead to the stars. Their falls enable them to rise.

In the realm of *Twin Peaks*, Mr. C has defied the high powers' command to return to the Red Room and is flying free to feed his ravenous ego. No repentance for him; he's not going to change course: it's all the way down the line on the demonic mystery train. Before Mr. C leaves the Farm to find the Dutchman's, we see the Farm denizens watching him execute Ray on the big TV screen. Among the criminal group is young Richard Horne, hanging out with his kind of sleazy people. Assuming that Richard is the spawn of Mr. C having raped a comatose Audrey, is a father-and-son reunion in the offing?

Part Thirteen catches us up on many couples. Chantal and Hutch are on a beeline from South Dakota to Las Vegas to do that "doubleheader" for Mr. C, presumably to kill Dougie, since everyone else has failed to complete that mission, and to blow away any other loose ends, like Mr. Todd, the man who knows too much about Mr. C's criminal empire. When Chantal and Hutch hit Utah, they exchange some classic Lynch-and-Frost absurdist dialogue. Chantal: "Utah. Mormons. No liquor, coffee, Coca-Cola, no sex before marriage." Hutch: "And men can have, like, six or ten wives." Chantal: "Funny there aren't more of them. I guess it's the drinks." Whatever you say, Chantal. As Sailor Ripley said to Lula Pace fortune in Lynch's *Wild at Heart*, "The way your mind works is God's private mystery."

Up in *Twin Peaks*, in that house where everything is old-fashioned, Audrey is frantic, at loose ends. The last time we saw her, she rained the power of her anger on her husband, Charlie. But now she's painfully vulnerable, coming apart. Previously, the narrative driving Audrey and Charlie was Audrey's strong desire to go to the Roadhouse and Charlie sadistically stalling and subverting her gratification. Now she sobs, "I want to stay and go—which will it be?" Charlie's "We've been over this" sounds like an understatement. There's a sense that Charlie is Audrey's therapist or guide. And she needs help: "I'm not me; I'm not sure who I am." A state of mind in which, over the years, a number of Lynch's characters find themselves.

Mark Frost has said he's a Jungian, referring to the seminal Swiss psychologist Carl Jung (1875-1961). Jung's early study of the medieval alchemists, who sought to transmute base elements into gold, gave him a metaphor for the human psyche's need to integrate its disparate parts and drives into a golden wholeness that can deal with life in a healthy, fulfilling way. Jung realized that we project powerful, often unconscious shadowy forces within us onto the world outside us: it's them, not me. As Lynch said of the Red Room, "It changes depending on who walks into it," and, another time, "The world is as you are." Some days morning is a cold, treacherous film noir place, but the afternoon is warm, invigorating, easeful. Sometimes we want to destroy, sometimes create, and every nuanced gradation in between the polarities. But like the balanced positive and negative particles that compose us, we need to counterpoise our various energies to optimally survive and thrive. It feels like we have many selves, multiple roles and storylines we act out, but they're chapters that form a single big book.

Audrey can't see or feel how everything fits. Her clashing, out-of-control stories don't emanate from a safe and secure center, an integrated self. Distressed, she asks Charlie, "Is this the story of the little girl who lives down the lane?" Unless there's a fairy tale or fable by that name that we haven't heard of, we assume Lynch and Frost are referencing Nicolas Gessner's quirky 1976 film, *The Little Girl Who Lives Down the Lane*," starring Jodie Foster as a very pulled-together thirteen-year-old girl who knows who she is and effectively maintains the world as she wants it to be, secretly living in a house alone. At this point in *The Return*, such a harmonious self-understanding eludes Audrey. In a later part, the question "Is this the story of the little girl who lives down the lane?" is related to Laura Palmer, and both she and Audrey will eventually reach their own stunning moments of clarity. But not tonight. Audrey and Charlie still can't break through their stasis enough to get to the Roadhouse.

Another *Twin Peaks* stay-at-home is Sarah Palmer, whose primary relationship seems to be with her TV set. And what sort of electricity powers that box glowing with swarming blue-lightning energy? Something's causing a very strange broadcast. We see a black-and-white boxing match, tinted blue, that keeps repeating the same passage over and over. One fighter clips the other on the ear, the referee checks him over, and they commence again. Very straightforward, but the announcer says, "Looks like rounds number one and two are underway." One round's supposed to follow another chronologically; two don't happen at the same time, at least in places other than Sarah's house. (This time scrambling at her house will figure in *The Return*'s final moments.) This place once housed her husband, Leland, a seemingly "good man" possessed by Bob's evil, who regularly raped and eventually killed their daughter, Laura. Laura the town's golden girl, who acted out her own shadow self.

Fire Walk With Me opened with blue TV static, which became linked with the paranormal convenience store denizens and the Red Room, like a crackling veil between dimensions and realities. There's a sonic static stutter between the repetitions of Sarah's boxing show, which recalls the repeating clicks of the stuck record playing in this room when Leland killed cousin Maddy (a dead ringer for Laura). And the sound reminds us of the click/voice on the Fireman's gramophone at the start of *The Return*, an audio pattern of dark energy. Sarah has had her own repetitive cycles: liquor bottle after liquor bottle, cigarette after cigarette, and the white horse she would see when Leland was secretly doing his dirty work with their daughter. The only time we've ever seen the white horse other than in close proximity to Sarah was when Cooper saw it in the Red Room, standing on a dark plane behind the red curtains that ruffle up in a wind as Laura is torn out of the room by some force. And later the Woodsman intones, "The horse is the white of the eyes," as he exercises his wickedness.

In the original *Twin Peaks*, Sarah was a grieving mother who had visions of Bob, and since *The Return* has shown her as a young girl being invaded by a loathsome frog-moth that's part of the alien chain of life that includes Bob, we suspect she hides dark inner depths. From *Fire Walk With Me* onward, we've known that the darkness feeds on human pain, fear, and sorrow, which Sarah has plenty of. Perhaps in the lonely decades since Laura and Leland have been gone her alien drives have strengthened, her circuit connection to otherworldly powers crackling blue. Maybe in Part Twelve, when Sarah, disturbed by a vision in the supermarket, warned, "Men will be coming," she meant the FBI, the good guys who are a threat to her kind.

In Lynch's unproduced screenplay *Ronnie Rocket* (1977), a city in the evil grip of high-voltage bad electricity can be saved only when the malignant circuit, the circle, is broken. In *The Return*, Sarah Palmer is enslaved by her paranormal repeating cycles, and we've noted the same-as-it-ever-was narrow tunnel vision of Ben Horne, who's chained to his parade of problems, and Dr. Jacoby, whose outraged mind dwells on every possible socio political-environmental ill that could possibly befall humankind. Ben chooses not to break out of his trap and embrace a romantic connection with his colleague Beverly. But Dr. Jacoby is motivated to reach out, at least via the airwaves, by broadcasting his ranting beliefs publicly. He wants people to get fired up about the world's problems and do something about them. As Jacoby symbolizes it, we're all mired in shit, and we need the golden shovel of awareness, resolve, and action to dig our way out. This equation can be seen as a metaphor for Lynch's belief in the golden technique of meditation as a tool for raising personal and world consciousness out of the morass of negative energy, to tackle problems small and large.

The Return's Part Four introduced the Sanskrit concept of dharma, a person's place in the universe, the path they're best suited to follow. Andy and Lucy's son Wally Brando is enacting his dharma by experiencing the open roads of America, while Sheriff Frank Truman's dharma is rooted in Twin Peaks, which he does everything in his power to protect. Dr. Jacoby is on his own unique journey, and from a high-altitude view, we see that Ben Horne is on an admirable path stretching from decades of villainy to the quiet everyday heroism of coping with mundane problems and choosing not to harm those close to him.

A person's dharma path can have unexpected branches. One night Dr. Jacoby is driving through town and sees a thrilling sight: one of his golden shovels, illuminated in a store window, framed by black curtains (an impeccable little David Lynch art piece). Something crystalizes for Jacoby: His broadcast persona, Dr. Amp, hasn't just been ranting in solitude; his passion has reached at least one anonymous town citizen—and it's Nadine! She's been his secret sharer, taking in his message and being inspired to change her life. This is her store, offering an array of curtains and her long-sought-for holy grail: silent drape runners. She and Jacoby haven't seen each other in seven years, and as they talk in the reflected glow of the golden shovel, there's a warmth of more than renewed friendship in the air.

The air onstage at the Roadhouse glows pink, like Cooper and Naido's love light (Part Two), as James Marshall, looking as boyish as he did twenty-five years ago, strums his guitar and sings. The song is "Just You," the simple, sweet love song he introduced in his girlfriend Donna's living room, with her and Laura's cousin Maddy singing harmony. His love, Laura, had been killed recently, and her look-alike, Maddy, soon would be. Today he lives the pain of those deaths and the disappearance of Donna from his life. He's had more downs than ups over the years, but he still wants to dream and sing about "together forever" love. In Part One, he made eyes at Shelly's friend Renee but turned away when his emotional outreach was not returned. But tonight, singing at the Roadhouse, his falsetto is like a mainline to Renee's heart, and she's deeply affected, wiping away tears as he finishes. She's really seen who James is now.

Back in his bad boy days, James loved Laura, and so, in his way, did Bobby Briggs. Bobby also had a hot affair with Double R waitress Shelly, who was married to Leo Johnson at the time. *The Return* has shown us that Bobby and Shelly were married at some point and that Becky is their daughter.

Bobby, having matured over the years and found the moral compass appropriate for the son of Major Garland Briggs, stops by the diner for his "usual" dinner, and maybe to be near Shelly. But tonight she's out, probably with that dangerous slickster Red. Bobby's outgrown his youthful swagger and bravado, and he humbly, almost shyly accepts an invite to sit in a booth with Norma and the original *Twin Peaks* character that Lynch and Frost have made us wait the longest for: Big Ed Hurley (Everett McGill.) In the 1990–1991 *Twin Peaks*, characters often shared a Double R booth. Such scenes are rare in *The Return*, and this one emanates that good-old-days aura that a number of viewers bitterly miss.

In *The Return*, Bobby's possible path to be with Shelly again is disrupted by Red. Big Ed has loved diner owner-manager Norma Jennings for decades but remains married to Nadine out of guilt and his sense of decency. Still, now here's Ed and Norma in a booth chatting, with Bobby along for the ride, until Ed's love train is derailed once more. In strolls grinning businessman Walter Lawford (Grant Goodeve), who kisses Norma's mouth as she strokes his arm, and Ed and Bobby retreat to a separate booth, their status certified: the lonely guys.

We learn that Norma and Walter are partners in romance and business. Norma has become the "face of the franchise"; there are now five Norma's Double R diners, but the Twin Peaks one is lagging behind in profits. True to *Twin Peaks* culture, it's all about the pies. Norma uses local, organic ingredients, but the other locations don't, so Walter says this diner's "spending too much per pie." This scene sounds like a rebuke to Carl Twede, the real-life owner of the Mar-T, who's complained publicly about the cherry pies costing so much to make. Walter's vocalized mindset encapsulates a rationale that Lynch and Frost must have heard from executive types over the years: "You're an artist, but love doesn't turn a profit. We want you to tweak the formula; consistency and profitability are important."

Walter isn't a money-sucking vampire; he's eager, soft-spoken, pleasant, and attentive to Norma's thoughts and concerns. And the two are definitely on for later tonight. Down the row of booths, Lynch has Ed facing in Norma's direction, and as she starts to talk to Walter, she catches Ed's glance for a second, then looks, beaming, at Walter and doesn't return her eyes to Ed.

Over the years, Lynch has said that Twin Peaks is "a town of desire and longing," where people have burning needs and wants that are often not fulfilled. In *The Return*, it's a harsher place than it was twenty-five years ago: less fun, more pain and sadness. In 1991's season two, Ed and Norma shared their love, body and soul. They were on the verge of marrying, with Nadine (in an amnesiac state of consciousness) agreeing that the former high school sweethearts should be together. But then Nadine popped back to her normal self, and Ed resumed his guilt and conscience-driven role as her long-burdened husband. And now that Walter's in Norma's life and Ed and Nadine are estranged, living apart, it seems that Ed is born to lose. Walter is Norma's main course now; these days Ed just gets little morsels of her warmth.

Lynch concludes most parts of *The Return* with the end credits rolling as a musical group plays, but he gives Ed's sadness (and Everett McGill's talent) its due in a quietly mournful final scene.

At the Double R, before Walter arrived, Norma served Ed his dinner. Now Ed, alone in dim light and silence, sits in his gas station office staring out the front window into the night, having some soup Norma sent home with him: a token of her loving sustenance, yet so far from what he needs. There are two tall paper cups of soup, but Ed doesn't sip it; he uses a spoon, making it last. Reflected back at him in the front window, his face is blank; he's depleted, whipped; he's got no agency in this situation, no moves he can make. There's a little scrap of white paper in front of him, maybe a love note he had planned to slip to Norma. He strikes a flame and burns it up.

A man sitting alone at night, two gas pumps on an empty road, like in one of the Edward Hopper paintings Lynch loves. A hell of a thing to feel like you're living in one of those damn lonesome country songs.

–CHAPTER TWENTY–

VOLTAGE RISING
(PART FOURTEEN)

The Return is always engaging, but its exploration of *Twin Peaks*'s primal mysteries and metaphors, the saga's unique core, ebbs and flows. In Part Fourteen there's a rewarding quickening. Side streams start feeding into a substantial river that we know will ultimately plunge us over the falls, down into that ever-blooming misty blue rose shape where the water collides with itself.

Gordon Cole, in his Buckhorn, South Dakota, hotel room, talks to Sheriff Frank Truman in Twin Peaks, learns of former Sheriff Harry Truman's illness and that Deputy Hawk has found lost pages of Laura Palmer's diary, which indicate that there are two Coopers.

A floor above, Tammy and Albert are in a larger room that looks like an FBI control center, with stacked servers and screens displaying the bureau's badge symbol. Before Gordon joins them, Albert reiterates the derivation of the Blue Rose concept, dispelling the term's evocative mystery, but providing useful information. (Maintaining mystery while providing information is *Twin Peaks*'s core balancing act.) In Washington State in 1975, the bureau's wonder boys, Gordon Cole and Phillip Jeffries, arrived at a motel room where a gut-shot woman, Lois Duffy, was bleeding on the floor. As she was dying, she said, "I'm like the blue rose." Dead, she disappeared. Standing in the corner was the shooter, Lois Duffy, who did not have a twin sister. In prison, Duffy hanged herself. This convergence of crime and the supernatural was Blue Rose Case Number One.

Albert quizzes Tammy: "What did dying Lois mean, 'I'm like the blue rose.'?" Once again, Tammy displays her depth of knowledge: "There's no blue rose in nature, so Lois was unnatural, a conjured being, a tulpa in Tibetan Buddhist terms. A thought form created by a powerful mind." In Colin Wilson's 1978 book on paranormal research, *Mysteries*, he speaks of a Greenwich Village house haunted by a black-caped figure with a wide-brimmed slouch hat. No person of that description lived or died in the house, but years earlier a writer named William Gibson had, and his best-known creation was the Shadow, who wore a black cape and wide-brimmed slouch hat. Wilson quotes Thomas Beerdsen's paper *Species Metapsychology*: "UFOs, fairies, angels, sasquatches, the Loch Ness Monster, etc., are tulpa manifestations from the unconscious—they are 'dreams' of the/our race." Comic book writer Alvin Schwartz (1916-2011) created stories and dialogues for magazines like *House of Mystery* and *A Date With Judy* (!) before beginning a seventeen-year creative relationship with *Superman* in the 1940s and 1950s. The Man of Steel was conceived by Jerry Siegel and Joe Shuster in 1938, but more than any other writer, Alvin Schwartz, year after year, pondered Superman's strengths and weaknesses and problem-solving abilities. He felt he was providing Superman's "sustaining energy," that the Man of Steel had "a life of his own"; "thinking of him as real made him real." (*An Unlikely Prophet: A Metaphysical Memoir* by the legendary writer of *Superman* and *Batman*). Schwartz felt Clark Kent was vital to the Superman legend, the bland everyman who has vast secret powers hidden within. Schwartz was familiar with the Tibetan tulpa concept and, in a fanciful mood, could imagine that Superman was a tulpa that humdrum Clark Kent created.

As Tammy and Albert conclude their tulpa topic, Gordon Cole arrives and says, "Diane is on her way." Director Lynch cuts to the room's window. The shade is drawn, but there's a disturbing human-shaped shadow outside, twisting at bizarre angles in the window frame, and a sobbing-screeching-screaming sound fills the room: the painfully amplified sound Cole hears as he adjusts his hearing aid. It takes a moment for us to realize that the creepy shadow form is a dangling window washer using his squeegee. In a compressed amount of time, Lynch has linked things perceived as other (Blue Rose cases, tulpas, a phantom window shadow and an eerie sound) with Diane's anticipated arrival. Is Lynch carefully, subtly, prefiguring the idea Diane = tulpa, or something menacing?

Diane joins the group with a jaunty "Deputy Diane reporting." (She's prickly, she's dangerous, but sometimes we've got to love her, those reminders of Cooper's good old FBI Diane). She reluctantly talks to the group about "that night" she spent with the man she thought was Cooper, but we know was Bob-infested Mr. C. (Was this liaison with Diane Mr. C's chance to get a strand of her DNA with which to make her tulpa?) She says "Cooper" mentioned Major Briggs, who'd seemingly died in a fire near Twin Peaks, and Cole tells her Briggs actually died here in South Dakota a few days ago. He mentions the wedding ring found in Briggs's stomach ("To Dougie with love from Janey-E"), and Diane says, "Oh my God, Janey-E's my half sister, but we're estranged." Cole tells the Las Vegas police to investigate Mr. and Mrs. Dougie Jones: "They're wanted in connection to a double murder." For all Cole knows, they may have killed Major Briggs and Ruth.

After Diane leaves, Cole relates Sheriff Truman's news that recently found pages of Laura Palmer's diary indicate that there were/are two Coopers. Cole's feeling a strong vibe of synchronicity, and he tells Tammy and Albert about his latest "Monica Bellucci dream," in which he and the gorgeous Italian actress were having coffee at a Paris café. With the gravitas and beauty of a Madonna, she intones, "We are like the dreamer who dreams and then lives inside the dream." This line from the ancient Hindu scripture the Upanishads is spiritually foundational for Lynch. He quotes it in his *INLAND EMPIRE* chapter in his book *Catching the Big Fish*. And when I stood next to him onstage in front of a sold-out audience at Seattle's Cinerama Theater before *INLAND EMPIRE*'s local premiere, he recited the line to the crowd from a little piece of paper. That night he included lines not in *The Return*: "We are like the spider; we weave our life and then move along in it." These thoughts resonate with Lynch's belief in karma and reincarnation: our actions, our good and bad choices, influence the shape of our lives today, a year from now, and in our next reincarnated lives. The *INLAND EMPIRE* themes of "actions have consequences" and "you reap what you sow" will have a profound bearing on *The Return*'s conclusion.

In *The Return*, after Bellucci speaks of "the dreamer who dreams and then lives inside the dream," she adds something not in the Upanishads: "But who is the dreamer?" In Hindu terms, we're weaving our life webs, enacting our life dreams, separate from each other. But the deepest truth is that this multiplicity of web weavers and life enactors is a manifestation of the single-point oneness of being, the single dream of universal consciousness, played out in multifarious forms. The final line of the Upanishads verse, after the web weaving and dreaming, is "This is true for the entire universe." Lynch spoke this line in Seattle, but it's not in *The Return*. The universe as God's dream, God born of the Unified Field, which can also be the void: each encompasses all.

As Cole relates his dream, there's some technical equipment with red glowing lights behind him, as though Lynch is pouring out his spiritual heart. Bellucci's "Who is the dreamer?" query, placed in the *Twin Peaks* context, where dreams have been important, and linked with David Lynch, who's known for being artistically guided by his subconscious, prompted some *Return* viewers to conclude that the show's narrative is one of the character's dreams (it's a given that the whole thing was dreamed by Lynch and Frost). Could *The Return* be Cooper's dream, while still trapped in the Red Room? This doesn't sound or feel right, but we have more events and people ahead to experience and consider.

Cole tells Albert and Tammy the rest of his dream. Monica Bellucci's line of sight, where she's looking, causes Cole to look over his shoulder, and see himself (in footage from *Fire Walk With Me*) in his FBI office twenty-five years ago, the day Phillip Jeffries mysteriously materialized, pointed at Cooper, and said, "Who do you think that is there?" At the time, this question seemed the utterance of a distraught, disoriented, confused man. But it did appear in a film in which Cooper could both be in the Red Room after Laura's death and not yet have arrived in Twin Peaks to investigate her murder. In *The Return*, the slipperiness, the malleability of time and space are major themes, and personal identity, the possibility of multiple identities, can be an open question. *Fire Walk With Me* established the idea that Jeffries was somewhere unstuck in time, unsure of when it was. Mr. C's and Ray Monroe's interactions with the voice of Jeffries, or someone pretending to be him, have deepened the paranormal traveler's mystery. We'll soon be on Jeffries's threshold and perhaps learn who he is and what he wants. He's a hard man to nail down. As Cole says to Albert and Tammy in 2016, Jeffries "apparently didn't appear" in Cole's office that day. As Cole ends his dream narration, which references Jeffries questioning Cooper's identity, he has an epiphany: "Damn! I hadn't remembered that." As with the Log Lady's many oracular promptings over the years, a wise woman (Monica Bellucci) has pointed our good guy seekers in a fruitful direction but left the full, broad challenge of their quest to them, as Lynch and Frost do for us.

Talk about the flux of time and space: when, from April, 1990 to June, 1991 we watched the *Twin Peaks* pilot and thirty episodes over fourteen months, it was easy to forget that the show covered one month of time in Twin Peaks. The day of the scene with Cole, Albert, and Tammy is the morning after the nighttime scene at the RR diner, with Bobby, Norma, and Ed. It's almost a surprise when Bobby tells them about finding some "stuff" that Major Briggs left for him and local law keepers, since *The Return* hadn't mentioned it for a month of weekly viewing time. Our time is longer than *The Return*'s time. At any rate, Lynch and Frost have built our anticipation for our heroes' trek into the heart of the Deep Story, as mapped out for them by Major Briggs on a little piece of paper twenty-five years ago.

With their backpacks, a compass, and the paper, Bobby, Sheriff Truman, Hawk, and Andy walk where there's no trail, in the green leafy light punctuated by giant, dark tree trunks, a sacred space that Lynch likens to "a cathedral" and that reminds him of dreamy times as a small boy with his father in the forest. As a boy, Bobby spent time with his father here, near the secret site where Major Briggs listened for sounds, maybe messages, from space and one night heard, "Cooper, Cooper, Cooper," linking Cooper and himself in an epic cosmic battle against evil. Our trekkers come upon Jack Rabbit's Palace, the looming twenty-foot-tall tree stump where young Bobby and his father used to swap "tall tales." As if to counterpoint Lynch's awestruck "cathedral" atmosphere, the stump's wide base has eerie ancient roots like blood veins into the earth, and its ragged, broken-off crown is topped with devilish horn spikes. In terms of *The Return*'s visual patterning, the towerlike stump reminds us of the Fireman's abode atop a rocky tower and the rock-based Mansion high above the purple sea where Cooper and Naido glowed pink together. In symbology, towers have a dual meaning: ascendancy and a deepening movement toward knowledge (Lynch dives deep to transcend).

The men proceed beyond Jack Rabbit's Palace and come upon one of David Lynch's most quietly magical tableaus, one of his dreams: a gentle green slope down into pale ground fog, sparking with electricity, misting away and revealing a pale circle in the earth, a pale barren tree, with a naked woman lying at its base. Over the *Twin Peaks* years, Lynch has shown us naked horizontal women in nature, perhaps inspired by Marcel Duchamp's 1969 art installation *Étant donnés*, on exhibit at the time Lynch lived in Philadelphia. Laura Palmer lay dead on a lake shore, Teresa Banks floated dead in a river, but this woman stirs; she's alive, and she's Naido.

As Naido, watched over by Andy, makers wordless, vulnerable-animal sounds and the electrical fog evaporates, we realize that this is a momentous occasion:

metaphorically, the Log Lady's log has gained another branch of knowledge; a continuum has gained a new element; a pattern has expanded. It makes sense that Naido's dress would have disintegrated as she fell through interdimensional space from her Part Two sacrifice for Cooper on the box in space. Did she just now land, cushioned by the fog, a pillow of atmosphere provided by the Fireman? What time is it? Frank Truman to the men: "It's 2:53, fellas." Just as Major Briggs's little map indicated, the men found Naido 253 yards from Jack Rabbit's Palace. Two fifty-three was the time when Mr. C evaded the cosmic edict to return to the Red Room and when Cooper was going through the giant electrical socket, transforming into Dougie. 253/2:53 in space and time. Since the time-linked activities involving Mr. C and Cooper happened weeks ago in our viewing time, the current 2:53 references with Naido really hit us with the feeling that all time is now, that Lynch and Frost are adept at layering realities.

The Fireman's primal power is asserted as a sparking vortex appears above Andy, whisks him up, and lands him in the Fireman's black-and-white stronghold, in the chair where, in *The Return*'s first moments, Cooper received clues about his path forward. The Fireman gave Cooper verbal information, but Andy is schooled visually. The Fireman raises his hand, and a device appears in Andy's hands. It has points like a star shape and is formed of layered triangles. (In Lynch's 1977 *Ronnie Rocket* screenplay, a "triangulator" device formed of intersecting triangles helps the heroes break the circuit of bad electricity.)

Lynch presents the Fireman and his realm to us in a soot-and-silver black-and-white that evokes old tintype photographs etched on metal. The Fireman's stately, slow movements, his bald dome of vast wisdom, his huge, shadowy abode and archaic furnishings give his doings the timeless air of alchemy, magic, fairy tale, fable. The star-pointed device that materialized in Andy's hands has a central spout, and a stream of translucent smoke rises from it like the genie emerging from Aladdin's lamp, like the 1974 light beam that uploaded masses of cosmic information into author Philip K. Dick's mind and the projector beam of spiritual adept Paramahansa Yogananda's (*Autobiography of a Yogi*) "Cosmic Motion Picture." Andy tips his head back to watch the rising smoke, and we see a glowing white circle recessed in the ceiling above him. It's movie time.

The Fireman shows Andy, and Lynch shows us, the most significant participants, the key, narrative-driving points of *The Return*'s deep story, an abstraction of its epic journey. The New York glass box-enclosed demon. The Dark Mother spewing Bob and maleficent eggs from her mouth. The scurrying Woodsmen readying the convenience store for the evil invaders. The head Woodsman intoning "Got a light?" Phone lines crackling with bad electricity, Laura Palmer's homecoming queen photo attended by two winged angels, superimposed on the Red Room curtains. Naido naked on the ground, in front of the Red Room curtains, a fusion of two faces: Mr. C and Cooper. The number six telephone pole in some location we've never seen before. Andy behind Lucy, hands on her shoulders, urging her forward like a waif child, then stepping back, leaving Lucy standing alone, her expression focused, distressed. And Andy sees himself, holding Naido's hand as he was a moment ago in the woods, as though she's a summation, an emblematic signpost to what's been and what's to come.

So much of the image parade is new to Andy: the glass box, Bob's "birth," the Woodsmen, Laura in a beatified state. Andy doesn't say "I understand" but we know Andy has absorbed deep meanings. In the opening moments of *The Return*, Cooper said, "I understand" after the Fireman gave him verbal signs indicating his role in the grand game that would proceed onward after Cooper left the Red Room. But Cooper, and we, didn't count on him getting electrozapped, space/time warped into being Dougie, a super-constrained version of our Special Agent: Dougie, like the Red Room, another form of entrapment for Cooper. The entrapment-by-body idea recalls, in Lynch's *The Elephant Man*, John Merrick's golden, refined soul encased within his misshapen cocoon of flesh. Cooper's journey in *The Return* is not the one we expected. But the more we see of what the Fireman can do, and the way the disembodied head/spirit of Major Briggs is in the air/consciousness of *The Return*, we sense that things are happening as they're meant to be.

In Lynch's *Dune* (1984), for which he wrote the screenplay from Frank Herbert's novel, a third-stage guild navigator, a long, insect-pupa-like body with a massive cranial dome head, had evolved from a normal man into a being with an extended life span, prescient vision, and the ability to bend space and facilitate intergalactic travel. The navigator exists in a controlled environment, never leaving a locomotive-sized glass-and-metal conveyance, but he wields vast power, manipulating people and worlds. In the original *Twin Peaks*, the Giant, which Mark Frost says was a Lynch creation, was a force for good who offered Cooper cryptic, evocative verbal clues like "It is happening again" and"The owls are not what they seem." The Giant would materialize in the environs of *Twin Peaks*, but it was up to Cooper to physically act on the imparted information.

In *The Return*, the Giant has evolved into the Fireman, who, like *Dune*'s navigator resides in his own atmosphere, influencing human doings indirectly, like the gods of yore. Maybe the Giant was a tulpa, the Fireman's mind creation, who could appear in the world Cooper was familiar with. In *The Return*, the Fireman's power has evolved to a level where he can bring Cooper and Andy to him at will, and we've seen him create the spirit being of Laura and send her to Earth before she was born. But like David Lynch, he likes to stay home, inside. Lynch, as though embodying the folklore of the supersmart person who doesn't know how to play catch in the backyard, has no exercise routine, and during the first run of *Twin Peaks*, he said, "The body exists to carry the brain around."

Dale Cooper, in the impaired state of being Dougie, may hold the information, the action plan the Fireman told him, somewhere in his psyche, but he can't access it until, somehow, he wakes up. But Andy's mindset of understanding is already in motion. In the original *Twin Peaks*, this good-hearted, decent, gawky, endearingly human fellow had some heroic moments, but now he's the man with the plan. Fragments of thought and experience have coalesced; forward-moving positive energy has been generated.

Andy, having been returned to Naido and his comrades in the forest, tells them she's very important and must be protected; people want her dead. He's in a commanding role, saying, "We'll take her back to town and lock her in a jail cell for safekeeping." With Naido in his arms, Andy leads the trek back. The other men have no memory of Andy having been transported away and returned.

True to Lynch's visual-emotional structuring of *The Return*'s narrative, Naido, safe in the sheriff's office jail cell, is wearing Lucy's pink bathrobe. Pink like the divine luminosity that enlightened author Philip K. Dick, like the light Naido and Cooper emanated when they met on Cooper's journey from the Red Room and communed with unstated emotion. Pink, the traditional color of love, which no longer glowed from Cooper's skin after Naido sacrificed herself to aid his progress and fell away in space.

In Part Four, we met Andy and Lucy's son, Wally Brando (Michael Cera), like Lucy a relatively small person, who's innocent of the big wide world but ready to test his wings, riding his big Harley into the adventure that is America. Maybe because Cera played the unlikely world savior in the cosmic battle of *Scott Pilgrim Versus the World*, it seemed he might circle back to help defend good against evil in *The Return*'s final battle. We know how much Lynch loves *The Wizard of Oz*, in which the self-described "small and meek" Dorothy emerges as a potent challenger of the Wicked Witch. Lynch and Frost have a gift for making atypical creative choices, like embedding their usually potent hero Cooper within the relatively ineffectual Dougie, so it seems likely they will break the traditional hero persona mold as they play out their tale. As the saying goes, the battle doesn't always go to the obviously strong. Alpha males and females don't always win the day. In *Twin Peaks*, rudely aggressive people like Officer Chad, even if they work for the sheriff, are frowned upon; they generate bad karma.

A couple of working guys wearing Great Northern security uniforms, one of them James Marshall, are sitting on the hotel loading dock at night, taking a break, chatting amiably, not smoking. It strikes us that Diane is the only *The Return* character we see smoking (one puff for Gordon Cole), a sign of 2017's social climate. It's good to see that James Marshall has a steady job, and we meet Freddie Sykes (Jake Wardle), an import from London's East End with an endearing Cockney accent. His first name is Lynch's homage to the gifted British cinematographer Freddie Francis (1917-2007), Lynch's friend, who shot *The Elephant Man*, *Dune*, and *The Straight Story*. At a distance you might mistake Freddie Sykes for Wally Brando: neither one is an imposing man of rugged girth. The sequence of images that the Fireman showed to Andy indicates that Andy and Lucy will figure prominently in *The Return*'s climactic section, so having Wally Brando also present might make it too much of an unlikely-hero family affair. But it's so like Lynch to bring in a character who's almost a double for Wally Brando: *The Return* is a vortex of echoes and mirrors.

In *The Return*, Lynch and Frost immerse us in a world where above, beyond, inside immediate surface reality we feel mysterious forces at work, energies that reveal themselves in scary, awe-inspiring, sometimes delightfully absurd ways. East Ender Freddie is in Twin Peaks, Washington, wearing a green British gardening glove on his right hand because the Fireman told him to. It's James's birthday this evening, so Freddie treats him to the tale. How, walking home from another night of drinking, the young man realized he was wasting his life; he should be helping people. With this life-changing thought in mind, Freddie was drawn up into a tunnel of air where he met the Fireman, who told him to buy the green glove, put it on his right hand, and go to Twin Peaks, Washington, USA, where he will find his destiny. Still in London, and attacked by an aggressive, belligerent bloke, Freddie punched the guy once and realized the glove had phenomenal power. A golden circuit has been formed linking the Fireman, Freddie's mind, his determination to do good, and his right hand of physical action. He literally can't take the glove off, and he says, "It's a part of me": the alchemical transmutation of positive thoughts into positive behavior. Freddie's green glove is like Doctor Jacoby's golden shovel, the physical manifestation of the positive inner force that can shovel away the shit sludge of negativity. Is the Fireman like Lynch's Maharishi, a being of spiritual power who can show us how to manifest universal positivity, to "find our destiny" doing good?

Lynch has always been a man of no, or few, words when it comes to saying anything about his view of his own work. We know he reflexively sees things in pairs and is super sensitive to "contrast," opposing poles of force in, or out, of balance. Speaking of *The Return*, he said, "You've got Dougie and you've got Bob, and there's a big difference between them. And you've got the frog-moth."

The Fireman can properly be characterized as "a presence of power and dignity." When young David Lynch saw photographs of Indian yogis meditating, he used those words to describe their faces. Through disciplined spiritual practice, the yogi seeks a state of mind in which their personal spiritual moral order is a reflection of universal, cosmic order. As Yogis gain more mental acuity and consciousness expansion, they develop extraordinary powers, many of which the Fireman exhibits: knowledge of the past, present, and future; knowledge of what is subtle, distant, and hidden; knowledge of the firmament; the ability to levitate. He possesses an irresistible will and is a beacon of goodwill.

If the Fireman shines a spiritual light, the frog-moth casts shadows, and as we intuited earlier in *The Return*, the morally corrosive shadows reside within Sarah Palmer. Lynch gives us a stunning certification of this fact when Sarah, an inveterate homebody in later life, goes out to a Twin Peaks dive bar one night. Maybe, like the *Wild at Heart* character Marcello Santos, her inner voice is saying, "I'm in a killin' mood." Though you'd never guess it as she primly takes a stool at the bar and quietly orders a drink. She is the town's Grieving Woman, living with the knowledge that her husband raped their daughter for years, then killed her and killed himself. She's tortured by loss, but also by presence, a white horse that appears and disappears in her house, as does the face of the one known as Bob, and decades after she lost Laura and Leland, her TV set seems stuck in a repeating space-time loop, like her endless days and nights of smoking and drinking, what Stephen King would call "the hell of repetition."

Leland acted out his evil impulses because he was possessed by Bob, who came into our world at the same time as the egg that hatched the frog-moth, which promptly crawled into young Sarah's mouth. Lynch has called Bob "an abstraction with a human form," a manifestation of evil as a mysterious entity that enlivens a fictional story. But he's serious business, a fundamental aspect of the human heart and psyche: our shadow side. It disturbs our egos, our preferred public personas, to acknowledge that we harbor dark, socially unacceptable thoughts and urges, the capacity to do evil. But whether it's due to original sin, our fallen natures, or the way our brains have evolved over millennia, we have a dark side. The point is to choose not to harm others with it; think about it, channel its energy, use its power, maybe make art with it, but center your selfhood on the gold that stands out against the darkness.

In Lynch's *Lost Highway*, the Mystery Man, a personification of the human shadow side, tells Fred Madison, "I don't go where I'm not invited." Without being fully conscious of it, Fred did invite the darkness in, yielded to his malevolent impulses, killed his wife, and was lost. In *Blue Velvet*, Jeffrey Beaumont flirts with the psychosexual violence personified in Frank Booth, but ultimately rejects it and chooses the righteous path. And, of high relevance in *The Return*, in *Fire Walk With Me* Laura Palmer, seemingly lost in a morass of drugs, sadomasochistic sex, prostitution, and self-loathing, became aware that the catalyst for her dark behavior was the Ur darkness of Bob, his hunger for her body and soul, acted out through his possession of her father, Leland. Wanting to contain the dark contagion and keep it from spreading to those she loves, she heroically sacrifices herself, letting Leland/Bob kill her. Her choice is beatified by Christian winged angels, and in her *The Return* post death state in the Red Room, she shows Cooper that behind her eyes, filling her being, she is pure white light.

Actor Ray Wise, who so affectingly portrayed Leland's menace, regret, sadness, and soul torment, told me that Leland was Bob's victim, just as Laura was, that Leland wasn't aware when Bob was inside him, making him do horrible things. In the original *Twin Peaks* and *Fire Walk With Me*, when Leland was being his baddest, we would see flashes of Bob's grimy face melded with Leland's visage.

In the last 1991 *Twin Peaks* episode, Lynch shows us Bob's face reflected back when Cooper, just changed to Bad Cooper, looks in a mirror. In *The Return*, Mr. C says to Bob in the mirror, "I'm glad you're still with me." Mr. C is the shadow side of Cooper, plus Bob, so since Cooper is a more self-aware, spiritually seeking person than Leland, it makes sense that unlike Leland, he would be cognizant of his dark passenger as a co-creator of his being. In *The Return*, Lynch and Frost, as they do with the concept of the Blue Rose, choose to make Bob less ethereal, more prosaically defined. He's a being/face in a bubble that we glimpse for a moment when the Woodsmen are repairing Mr. C's bullet-ripped midriff. Perhaps beneath our own conscious awareness, we know that a computer-generated image is no Frank Silva.

Bob and his Dark Mother entered our world when the sky was torn by the first atomic bomb explosion, loosing an alien-dimension flood of horrors into the New Mexico desert. Among the invading spew was the egg that hatched the frog-moth, the creature that crawled into young Sarah's house, into her mouth, into her head. In the early 1970s, before Lynch made *Eraserhead*, he wrote a script called *Gardenback*, in which Henry and Mary live happily in their home. But one day Henry "looks at a girl, and something crosses from her to him. That something is an insect, which grows in Henry's attic, which is like his mind. The house is like his head. And the thing grows and metamorphoses into this monster that overtakes him. He doesn't become it, but he has to deal with it, and it drives him to completely ruin his home."

Lynch grew up in an idyllic world that he saw as vulnerable to "a sort of wild pain and decay." Everything was beautiful, but "you just look a little bit closer, and it's all red ants." To this day, Lynch protectively buttons the top button of his shirt and is uneasy about leaving his house, the security of his "perfect setup," where he can get ideas and shape them into art, the products of his head. Over the years, in his drawings, paintings, prints, photos, films, and TV shows, heads (which read pictorially as two windows and a door) and houses are invaded by dark thoughts and forces, wounded and haunted. Lynch feels he hides his fears in his work, in which the mind's/home's vulnerability is primal. Aside from death, Alzheimer's disease is humankind's main fear, the terror of losing your personhood. *Twilight Zone* creator Rod Serling felt that the base theme of the show was the fear of not being able to trust your own thoughts and memories, your sense of reality.

To have *The Return*'s young Sarah be the New Mexico girl invaded by the insect creature from the dimension of Bob and the Dark Mother was a brilliant artistic choice, which synchronized perfectly with the Sarah we've known since the 1990s. Grown-up Sarah was unease personified: anguished with loss and guilt after Laura and Leland's deaths, but earlier disturbed by things she saw and heard that others didn't, with an inner turmoil she didn't understand that twisted her smile into a grimace. Living in a pure white colonial home where, just behind her conscious mind, the dark spirit of Bob was having his way with her husband and daughter, Sarah could sense something stirring and squirming: "What is going on in this house?" And in her?

Twenty-five years after asking that question, Sarah has long been alone, in her house of dim light and phantom sounds, where the TV repeats cycles of animal and human violence, where she senses oncoming waves of shadow, the unending "bad story." When Leland was a boy who wanted "to play with fire," he was morally weak, open to temptation, and he let Bob enter his spirit. As he committed his heinous adult actions, he was both predisposed to violate moral boundaries and innocently possessed by an evil entity: darkness from inside and outside. In *The Return*, young Sarah is innocence invaded and violated, as her future daughter, Laura, will be. As a young woman, Laura learned the nature of her tormentor, defied him, and chose to escape in death. And Leland, finally aware of the horrors he had perpetrated, took his own life by bashing his head and was forgiven by Laura in the afterworld. So how aware is the aging Sarah of her dark passenger? And aside from its general evil nature, what is it really? Some kin to Bob, or to a Woodsman, or . . . ?

When an unwanted resident entered Sarah in girlhood, beneath her conscious awareness, some part of her spirit was absorbed by a dark web of alien intelligence, a malignant hive mind. In the original *Twin Peaks*, something vague and disturbingly undefined was roiling within Sarah. Now, in her later years, she still feels existentially disoriented, but she's familiar with the dark force within her and knows how to use it.

Lynch has always loved the pictorial drama of showing figures emerging out of darkness, and we see Sarah step out of the shadows and approach the entrance of a dive bar on the outskirts of town. She and her home are so symbiotically connected that it's surprising to see her out late at night. Maybe it's feeding time.

She sits at the bar in the back room. Compared with the lively Roadhouse and Double R diner, this place is almost dead. Her (appropriate) Bloody Mary arrives, and so does an unwelcome companion, an aging, sleazy, belligerent guy who's almost a caricature of toxic masculinity. He comes on to her in gutter language, and when she spurns his advances, he rages that she's a "lesbo." Her manner has been soft-spoken and polite, but she says, "Do you really want to fuck with this," and, as Laura did in the Red Room with Cooper, Sarah pulls aside her face to reveal her inner essence. Laura's was the righteous white light of pure goodness. Behind Sarah's eyes is the black circle mouth of the glass box devouring demon, with a darting serpent tongue like a lightning flash. And there's a big white left hand, the symbol of enacted intent, with a black ring finger (in Part Four Gordon Cole noted that this "spiritual mound" finger of Mr. C left a reversed fingerprint), then a grinning mouth showing weirdly perfect teeth, the facade hiding Sarah's evil. In an instant, the peek inside Sarah is gone; her mouth seeks her harassing bar mate's throat, and tears it out. She screams, pretends to be horrified; the bartender looks down at the dead man with no throat in his pool of blood. The bartender's suspicious of Sarah, but she's an old lady with spotless lips.

The 1945 New Mexico atomic bomb blast opened a thrust of alien, extradimensional, maleficent entities from some other place into our world. Just as the spectrum of American criminality can include dapper Al Capone and grubby Charles Manson, the evil denizens include Bob, the Woodsmen, the Dark Mother, and her hungry demon. They came on strong a few decades ago, but how far have they advanced their cause? They've killed a few people, corrupted some souls, but how does that stack up against the bomb America dropped on Japan or Japan's sneak attack on Pearl Harbor? Mark Frost has said that "the frog-moth brought the evil that we've been dealing with for twenty-seven years in *Twin Peaks*." Frost has said that none of *The Return*'s main plotlines are out of sequence, that most of what we see is happening chronologically. The Fireman and Dido send Laura's golden spirit to Earth before we see the frog-moth hatch and enter young Sarah. It's a given that *Twin Peaks* is full of secrets, things that happen hidden inside people's heads/offscreen/ somewhere in the cosmos, that may or not be revealed over time, and time itself can be a looping roller coaster ride. But perhaps both the frog-moth/Judy force essence and the golden Laura essence have been deposited in Sarah, who births corporeal Laura. It's common to feel like various aspects of ourselves, our sacred ideals and wayward impulses, are at war with each other, but we strive for a unified harmonic balance that's a life's work to maintain. It's a rare *Twin Peaks* character who does not exhibit a multi-faceted nature. Judy, Bob, the Woodsmen are unalloyed agents of darkness; the Fireman, Dido, and Major Briggs bring only light. Multivalenced Cooper, who shows up as a number of separate people in *The Return*, is the mediator between darkness and light, the human being who can attempt to facilitate a reconciliation between powerful physical, moral and spiritual forces. Just as the Fireman, thanks to his panoramic vision, has made past moves that we're finding out about now, maybe grandmaster Cosmic Evil sent Bob into Leland to snuff out Laura, but she outsmarted them, evolving through death towards her golden potential.

So if Sarah, ostensibly a good, grieving mother, actually harbors the body-shredding, soul-harvesting Dark Mother, will this Matriarch of Damnation battle daughter Laura in *The Return*'s finale? Will we even see Laura, who's "the One," again? She's been gone for twelve episodes.

Part Fourteen ends at the Roadhouse, with the group Lissie: three electric guitars, a woman (Elisabeth Corrin Maurus) singing. Her hair is long and blonde like Laura Palmer's. Is Lynch reminding us of *Twin Peaks*'s long lost muse, giving us a foretaste of where *The Return*'s journey is going? The woman strums her guitar, the color of the yellow rose of Texas. What if in Lynch's and Frost's minds, Laura wasn't in Twin Peaks or the Red Room, but in a West Texas town, with all her familiar problems and situations? Maurus sings of a woman who's "been living with the firelight," and "living life on the edge/Slip and fall if I take one more step"; she's "going rogue in the wild, wild west." The woman is "so far from my home"; if she falls, "who's going to catch me?" Maurus has spent time with Lynch, and her creative mindset is akin to his: "I want my songs to be able to go to dark places, but there is always hope there," she told *Headliner*. The woman in the song believes there's a world where "All that you lost you get back." It's a fine dream, but the night is long: "Are you out there to take away my fear?" Can you hear her, Dale Cooper?

Juxtaposed with *The Return*'s "Wild West" song on Maurus's *My Wild West* album is the song "Hollywood," which hints at an ultimate destination for *The Return*: "Mamma, come meet me at the station/I'm coming home for a while/I'm ready for that conversation/About the way I'm running wild/And suddenly, I'm a child."

–CHAPTER TWENTY-ONE–

GOLDEN LOG, ELECTRIC FORK
(PART FIFTEEN)

War, pestilence, famine; pollution of air, water, food; greedy, arrogant corporate vampires sucking the world dry: a swamp of shit for Dr. Jacoby to dwell on. He's a seasoned spiritual traveler with an all-encompassing mind, and rather than feeling powerless and defeated, he embraces problems, pain, and misery with the attitude of Tibetan Buddhist Chögyam Trungpa Rinpoche: "Without your help I would not have any way to work with my journey at all." Awareness of self and world stimulates the confronting of negativity with good, positive action, symbolized by his hand-produced gold shovels, to "shovel your way out of the shit." The shovels can be seen as a metaphor for alchemy, transmuting base materials into gold, and for meditation, converting the stuff of life into bliss consciousness, which inspires positive actions in the world. In *The Return*, have Lynch and Frost, consciously or subliminally, produced life lessons, a teaching tool for spiritual growth?

Nadine, with her years of emotional travails, has been absorbing Dr. Jacoby's ranting, motivating broadcasts, and they've enlivened a spirit of calm reason and compassionate resolve within her. Part Fifteen opens on a sunny Twin Peaks day, with Nadine, even with one eye patch covered, striding straight and confidently toward us, carrying a gold shovel on her shoulder like a badge of honor. Her destination is Big Ed's Gas Farm, to see her estranged husband, Ed, the man who accidentally shot out her eye, who's been in love with Norma Jennings for years but has stayed loyal to Nadine out of decency and guilt and endured all her wild emotional ups and downs.

They face each other in the sunshine, both wearing life-affirming red. Ed and Nadine care about each other, but they've been stuck for years, unable to move on with their lives. Now, sweetly, with her comical earnest intensity at a nonpathological level, Nadine releases them both. *Twin Peaks* has presented a "new Nadine" at various times over the years, but this is the settled and serene real thing. She confesses to being a "manipulative bitch," while Ed's been "a saint," and urges him to enjoy a happy life with Norma. They part with a loving hug, and Nadine marches off home, a loyal member of the gold shovel brigade.

Lynch arcs his visually and emotionally warm red-and-gold theme to the Double R diner, where Ed parks his gold pickup truck and then parks himself at the counter on a red-circle-topped seat. Finally, his dream of love will come true. But Lynch and Frost love to foil our expectations, keep us off balance; that's life, after all. They give us a pause when Walter enters and Norma greets him warmly. Ed bitterly tells the waitress that he'd like a cyanide tablet with his coffee. But he's amassed so much good karma over the years that the universe seems to be rooting for him. In her never-unpleasant manner, Norma tells Walter that she's buying out her multiple-Double R-locations franchise. So that's that, and he departs. When Walter sat down in a back booth with Norma, Ed dropped his eyes, stopped watching. His eyes are still closed; he doesn't know that Norma's dismissed Walter.

Lynch knows that reality is in layers, and from the moment that Ed arrives at the Double R, his time there is sonically supported, upheld, by the soundtrack bedrock of Otis Redding singing "I've Been Loving You Too Long," his voice quavering with gut-wrenching passion. Sometimes in films the mood of a pop song is used as a counterpoint to the tone of the scene or a character. Lynch has spoken to me about his intuitive artistic certainty when elements come together "correctly"; he senses that "the harmonics" are correct, as though composing and balancing a painting. Singer-songwriter Otis Redding wrote his melancholy lament in 1965, weary of touring from town to town, always far from home. We all know the feeling of having a song from our past pop into our heads, evoked by an emotion or a situation we're experiencing right now: one of Marcel Proust's "involuntary memories." Ed must have heard "I've Been Loving You Too Long" when he was a teenager, fifty years ago, and it's like his emotional autobiography. Now he's sitting, eyes closed, at the Double R counter, free from Nadine but once again convinced that he and Norma will never be together; the song expresses his heart and soul. He's tired; his time with Norma has been "so wonderful," but her "love is growing cold" while "my love is growing stronger . . . I can't stop now. Please, please, please don't make me stop now." As the torn-voiced words fill our ears, Lynch holds the shot of Ed with eyes closed, lost in his sad, yearning reverie. But into the shot comes a woman's hand, gently touching his shoulder. His eyes open (the sleeper awakens), and his long-held dream comes true.

Ed says, "Marry me," Norma says, "Yes," and they smile and kiss. Shelly stands holding a pot of steaming coffee (*Twin Peaks*' sacrament), blessing the moment with her awe-struck smile. Lynch knows that the world is full of "wild pain and decay," but also that the world is based on the ultimately stronger power of love. As Ed and Norma embrace, we hear Otis Redding swooning, repeating the refrain "I love you." The "I love you" continues, blanketing an exterior shot of the Double R and its twin mountains backdrop in warm light. Then, to Redding's "Good God almighty, I love you," a shot of blue sky, wispy white clouds like divine brushstrokes: an abstraction of Lynch's love for people, for nature, for the artistic reality he's created, for all that is.

Of course such sublime, luminous moments are but half of *Twin Peaks*, if that:

night must fall. From the blue skies that are like a protective dome above Ed and Norma's union, Lynch cuts to an equally beautiful image of darkness. We're on a road, deep in the night. An endless repetition of black telephone poles and wires, barely discernible against a charcoal sky, whooshes by, accompanied by that electrical clicking rhythm. The vibrant circuit of bad electricity must span the globe by now: people stuck on lost highways, phonograph needles stuck on grooves of bad karma, your nightmares endlessly rerunning on your TV screen.

We've seen the dark, sooty image of phone poles and wires before. It was part of the visual information that the Fireman showed Andy, and it certifies that the Fireman can see the Future, including the dark side's point of view, for it's Mr. C we're riding with, seeing the dark poles and wires go by. We've viewed the convenience store before, when the pixilated Woodsmen scampered around readying it for Bob and the extradimensional invaders. But now we're there, as Mr. C gets out of his truck by the twin gas pumps and the wood structure charred by ineffable fires.

Lynch establishes the wide-view pictorial reality of the store and Mr. C and his truck against the forest background before floating us through shifting planes of reality to the presence of the "long lost Phillip Jeffries," as Gordon Cole once called him. A grubby Woodsman, like a shadow with pale eyes, leads Mr. C up a staircase on the side of the building, the two figures flickering away in mid-climb. We hear the Trinity-blast discordant violins of Pendrecki's "Threnody for the Victims of Hiroshima," like the sonic afterbirth of the A-bomb-spawned arrival of the store and the Woodsmen. As Mr. C advances, we see a couple of the convenience store denizens from *Fire Walk With Me*. A Woodsman throws a switch that flashes some electricity so that Mr. C can proceed. This seems like a major clue: Mr. C and a Woodsman in the same frame, interacting on the same plane. So in the Zone, Mr. C could have shot Ruth in the eye, then the Woodsmen segmented her and Major Briggs and deposited and posed their body parts in Ruth's apartment. Maybe some mystical electricity transported Mr. C away before he could read Ruth's coordinates, and Bill Hastings was face down so he couldn't have seen all this action.

Back at the convenience store, on his way to see Jeffries, Mr. C glimpses a red-suited figure wearing a white mask, accompanied by a high whining sound. Lynch fine-tunes the soundscapes of his films as carefully as he composes his images, and the hearing-impaired subtitles for *The Return* are very specifically detailed, just like the few pages of the show's sound cue script that have leaked out. The red figure's garb evokes the Red Room curtains, his white mask recalls the inner white light behind Laura's face; but we also remember that in *Fire Walk With Me* a monkey face behind the mask said, "Judy" (always the potential for darkness and light in Lynchland). The sound subtitle accompanying this image says "high-pitched rewinding." Of course, that's the high, almost screaming sound of a VHS tape rewinding at top speed, vibrating your machine as though it's going to fly apart. Rewinding, playing it again: former reality existing now. In *Mulholland Drive*, Lynch used a tape recording of a song still playing on after the singer went silent and collapsed to the floor as a metaphor for a soul persisting after death. *Mulholland Drive* itself was an homage to Lynch's beloved *Sunset Boulevard*, an entire film narrated to us, and relived, by a dead man. In *Lynch on Lynch*, Lynch said, "It's interesting doing something twice—the same piece of material two different ways. In *Blue Velvet*, the song 'In Dreams' is played twice, and it's got a completely different feeling each time, and a different meaning. Or maybe it's the same meaning, but you see it a different way. All the characters are dealing with questions of identity. Like everyone." These words, from years ago, and *The Return*'s high-pitched rewinding, the idea of things happening again, differently, foreshadow the further story of the blonde girl who lived down the lane: Laura as she was then (1990-91), and as she is now (2016). And hidden aspects of Sarah, her face at one point juxtaposed with the white-masked face, are coming to light.

In the depths of the convenience store, the Woodsman guides Mr. C through the room with flowered wallpaper that appeared in Laura's dream in *Fire Walk With Me*, which mirrored the room in a painting in which she saw herself reflected—in two places/states of being at once (as Laura says in *The Return*, "I am dead, and yet I live.") Mr. C and the Woodsman pass through a space where forest trees and a dark room blend together, then they climb a staircase and open a door that leads to the dim, empty courtyard/parking lot of a large motel. This is the Dutchman's, and a woman takes Mr. C to the door of Room 8 and lets him in. His progression has been like a dark ceremony, and he's arrived at a dim, barren room with sourceless flickering light and an electrical buzzing/crackling sound. In front of Mr. C: an old iron radiator against a dirty brown wall. Just as we remember that forty years ago, in *Eraserhead*, troubled Henry found a delivering angel in just such a radiator, the radiator and wall in front of Mr. C fades in and out of the room Jeffries occupies beyond, reminding us we're in a mysterious, complex space-time matrix, which can also be called David Lynch's head, a compendium of his artistry.

Actors Frank Silva (Bob) and Don E. Davis (Major Briggs) had died well before Lynch started shooting; David Bowie (Phillip Jeffries) just before, and Michael J. Anderson (the Man from Another Place) was not asked to be in the production. Lynch chose to represent Silva and Davis photographically; we see their heads and faces. For the Man from Another Place, Lynch entered the realm of biomorphism and presented us with an evolved form: a pale, sycamore-like tree sparking with electricity, topped by a blobby "head" with a mouth hole. The thing resembles an anatomy book "brain tree" illustration of the human nervous system: a tree form of nerve tendrils topped by the brain, electricity implied in the illustration.

For the nonextant Bowie/the "nowhere" Philip Jeffries, Lynch went the biomechanical route. And he gave us a little visual foreshadowing as Mr. C walked across the motel courtyard toward Room 8; there was a dissipating steam cloud in the dark air. At one point in Lynch's *The Grandmother* (1970), the old dear flits around a room making a whistling sound like a boiling tea kettle, and in *The Return*, Phillip Jeffries's essence is contained within a black metal teapot form bigger and taller than a man. The massive core form, with its perpendicular jutting armature spout, does look like a teapot, but Lynch calls it a machine. And Lynch feels that his favorite themes, motifs, and mechanisms of expression are his particular machinery. Growing up in the evergreen, organic bower of the Northwest, and being hypersensitive to contrasting polarities, Lynch was struck by the otherness, the surging power of inorganic machines, the metal shapes containing the forces of fire, smoke, steam, electricity that could make things. They were alive, animated by processes, like people, like the Tin Man in *The Wizard of Oz*, like the factory of the cosmos.

When Lynch was a young art student in Philadelphia, he must have seen Marcel Duchamp's renowned painting *The Bride* (1912) at the Philadelphia Museum of Art: a woman portrayed as metallic, geometric shapes linked by a plumbing system both mechanical and biological. As Duchamp said in a lecture, *The Bride* is a "juxtaposition of mechanical and visceral forms." In the early decades of the twentieth century, Duchamp was aware of the recent discoveries of radioactivity and X-rays, with their power to transform matter and make visible the invisible, and he could see his *Bride* as what Duchamp biographer Calvin Tomkins calls "a three-dimensional projection of a four-dimensional being." In that era, Picasso spoke of painting "not what you see but what you know is there," and Lynch feels that an artist can capture a bigger picture than he can perceive. Duchamp felt artworks were not understood through words and the intellect, but by way of the "esthetic echo" of the work, an experience like "religious faith or sexual attraction" (*Duchamp: A Biography*). In a single word, emotion. A state of experiential/emotional understanding that Lynch told me was an "inner knowing." A circuit of energy flows between the art object and the spectator; the spectator completes the art work.

In his 1984 film, *Dune*, Lynch presented the third-stage guild navigator, a huge, pale sluglike creature that had evolved from a normal man, living in a metal-and-glass cylinder that was part of its being. *Dune* also presented a metallic-electrical machine whose structure included a meowing cat. As Lynch once told me, he's moved by "the organic and the inorganic together." Today the design look of *Dune* is seen as a progenitor of the steampunk sensibility and aesthetic, which arose in 1987. A strain of science fiction literature began dwelling in a world where technology was at the steam-and-early-electricity stage, and people dressed like Victorian ladies and gentlemen. No computers, no plastic. Things were made of wood and brass and primal mechanical-industrial processes, formed right in Lynch's wheelhouse: steam and sparks, exposed gears, belt-driven wheels, man and machine. Steampunk culture grew; more fiction was produced; aficionados dressed and decorated their houses in the style; men and women got tattoos that made them appear to be driven by internal gears. Artists and crafts people had a field day, creating light fixtures that would fit perfectly in Baron Harkonnen's factory-planet in *Dune*, and contraptions that melded machines with human brain tissue, eyeballs, and wombs with their fetuses.

The C in Mr. C could stand for Cool. He seems unsurprised to see Phillip Jeffries in this machine form in a motel room off a large asphalt courtyard dimensionally above a small convenience store that's surrounded by trees and open air. The space Jeffries occupies has an arched, coved ceiling exactly like the purple sea-realm Mansion's living room, where Cooper fell to from the Red Room, where he, pink glowing, encountered pink-glowing Naido and the huge electrical outlet, and American Girl warned that a powerful "Mother" was pounding on the door to get in. Lynch's scale shift from small convenience store leading up to the big motel courtyard is a mirror opposite of the fortresslike Mansion leading up to the small box in space. Besides the Mansion, the only structure in the purple sea zone is the Fireman's tower-top abode, whose interior is black-and-white. In the motel Room 8, Mr. C and his space are in naturalistic color, but Jeffries and his space are black-and-white. So can we conclude that Jeffries is in the Fireman's realm, some room in the White Lodge, and hence on the FBI side of the righteous and the good, not converted to darkness like FBI man Windom Earle had been in the original *Twin Peaks*? Jeffries's machine consists of a big black bell form like the one atop the Mansion's box in space and those in the Fireman's house, which are linked to massive electromagnetic power. The core has a spout-like arm jutting from it, and out pours a flow of steam when Jeffries expresses himself.

A core principle of *Twin Peaks*, and Lynch's worldview, is that reality is in layers: now/then, inner/outer, above/below, foreground/background, macrocosm/microcosm. Mr. C's tableau view of machine Jeffries is unchanging, static, except for the steam pouring from the spout and hanging in the air. We never get any closer; the angle doesn't change. At first it looks like the steam is floating within a bubble. We've previously seen Bob and Laura Palmer in bubble forms, so is this one Phillip Jeffries's essence? But we realize that the "bubble" we're seeing is composed of the steam and a circle on the wall a few feet behind Jeffries's machine; our eye/mind wants to make two separate things "one and the same," to quote the Giant (*The Return*'s Fireman) in the original *Twin Peaks*. The circle seems drawn or painted on the wall, or maybe it's some kind of metaphysical light source: it gleams. It's really two circles, a dark one within a lighter one; in other words, it looks like a doughnut. We're really in Lynchland here.

In addition to munching those tasty circles of fried dough, Lynch likes to say, "Pay attention to the donought, not the hole," meaning the essential things, your work, your calling, the signs of Providence in the world. Lynch the artist appreciates the linear perfection of the circle. He once summed up his assessment of his beloved daughter Jennifer by saying to Catherine Coulson, "Cath, she's round as a ball." Lynch sees the world in polar-opposite dualities, and also in circuits: energies in circular, repeating, cycling motion, as with electricity. He speaks of how "the world is as you are," meaning that we're on a circling line that goes from us to the world and back. We perceive our psychic energies in the world; it mirrors us. The Red Room is what you bring to it. Your karma makes the world you're in. And all of us, all the individual forms of karma, are contained within the circling wheel of time, the cycle of birth/death/rebirth. In symbolic terms, the circle, the complete, perfect pathway of energy, connotes the return of multiplicity to unity: Lynch's Unified Field, his "big home of Everything."

In Lynch's unproduced screenplay for *Ronnie Rocket* (1977), the Donut Man character says, "Life is a donut." Another character says, "Things keep going round and round," and in the *Twin Peaks* Pilot (1990), the idea is expressed as "What goes around comes around." In the world of multiplicity, *The Return* presents both Laura Palmer and Bob in circular bubbles: hers is golden, his is shadowy. In the original *Twin Peaks*, before the One-Armed-Man broke from Bob and embraced goodness, they killed together, forming "a perfect relationship of appetite and satisfaction. A golden circle." And in *Ronnie Rocket*, the villains control a big city by maintaining circuits of bad electricity until the good guys figure out how to break the circular flow of evil power. In *Lost Highway*, Fred Madison does a very bad thing and is doomed to recycle a life of suffering for a long, long time.

So what does the circle within a circle on machine Phillip Jeffries's wall signify? Maybe it's Jeffries's mandala, representing his spirit essence as the center point of wheeling space-time, of his being safely armored within his machine, part of the Fireman's protectorate. Jeffries's dialogue with Mr. C, though ambiguous, indicates he is on the side of good, making moves to destroy the Bad Cooper. Aside from getting Ray to shoot Mr. C (Part Eight), maybe, in Part Two, on the phone with Mr. C, Jeffries pretends to be someone pretending to be him, thus sowing confusion in Mr. C's sense of reality, clouding the nature of the forces he's dealing with. Though Jeffries has alchemized into a machine, he can make big things happen. The circle on his wall is like a clock without hands. A circle that implies motion: forward (clockwise), backward (counter-clockwise).

Jeffries responds to Mr. C's presence, "Oh, it is you; thank God." Is the "you" he recognizes Cooper or Bob? Would he say "God" if it was Bob? Mr. C says, "Why did you send Ray to kill me?" Jeffries sounds surprised: "What?" he says, though he could be acting. Then he says, "I called Ray," and Mr. C concludes, "So you did send him after me," which Jeffries doesn't respond to. Mr. C says, "Did you call me five days ago?" referring to the ambiguous conversation in the motel where Mr. C kills Darya, in which the "Jeffries" on the line spoke of "being with Bob again," maybe working some personal scheme. Jeffries says, "I don't have your number," so it must have been some imposter. Jeffries adds, "We used to talk," and Mr. C adds, "Yes," alluding to the 1989 day Jeffries arrived in the Philadelphia FBI headquarters and said, "We are not going to talk about Judy," and seemed to question Cooper's identity ("Who do you think that is there?") Remembering that day, machine Jeffries says, "So, you are Cooper?" meaning the man in front of him (or some percentage of him) was in the office that day. Jeffries's question could also mean "So, Bob, you are Cooper." Mr. C shows more emotion than ever before: "Why didn't you want to talk about Judy? Who is Judy? Does she want something from me?" Phone numbers float up from Jeffries's steam cloud, and he says, 'Ask Judy yourself. You already met Judy." It sounds like Jeffries has confirmed to himself that Mr. C is an evil conglomeration of Cooper and Bob, who has "met" the Dark Mother who birthed him. Or maybe Jeffreies is referring to the Judy-linked red-suited white-masked being who brushed past Mr. C on the stairs.

As Mr. C becomes more agitated asking about Judy, a phone on a table in his space starts ringing. As he grabs the receiver, there's a flash of electricity, and Jeffries and his space fade away. Mr. C's form flickers, and he appears in the phone booth outside the convenience store. The receiver's in his hand, but who or whatever is on the line hangs up: another click sound of metaphysical doings, of powers beyond Mr. C's grasp.

A core lesson of *The Return*: all is change, fluidity, flux. Physical and cosmic forces shift toward darkness, shift toward light. Young Richard Horne thinks he's got the power. He steps from the shadows holding a gun on Mr. C outside the convenience store. But Mr. C quickly disarms him, orders him to get in the truck. Richard says he's Audrey Horne's son, so Mr. C, having raped the comatose Audrey twenty-five years earlier, realizes he's in the presence of his offspring, though he doesn't speak of it. And the youth must have inherited some percentage of Cooper's sleuthing DNA, since, having seen Mr. C in action at the Farm, he has somehow tracked him here. Richard's concluded that Mr. C is with the FBI, having seen Audrey's photo of Cooper in his black bureau suit. But really, how did Richard get here tonight?

Alfred Hitchcock used to say that he made cinematic dreams, not documentaries. He told François Truffaut: "To insist that a storyteller stick to the facts is just as ridiculous as to demand of a representative painter that he show objects accurately. . . In the fiction film the director is god; he must create life. And in the process of that creation, there are lots of feelings, forms of expression, and viewpoints that have to be juxtaposed. We should have total freedom to do as we like, just so long as it's not dull. A critic who talks to me about plausibility is a dull fellow." Clearly Lynch, with his need for "room to dream" and his desire to stimulate the imaginative faculty of his audience, is a fellow traveler with Hitchcock. At the convenience store, Richard Horne is just there. But how do we stop our minds from seeking all the details of meaning? Was Richard hiding in the truck bed?

After Mr. C and Richard drive off, the convenience store, seen in a wide, tableau image, sparks and flashes, fills with crackling-electricity light and billows of white smoke that thin and drift away as the store dematerializes and vanishes, leaving just the pale ground, over which a dark shadow drifts. We've seen air-tunnel vortexes appear in South Dakota and Washington State, and it seems that the convenience store is an extradimensional gateway that can appear here and there.

Love may have blossomed into fulfillment for Big Ed and Norma at the Double R, but it's torturous and dangerous for Gersten and Steven in the woods of Twin Peaks. These two, plus Steven's wife, Becky, form a high-tension triangle. Becky seems most useful to Steven as a money source for stoking his drug habit. She loves-hates him with a passion and has fired bullets through a door she thought he was behind. Both Becky and Steven are hot-tempered, capable of blind fury, while Gersten is more calm and balanced. Whether she's in lust or love with Steven, we sympathize with this grown-up daughter of good old Doc Hayward. And because Gersten cares for Steven, we're concerned for this desperate, troubled punk who seems born to traumatize the women in his life.

Young Gersten and Steven sit on the ground at the base of a giant, centuries-old evergreen tree. Steven's eyes are drug fevered. His point of view is a green blur of trees. He's agitated, semicoherent. He's holding a loaded pistol. He points to his head, talking about ending it all. She holds him, tries to grab the gun, worried for her safety as well as his. He wonders, if he takes himself out, will he be with the beast ("the rhinoceros"), the light ("lightning in a bottle"), or will he "be turquoise" (the package color of Lynch's American Spirit cigarettes). Imaginative metaphysical systems sprout like toadstools in *Twin Peaks*.

At the point of highest tension, a guy walking his dog strolls by. Steven hides the gun. Gersten grabs the existential moment, jumps up, leaps to the side of the massive tree trunk that's opposite Steven. The walker keeps going. He's Mark Frost, making a cameo appearance. Mark's father, Warren Frost, played Doc Hayward, Gersten's father, so in a metapoetic way she's Mark's "sister," and his sudden appearance has saved her life. Her back against the tree, she hears a single shot. She repeats, "No, no," and looks upward for answers. The open sky is blotted out by the tree canopy. Forces stir in the ominous music. This is Ghostwood Forest.

Hours later, in the Roadhouse, forces are also stirring as James and Freddie show up for the evening. Previously, Freddie emphasized to James that Renee, the woman James is infatuated with, is a married woman. James knows that, but a guy can hope, and this guy's a romantic. Again tonight he gives her a longing look, speaks his heart, "It's good to see you, Renee." The man sitting with her is her husband, Chuck (Rod Rowland), who glares at James and snarls, "You got a death wish? Don't talk to her." Good old sincere James goes on, "I was very polite; I like her." Chuck leaps on James, pounds him to the ground, keeps on pounding. Freddie steps in, doesn't even do a windup, just meets Chuck's face with his superpowerful green garden glove, and Chuck is down, foaming at the mouth; a witness says Chuck's "eyes are funny."

Deputies Bobby Briggs and Hawk both have an experienced, nuanced sense of right and wrong, but they lock up James, the victim, with Freddie, while Chuck is sent to intensive care. Having James behind bars allows Lynch and Frost to strike resonant echoes with a standout scene from the original *Twin Peaks*. In those days, Bobby was a bad boy, and he and his pal Mike were locked up for barroom brawling. In the cell across from them was James, being held for questioning. James, in the scene where he was attacked by Chuck in *The Return*, is a victim of animalistic fury. And decades ago, James, in jail with Bobby and Mike, cowered as the two, their teeth bared like hungry bestial predators, snarled and growled at him. Now, benign lawman Bobby locks up James and leaves, but there are again strange vocalizations between people caged in cells.

In the happy orchard of sheriff's office culture, Deputy Chad is a bad apple. He mocked Frank Truman's emotionally distraught wife, jeered at sweet, guileless Deputy Andy, and did not follow lunch protocol, and we know he had shady doings with Richard Horne and others. Turns out the good guys knew too, and it's satisfying to see his colleagues lock him up. In addition to being incarcerated, Chad is sonically tortured by the drunk in a nearby cell, played by Lynch's former assistant Jay Aaseng, whom I often dealt with. The drunk's been in a nasty fight, and drooling and dripping blood from his face, he slurringly repeats any vocalization he hears. These include Chad's angry, exasperated outbursts and the plaintive, nonverbal sounds made by Naido, locked up to protect her from cosmic/interdimensional threats. These three in full voice create a bizarre cacophony reverberating amid the steel bars, which, combined with James's notice of Naido's face with just skin where there should be eyes, causes him to respond, "What the hell?"

In terms of *The Return*'s sequential presentation, Audrey and her husband, Charlie, began a conversation in Part Twelve that's still going on in Part Fifteen. If Lynch and Frost want to make us feel the irritation and frustration that Audrey and Charlie have with each other, they're doing a good job. Actors Sherilyn Fenn and Clark Middleton make us live every stretched-out moment of a marriage gone sour. If the estrangement between *Lost Highway*'s Fred and Renee Madison was slow building, often silent, with resentments floating like amorphous clouds in their spacious house, Audrey and Charlie are engaged in an endless, heated, claustrophobic dialogue: stuck in the middle with you. Energies that cycle and repeat have always been part of *Twin Peaks*. In the first, 1990 season, Mark Frost, a master of structuring episodic TV, directed short segments of a mock soap opera (*Invitation to Love*) that appeared on the TV sets of Twin Peaks homes. Frost once recalled with a laugh that "it was the town's favorite show, but it was in constant reruns." Each "episode" of the Audrey and Charlie Show has different dialogue, but the sense of emotional acrimony and stasis is uniformly oppressive.

There's a sense that Audrey and Charlie are each other's best audience, each acting out their darkest selves, stuck on a stage they've crafted, humiliation upon insult upon fuming rage. But it's not a fair fight. She needs him to do things he won't do and is wounded by those he does. His power is existentially threatening; he speaks of "ending your story." And he takes sadistic pleasure in manipulating her story, always with a deadpan "I'm not to blame, you are/I'm innocent, you're wacko" expression. In the previous "episode," Audrey voiced the toxic effect of their psychodrama: "I'm not sure who I am," the most horrifying predicament in Lynchland. Now, in Part Fifteen, they're closer than ever to actually leaving their crucible of stasis to go to the Roadhouse to look for Billy, with whom Audrey has found love. But once again Charlie halts their forward motion. In a crystalizing moment of insight, Audrey sees beyond her reactive ego and understands what Charlie's been doing. He's the one in question, not her: "Who are you, Charlie?" Her old Audrey spunk jolts her; she leaps on him, grips his neck in a strangle hold, and growls, "I fucking hate you, Charlie."

Even though the toxic twosome of Audrey and Charlie don't make it to the Roadhouse tonight, there are plenty of bad vibes in the air there. The music is a spiritual-existential lament ("Oh, my soul"), and a small young woman (Ruby: Charlyne Yi) in a booth alone is intimidated into giving up her seat when two hulking bikers loom above her, waiting for her to slink away. The pain in her head and heart are so heavy that she slips onto her knees and starts crawling while everyone around her is dancing. Lynch's gift for abstraction is operating at full force. The camera is at the woman's level as she crawls toward us in an unbroken take, her small, struggling body hemmed in by dark legs like menacing tree trunks in a forest: a piercing image of the sheer burden, the entrapment, of being alive, like Sisyphus continually trying to roll a rock up a hill, or some endless Kafkaesque labyrinth.

How good is the chocolate cake at the house with the red door? In Las Vegas, where Dougie, Janey-E, and Sonny Jim live? It's delicious, baked with care by Janey-E, whose love for Dougie has grown and beams like the desert sunrise. Dougie, who talks less than he used to, when he was busy drinking, gambling, and whoring his life away. But now he seems to move in slow motion, just coming up with a word now and then, and radiates a calming childlike innocence and warm affection for his wife and son. Though he's a misfit in the speedy, hyper busy mainstream world, he's brought prosperity to his family and saved his and Janey-E's lives when an assassin attacked. Things couldn't be better under their suburban roof tonight. But yes, they could.

Lynch characterizes himself as a homebody and has spoken of his childhood, when the world was just his house and the immediate neighborhood, and as he grew he sensed a force "of wild pain and decay" in the broader world, scary, threatening things at work beneath the surface. In Lynchworld, the surface is often sunny, masking a dark undercurrent. But in the Dougie Jones house, the happy, fulfilling surface hides/hinders/cocoons a transcendent beneficent force that needs to be released. Having Cooper-as-Dougie has been good for everyone he's interacted with. Which is ironic, since Mr. C created Dougie as a trap for Cooper, to curtail him and position him as an easy target for death. Mr. C still wants Cooper permanently gone, but he hasn't accomplished that yet. In the broader cosmic picture, higher forces want a balance restored. The One-Armed Man keeps urging Cooper-as-Dougie to "wake up"; the überbeneficent Fireman needs Cooper to fulfill his mission: kill Bob, who's within Mr. C, and save Laura, who's in the interdimensional winds.

When Lynch was in is early thirties, every day at three p,m. he'd sit in LA's Bob's Big Boy diner, relish a chocolate milkshake, and enjoy the ideas that bubbled in his brain. He'd chase the shake with a cup of coffee, and we know how passionate Cooper is for that "damn fine" elixir of the body and spirit. Lynch has said that "there's a fair amount of me in Cooper," and his first wife, Peggy Reavey, told me that "David would crave chocolate milk after sex." In Part Ten of *The Return*, Dougie was eating Janey-E's thrilling chocolate cake, barely aware that she was giving him a feverish, hungry look. Then, in bed, he was on his back, she was naked, moving up and down above him, until everything exploded in GOODNESS and he flapped his arms like a soaring bird. That time, eating chocolate cake culminated in what we recognized as Dougie's orgasm. So where will the chocolate cake portal take him this time?

It's another night in the Jones house, and Dougie is alone at the dining table enjoying a big helping of chocolate cake. He's silent, of course, and savors every bite. The TV remote control is on the table, and he keeps pushing the buttons. Nothing happens, a metaphor for Dougie's impaired state; he hunts and pecks his way through the world. He presses some more, and I hear a familiar voice: real-life legendary film director C. B. DeMille, playing himself in Billy Wilder's *Sunset Boulevard* (1950), one of Lynch's favorite films. It's the scene where once-great, now has-been star Norma Desmond (Gloria Swanson), thinking the movies want her back again, comes to the Paramount Studios, the site of her long-ago triumphs. But as in Lynchworld, the reality is different from what it seems. Some Paramount functionary named Gordon Cole (!) was interested in using Norma's antique car in a film, but the communication got scrambled, and Norma misunderstood, thinking, "It's Hollywood calling!" DeMille doesn't know anything about the car, so when Norma shows up, though he's surprised and puzzled, he graciously gives her a reunion tour of his current production.

Dougie's come into the action where DeMille's bidding Norma goodbye. The situation is poignant, tragic, but DeMille's a kind gentleman, and he gives her a warm send-off. Norma, misinterpreting, is ebullient, "How wonderful, the old team together again!" As she drives off, DeMille fumes, "Get me Gordon Cole!" "The old team together again," "Gordon Cole": these words have deep resonance for us viewers, but what about Dougie? He's stopped eating, and he blinked when the man on the screen said "Gordon Cole." He hits the pause button, and DeMille's round-moon bald head floats in the TV frame, just as Major Briggs's disembodied head floated in space when Cooper stood atop the box in space where Naido threw the switch and plummeted away. And in the vast vocabulary of images, DeMille's head rhymes with Major Briggs's head rhymes with the round floating head of *The Wizard of Oz* in another of Lynch's most cherished films. We prosaically say "pattern recognition." Nineteenth-century French poet Charles Baudelaire wrote of "correspondences": "Man passes through these forests of symbols which regard him with familiar looks."

Maybe it's the cake: stimulating sugar and cocoa (with its caffeine content). Maybe it's Cooper's detective/seeker essence, even though it's diminished, constrained, entrapped in Dougie's oh-so-slow form. Perhaps because Cooper/Dougie's in such a safe, secure, relaxed place with Janey-E and Sonny Jim, Dougie has a subtle yet significant air of enlivened attentiveness. Lynch, a poet of images, has placed Dougie in a forest of signifiers, little bits of meaning that are coalescing. In addition to "The old team together again," "Gordon Cole," and DeMillle's Major Briggs-like round floating head, there's another shape from Cooper's past. When Dougie began eating his cake, one hand idly moved a salt/pepper shaker near the TV remote control. The dark ceramic object was similar in form to the big, dark, electrified bell-shaped machine atop the box in space with Naido. Does some part of Dougie perceive this path of psychic energy, this abstraction of Cooper's quest?

As he did in the Las Vegas police station in Part Nine, Dougie notices a humming electrical outlet on the kitchen wall. In contrast to Ruby at the Roadhouse, who crawls on the floor in torment, Dougie follows some vector of desire, gets down onto the same plane as the outlet, and crawls forward. Does he know why he's doing this, what he did before this, what he needs to do? His cake fork is still in his hand. Being Dougie, he tries to stick it into the humming outlet tines first. Nothing happens.

The other end of the fork is the key to the passageway. He inserts it: crackling cacophony, the brightness of a lightning flash in a suburban kitchen. Smitten, he collapses. Janey-E screams; Sonny Jim yells in alarm. Lights out.

Experiencing the linking signs and meanings of the two minutes of Dougie's cake night, I recall the first time Linda and I visited Lynch's house. The way *Sunset Boulevard* happened to be on TV the night before, and Lynch and my interaction over the quest to find the driveway to the film's mansion. It's a delicious night of cake layers indeed.

Is Cooper/Dougie gone for good? We can't believe that. Lynch may admire Alfred Hitchcock's *Psycho*, in which the prominent woman protagonist, the heroine, whose story and point of view we're immersed in, is killed in the film's first third. But Lynch and Frost are acutely conscious of living in a spiritual-moral atmosphere, within themselves and the world, and they want to tip the balance toward positivity. In their minds they're the heroes of their own life adventures, and their artistic story needs a hero, an embodiment of righteousness. Every day in the mirror we see angels and devils at work, the battle between life and death. The oldest story, striving to make goodness triumphant, absolute. But achieving finality is elusive, an ideal to be sought; the battle goes on. Fighting for goodness, within and without, is a vital, noble dharma. This time the ancient story is in Twin Peaks, and it involves Cooper, Laura, and the devouring darkness.

A beacon of light, Catherine E. Coulson (Margaret Lanterman, the Log Lady), lived long enough to work the case with Hawk one more time. Their late-night phone talks conveyed their warm bond with each other and with us: a communion of heart and soul. Lynch and Couslon had been dear friends for four decades. They took up meditation together, and Lynch saved her life when she was seized with illness in the *Eraserhead* days. He can't save her now, but they both know, as the Log Lady tells Hawk, that "death is a change, not an end." Throughout the *Twin Peaks* epic, the Log Lady has emphasized that "Laura is the One." Beginning with the opening images of every part of *The Return*, Laura is the golden woman in a golden orb. Now Margaret Lanterman (Hawk calls her Margaret at this point), whose words have always had profound meaning, tells him, "My log is turning gold." Then, as we perhaps visualize an imminent spiritual threshold crossing glowing gold, Margaret and Hawk sign off with "goodbye." It was always "good night" before.

The antique lamp next to Margaret has a simple, straightforward on/off switch. After she and Hawk say goodbye, Lynch shows her cabin, small and dark against the darker forest surrounding it. The warm light from her little window doesn't just stop, go away. Lynch shows the glow fading slowly, gently merging with somewhere that's always here.

June 22 1992

Dear Greg,

Thanks for sending me the info. about the TWIN PEAKS FEST. It sounds great, and I'm looking forward to

–CHAPTER TWENTY-TWO–

CHANCE, PROBABILITY, CERTAINTY
(PART SIXTEEN)

I'm writing this the morning after I screened Swedish writer-director Ingmar Bergman's film *Cries and Whispers* at the Seattle Art Museum. The film came out in America in 1972, when Lynch was a student at the American Film Institute in Beverly Hills and saw many more films than he does now. *Cries and Whispers* centers on two sisters attending to their dying sister; much intense drama is in the air. The story unfolds in a mansion in which every room is covered in red fabric (*Twin Peaks*'s Red Room). At one point, a furious character says, "Don't look at me!" (Frank Booth in *Blue Velvet*). Agnes, the ill sister, dies; there's a funeral—but she's not dead (Laura Palmer in *Twin Peaks*). Bergman's notes on the film say, "A human being dies but, as in a nightmare, gets stuck halfway through and pleads for tenderness, mercy, deliverance, something. . . . Agnes is dead, with all the necessary sharpness of details. Agnes is not dead. What happens when Agnes is not dead but calls for help?" (Laura's death/postdeath situation, Cooper her helper/protector/savior).

Three elements in *Cries and Whispers* that resonate in Lynch's work. Did they live beneath his conscious mind after seeing the film in the early 1970s, assuming he did see it, and seep into his creative dreams over the years? As Jerry Horne says in the original *Twin Peaks*, before he was as drug addled as he is in *The Return*, "We're one-hundred-percent certain that we're not sure." But a cop in *Lost Highway* says, "There's no such thing as a bad coincidence." And Cooper has spoken of "curious linkages" and things considered to be separate entities that are "actually complementary verses of the same song." It's a convention of mystery stories and police procedurals that "coincidences" are solid, meaningful pathways.

Mr. C is facing a dilemma. In his quest to gain power that transcends the mundane, temporal world, to interact with Judy, he's obtained coordinates from Ray Monroe, Diane Evans, and Phillip Jeffries. Three sets, two of them the same. Stands to reason that the ones that match are the right ones. But what if that's a trap; there are nebulous forces out to get him. He needs to have someone else test the coordinates, like the kid sitting next to him as they drive on a dirt trail through night wilderness, his son, Richard Horne. Richard the criminal spawn of Mr. C's rape of the comatose Audrey Horne. Mr. C and Richard have never met before; there's no hint of kindred fellow feeling in their stony faces. Each man spinning and devouring in his own self-reflecting circle of appetite and satisfaction. And in a moment, Richard will unknowingly close a circuit of bad electricity. With his body.

Mr. C speaks with dark reverence of "this place" he's seeking, which we know is somewhere beyond this world. He sends Richard up a slope that's topped by a huge rock. Richard stands tall in the black air, holding an electronic homing device in his hand. When he's at the right spot at the right moment, the air crackles—and he ignites, with the piercing brightness of a welder's torch. Lynch renders this as a beautiful/horrific tableau, distant like a painting in a frame, an ungodly occurrence in a scene of nature. From Mr. C's point of view, we see the rock and Richard's searing form. But Lynch, knowing there are multiple aspects to everything, makes an inspired choice. He shows us the point of view from the backside of the rock, and it's weirdly different. No broiling air and flaming figure; Richard is a black shadow in black smoke; Hellfire in front, hell smoke in back. (Lynch may have been subconsciously influenced by archetypal LA artist Ed Ruscha, famous for his many paintings of the iconic Hollywood sign, always viewed from the front, the letters prominent and lit up. But in his painting *The Back of Hollywood*, Ruscha showed the letters black, from the backside, the front's dark double. The sign reads DOOWYLLOH. Ruscha created this image in 1977, a decade before Lynch and Frost made *Twin Peaks*, but could it have inspired the series's backward-speaking motif?)

Back to Mr. C's front view, Richard crumbles away in ash and sparks. Mr. C says, "Oh. Goodbye, my son." Cold, but somehow poignant. Mr. C is a thorough blackguard, but he's lost what would be an emotional touchstone for a normal human being. Because he looks like Cooper, do we want to humanize him? That's about as possible as mayhem viewed through a pair of binoculars having been caused by the binoculars. Roving Jerry Horne, in proximity to, but far away from, the person on the rock igniting like a light bulb filament, views the event through binoculars held topsy-turvy, so the image was a tiny flare in the night. Like a counterculture leprechaun, his brain marinated in marijuana, Jerry has popped up seven times in *The Return* as comic relief and to add further worries to his brother Ben's extensive list of troubles. Because we first saw Jerry and Ben in the Great Northern, we've assumed all of Jerry's woodland appearances have been in the Twin Peaks neighborhood, but here he is near Mr. C and Richard Horne, way east of Twin Peaks (Montana? Idaho? Mr. C and Richard don't seem to have driven too far). Our being unsure of Where's Jerry? (he wears stripes like Waldo) mirrors Jerry's aura of confused disorientation and misperception of reality. Jerry does blame his binoculars for causing/showing him a horrible sight, and he beats them against the ground, saying, "Bad binoculars! Bad binoculars!"

It's easy to laugh at Jerry's pixilated antics, but the man is suffering. At various times we see him screaming, running through the woods, pursued by the shadows of his own mind. In Part Nine's disturbing, creepy Jerry segment, he thinks that his own foot is other than him, alien. It won't move when he wants to go; it talks to him in an eerie high voice. The slipperiness of identity, the horror of depersonalization are Lynch's artistic home turf. It's as though he's found as many ways as he can to portray the disturbing identity-loss essence of the Wicked Witch's words in his beloved *The Wizard of Oz*. After Dorothy pours a deadly bucket of water on the Witch, she cries, "I'm melting, melting." In *The Return*, a scary, unsteady sense of selfhood torments Audrey, Jerry, and right around the corner, Diane.

After Richard Horne goes up in smoke, Mr. C sends Diane a text: "—)ALL." She's sitting at the hotel bar in Buckhorn, South Dakota, idling her time away. The text comes in, and she's stricken. Her shoulders and head slump forward as she reads, like she's pierced by a mortal blow. "—)ALL." I'm looking at a piece of paper that David Lynch typed some words on. It's a Xerox of the Log Lady's *Twin Peaks* pilot introduction that he wrote and Catherine Coulson sent me. It says that the stories in *Twin Peaks* have "a sense of mystery—the mystery of life," ALL indeed. That word with a subtraction sign puts Diane on the cutting edge of life and death. Does she have any say in the matter? Is she or Mr. C guiding her moment-to-moment choices? Lynch and Frost's script, plus Laura Dern's fine performance, conveys Diane's wavering consciousness. Lynch shows us a close-up of the "—)ALL" message, and we note that the time is 16:32, which in Lynch's numerologically inclined mind, adds to three. So the full message is subtract all three, and the three (Gordon Cole, Albert, Tammy) are nearby in the FBI field station/hotel room. Diane squares her shoulders and fiercely heads down the hallway, moving to the piledriver beats and guttural vocals of badass music we haven't heard since it introduced Mr. C in Part One; she's on his mission. Whether Albert intercepted the "—)ALL" message or whether Gordon Cole can feel the heat of her approach, he says, "Come in, Diane," before she even knocks.

She enters, takes a chair and a drink, and, like the true-blue, incorruptible Diane of old, gives her comrades her heartfelt account of the night Cooper (Mr. C, as we know) came to see her. It was four years after he'd disappeared. He quizzed her about FBI information, and they kissed. But something wasn't right; his coldness scared her. He sensed her fear, gloated, smiled, and raped her. She sobs in the telling, a good woman violated by the worst of men. Then he took her somewhere, "an old gas station," which suggests the convenience store, a generator of alien power where Mr. C must have brought her under his influence/command, but not complete control. Sitting in the hotel with Gordon, Albert, and Tammy, distraught from the emotional turmoil of reliving her past trauma and being on Mr. C's kill mission, Diane exhibits dual aspects. One moment she's talking about that gas station, then she says, "I'm in the sheriff's station. I got him those coordinates. I'm in the sheriff's station." When Diane was sitting at the bar, before she set off resolutely down the hall, she'd said aloud, "I remember, Coop. Oh, Coop, I remember. I hope this works," and sent coordinates on her phone.

We're witnessing the body of a woman whose good soul is being overridden by an evil, alien will. She sobs, trembles, gasps. Her hand grips the pistol in her purse, pulls it out, but Albert and Tammy are quicker. Their gun blast sounds fill the room. The bullets jerk Diane to the side, and she whoosh vanishes out of the room. In the poetics of Lynch's universe, *this* can also be *that*; things can be here and there simultaneously. In quantum physics, the way that a subatomic particle can exist all over the place at the same time is called superposition. In *The Return*, Lynch devises a visual metaphor for this process, a plastic expression that he employs when Cooper leaves his audience with the Fireman (Part One), when Andy leaves his Fireman session (Part Fourteen), and when Mr. C climbs the convenience store exterior stairs (Part Fifteen). With a blinking quickness, the figures become triangular/curve-edged fragments that depart one after the other—in less than a second. They're both here and where they're going. This artistic superpositioning also qualifies as Cubism, a meta representation of matter in space and time familiar to Lynch since his youthful art student days. The just-shot Diane departs the hotel room like a scrap of paper whisked away by a powerful wind, similar to the way Laura was jerked away from the Red Room the last time we saw her, though her flight path was straight up while Diane's is to the side. Unlike the men, these two blonde women don't flicker and fragment when traversing dimensions. Is this a reflection of Lynch's reverence for Laura and Diane, his feeling that women are more whole, solid, complete than men? (Males Dougie and Ray Monroe didn't go cubistic when they left the Red Room: they were wearing the jade ring.) Albert and Tammy fired on Diane. Gordon Cole didn't even reach for his gun: "I just couldn't do it."

In *The Return* identities are in superposition. After Diane vanishes, Tammy confirms she was a tulpa, a thought being created by a powerful mind, which we know belongs to Mr. C. He must have accomplished that process when, postrape, he took Diane to the "gas station," which signifies the paranormal convenience store. In *The Return*'s concluding parts we'll see that tulpa creation involves a golden seed like the one that remained after tulpa Dougie disintegrated in the Red Room, plus some DNA from the one to be duplicated, and jolts of supernatural electricity. After Mr. C and Diane's sexual encounter, he certainly had some of her DNA at hand. (Once, hours after David Lynch had hugged me, a woman friend of mine said, "You've got David Lynch's molecules on you": a scientific truth, a metaphor for the spiritual, invisible unity of All). When tulpa Dougie found himself in the Red Room, before devolving into the golden seed, he was befuddled, enervated. Tulpa Diane is tough and feisty to the end. When the One-Armed Man speaks his refrain "Someone manufactured you," she snaps, "I know. Fuck you."

When Tammy certified that Diane was a tulpa, Gordon Cole didn't respond. He's a seasoned spiritual warrior and takes this as a given. What shakes him, sets him to pondering, is when Diane said, "I'm in the sheriff's station; I'm not me." Was she seeing the future? Or are Lynch and Frost prefiguring a significant linkage between Diane and one of the two most prominent women in the sheriff's station: Lucy, Naido? Naido is Asian, and Diane's apartment is decorated with Asian art and objects; the turquoise sweater she wears as she sits in the Red Room has neckline embroidery like the design motif on an ancient Chinese vase. As with Dougie's tulpa, the black smoke essence inside Diane exits up from the gap where her head just was a moment ago, and she's gone, leaving a golden seed in the chair.

Mr. C's lost his number one special agent, but Chantal and Hutch are still on the job. They've eliminated those who have knowledge of Mr. C's criminal empire, and they're sitting in their van across the street from Dougie's red-doored Las Vegas house—but where is he?

Having survived a major jolt of fork-to-socket-induced electricity, Dougie is hospitalized in a coma. Supine, he's the horizontal element in a tableau that recalls the ending of the 1991 *Twin Peaks*, when Cooper, in bed after a punishing session in the Red Room, was surrounded by his concerned friends. The image also serves as an homage to Lynch's beloved *The Wizard of Oz*, which concludes with Dorothy back home in Kansas after her fantastic adventures, in bed with her family and friends gathered around. It's a potent image of communal love. On her journey, Dorothy discovered her dependable, powerful inner resources, whereas 1991's Cooper got taken over by his fears, dark drives, and Bob. The figure in the Las Vegas hospital bed, unmoving, with closed eyes, could be Dougie or Cooper the champion, the sleeping prince. He's surrounded by Janey-E, Sonny Jim, Bushnell Mullins, and later arrivals the Mitchum brothers and their Pink Ladies, who make the room overflow with harmonious fellowship—and a platter of finger sandwiches. As Bradley Mitchum regards the man in the bed who's dead to the world, he makes what qualifies as an understatement in Lynch's world: "Something to do with electricity?" That's an easy yes, but Lynch and Frost make us wait a bit longer to learn Dougie/Cooper's identity status.

David Lynch's sense of the absurdity, the surreality, the sheer wackiness of life is always at the ready. It's rare in a Lynch film to have two characters, and their behavior, seem like they're visiting from another auteur's cinema. Maybe it's because Tim Roth (*The Return*'s Hutch) has been in three Quentin Tarantino films and Jennifer Jason Leigh (Chantal) in one. Tarantino movies feature amoral, lovin'-and-killin' male-female couples or male-bonded guys who do their work with a cruel, casual attitude and philosophical chatter while relishing comfort food. As Hutch and Chantal drive from kill to kill, Chantal's pout and Hutch's lean-and-mean air are pure Tarantino. But here they are in Lynchland, staked out by Dougie's house, watching a carnivalesque, Felliniesque parade of gangsterish guys (the Mitchum brothers), three Pink Ladies, and delivery men head into the house with a cornucopia of provisions.

Lynch's belief in karma is also at hand. As Chantal and Hutch scan the horizon looking for Dougie (Mr. C has told them that their target "looks like me"), Hutch says that a guy he owed money to just died, so he has nobody to pay. But money isn't everything. What about the wages of sin, the value of your soul? The karmic path that these two have been walking arcs steeply downward. As Lynch has told me, "It may seem like some people get away with murder, but when you factor in reincarnation, it becomes clear, there's perfect justice in the world. Because whatever wrongs you commit will visit you in exactly the same form."

Just as Lynch has made affectionate references to France in *The Return* (French flags, Gordon Cole's French girlfriend and Paris-set dream, the children's film *The Red Balloon*), he honors Poland by having the agent of Hutch and Chantal's retribution be a Polish accountant (Jonny Coyne). (Lynch shot some of *INLAND EMPIRE* in Poland, and he's friends with a group of Lodz artists, musicians, and filmmakers he calls the Camerimage Gang in reference to the city's Camerimage Film Festival, which is devoted to cinematography).

The little bald man's white Mercedes says "Zawaski Accounting, Inc." on the driver's door. He lives across the street from the Jones house. Coming home, he sees a white van parked in front of his driveway, and he asks the occupants to please move their vehicle. Chantal replies with hair-trigger anger: "Not even close, asshole—go fuck yourself." Zawasaki says, "I move car," stomps on the accelerator, rams the van, keeps the pedal floored, tires smoking, the Mercedes's nose melded with the van's bumper.

Beyond the absurd irony of two "parked" vehicles having a road rage incident, this spontaneous, instantaneous escalation of reptile-brain confrontation is an abstraction of sociocultural malaise. Since the mid-eighteenth century, when the industrial revolution got rolling, the incidence of mental and emotional disorders has risen steadily. These days, in the era of Donald J. Trump and the COVID pandemic and continuing threat, there's the sense that anxiety, depression, and loneliness are invading more and more lives. Lying bullies running the show; toxic food, air, water; a future of downward mobility; some fucker steals your parking place. *I* don't reach out to another person for consolation and comfort; my hand seeks that cool, sexy, curvaceous steel with a trigger and a big magazine of bullets. I'll blast hot splinters of anger into their guts; the disease will burn them up. The disease that was in Frank Booth in that *Blue Velvet* movie, that got into Dorothy Valens and that Jeffrey kid: the atavistic lizard brain surge of dark thoughts, anger and violence.

Lynch feels that over his decades of meditation, his creative consciousness has expanded, and his capacity for volcanic anger has diminished. (Some of *The Return*'s DVD special features show that he's still capable of lashing out over work-related matters.) He understands that rage can be an expression of fear and powerlessness, and he uses it to great effect in his art, from comic strips to paintings to film and TV. Some of his characters seem to have big, red, roiling clouds of steam inside that they can barely contain and that burst out in absurdly intense ventings.

Hutch and Chantal may remind us of Tarantino characters, but with the Polish accountant they don't hit the pause button for one of Quentin's typical Mexican standoff interactions, with guns drawn and pointing but not used while lots of speechifying goes on. They jump right in, guns blazing. But like flames flash-jumping across highways in the LA-SoCal burning season, Zawaski blazes too, and his gun delivers more bullets, quicker. Hutch and Chantal's van, and their flesh, are pierced with many bloody bullet holes. She's dead at the wheel as the van bumps to a stop at the end of the street. The gun battle commotion drew the Mitchum brothers out of the Jones house, where they'd been stocking the shelves. As the out-of-control mayhem in the street concludes, they nicely sum up Lynch and Frost's point: "People are under a lot of stress these days."

Hutch and Chantal are free of their bodies now. But their karmic track record is so bad. Maybe they'll reincarnate as subhuman, dusty roadside lizards, skittering past a blood-spattered bag of Chantal's Cheetos.

In Part Fourteen, Gordon Cole, after learning that Diane is Janey-E's half sister and that Janey-E's wedding ring was found inside the murdered Major Briggs's stomach, which was found next to Ruth's severed head, ordered the Las Vegas FBI to investigate the Douglas Jones family. So there's an FBI stakeout crew down the street from the massacre, and Agent Wilson is handily there to arrest the Polish accountant with his still-smoking firepower.

It's quiet on Dougie's Las Vegas street. The deadly threat of Hutch and Chantal is gone for good. Zawaski, the temperamental shooter, is in jail. The beneficent Mitchum brothers and their Pink Ladies have gone home, leaving the Jones family home well stocked with the accoutrements of the good life. But no one's home to enjoy them.

Janey-E and Sonny Jim are wracked with worry and distress, sitting at comatose Dougie's hospital bedside. Dougie, who contains Cooper, who was created by Mr. C as an entrapping body, a barely moving target for easy elimination. Dougie, having been formed from Mr. C's spiritually debased DNA, then suffered some "accident" that left him a still-more-impaired vessel. And Cooper's journey to being/inhabiting Dougie had been severely punishing. Cosmic law dictated a smooth physical-spiritual transaction for Cooper in the Sycamore woods by the red curtains, like an extradimensional revolving door, with Bad Cooper going into the Red Room and Cooper coming out. But Bad Cooper went rogue, stayed outlaw. And Cooper, "tricked" by the wicked aspect of the electric tree, left the Red Room in free fall, experienced nonexistence and the sort of pummeling by electricity that Lynch detailed in his unproduced *Ronnie Rocket* script (1977).

Lynch has had electricity on his mind since boyhood, when he saw it as a magical, invisible force that hummed and snaked behind the walls of his house. Growing up, Lynch was fascinated by the wizardly electricity scientist-inventor Nikola Tesla, and as an artist he made enlivened electrons a visual and thematic motif in many of his fictions—never more so than in *Ronnie Rocket*, which introduced the idea of bad electricity, which villains use to manipulate, control, maim, and kill innocent people. In the screenplay, electricity is also used to power Ronnie Rocket himself, a boy "with physical problems" whom doctors try to help. (From *The Grandmother*'s [1970] Boy to *The Return*'s Dougie [2017], Lynch has had a poignant feeling for people with special vulnerabilities.) One of Ronnie's physicians is Dr. Pink, Lynch's first association of that warm, loving, calming, stimulating color with positive energies; *The Return*'s Cooper and Naido radiated pink light when they met and interacted. Ronnie needs to be plugged in periodically to maintain his vitality. The strange vibrations he emanates resonate with musicians and their instruments onstage, and Ronnie becomes a rock star. But money-grubbing promoters often crank his voltage too high and damage the poor kid.

Ronnie, like Cooper, wears "a great black suit." When the heaviest pressure of electricity is on him, he gags and vomits, as did Mr. C and Dougie at the moments when Mr. C defied the Red Room and stayed out, and Cooper became Dougie. The electricity theme is a major component of *Ronnie Rocket*'s architecture, and *The Return*'s giant electrical socket that Cooper has to get sucked into could have come from its world. The voltage there is of such a punishing magnitude that it causes a detective to visually distort, his heart swollen and smoking, which sounds like Cooper getting too close to *The Return*'s big socket. And the kid Ronnie Rocket really suffers. The electricity makes him twitch and flip, spark, smoke, and scream. And when it's off, he's semicomatose, barely speaks, has "a dopey look" (a progenitor of Dougie?). At one point, he crawls on the floor toward an electrical wall socket. Consciously or subconsciously, Lynch has worked some of *Ronnie Rocket*'s aesthetics and themes into *The Return*. Indeed, earlier in the show, when Gordon Cole, Albert, and Tammy were setting off on their adventures, Albert said they were pursuing "the absurd mystery of the strange forces of existence," which is the subtitle of Lynch's *Ronnie Rocket* screenplay. An efficient artist, Lynch knows good ideas shouldn't go to waste.

So, both Ronnie and Cooper, in their black suits, have been battered by punishing paranormal electricity, leaving them dazed, their recovery periods of varying lengths, outsiders from "normal" life. In 1990, a few years after Lynch wrote the "sleeper must awaken" speech for *Dune*, he said, "A jolt of electricity at a certain point of your life is helpful. It forces you a little bit more awake" (*Lynch on Lynch*). High-voltage survivors Ronnie Rocket and Dougie-housing-Cooper are outsiders who have gifts and wisdom that others must awaken to. Ronnie has the key to defeating evil in his world: the circle, the circuit, of bad electricity must be broken, and so it happens. And Cooper, when his eyes open and he's fully functioning, will hunt down evil and protect and champion the good, perhaps enacting the Fireman's instructions; a strategy worked out with Gordon Cole, Major Briggs, and Phillip Jeffries in the flux of space-time; or, following his idiosyncratic intuition, some Tibetan method of his own.

In the early 1980s, Lynch had an awakening of his own when he read Frank Herbert's novel *Dune* in preparation for writing the film's screenplay. He felt the book "captures fantastic ideas," and it "leaves a lot to the reader's imagination; he gives you a feeling and your mind takes over from there" (*Cinefantastique*), which is the way Lynch wants us to experience his work: in the "room to dream" that he gives us. In the book, Herbert says that in order to understand a phenomenon or a dynamic, don't stop it and freeze it for cerebral examination. Instead you must "move with the flow of the process, join it and flow with it."

Lynch lives in a misty realm of thought and feeling, leaning toward visionary notions of abstraction. He said he'd "like to make *Dune* a long poem. Just let it be abstract in some places, with no dialogue, and let it be more of a mood" (*The Films of*

David Lynch). But there was hard concrete within the poetic mist, a potent metaphor that's been meaningful to Lynch for decades: "the sleeper who must awaken and become what he was supposed to become" (*Lynch on Lynch*), the trajectory of Laura Palmer's journey in the *Twin Peaks* saga. He'd been meditating for ten years when he put the phrase in his *Dune* screenplay. Familiar with the feeling of newfound spiritual alertness and aliveness, Lynch has Paul Atreides's father speak to him about the need for change as a catalyst for growth, how without new experiences, "something sleeps inside us, and seldom awakens. The sleeper must awaken." Though, as Lynch says, many of his characters have to go through hell to get there, they have awakening moments of illumination when the clear, fresh, fulfilling path is right there to be seen and chosen. For Lynch, awakening also has the connotation of reincarnation, for dying "is like going to sleep: you wake up in the morning and you start a new day. You die and you have a little time in a dream and, *by golly*, you come back!" (*Lynch on Lynch*).

In 1955, ten years before Frank Herbert published *Dune*, his novel *The Dragon in the Sea* advised that in order to recognize the rewarding path you have to "understand currents, to know what's required in different waters." Paul Atreides in *Dune* and Dale Cooper in *Twin Peaks*, both Lynchian metaphysical detectives, learn to ride waves of shifting circumstances and read dream visions as they puzzle over existential fragments, seeking meaning. Paul and Cooper have to come into their own, become aware of their full powers, their significance as agents of goodness in various worlds.

In the complexly plotted universe of *Dune*, Paul drinks the poisonous Water of Life, and the resulting physical-visionary jolt makes him understand that he can control the giant sandworms and the production of the valuable spice, defeat the wicked Harkonnens and the Emperor, dictate terms to the Spacing Guild navigators, avenge his father's killing, and help the Fremen create a paradisiacal world. He recalls his father's words to him from earlier in the film and cries out with firm resolve, "Father, the sleeper has awakened!" *Dune* being a grandiose epic, Paul's declaration of awakened selfhood is attended by towering phallic sandworms (seven) standing erect in fealty. But this allusion to male power is only half the story of Paul, Cooper, and David Lynch. Herbert's book has been a resonant, international classic for decades because it is vibrant with the interplay of both male and female energies, a stealth matriarchy within a patriarchy, the womanly spirit within Paul's male spirit. The book tells us that Paul becomes the fulcrum between male taking forces and female giving ones, the balancing point. Absorbing this idea in the early 1980s may have sparked Lynch's belief, voiced over the decades, that "divine mind" is gained through "knowledge and experience of combined opposites" (*The Prints of David Lynch*). Certainly Cooper, like Paul, is a potent blending of anima and animus, energized by empathy, intuition, dream visions, and female guidance as well as by physical prowess and fortitude, moral righteousness and codes of male honor.

Lynch has told me that when he's immersed in the process of making his films, "Ninety percent of the time I don't know why I'm doing what I'm doing." He's "sort of on automatic pilot," intuitively tapping into his subconscious. Sure, the script provides guidelines, but the process is fluid, there have to be "openings for other forces, you know, to do their thing" (*Lynch on Lynch*). Ideas come to him as fragments charged with emotional and aesthetic promise, and sometimes it's an agonizing wait for a unifying form to emerge. These creative resolutions seem like mysterious conjurings: "How in the world did this happen?"(*Catching the Big Fish*). "Sometimes you can do things that are smarter than you actually are and you'll capture a bigger picture than you really are perceiving, and that's the beautiful thing about intuition." (*Reel Conversations*).

Lynch's psyche, his conscious/subconscious mind, is a compendium of his biology and everything he's seen, heard, smelled, touched, dreamed, and imagined. And, perhaps "forgotten," but embedded in his neural network, are the imaginings of other creators he's encountered. Over a period of years, Lynch read Frank Herbert's *Dune*, thought about *Dune*, wrote a *Dune* screenplay, learned that *Dune* was Kyle MacLachlan's "bible" when he was a youth, and made a film of *Dune*. And while Lynch was immersed in this process, he was writing a screenplay for a second *Dune* film, which would encompass Herbert's *Dune Messiah* and *Children of Dune*. The financial failure of the first film put a stop to Lynch's *Dune*-world forward momentum. Simply put, Herbert told Lynch "anything and everything David wanted to know about *Dune*" (*The Making of Dune*). And then, in the mid-1980s, it was all over.

In 1986, thanks to financial help from *Dune* producer Dino Di Laurentis, Lynch crafted one of his masterpieces, *Blue Velvet*, which returned the writer-director to his most rewarding artistic home turf: small town/neighborhood life as a psychological journey. And the young man taking the trip was Paul Atreides, that is, Kyle MacLachlan. As a kid, MacLachlan had worshipped *Dune*; he "was Paul in my imagination for years" before he ever met Lynch. Lynch likes to say, "It's a learning world," which Herbert states as "every experience carries its lesson" in *Dune*. Lynch's screenplay has Paul say to his mother, "Your teachings have changed my consciousness." *Dune* imparted lessons for life and art to Lynch and MacLachlan, and some of them are on display in their thirty-year *Twin Peaks* saga.

Dune gave Lynch the experience of a mythic, poetic story system, a mesmerizing multidimensional world with a vivid, unique sense of place, character, and properties of physics and metaphysics, words that apply equally to *Twin Peaks*.

So what are some of the elements common to *Dune* and *Twin Peaks*? *Dune* posits a safe, sacred place like Twin Peaks that's "touched by anarchy from the outer dark," in the form of a "female immanence filled with ambiguity and with a face of many terrors." Sounds like *The Return*'s mysterious dark threatening force Judy. Both epics have "beast demons" in the desert, a "horned goddess," a female vomiting "the most lethal poison in the universe" (*The Return*'s vomit stream of Bob and the eggs), devouring circular mouths, "sorceresses with great powers." In *Dune*, Paul is antagonized by a Bene Gesserit witch, a female spiritual leader who seeks to control his fate. In *The Return*, Cooper is pitted against the power-hungry Dark Mother Judy. In *Dune*, evil schemers sow infectious fears that grow in people and can be fed upon—the favorite nourishment of Bob and his kind, their food chain of "appetite and satisfaction, a golden circle."

In *Dune* and *Twin Peaks*, characters are named for their qualities, what/where they are, names that sound like archetypes: Demon Ruler, Voice from the Outer World, the One Who Will Lead Us to Paradise (all from *Dune*); the Man from Another Place, the One-Armed Man, the Giant/Fireman, the Log Lady (all *Twin Peaks*).

In *Dune*, Paul's stirring declaration "Long live the fighters!" encapsulates the credo of those consecrated against evil, a like-minded group comparable to *Twin Peaks*'s Bookhouse Boys and the FBI's Blue Rose Task Force, which, like Paul, has been schooled in esoteric knowledge and "dangerous facts."

Dune and *Twin Peaks* relish coffee as an elixir and social bonding agent. On the planet Dune, Paul coins a term expressing great awe, "I am profoundly stirred"; in other words, an Oh, wow! moment. Sounds like Cooper enjoying coffee and pie. Throughout Lynch's *Dune*, we hear Paul's voice expressing his inner thoughts; in *Twin Peaks*, Cooper speaks his thoughts into a tape recorder for Diane. *Dune*'s beneficent Atreides family lives in a fortress on a cliff above a sea, as do *The Return*'s Fireman and his Lady Dido. *Dune*'s Truthsayer character can quickly determine a person's veracity by studying their words and body language, a skill that Agent Cooper often employs.

The Return has tulpas, thought-created beings, and *Dune* has "ego-likenesses," shaped by the power of human thought, and "Face Dancers" who can put on another's appearance and inhabit their psyche. *Dune* has vast electrical generator rooms, and we'll see one at the Fireman's fortress soon. *Dune* speaks of the electrical fields within people and the environment, an essential component of Lynchland. Sometimes in *Dune* and *Twin Peaks*, communication is distorted; what Frank Herbert notes as "voice was blurred" is common to both epics, and Herbert's "magnetic language" suggests *The Return*'s vocal-electrical-mechanical sounds.

In both *Dune* and *Twin Peaks*, human beings can sense metaphysical realms, mental powers can bridge space and time, and actions are initiated by the spirit world. Both sagas have an expansive reach of space-time scale, of multiple, simultaneous planes of reality (*The Return* more than the original *Twin Peaks*).

Dune posits an ecumenical spiritual system that blends Western and Eastern traditions in the "common belief that there is a Divine essence in the universe." And *The Return* is an amalgamation of Christian and Asian traditions, though Lynch is partial to Hinduism. The holy Vedas state that all of creation, from atoms to the farthest galaxies, began with a single point, a dot. And both *Dune* and *Twin Peaks* have a focal point: "the One." A transcendent deliverer who will defeat evil and guide a rebirth of goodness in the world. In *Dune*, The One prophezied for centuries turns out to be Paul. In *Twin Peaks*, the Log Lady, who can see beyond the realms of life and death, reminds us, and her spiritual comrades, that "Laura is the One." In both epics there are clear, righteous paths to be found and followed. But even in the best people, there is uncertainty, fear, doubt, misperception, inaccurate judgment, forgetfulness, laziness. In *Dune*, the common commandment held by all is "Thou shalt not disfigure the soul," your own or others, which is the essence of Lynch's "I must have final cut of my work" credo. In his life and his many fictions, Frank Herbert counseled us and his protagonists to not let heroism go to our heads, to beware of hubris, the seductive spells of charismatic leaders who might be protodictators eager to impose their "perfect" plans on the rest of us. Sadly, as the *Dune* saga expands, powerful Paul will embody that dynamic. With so many correspondences between *Dune* and *Twin Peaks*, might Cooper harbor some totalitarian plan of his own?

In *Dune*, there's a psychic chemistry that can unravel time, the idea of meddling in "all the futures I could create," since "I am a net that can sweep future and past." But enacting a righteous plan, "reaching for a new thing, he might fail what was most precious—receding, never to be recaptured again. Nothing, nothing can be done." Will these *Dune* ideas haunt the ending of *The Return*? Right now, Cooper has to follow Herbert's advice to let action banish stagnation, and ambition triumph over fear.

For Lynch, the essence of *Dune* is Paul awakening to his destiny as a beneficent force within a matrix of roiling power systems and metaphysical forces. And in *Twin Peaks* and *The Return*, the program for Cooper is the same. Lynch stages Paul's coming into full consciousness of his powers and his mission as high theater, in the desert, a site of history's timeless fables, where Paul is surrounded by the woman who loves him and towering sandworms rearing up at attention to pay him homage as he declares, "The sleeper has awakened!"

Lynch stages Cooper's awakening as relatively more subdued theater, without symphonic accompaniment. Cooper lies comatose, no one else in the room. For the third time in *The Return*, we hear that humming-ringing sound that was in Ben Horne's hotel office and that James heard down in the dark hotel boiler room near a mysterious closed door. Now the sound gently permeates Cooper's hospital room; Lynch is laying down aesthetic-narrative stepping stones, like a sonic yellow brick road. Over the previous hours of *The Return*, the cosmos have been out of balance. Mr. C, Cooper's bad self + Bob, didn't come back in the Red Room when he was supposed to, and Cooper's good self was embedded in the halting, impaired, barely speaking Dougie. Frank Herbert states that one "who has spent his life creating one particular representation of his selfdom will die rather than become the antithesis of that representation." The One-Armed Man has tried in vain to penetrate Dougie's slow wits with the message that the good Cooper within him needs to wake up and destroy evil Mr. C. And he's sent Dougie helpful signs that have enabled him to win casino jackpots and mark those insurance papers in a way that uncovered corruption in Bushnell Mullins's organization. The One-Armed Man has been able to monitor Dougie's doings, and now, after Dougie gave himself that massive electrical shock, perhaps the Cooper "sleeping" within him has been stirred to the brink of full consciousness.

At last. Cooper's eyes open, he sits up in bed and talks to the One-Armed Man, who's materialized at his bedside. The One-Armed Man reiterates that the "other one" (Mr. C) is still out and will have to be eliminated. Cooper knows the score.

He's "one-hundred percent" awake, and we sense that he comprehends the physical/metaphysical status quo and what needs to happen next to help accomplish the Fireman's visionary plan. Cooper takes the jade ring from the One-Armed Man so that he can use it to transport Mr. C/Bob back to the Red Room. He confirms that the One-Armed Man has the little golden tulpa-making seed that we've seen in relation to tulpas Dougie and "Diane." Cooper plucks a few hairs from his head (DNA) and gives them to the One-Armed Man, telling him to "make another one," meaning a "good Cooper" Dougie, to be husband and father to Janey-E and Sonny Jim, who love him so much. The first tulpa Dougie, made by Mr. C from Cooper's dark-side spiritual makeup, was a degraded, wastrel Cooper.

We've witnessed the deep familial and romantic love and support Cooper-as-Dougie has received, for the first time in his life, from Janey-E and Sonny Jim. So why would he send a simulacrum of himself to be with them? Maybe the pure-Cooper tulpa would be a placeholder while he's completing his mission ("two birds with one stone": kill Bob, find/save Laura). The words "I understand" and a nod concluded Cooper's early briefing session with the Fireman in Part One, and they conclude awakened Cooper's chat with the One-Armed Man, who vanishes. So how will Cooper proceed?

Lynch's method, ever since he began making art as a youth, has been to present contrasts and dualities. If Dougie was slow, quiet, severely limited, the awakened Cooper is adroit, tuned up, and ready to go in mind and body. Technically, Cooper awoke a few minutes ago, when his eyes opened. But his true "The sleeper must awaken" moment comes when he interacts with Bushnell Mullins, Dougie's boss and friend, who tells him, "The FBI is on its way here." And Cooper, in a thrilling affirmation of the *Twin Peaks* spirit, declares, "I *am* the FBI!"

Janey-E and Sonny Jim are momentarily disconcerted but happy and excited that Dougie has suddenly expanded to heroic proportions. He now talks a lot, he walks briskly; he, not Janey-E, gets in the driver's seat of the BMW the Mitchum brothers gave them and proceeds to weave in and out of traffic like a racing pro.

As the Douglas Jones/Cooper family speeds away from the hospital, there's a delicious culture-shock moment that crystalizes the contrast between *The Return*'s new realities and the expectations fostered by the original series. The midday Las Vegas desert sun beats down; it's eighty-four degrees, the BMW's convertible top is down—and the *Twin Peaks* "Falling" theme music is playing. Music that for twenty-seven years has accompanied only rain-dripping forest trees and shivery temperatures. Composer Angelo Badalamenti's mesmerizing chords have enveloped the Northwest like fog, but now they propel Cooper and company fast over Southwestern sands. Lynch and Frost have done it: they've successfully expanded the *Twin Peaks* sensibility and culture as their own personal and artistic world views have broadened and deepened.

When Cooper left the hospital, he told Bushnell to send a message to Gordon Cole, and Cole sends one to the Mitchum brothers: get your private jet ready; we're heading to Spokane, Washington, the nearest airport to Twin Peaks (and one of the Northwest cities the Lynch family lived in when David was young). Cooper's speeding forward on his mission, pulling strategic elements into position, but he doesn't outpace his heart. He holds Janey-E and Sonny Jim close, looks them in the eyes. Through the strange process of being embedded in the life of one Dougie Jones, Cooper has experienced what he never did in the original *Twin Peaks*: the love of a good woman and child, a supportive, nurturing domestic life. We've often seen the three of them together, and it's poignant when Cooper goes off alone. But he's one-hundred-percent Dale Cooper, and he knows that should he not survive, the One-Armed-Man's way with the golden seed and a bit of Cooper's hair (DNA), and some magical electricity, will bring the Cooper whom Jane-E and Sonny Jim love back to them. Cooper assures his family that he'll be with them again: "I'll be back through that red door and be home for good." Maybe in Lynch's visual language, the safe and happy family behind the red door was the pinnacle, the peak experience prefigured by the red balloon at the top of the white mountain sculpture outside the building where Dougie worked, at the Lucky 7 Insurance company, what that bronze peacekeeper statue was actually pointing toward.

In the movies Lynch and Frost grew up watching, men on missions often said, "Let's synchronize watches," before they proceeded. During the time Cooper's been living with Janey-E and Sonny Jim in the Jones house, he's been out of synch, out of phase with himself, his willpower short-circuited. Now that he's restored to full-functioning Cooperhood, it's clear that he absorbed everything he experienced while being Dougie. He sees the full, correct picture and can act on it. He can briskly tell the Mitchum brothers, "I read you one-hundred-percent." He can resolutely press forward, convinced that his ideas are correct. But the world of *The Return* is far more complex, nuanced, and ambiguous than that of the original *Twin Peaks*. Even members of the Blue Rose Task Force make erroneous assessments of data, miss clues, forget things. Hopefully on his coming mission, Cooper's reading of reality will be properly balanced; he'll know what the right time is.

Part Sixteen has one more awakening for us. Audrey Horne is one of Lynch's traumatized people. She barely survived a bomb blast, was raped by Mr. C, and has endured having the child she gave birth to be raised by those deemed more competent. Now she and her husband, Charlie, are at tense, angry odds with each other. He has the power of money, a marriage license, and a malicious will over her. She has her rebellious spirit and a passion for Billy, whom she loves and has sex with, and whom we never see. We've seen Charlie manipulate her for sport and Audrey fight back with growing animosity.

In previous parts, in the midst of their venom spewing (Charlie cool, Audrey scorching hot), they talked of going to the Roadhouse so that Audrey can look for Billy, who's been in past trouble and has disappeared. In the mode of *Waiting for Godot*, it seemed they'd never leave their house, but here they are, in the midst of a Roadhouse evening. Characteristically, Charlie toasts "To us," and Audrey raises her glass "To Billy," as she scans the room for him in vain.

When they came in, Northwest rock god Eddie Vedder of Pearl Jam was singing his lament "Out of Sand" in his tear-your-heart-out voice. The poignant words make us think of Audrey, Laura, ourselves, all of humanity. Time is gone, or fast going. Who I was won't come again. There were right roads not taken, but the chance is gone now; it's too late. Vedder's words paint a sad, hopeless picture. But the title "Out of Sand" references an hourglass, which, when the sand runs out, gets turned over, bottom to top, so that time flows in the opposite direction, a new beginning. The song's general sense of loss is counterbalanced by a very Lynchian/*Twin Peaks* mention of "another us around somewhere with much better lives," the glimpse of heaven in the midst of hell.

Vedder had been alone onstage with his acoustic guitar, but now, suddenly, there are five musicians, bathed in the reddish blue light with which Lynch illuminated Isabella Rossellini singing in *Blue Velvet* and Julee Cruise singing in *Fire Walk With Me*.

As in a wish-fulfilling dream, the announcer says, "Audrey's Dance," and the crowd clears the floor. We hear familiar, cool-jazz Angelo Badalamenti sounds that twenty-five years ago, came from the Double R diner's jukebox as teenage Audrey danced dreamily, her whole life ahead of her. The music moves her away from Charlie, to sway and twirl in a gentle ecstacy, eyes closed, smiling, her extended hand sculpting the air in graceful arabesques. There's a white spotlight on her, and pink light beams are near, but she doesn't glow with blessed pinkness like the illuminated Naido and Cooper did in Part Two. Audrey's blissful respite from her hellish life ends when two rough guys start pounding each other. She clings to Charlie in fear, vulnerable and dependent as ever: "Get me out of here!"

In the art of cinema, one shot can cut to another so smoothly that we don't even notice the change. Or a cut can shake us to our roots. From the dimly lit action of the Roadhouse, we're suddenly in bright whiteness; there's the black, oval frame of a mirror, which reflects, close-up, the pale face and black hair of Audrey. She looks utterly confused, aghast, and gasps, "Wha—what?" A white, smock-like hospital gown frames her face. The shot lasts maybe a second and is accompanied by an electrical crackling and the biomechanical scraping/clicking that indicates realities/dimensions interfacing.

Audrey is in a care facility, living beyond harsh realities in memories/flashbacks of her dramatic, heartfelt life in Twin Peaks with Charlie, Billy, Tina, dancing to the music of her soul. Has Lynch returned to *Oz* again, taken a woman from a bleak black-and-white place (Dorothy's Kansas/Audrey's hospital) to a colorful inner land (Oz/Twin Peaks) where she can strive, wrestle with challenges, discover her inner resources and strengths, and return home stronger and wiser?

We won't see Audrey again in *The Return*. She has certainly suffered, like another daughter of the North woods, the blonde one. The one gone twenty-five years ago and gone now, the Mystery. And we know the detective who thinks he can find her, solve her.

–CHAPTER TWENTY-THREE–

SHERIFF'S OFFICE/UNOFFICIAL (PART SEVENTEEN)

Writer-director Monte Hellman (born 1929), who made the existential westerns *The Shooting* and *Ride in the Whirlwind* (both 1966) and the cult-classic existential car movie *Two-Lane Blacktop* (1971), once told me about a western he planned to make. The title would have encapsulated the idea that There Are No Soft-Hearted Gunfighters, because if you hesitate, you're dead.

Gordon Cole sits in the Buckhorn hotel room where tulpa Diane has just vanished, off to the Red Room to dissolve into the golden seed. Gordon's gun is in his hand, unfired: "I just couldn't do it." But he's alive. When Diane drew her gun, Gordon could rely on his partner Albert to take her out. And besides, how could he pull the trigger on Diane, even if she was under a bad influence?

In *The Return*, Lynch and Frost have made Gordon and Albert more complex and more deeply human than in previous *Twin Peaks* outings. The FBI partners are older now; they can forget things, get things wrong. For years, Albert kept a secret from Gordon, that he had authorized Phillip Jeffries to give "Cooper" (actually Mr. C) information that resulted in an agent being killed. It took some emotional work on Gordon's part, but he and Albert got through this crisis with their relationship intact.

In this space where Albert and Tammy have just shot "Diane," Gordon has seen the woman so like the woman he has known for decades die. It's a moment of terrible awe. Emotions are raw, vulnerable; defenses are down, and Gordon makes a confession. For twenty-five years he has kept something from Albert, and us: nothing less than the constellation of elements, the metaphysical clockwork, the secret knowledge of *Twin Peaks*'s branching tree of good and evil.

After a dramatic pause, Lynch/Gordon Cole lays it out. Two decades back, before Major Briggs disappeared, he told Cole and Cooper that he'd become aware of "an entity, an extremely negative force," called Jouday in ancient times, now known as Judy. Briggs, Cole, and Cooper then put together a plan that could lead them to

Judy, theoretically to curtail her power, even eliminate her.

The Devil is a male, but there are plenty of evil females in the world's myths, religions, and cultures, ancient and modern. Lynch's Hindu spiritual system has the devouring goddess Kali; the Bible's Book of Revelations has the Whore of Babylon, mother of abominations. There are wicked queens, witches, and sorceresses; sleep-invading demons, film noir femme fatales; Cruella De Ville; evil stepmothers: the whole symbolic notion of the vagina with teeth inside.

Of Lynch's sixteen primary film and TV fictions, nine present threatening, treacherous, sometimes murderous women, but none of them can even dream of the dark power of Judy, spanning time and space in burning clouds of nuclear fission, superior to Bob, the object of ultimate desire for Mr. C, who's already mastered worldly evil. Lynch's most potent physical/metaphysical/spiritual malefactors have been male. In the original *Twin Peaks*, Lynch saw Bob as "an abstraction with a human form," and Albert called him "the evil that men do." Ravenously raping Laura Palmer and hungering for her soul, Bob was the darkest male energy incarnate. Lynch gave us a scary taste of abstract female evil in *Mulholland Drive* (2001), where a sludge-encrusted being (Bonnie Aarons) whose black smudge of a head, suddenly seen emerging from behind a wall, causes a man to drop dead. Before he was scared to death, the man said the being was "causing it all," meaning "the god awful feeling," the web of fear and negative energy poisoning the world. At the time he was making *Mulholland Drive*, Lynch did a large painting called *Bob Sees Himself Walking Toward a Formidable Abstraction*, in which a small Bob approaches a huge floating, irregular-edged black smudge of God-awful feeling, of devouring evil energy that can take any form, the empowering essence of dark intention that can suck the light from the world. This is the shadowy being in *Mulholland Drive*, the dark smudge on Mr. C's playing card, Judy, nonexistence, nullity, beyond naming.

In Lynch and Robert Engels' 1991 *Fire Walk With Me* screenplay, Phillip Jeffries refers to being "in Seattle at Judy's" and adds that "Judy is positive about this," referencing Jeffries's encounter with strange denizens, finishing with "I'm not going to talk about Judy; keep Judy out of this." In footage shot but not included in the final cut, Jeffries, in a Buenos Aires hotel, asks, "Do you have a Miss Judy staying here?" He's told that "a young lady" left a note for him. This Judy sounds like a human being, a compatriot/companion/colleague of Jeffries's, not *The Return*'s extradimensional abstraction of evil, an emanation from the dark stars. In the film (1992), when Jeffries enters Gordon Cole's office, he says, "I'm not going to talk about Judy; in fact we're not going to talk about Judy at all," connoting that Judy is a corporeal person, not the "extreme negative force" she is in *The Return*. Moving forward from the *Fire Walk With Me* days, Lynch and Frost have expanded Judy's power and status to that of a dark goddess. *Twin Peaks* can have Judy both ways, since Jeffries's words about her as a person fit *The Return*'s Judy-as-force context. And there's a bridging, linking harmony between *Fire Walk With Me* and *The Return* in the way Albert first hears about the full Judy narrative in 2016, even though he was in Cole's office in 1989, where Jeffries emphasized that he, Cole, and Cooper weren't "going to talk about Judy" in front of Albert. Like *Twin Peaks* viewers, Albert will wait a long time to see how the story plays out.

Lynch wrote *Fire Walk With Me* with Robert Engels and *The Return* with Mark Frost, so how did Judy become the metaphysical essence of metastasizing evil over twenty-five years? Before *The Return* aired, Lynch said that *Fire Walk With Me* was a key to the new *Twin Peaks*, and Robert Engels agrees. He confirms that he and Lynch conceived of Judy as a flesh-and-blood person; in fact she was named after Engels' sister-in-law. In this early narrative, Judy was Josie Packard's sister; the two interacted with arch villain Windom Earle, and Phillip Jeffries was on the scene. None of this is in *Fire Walk With Me* or the original *Twin Peaks*; Jeffries just mentions Judy cryptically in Cole's office. And later a monkey's face that had been hiding behind a mask whispers, "Judy." Engels says this was done to keep the idea of the Judy character alive for potential future story threads, but this would be the woman Judy, not *The Return*'s Wicked Mother of fairy tales, legends, the dark side of our psyches and, sadly, some of our living rooms.

So how did Judy, written as a woman character in 1991, become Judy/Jouday, *The Return*'s invading, pervasive force of evil? I haven't done deep Library of Congress research, but to my knowledge no other Lynch commentator has posited the idea I wrote in my 2008 book *David Lynch: Beautiful Dark*. Writing about *Fire Walk With Me*, I was pondering the power dynamic between Bob and the One-Armed Man and the gathering of extradimensional invaders above the convenience store: the mystery of why they came to our realm, what they were seeking, what their mission was. Or were they not here by choice, exiled, but by whom—who was running their show? I wrote that maybe Judy was the ultimate authority/spiritual figure in Bob and the One-Armed Man's world. I wondered if Bob was an underling to a dark female goddess. Was this idea a blueprint for *The Return*'s Judy/Jouday? It's conceivable. I sent a copy of my book to Lynch, who by all accounts does not read widely, in the fall of 2008, four years before he Mark Frost started writing *The Return*. Those close to him say he "read every word of your book." Lynch says, "Ninety percent of the time I don't know what I'm doing" when he's creating. The fundamental energies/impulses/structures of the human psyche produce "original thoughts" common to human consciousness. Lynch synthesizes the elements in his mind in an alchemy both dark and golden.

So *The Return*'s Judy would be the dark goddess invading our world in 1945 through a nuclear fission portal, spewing her creepy-crawly agents forth to blacken human souls and devour them, sucking the essence of goodness into the abyss of nonexistence. Clearly human beings have had the capacity to manifest evil throughout centuries of preatomic bomb history, so Judy and her crew would amplify the psyche's inherent dark shadow currents and meld with existing sinister narratives like those that have long haunted *Twin Peaks*. The power struggles between dark and light impulses in our heads will always be enacted outside us in the world; *The Return* would have a dark Wicked Queen propagating fear and destruction, so who could be a female counterforce championing golden goodness, a righteous angel with a flaming sword? The Fireman sent Laura's spirit to Earth to be that one. She sinned, sacrificed herself heroically, and was in a sanctified, light-filled state when she was torn away from the Red Room. In *Twin Peaks* Cooper is born to seek her, to help shape some cosmic plan that's in motion, full of danger and great promise. But he must revive to help form the future.

Mark Frost, in his books *The Secret History of Twin Peaks* (pre-*The Return*'s airing) and *Twin Peaks*: *The Final Dossier* (post-*The Return*), links Judy/Jouday to the Middle Eastern desert regions of ancient Sumer and to the American Southwest, where real-life Jet Propulsion Lab scientist Jack Parsons, English magus Aleister Crowley, and science fiction author L. Ron Hubbard focused their efforts on opening portals to powerful secrets from Beyond. Did Frost follow these ideas into the desert and link them to the historical 1945 atomic bomb blast as a way of bringing Lynch and Robert Engels's Judy into *The Return*? Had either Frost or Lynch seen the 1977 film *The Chosen*, in which a scientist (Kirk Douglas) who designed seven nuclear power plants fathers the Antichrist, who plans to destroy the world with atomic blasts? Douglas has a biblical nightmare in which the *Book of Revelations*'s beast with seven heads obliterates the world. In *Revelations*, this beast serves as transportation for one of the biblical Dark Women, Babylon, "mother of harlots and of earth's abominations." Both Lynch and Frost have long been fascinated by the *Book of Revelations*, so this wicked female creature birthing abominations in the desert seems a direct inspiration for *The Return*'s Dark Mother.

The name Babylon (Babalon in Aleister Crowley's myth system) is nowhere in *The Return*. Throughout literature, there are various versions of Babylon and the beast, including my *Beautiful Dark* idea that she is Judy and Bob is the beast. In some accounts, the female creature is called Mystery, or alluded to as an amorphous, virulent dark quality that has no name. Lynch has long revered the visionary English poet-painter William Blake (1757-1827), whose prodigious imagination created a unique cosmology of images and words, partly based on biblical dynamics. In Blake's *The Sea of Time and Space* painting Mystery represents the dark anima of the female principle, the feminine counterpart of Satan, and Blake portrays her wearing the crescent moon horns of Artemis, the lethal night-hunting goddess aiming her killing bow and arrows. In *The Return*'s Part Eight Lynch linked a crescent form to the Woodsmen preparing the convenience store for the dark invaders, and the female creature spewing out Bob and a contagion of eggs into our world. For ages storytellers have portrayed monstrous threats from the outside coming at us, out of the black reaches of space or from a dark city alleyway. But Blake sensed that exterior threats were forms of our own shadow side, our dark unconscious projected onto the world. In his poem *The Human Abstract*, Blake posits that the miasma of human self-deception, ignorance and evil feeds on Mystery, a psychological structure, a Tree in the Human Brain, an expansive idea far beyond Blake's *The Sea of Time and Space* Mystery just representing the dark female principle. This inner obstacle keeps us from perceiving and regaining the unfallen world of paradise, and Lynch believes the tunnel vision of negativity can be transcended through meditation and an expanded spiritual consciousness. Blake wrote of "the Gods which Came from fear," who can "bring forth mighty powers." Throughout history, there have been devouring creatures, dragons, the serpent of the Scandinavian Völuspá epic vomiting poison over the earth (in *The Return*'s desert?), and heroes attempting to slay them (Beowulf, the Red Cross Knight of Spenser's *The Faerie Queene*, Special Agent Dale Cooper?) Evil and a countering goodness, abstracted in visual and storytelling art, and William Blake was a master of both. I've thumbed through beautiful art books of Blake's work at Lynch's studio and been struck by the eighteenth-century artist's cosmos-spanning sense of scale. Blake's *The Angel of the Revelation*'s (1803–1805) head is big as the sun; huge allegorical figures float above earthly landscapes; spirals of souls span galaxies; a figure contains the sun, moon and stars; there's an ocean of dark waters, *The Sea of Time and Space* (*The Return*'s dark purple sea?). As usual in Lynch's work, the outside echoes the inside, the microcosm mirrors the macrocosm: both artists know that small, particular things are, as Blake says, "Portions of Eternity."

I was an English major, and Blake has been on my mind since school days. A man who could see literal angels in the air above industrial England, Blake believed in "worlds on worlds," layers and waves of reality beyond the everyday, the ordinary. In the original *Twin Peaks*, Bob was always ferocious, fearsome, mysterious, other, but he became standardized, an expected part of the *Twin Peaks* universe. My thought in *David Lynch: Beautiful Dark* that there was a greater, dark Judy power above and beyond Bob came from my conception of Lynch's sensibility. His Blake-like feeling that there was Something More in the mundane world, that "sense of wild pain and decay" he could feel but not see, combined with his belief in angels, guiding powers, the larger-than-life rages and loves in his life, his Hindu view of spiritual life, and the universe, being-ending-being forever, like the goddess Shakti blinking her eyes.

In Western tradition, the archetypal image of evil is the serpent, whose sinuous form is composed of many glistening scales. Bob is one of the scales; Judy is another (Blake called the dark female power "A Woman Scaly"), but they're just part of an expansive evil beyond comprehension, which Lynch keeps alive, ferocious and terrifying through his perfectly balanced artistic orientation toward abstraction and restraint. Obscuring, diffusing, superimposing smoke, curtains, veils, flashing light: Who do you think that is there? What time is it?

Maybe it's time to read Stephen King's novel *The Revival*. It's not about Lynch and Frost reviving Twin Peaks . . . but maybe it is. Lynch and Frost started writing *The Return* in 2012 and began filming it in 2015. *The Revival* was published in 2014 and contains elements germane to *The Return*. *The Revival* has a supremely powerful female force of negativity that seeks to enter our world: "Mother will be here soon." And at one point she's pounding on a door, which parallels, in *The Return*'s Mansion by the Purple Sea, the American Girl warning, "Mother is coming," as that malevolent Mother pounds and pounds. Did Lynch and Frost lift this from King? Or did movie fan King see Lynch's *Mulholland Drive* (2001), in which an abstraction of a woman's guilt and bad karma pounds on her door? And King may have transformed Lynch's concept of bad electricity (*Ronnie Rocket* screenplay, mid-1970s; *Fire Walk With Me*,

1992) as a conduit for, and manifestation of, evil energy into *The Revival*'s "special electricity." Who can explain how creative people of prodigious imagination can sense the same things in the air?

Mr. C, though composed of Bob and Cooper's dark side, is still a detective, a seeker like Coop. He needs to find Judy, know her power, fuck it out of her if he has to, steal it, own and command the supreme energies, beholden to no one, totally free—or maybe find a situation that can give him some resistance, a challenge, keep some kind of game on.

In the Buckhorn hotel room, Gordon Cole tells Albert and Tammy that twenty-five years ago Major Briggs, Cooper, and Cole devised a "plan that would lead to Judy." But then Briggs and Cooper disappeared, as did Phillip Jeffries, who also knew about Judy. The last thing Cooper said to Cole was "If I disappear, find me; I'm trying to kill two birds with one stone." Intriguing words, which we first heard when, in Part One, the Fireman boosted Cooper from the Red Room for a briefing. The Fireman said the nine words to Cooper, who seconded them with "I understand." We know that Mr. C is an independent cuss who likes to deviate from what's prescribed for him and go outlaw, and Cooper likes to be guided by his own lights. (In *Fire Walk With Me*, when Carl Rodd is methodically showing Cooper the trailer park, Cooper vectors off in another direction, saying, "I'm going over here," which could be individualistic Lynch's motto in art and life). Kyle MacLachlan and Lynch have both said that there's a fair amount of Lynch in Cooper's character. And a number of Lynch's cowriters, actors, camera people, and assorted crew members will confirm that Lynch can treat a film shoot like one of his paintings in progress, spontaneously responding to fresh ideas and aesthetic impulses in midproduction. And in the creative fever of shooting, he can alter or drop already scripted material.

So twenty-five years ago, Briggs, Cooper, and Cole hatched the *official* plan to find Judy, and Cooper had his additional, *personal* plan. He would be the stone, the agent who would kill Bob and find and save Laura. Of course Cooper and the Fireman's "two birds with one stone" is symbolic language; as with so much of *The Return*, what seems to be a mutual understanding may have a different meaning to each party.

Cole keeps giving Albert and Tammy full knowledge of the situation. Mr. C's gang member Ray Monroe was an FBI informant who learned that his boss was looking for coordinates from Major Briggs, another confirmation that Mr. C was not in the Zone when Ruth was killed, since the coordinates were written on her arm. Ray also confirms that he and Phillip Jeffries were on the side that wanted Mr. C killed, but the question of the alternative-Jeffries phone voice that Mr. C heard remains.

The Las Vegas FBI's confusion over Who's Dougie, Who's Cooper, Who's in the FBI? is cleared up when Bushnell Mullins, standing next to Dougie/Cooper's empty hospital bed, tells Gordon Cole (in South Dakota) Dougie/Cooper's message. These facts are hyper meaningful to Cole: Cooper's heading for Sheriff Truman's office in Twin Peaks, and the timestamp of his message adds up to ten, the "number of completion."

When two guys are as simpatico with each other as Cole and Albert are, Cole knows he doesn't have to apologize for keeping the hugely significant Judy thread secret for decades, but he does. And Albert, who spat fire in the original *Twin Peaks,* graciously accepts. Besides, a balance has been righted, for in Part Four, Albert revealed that years ago he'd kept a secret from Cole, that he'd authorized Jeffries to give Cooper (actually the unrevealed Mr. C) information that resulted in an agent being murdered. Lynch as writer-actor is at ease with showing Cole as a vulnerable, forgetful, sometimes confused human being. As Cole, Albert, and Tammy pack up to head for Twin Peaks, he says, "Dougie is Cooper? How the hell is that possible?"

In Part Sixteen, before the divided Diane tried to kill her fellow Blue Rose Task Force colleagues, she sent Mr. C coordinates, saying, "Oh, Coop, I hope this works." In Part Seventeen, Mr. C is on the road, following the coordinates; Cooper, the Mitchum brothers, and their Pink Ladies are flying toward Twin Peaks, as are Cole, Albert, and Tammy. Lynch and Frost are unfolding a legend for us, and their approach to the big showdown maintains a stately rhythm, the imminent drama of the congregation at Sheriff Truman's is self-evident: the creators don't need to hype up suspense by whip-cutting back and forth between the various travelers.

Mr. C goes where Diane's coordinates guided him: the forest near Twin Peaks, Major and Bobby Briggs's Jack Rabbit's Palace and the locus of mystery beyond: the meadow, the single tree, the circle of liquid at its base, a white smoke softly flashing with electricity. The Fireman seems to know this zone well. From here he pulled Andy into his realm and showed him a deep-story image parade of past and future: Laura, her beatification, bad and good Coopers side by side, Lucy's prominence in some coming action, the number "6" telephone pole. And on the grass by the single tree and stone circle was naked Naido. Perhaps the Fireman softened her fall from space after she threw the electrical switch that helped Cooper on his journey from the Red Room. Andy had been imbued with knowledge of Naido's mythic importance and taken her to the Sheriff's Office for safe keeping, which is where she is now.

Mr. C stands where Diane's coordinates sent him, by the circle and tree. The air whooshes; he experiences superpositioning, microsecond blinking in and out of the landscape at different spots. A spiraling vortex forms above his head—and he's gone, and it's the Fireman's doing. We're in the vast black-and-white space of the Fireman's theater-studio-workshop, with the big screen and proscenium arch centered in the image. In a cage on the left is Mr. C, his essence behind bars. His face fills the cage, as Bob's face fills his globe-shaped container in *The Return.* On the right floats the moon face of Major Briggs, recalling the Wizard of Oz's presentation in the Lynch-loved film ("*The Wizard of Oz* is a cosmic film, meaningful on many levels," Lynch told the Guardian's Killian Fox in 2019). This is the place where evil-fighting, beneficent spirits and wills are at work, and carefully laid plans are enacted. Twenty-five years ago, did Major Briggs and the Fireman, aware of a dark Cooper, devise a strategy to lure Mr. C to the Jack Rabbit's Palace realm, where he'd be vulnerable and paranormally grabbed? Since Cooper was in the Red Room twenty-five years ago, and Major Briggs was in hiding, did one of them, perhaps helped by mojo from the One-Armed Man, communicate to Diane, in a dream perhaps, the way to set up Mr. C? And even in her allied-with-Mr. C tulpa state, did Diane receive the righteous message and act on it? "Oh, Coop, I hope this works." It did. But where is Diane to celebrate?

Mr. C fathered Richard Horne the usual, genetic way. Mr. C made tulpa Diane from some of her DNA (hair, saliva, etc.) Tulpa Diane went to the Red Room when restored Cooper came on the scene, and dissolved to a golden seed. With our human tendency toward fuzzy thinking, sometimes when we watched Dougie it was easy to feel like Cooper was possessing/possessed by Dougie, who was a tulpa created by Mr. C. Dougie was gone, to the Red Room, back to a golden seed. But journey-battered Cooper, his self-awareness and communication abilities almost zero, was living Dougie as a community-and-family-established social role; all his DNA was Cooper's. So if Mr. C used Diane's DNA to make tulpa Diane and the tulpa's dissolved to the golden seed, the real Diane must be somewhere.

For now, the Fireman floats like a high-levitating yogi near his work-space screen, as when he synthesized Laura's golden globe and sent her to Earth in 1956. The black-and-white image of the forest that Mr. C vanished from fills the screen. The pale tree, the ground circle, and we notice that the number of big evergreen trees in the background is seven; this truly is an auspicious spot. The Fireman exercises his power with majestic grace, sweeping his hand in the air and causing an image of the Palmer house to take the screen. That will come later. He moves on to the scene of an asphalt parking lot surrounded by evergreens. This is the next step in the plan.

With Lynch's usual perfect, strange blend of mechanical-electrical sounds, Mr. C's cage moves toward the screen. His essence is extracted into the golden, saxophone-curved apparatus that sent Laura earthward, and he appears in the scene on the screen, his back to us, small in the Fireman's vast expanse. Then director Lynch, the cinematic magician, dissolves to a color image of Mr. C's black leather jacket and black hair filling the frame, gleaming in the pale Northwest sunshine. He's just been manipulated by the Fireman, but he's huge, bristling with his own dark power.

He's landed in the Twin Peaks Sheriff's Office parking lot, and there's Andy getting stuff out of a car. Andy's always had a beautiful smile, and his face lights up: "Agent Cooper!" And Mr. C answers, "Hello, Andy." The power of familiarity and the complexity of the human psyche are on full display. This evil creature, whose eyes are black orbs the color of Satan's deep well, is still Cooper to Andy and, in some small, strange way, partly to us. Do we imagine that there's a slight softness of affection in Mr. C's greeting to Andy? And Andy's genuinely happy to see his old comrade. But previously, the Fireman showed Andy the images of the regular and the long-haired Cooper side-by-side; maybe Andy interpreted that as a then-and-now display, not a moral/spiritual portrait of light and darkness.

Lucy at her reception desk is thrilled to see "Cooper" too. Sheriff Truman comes out, Mr. C offers his hand, they shake, and Truman explains about Harry, whom

Cooper interacted with so much years ago, being ill and absent. They go out of frame, to Truman's office, and Andy stands beaming at Lucy, overflowing with sweet joy over their family-feeling reunion with Coop. Andy's always been lovable because he leads with his emotions. But now a memory kicks in, the Fireman's image parade, something disturbing with Lucy, Andy holding her shoulders, positioning her somehow, then running off. Now, at Lucy's desk, her nest within the Twin Peaks peacekeepers professional family, Andy's smile fades.

But Andy still seems to think that that's Cooper there, standing in front of Sheriff Truman's desk like a cold, dark monolith in the honey-gold-toned room. Andy reverently gets a chair for him to sit in and asks if he'd like some coffee. "Cooper's" "No thanks," his refusal of the bonding agent of everything good in Twin Peaks, should trigger alarm bells in Andy, but he's still bubbling with excitement, and he rushes off to tell Hawk about their visitor. After his "No thanks," Mr. C added, "I'm all right": a terse summation reminder of his self-referential circle/circuit of evil.

When Mr. C materialized at the sheriff's office, sent from the Fireman's holding cage, he realized he'd been manipulated and was in danger. He touched his black leather jacket on the left side; he could feel the shape of his hidden gun. In Part Two, he realized that "the game" was beginning, temporal and metaphysical forces in conflict, and he a major player. But the outcome of a game is uncertain. Mr. C is ever confident, but here, in the sheriff's office, Kyle MacLachlan gives him a subtle, perfect edge of wariness, his formidable powers calculating moment to moment.

Sheriff Truman has been schooled on the idea that there are two Coopers, and he stares at this one, who says he's back in Twin Peaks on unfinished business. Truman's phone lights up. It's Lucy with an incoming call. Her voice is agitated; she insists he take it. Cut to Cooper in a vehicle with the Mitchums and the Pink Ladies. He's percolating with happy energy: "Harry, this is Coop. We're just entering Twin Peaks. Is the coffee on?" We have a Lynch-Frost confederation of multi-identities: two Trumans, two Coopers, and a new, unexpected role for Lucy. Frank tells Cooper he's not Harry, and Mr. C goes on high alert, his eyes locked on Frank's. Frank gives no hint that he's talking to the real Cooper, but Mr. C's calculating brain and Bob's animal instinct say, It's go time. Mr. C fires, misses Frank. Frank draws his gun, but before he can trigger it, there's a blast, and Mr. C falls out of his chair, revealing Lucy in the doorway behind him: fluffy pink sweater, her hands in the prescribed law-keepers' two-handed grip on her smoking pistol.

So this is why Lucy was a prominent part of the image parade the Fireman showed Andy. And why Andy knows to bring Naido (who chattered and chirped in alarm when Mr. C entered the building), Freddie with his green glove (which smacked down Officer Chad, who was trying to escape), and his pal soulful James all up to Truman's office, where Hawk arrives and beholds the dead, dark Cooper with wonder and understanding. Good Coop is still on the phone line. He's plugged into the *Twin Peaks* energy/knowledge circuit and warns, "Don't touch that body." Lynch once told me a simple equation: "To get rid of darkness, you just turn on the light." But in *The Return*, not so fast. The light in Sheriff Truman's office seeps away to shadow; the room is suffocating with otherness as the dim forms of Woodsmen materialize and go to work on Mr. C, as previously, after Ray Monroe shot him, pushing and prodding his chest, bloodying their hands as those muffled, drowned-piano chords accompany some death/life process beyond understanding.

In *Blue Velvet*, an evil man's moral-spiritual "disease" infected a woman and a young man. And in *The Return*, Lynch shows the powerful darkness within the sheriff's office staining the air and even the light outside as Cooper's SUV arrives and deposits him on the sidewalk. (It's midday at the sheriff's station, but Lynch filmed Cooper arriving at twilight to match the paranormal half-light of Truman's office.)

Cooper enters as the Woodsmen vanish and the black, planetlike orb containing Bob rises from Mr. C's smoking, gaping chest. The long-anticipated showdown is here. Mr. C, the man who looks like Cooper, is dead. Bob, the alien spirit who caused Cooper's shadow side to split off into Mr. C, is at full, ferocious power, causing the ceiling to waver like a mirage as his globe hovers there. Lynch and his technical collaborators effectively made the snarling face of Bob (Frank Silva, who died in 1995) appear to be encased within a rough, rocky globe. He elicits awe, but not the visceral dread and fear that his full body and face (a "human" presence that is not human) stirred in us as he crept and crouched like an animal in the original *Twin Peaks* and *Fire Walk With Me*. Nothing in *The Return* matches the visceral horror of Bob putting his hands on Laura. And at the level of today's technology, Bob could have had a misty, computerized body instead of a globe. As Lynch has said, things that look human but aren't are deeply frightening. But the Bob-as-globe choice was made. If Bob is *Twin Peaks*'s resident evil, its goodness is Laura, and her glowing face in her golden globe is affectingly resonant. Lynch, in having both Bob's and Laura's faces encircled, creates an aesthetic/moral/spiritual balance. Perhaps an endurable balance between darkness and light is the best we can hope for.

Were we picturing, at the end, Cooper and Bob physically grappling, man to demon? Lynch and Frost surprise us by having Lucy snuff out Mr. C, but it didn't surprise the Fireman, the Übermensch, the high-in-the-sky being with a view of the Big Picture, who gives us humans hints, foreshadowings, and lets us marshal our personal resources to confront evil. In the original *Twin Peaks*, there was an overview sense that Bob violated a whole community when he invaded Leland, enlivening his dark side. And the good-hearted people gather in Sheriff Truman's office: Cooper, Naido, James, Andy, Lucy, Frank Truman. In the past, did the Fireman picture these participants, this scene, embed it as a spark of destiny, divinity, in human beings?

One of Cooper's life objectives is to eliminate Bob, but in *The Return* he's older, more humanized and vulnerable; he's happy to have help. The snarling, roaring Bob globe comes flying at Cooper, and the sheer terrifying sound knocks Coop on his back. (Weaponized sound, wielded by Kyle MacLachlan's character, is a hallmark of Lynch's *Dune*.) At *The Return*'s start, the Fireman gave Cooper coded hints about the future, but he didn't mention Freddie, yet now Cooper, struck down by Bob, knows to ask, "Are you ready, Freddie?" In *Twin Peaks*, knowledge comes to people in dreams, visions, and intuitions, so maybe the Fireman has updated Cooper somewhere along the line. Or maybe Cooper's ability to read a room is stronger than ever.

Cockney Freddie knows this moment is "me destiny," and he takes on Bob, punching with his powerful green gardening glove. The Bob globe bloodies Freddie's face, smacks him to the floor. Freddie hits the globe so hard it goes through the floor in flames, but it rises, charred and angry. Freddie's final blow does the trick: the globe shatters into hard black shards like gleaming black bits of coal, or cinders, that drift up toward the ceiling and vanish. In 1998, Lynch, with musician-singer Jocelyn Montgomery, recorded *Lux Vivens* (*Living Light*), based on verses by St. Hildegard von Bingen, the 12th-century German visionary writer and artist. As with Lynch, Hildegard's focus was the battle between good and evil, and her painting *The Fallen Stars* shows wicked Lucifer "turned to cinders and tossed in a whirlwind towards the abyss." Hildegard also painted a stunning depiction of a Dark Mother, "sullied with scaly blemishes and a monstrous head of Antichrist," emerging between her legs. Not vomited from her mouth, as Bob and the eggs were in *The Return*, but could these images have inspired Lynch? Hildegard did write of "the old serpent" vomiting "chunks of infected throw up all over the people." The revolting black vomit splattered on the earth, and in it Hildegard "saw seven sins." She also painted an image of the powerful female, light filled, with golden wings and hair, which recalls the Fireman's golden, glowing Laura globe sent to Earth.

In the Twin Peaks Sheriff's Office, the forces of light and goodness, the long-held plans of Major Briggs, Cooper, Gordon Cole, and the Fireman, have triumphed. Freddie, dazed after landing the killing blow on Bob, wonders, "Did I do it?" And Cooper, proud of the lad and savoring the moment, says, "You did it, Freddie." And since we're in Lynch and Frost's universe, it's a complex moment. A strategy that combined an elegant, reasoned design and visionary, intuitive guidance has worked; as David Lynch would say, "It's a beautiful thing." Cooper does what he needs to do, kneeling by Mr. C's corpse and sliding the jade ring on its finger. (What does it feel like to take your two hands and touch another hand that is also you?) The black form and bloody face of Mr. C fade away; the ring clatters on the Red Room floor.

A second SUV arrives outside the sheriff's station. Gordon Cole, Albert, Tammy, plus the Mitchum brothers join the office group, and we see and hear a sweet moment: Cole and the real Cooper, for the first time together in *The Return*, greeting each other verbally across the room. It feels like the spirit of some strategy devised by Major Briggs, Cole, and Cooper spans the space. Cooper notices Naido, standing silently in her pink robe. Lynch gives us alternating close-ups of their faces, finishing with a frame-filling close-up of Cooper that lingers as his head turns away from Naido and back to the group. Cooper's large, serious face remains superimposed over the scenes that follow, emphasizing his visionary abilities and glorifying his hero's journey and return: his Mount Rushmore status in the *Twin Peaks* legend. Lynch is also pictorializing a psychological-emotional nuance, the way we can be outwardly engaged with people in a room while simultaneously being stirred, captivated by a memory, a piercing thought. It's a Proustian remembrance of things past for Cooper:

Naido, his journey, her in it, glowing pink, plus something deeper in his heart. Lynch can communicate this state of consciousness without flashbacks, just Cooper's face large, transparent, included with his interactions with the group.

With a nod to Bobby Briggs, Cooper says that Major Briggs was "well aware of what's going on here today." So decades ago, when the Major, with his deep knowledge of paranormal forces, became aware of the Bad Cooper, he devised, with the Fireman's help, a plan to eliminate Mr. C and blast Bob to smithereens. If recently Briggs has needed a safe home, we know that he now has one with the Fireman.

Cooper, in his most serious demeanor, says, "There are things that will change," and the spiritually wise Hawk nods. Cooper adds that "the past dictates the future." Since we're in Lynchland, where karma counts and actions have consequences through multiple lifetimes, what we do now shapes our future; we climb the ladder or fall back. Lynch's revered, ancient Hindu texts don't talk about time travel; things change in a forward-flowing stream of time. In the Vedas and the Upanishads, divine entities don't come from the future to alter the present, thus shaping a better future, as in Philip K. Dick's visionary writings. But a key question of *The Return*: right now, "Is it future or is it past?" In Lynch and Frost's zone, Who? What? Why? When? Where? are in flux, and the characters' answers to those questions—and ours—are a function of mindset and angle of perception. It's a purple sea of possibilities, but we have to stay awake, step up, chart a course, do what we know is right.

Cooper credits the culmination of Major Briggs's grand design, but Cooper is the major voice in this room, the man who knows where he's going, what he needs to do. But there's something. . . . Naido surges forward; he steps forward to her. Their open palms touch. Throughout *The Return*, the transformational process of one being becoming another has involved the Red Room and been accompanied by saturated black smoke, which now pours from Naido's face with an egg-cracking sound. We see the Red Room through the aperture of her face, then the whole room, into which floats a dark, ovular shape that's a surrealistic combination of organic and inorganic elements. It looks like a rock with a womb-like cavity and recalls the massive gravity-defying single rocks that float in the paintings of master Belgian surrealist René Magritte 1898-1967), especially *The Glass Key* (1959). One of Magritte's famous paintings shows a huge floating rock with a small hat on top; Lynch, who's familiar with Magritte's work, has crafted prints of single rocks that seem sentient, and he's done a painting called *Rock with Seven Eyes* (1996). The cavity within the Red Room rock is filled with Diane's face—and then she's standing in front of Cooper in the sheriff's office, where Naido used to be.

Diane is pretty in pink, and Lynch's accumulated color coding is eloquent. She's wrapped in a pink robe, like the pink glow that illuminated Cooper and Naido when they first met and communed in the mauve zone. The pink that accompanies the coming and going of *The Wizard of Oz*'s Good Witch; the pink gown of Sheryl Lee as the Good Witch in *Wild at Heart*; the pink of resplendent femaleness, romantic and sexual; the "Pink House" that Lynch lives in; the "Pink Light," a euphoric, tangible quality that blesses the skies of Los Angeles, as LA secular saint Eve Babitz notes;

Philip K. Dick's pink light of universal enlightening intelligence. And amid this swoon of pinkness, Diane stands where Naido just was, her ruby-red bobbed hair the color of the gown Naido was wearing when she and Cooper glowed pink, the ruby red of Dorothy's transportive magic slippers in *The Wizard of Oz*. Cooper and Diane are not home yet. They have more adventure traveling to do. The clock in the Sheriff's office is stuck, not quite reaching 2:53, which, as Cooper said, adds up to ten, the number of completion. But for now, this is the real Cooper, the real Diane, no small thing in the fluid world of *Twin Peaks*, and we glory in their first kiss after many travails and years.

Lynch is a romantic who believes you can get in an elevator, lock eyes with a stranger, and feel the lightning bolt of love. He follows his heart in his art and life. It's an easy equation; it feels right and good and keeps on feeling that way. It's the Garden before the Fall, at least a scent, a taste of blissful eternity. And Diane tastes so fine, body and soul. Their embrace is so transportive for Cooper that his superimposed, man-on-a-mission close-up image vanishes while they kiss, then returns. Hearts and flowers—and a disturbing note: maybe Cooper's huge overview face vanishes during the kiss because down the road Diane won't be part of Cooper's Big Plan. Maybe that unexplained "Richard and Linda" business that the Fireman mentioned to Cooper early on will muddy future waters. Banish the thought, but?

It's been a surprise: the Asian woman who helped him in the pink light has become Diane. Unexpected, but with a sense of destiny being fulfilled, a reawakening to the Big Picture. We remember tulpa Diane, whom Mr. C created to help his kill-Cooper cause, yet whose divided loyalty caused her to say, "Oh, Coop, I hope this works," as she sent coordinates that ultimately delivered Mr. C to Twin Peaks to be killed. For millennia, human beings have sought knowledge that will guide them on the best, most fulfilling path through life, and beyond. For twenty-seven years, Lynch and Frost, in *Twin Peaks*, have made that quest a challenging, complex journey. Both men are smart as can be, but they're artists; they lean away from Aristotelian logic, toward the wisdom of the senses, dream logic, intuition, metaphysical signposts, and the malleability of time and space. This sounds like just anything goes, but *Twin Peaks*'s creators maintain an engaging, evocative balance between the mechanics of plot and sheer magic. Lynch and Frost imply that intellectual strategies, detective work, dream communications, wishes and prayers have kept Cooper/Dougie, the good aspect of Diane, the Blue Rose Task Force, the Fireman, Major Briggs, and Andy in some primal contact, generating the energy that fights evil.

Good thoughts and intentions are contagious, as are the creeping, devouring machinations of Mr. C and his minions, the Woodsmen, Bob, Judy. And we can add the Red Room's wicked electric tree, the one that attacked Cooper, "tricked" him into a fall toward "non-exis-tense." We remember that the Fireman knew about Naido's significance and communicated it to Andy, who became her keeper-protector. The Fireman created, or evoked, Laura's golden spirit (is she waiting to be activated in history's times of greatest need?) and sent it to America. Did he also create Naido as a vessel in which to safely hide Diane? She couldn't just stay at the Fireman's fortress/

White Lodge; she had to be out in the mauve zone to help further Cooper's journey. The Red Room has been established as a transportation hub of interdimensional coming and going, and the womb-like rock sheltering Diane was there. So maybe the wicked electric tree blinded Naido and stole her ability to speak, putting Diane-as-Naido in an imperiled state parallel to Cooper-in-Dougie.

We can tell that this is the real Diane. Her face is relaxed, warm, open. And maybe with the song line "It's in his kiss" flitting through her mind as their lips part, she knows this is her Coop. First a kiss, then a mutual verbal affirmation: "Diane"; "Coop, the one and only." Then he asks, "Do you remember everything?" She says, "Yes," and they both notice the stuck clock that can't advance to the completion number of 2:53 = 10. (Do we remember that Lynch, working without Frost, introduced the 2:53 stuck clock idea decades earlier in *Fire Walk With Me*?) *The Return* has often reminded us that time is slippery ("Is it future or is it past?"), and some commentators feel that the show's true ending is Cooper and Diane's happy reunion kiss, that things presented in the remaining hour and a half of the series, the "everything" that they remember, has already happened in some alternate time and space. Lynch hasn't offered even a peep about such an idea, but Mark Frost has. He refers to "viewing the show as chronological in time and space" and says that things "happen in sequence": we're watching the characters experience events in the order they happen. So we move on to the further adventures of Cooper and Diane. Even in her tulpa state, psychically enslaved by Mr. C, Diane sent out coordinates that enabled the Fireman to trap Bad Cooper and send him to *Twin Peaks* to be killed. Perhaps, as we saw with Cooper, Diane received some form of briefing from the Fireman, something cryptic about a "Richard and Linda," people they might encounter up ahead.

In *Fire Walk With Me*, Phillip Jeffries emphasized, "We live inside a dream," and Cooper's voice, in the sheriff's office after Mr. C's and Bob's deaths and Diane's return, intones those words without moving his lips. Now that he's operating at full power and things are going his way, he wants to keep living the dream plan he's strategized in his mind. To the assembled group he fondly says, "I hope I see every one of you again." Then, strangely, the light level falls in the room, Cooper and Cole call out to each other, and the two of them, with Diane, proceed in darkness, with Cooper's large face overlaying the scene. It's the face that Cooper presented to the Fireman when he said "I understand," at *The Return*'s opening briefing, which certified Cooper's deep mission. Perhaps the sudden darkness, Cooper, Diane, and Cole's pathway of shadow, is the Fireman moving the master plan along: what seems disruptive in one plane of existence can actually be the Fireman's smoothly functioning cosmic mechanism. In terms of screen time (and Mark Frost's sense of things happening "chronologically in time and space"), one moment we're in the sheriff's office, then shadowland, then the dark boiler room of the Great Northern, all in forty-some seconds.

Cooper knows where to go: the mysterious door deep in the boiler room shadows, where James had heard that ringing sound, the elusive one that had beguiled

Benjamin Horne in his office. When Cooper awoke in the Las Vegas hospital, he got dressed in the black suit Dougie Jones wore and flew up to Twin Peaks, so during the action in the sheriff's office, he wasn't sporting his official FBI pin. But from the boiler room scene to the end of *The Return*, the pin gleams on his black suit coat, a small illuminated shield against massing spiritual darkness. Cooper may have lost his shoes when he disappeared into the giant electrical socket and emerged as Dougie, but he still had his Great Northern hotel room number 315 key in his pocket. In his first, befuddled moments in Vegas with Jade the prostitute, he gave her the key; she mailed it back to the hotel; Ben Horne gave it to Frank Truman to give to Harry Truman as a memento, and an awakened Cooper knew to ask Frank Truman for it. In the original *Twin Peaks*, the key gave him access to the room where he slept and dreamed of a Red Room and a living/dead blonde woman, and again the key will ultimately lead to her. He tells Diane and Cole not to follow him, hugs Diane, shakes hands with Cole, who wishes him well, and Cooper says, "See you at the curtain call." (Lynch loves curtains "because they hide something . . . and you don't know if it's good or bad," he writes in *Room to Dream.*) So even when the play is over, mystery will prevail. As the ringing sound intensifies, the large overview image of Cooper's face fades. He has thought, planned, watched, and spoken; now he steps forward alone into some grand design, the door closing behind him.

One of Lynch's favorite visuals, which projects spiritual overtones, is a figure emerging from darkness into light: another way to communicate awakening. Cooper comes forward from formless blackness, and there's the One-Armed Man. They're face-to-face, in the flesh, unlike all the times the One-Armed Man was a hazy hologram trying to communicate with Cooper-in-Dougie from the Red Room. Lynch came up with the idea for the Red Room, a signature component of *Twin Peaks*, while leaning against the warm metal of a car in the LA sun. And some verses found their way into Lynch's brain, which he has had the One-Armed Man recite at various times over the years. The words encapsulate the *Twin Peaks* universe of dualities and space-time fluidity, and he now recites them to Cooper: "Through the darkness of future past, the magician longs to see. One chants out between two worlds, fire walk with me." In *The Return*, the One-Armed Man emphasizes to Cooper that what seems to be the present moment is in question: "Is it future or is it past?" Cooper seeks knowledge; he wants to see, to penetrate the veil of time, to cross from world to world. Fire is dangerous, devouring, the color of devils and war, the infernal energy that Bob summons. But it's also the goodness of light and heat, purifying and destroying evil, the vital flame of imagination and creativity that empowers Lynch, Frost, and Cooper. These are names to conjure with, and they excel at generating an atmosphere of ambiguity in which we think we know what's going on, but we can't be sure.

By now we know that when Cooper had his briefing with the Fireman at *The Return*'s beginning, he had known about the evil entity Judy for decades and was part of a plan (involving Major Briggs and Gordon Cole) to track her down. (We didn't learn about Judy and the plan to get her until Part Seventeen). When the Fireman mentioned "two birds with one stone," we assumed Cooper was the stone and his two objectives were to kill Bob and find Laura/save Laura. Now Cooper is free of the Red Room and Dougie and is following his plan, but is it the one the Fireman intended?

Cooper's first step is to confer with Phillip Jeffries, and the One-Armed Man takes him there, through the dimensional passage connected to the convenience store, the forest, the motel courtyard, through door number eight, to the steam-spouting machine enclosing Jeffries's essence. Jeffries sees and recognizes the real Cooper, and he probably assumes he's there to further the master plan to take down Judy. But Cooper has something else front-of-mind. He tells Jeffries he wants to go to February 23, 1989, the date Laura was killed by Leland, so his personal objective is confirmed. But as Jeffries manipulates symbols in the air, he says, "This is where you'll find Judy." Are these good guys working at cross-purposes?

Jeffries's informational images float in the white steam. The Owl Cave symbol (a central diamond with two side mountain peaks, suggesting a head with horns: the desert demon spewing out Bob and the eggs) metamorphoses into a white numeral eight. The line that forms the numeral is wide, like a ribbon; it's as though we're looking down on a figure-eight highway. If we view the lower loop of the eight as a clock face, there's a black ball at the three o'clock position. The face of the figure eight turns to the left and locks in place, so the black ball is now in the nine o'clock position. The plane of information, of reality, in which it was three, has turned backward, to the backside plane, where it's nine. The ball then travels around to the five o'clock position (in the backside plane), which would be seven o'clock from the front plane, the one Cooper and we are viewing. Jeffries announces, "It's slippery in here": manipulating time and space is tricky; it's an art, an inexact science. We can view the earth's surface as a common space/plane with different time zones (as Jimmy Buffett sings, "It's five o'clock somewhere"). But Jeffries's manipulation of some cosmic mechanism shows the existence of nearby/coexistent planes of space-time that aren't the ones we know. The way Cooper's journey intersects with this double reality will generate *The Return*'s final moments. Like Phillip Jeffries, David Lynch dwells in the bubbling, steamy teapot of his own head, conjuring paintings and movies about powerful forces in opposition. But his deeper, unifying themes are consciousness, subjectivity, relativity, the way each pole of force, each viewpoint, sees the world as its own reflection/projection. As in the way Jeffries sees his and Cooper's focus as talking about Judy, the Blue Rose Task Force's long-term goal, while Laura is in Cooper's mind and heart. Jeffries seems to catch a whiff of Cooper's unspoken Laura thoughts: "There may be someone . . . did you ask me this?" Their session concluded, Jeffries says, "You can go in now." Unknowable forces pull on Cooper; his form strobes here and there in superposition and vanishes.

Then, once again, *The Return* breaks through the fourth wall into my life experience, as when, in Part Ten, Rebekah Del Rio sang "No Stars," the song Lynch played for my love Linda and me at his house seventeen years earlier. It's probably paradoxical to think of the Maharishi/Lynch's Unified Field of Everything in portions, but there's a grouping, a gestalt, a connection between the deeply felt artistry of David Lynch and the lives of my father, myself, and Linda in the *Twin Peaks* region. I've mentioned how my father, as a young man, was a lumberjack in what would become the *Twin Peaks* woods, how Linda and I grew up east of Seattle and observed the creative process of Lynch and company in Washington State in 1991 and 2015.

Because of my flexible work schedule, I was able to watch more of the *Fire Walk With Me* production than Linda. Amid the bustle of a large crew and the actors, I remained anonymous to Lynch but was acknowledged by his assistant Gaye Pope. It was okay for me to be there. And one late night at the end of September, in the dark woods above North Bend, I stood silently with the crew watching a key scene being filmed. It's Laura's last night alive. She can't escape Bob; she can't flee with James to some Paradise of safety and love. She's soiled, damaged, wounded. James doesn't know the depths of her darkness. She has to protect him and those she loves from the devouring shadows. The escape door is her death. But she loves life, loves James. And what will be their last moments together are played out after midnight in the woods, with David Lynch, cinematographer Ron Garcia, and crew, me included. We're hemmed in by trees and foliage, so near to Laura and James that we could reach out and touch them. Sheryl Lee and James Marshall are immersed in such torturous emotions (screams, tears, slaps, kisses) that I have to avert my eyes.

Months later, when Sheryl Lee returned for the *Fire Walk With Me* premiere, she spoke of the atmosphere of "mystical connections" in the Snoqualmie Valley. And when, in March of 2017, she appeared at the Seattle Art Museum before *The Return* was broadcast, she may have felt a mystical connection she scrupulously didn't mention when she and I talked privately. She was moved and intensely focused when I told her about being right next to her and James Marshall when they'd filmed their big scene in September twenty-six years earlier. And then, when I watched *The Return*'s Part Seventeen in September 2017, I realized how admirably faithful she'd been to Lynch's secrecy pact regarding the show's details. For the *Fire Walk With Me* scene she and I had emoted about in March at the museum was playing again. Over the one hundred-plus years that motion pictures have existed, people have commented that films are like dreams. And also like memory, the way we consciously, or unconsciously, edit our recollections for emotional and thematic impact, making the past exist now, as film does.

James, on his motorcycle at night, picks up Laura at the Palmer house, and they blast off, with Leland, from an upstairs window, glaring down at them like the Devil himself. They drive deep into the dark woods, stop, and have the sad wrenching exchanges I'd stood in arm's reach of. In 2017, I was electrified, reliving a personal memory while wondering how and why Lynch was making the scene part of *The Return*. "Reliving" is the word. As Lynch says, "The same, but different." In *Fire Walk With Me*, in the midst of Laura's and James' anguished words to each other, Lynch gives us one of the scariest moments in his work. The camera's on Laura's face; her thoughts and feelings are roiling, fragmented. Her eyes are looking toward James, and us, but suddenly her line of sight shifts—behind James/us something's in the blackness—and she screams in terror. It's as if, for a second, she's seen-sensed the dark forest evil of every legend and tale ever told, waiting for her at the end of this night.

Laura and James conclude their punishing exchange; she jumps off his motorcycle, screams "I love you, James," her voice tearing, and she goes off to let herself be killed, thus defying Bob, being beatified by her guardian angel and watched over by Cooper in the Red Room. When Lynch uses this *Fire Walk With Me* sequence in *The Return*, when Laura screams, she isn't responding to some primal abstraction of evil, she's seen a flesh-and-blood person watching in the shadows, someone who quickly hides. We recognize the dark shape as Dale Cooper, arrived from 2016. So Phillip Jeffries has done it, gotten Cooper to the right place and time before Bob/Leland kills his own daughter.

Now Laura and James have their sad parting; Laura heads off in the woods, and Cooper steps forward. She recognizes him from her dream, where he was in the Red Room, warning her, "Don't take the ring, Laura" (the transportive Owl Cave jade ring, linked to death-by-Bob). In *Fire Walk With Me*, she took the ring and moments later was stabbed to death by Leland. But Cooper won't let her get that far this time; he's doing a major intervention. He doesn't say his name, but he emanates deliverance and safety. She takes his hand, and he leads her through the woods as the resplendent Laura Palmer theme plays—and her corpse, wrapped in plastic on the lake shore, one of *Twin Peaks*'s most iconic images, disappears!

Cooper's done it: she won't be killed; she'll live. But then she won't die in spiritual victory, becoming a Red Room being filled with pure light (Part Two). Cooper says, "We're going home," but what about the "home" of *Twin Peaks*, the long story of Laura that lives within the show's fans? If this is Cooper's ultimate triumph, why does it feel like non-exis-tence? Sarah Palmer's not taking it well, moaning and smashing Laura's picture with a liquor bottle. But if Laura didn't die, and neither did Leland, why is Sarah in such a state?

Lynch and Frost add more mystery. As Cooper proceeds through the woods, a gallant knight guiding his rescued lady, we hear that almost vocal clicking sound of some cosmic mechanism, perhaps related to the clanging paranormal machine that Phillip Jeffries now is. And Laura vanishes, screaming as she did when whisked from the Red Room in Part Two. Lynch holds on the dark woods. Laura's gone, and Cooper has moved beyond the frame. We hear warm Angelo Badalamenti chords in the black trees, and a deep red like the inner chamber of a heart suffuses the frame: black has not devoured red.

Somehow we knew that David Lynch would give the honored spot of *The Return*'s final musical performance to the original, angelic voice of *Twin Peaks*, Julee Cruise. With her platinum blonde pixie hair and delicate, tender hand gestures, Cruise stands in the red glow and sings "The World Spins" (Lynch's lyrics, Badalamenti's music) from her 1989 *Floating into the Night* album, which made the world fall in love with the music of *Twin Peaks*. Julee herself floated in the night, suspended by a wire, in 1990 at the Brooklyn Academy of Music performance of Lynch and Badalamenti's song cycle-stage narrative *Industrial Symphony No. 1: The Dream of the Brokenhearted.* She portrayed a damaged, heartbroken woman (one of so many in Lynch's art), who mourns her lost love but concludes with "The World Spins," which, though deeply sad, reminds us that life goes on in ever-renewing cycles.

As the last hour of *The Return* approaches, Lynch emphasizes the song's sadness and loss, someplace far from hope and uplift: "Things I touch are made of stone/ Falling through this night alone." The singer begs, "Love/ Don't go away/ Come back this way/ Come back and stay/ Forever and ever." It feels like the singer's world is over, yet in conclusion, "the world spins."

Cooper has saved Laura—and now she's gone again. It feels like the compass points of the *Twin Peaks* we know are spinning wildly; the ground is tilting, trembling. Is Cooper going to fall again? Has he been "tricked" again? Cooper has changed the past, so what will be the way of the world now? Lynch wrote that "the world spins," but also of a place "between two worlds."

–CHAPTER TWENTY-FOUR–

HERE AND NOW AND ALWAYS
(PART EIGHTEEN)

Steeped in Hindu philosophy, cosmology, and legends, Lynch's mind dwells in vast cycles of time and space and change. Through decades of meditation, he's sensed these cycles in his body, pondered the singular karmic human essence progressing through story upon story of death and rebirth, and spinning galaxies doing the same. He's an artist who puts frames around bits and layers of reality and shows them to us: his reality, which, he believes, is our reality, the way that life, death, world, and spirit are. Lynch's focused, particular portraits of reality imply expansiveness, narratives moving on, beyond the frame line, as he says, "continuing stories." He spoke to me once about how in *Lost Highway*, Fred Madison has done deeply bad things, has tried to imagine himself out of the karmic debt he owes, and failed. As the film ends, he's speeding down a desert road to perdition. But Lynch says that's just where the film ends; Fred's redemption, over future lifetimes of better actions that improve his karma, is possible. We can leave his ultimate outcome to our imaginations.

After *Twin Peaks* was canceled in 1991, Lynch couldn't leave Laura Palmer to his imagination. He brought her back in *Fire Walk With Me* (1992) and gave her a glorious, beautiful ending, sacrificing her life to protect her community from Bob and being heralded by her guardian angel and attended by Agent Cooper. Cooper, retraumatized every time he thinks of his lost love, Caroline, haunted by the way he failed to protect her, his last embrace of her blood-gushing body. Caroline, her flesh blade-pierced, and Laura the same. Caroline's gone; he can't save her now. But Laura is the special One, touched by the divine; she's a spirit-essence in some metaphysical circuitry, in a network of circling time that Cooper has some understanding of. Cooper can expiate his sin, his weakness, fear, and failure, with Caroline by saving Laura the warm-flesh-and-blood woman. His heart and mind tell him he must, even though he's witnessed Laura in her gained-through-death spiritually exalted state, as an evolved entity filled with light. The *Twin Peaks* saga shows us that there's just a wispy veil between life and death, but Cooper's dharma, his life path/calling, has been devoted to saving the living. And saving Laura, keeping her from being killed, will somehow save him.

But is Cooper going rogue, like Mr. C, who didn't want to go back in the Red Room when he was supposed to? Is he going off-script, violating the big plan in the sky? One of the grandest plan makers we encounter in *Twin Peaks* is the Fireman. He's a man of few words, so those words seem as potent as scripture, as though they're sharply chiseled in stone, but they're open to paradoxical interpretations, with key terms and elements not specifically defined, though perhaps decipherable, even status quo knowledge, to those of highest consciousness. It's as though Lynch and Frost employ some algorithm that generates multiple possibilities for their narrative components. Their minds, following the principles of particle physics, remind us that it's a world of simultaneously this-and-that. But we're also born to choose, to select our own meanings and act on them. Are there "wrong" choices? Cooper's decisions have caused harm to himself and the one he cared most about, but his will to do good in the world is almost superhuman. He has helped many; his sheer joy of being alive has brightened lives. He follows his inner light, and as Hawk told him in the original *Twin Peaks*, "You're on the path. You don't need to know where it leads. Just follow."

But still, Cooper choosing, and acting, to keep Laura from dying stole her from a state of light-filled grace, of being a female power evolving on the angel-illuminated path to countering the Dark Mother Judy's evil energy. Laura's exalted state was like a momentary glimpse of heaven in a fallen world. As French existentialist Albert Camus wrote, it's like a poignant patch of blue sky in a dark storm: "A torture for the eyes and for the soul, because beauty is unbearable, drives us to despair, offering us for a minute the glimpse of an eternity that we should like to stretch out over the whole of time." Maybe it's enough that Lynch gave us one of the most stirring passages of spiritual exaltation in film history. It's a glimpse of the transcendence he knows is possible. He envisions cinematic abstractions when he meditates and flashes them at us in peak film moments: the highest highs of love, floating in dreams, trying to outrun death on a flaming highway, being both the hell-spawned one and the angel, the hero trying to save the girl and the girl, herself a hero.

In the sheriff's office showdown, Freddie's winning punch shattered Bob into fragments that blew away, into nowhere. Part Eighteen starts with Mr. C, Cooper's shadow side, sitting flaming in one of the familiar Red Room chairs. There's no expression on his face. He's dead, but Lynch cuts away before we see him vanish.

The One-Armed Man places a golden tulpa seed on the chair with some of Agent Cooper's hair that Dale gave him. He applies some electricity, and the seed becomes a head-sized golden globe like the gold-globe head of Laura that the Fireman made, reinforcing the idea that the One-Armed Man and the Fireman are paranormal agents of goodness. Cooper's globe metamorphoses into his amused face sitting atop his black-suited body. Mirroring the bewildered Dougie, who occupied the chair in Part 3, he says, "Where am I?" This all-good Cooper was also "manufactured for a purpose," the homey purpose that resides behind the welcoming red door of a tract house in Las Vegas. Janey-E opens the other side of that door, and there stands the tulpa-Cooper Dougie, the one who's good and smart and walks and talks like most people, the improved model of the one she and Sonny Jim love, and who loves them. The three embrace, and Dougie says, "Home." This may be the only home that any part, any aspect, of Cooper will ever know. This Cooper is one heck of a nice guy, but will Lynch and Frost still give us a fully integrated Cooper, a body and mind and consciousness energized by both darkness and light, in balance? As William Blake phrased it in *To the Public*: "Heaven, Earth, and Hell, henceforth shall live in harmony."

The eliminate-Bob-and-Mr. C part of Cooper's mission seems to be over (we have to say "seems" in respect for Lynch and Frost's ability to spin future *Twin Peaks* tales). As for the Laura part, we've seen Cooper guide her away from her appointment with death in the dark woods, then vanish from his protective grip, screaming. Suddenly, Cooper's back in the Red Room chair next to the One-Armed Man, who repeats his "Is it future or is it past?" refrain. Cooper notes that the chair Laura usually occupies is empty, so if she wasn't killed, she never came to the Red Room.

The One-Armed Man takes Cooper to the electric tree, the good one, not the wicked one who attacked him and toppled him toward "non-exist-ence." The tree repeats its litany, "Is it the story of the little girl who lived down the lane?" This is *Twin Peaks*, so we have to wonder, Which girl? We've seen one story of Laura; we've seen Cooper act to alter it. But there's a blonde woman who lives on a different street, in a sunbaked landscape. Cooper doesn't know her, hasn't met her yet, but she's part of his and Laura's legend.

In the Red Room, Cooper, after listening to the electric tree, passes by Leland, who repeats his singular *The Return* message, "Find Laura." We've noted that Lynch sees the eighteen parts of *The Return* as one long film, a composition, a cinematic painting that transcends typical plot logic, a narrative composed of elements of emotion and energy that combine and progress a certain way because they "feel correct" to Lynch: they emanate "an air of euphoria"; they speak human truths. What about logic? Cooper has saved Laura; Leland didn't kill her. The One-Armed Man brings Cooper into the Red Room to make some key points, to reset his mission (Future? Past? Little girl down the lane?) And there's Leland, where he went after he killed Laura. And in some separate Red Room chamber, there's Laura, whispering something in Cooper's ear. As Dorothy in *The Wizard of Oz* says, "People come and go so strangely here." As for Leland and his relationship to Laura, it was abusive for the years preceding Cooper's intervention to prevent her killing. Their father-daughter interaction bore a resemblance to William Blake's poem *A Little Girl Lost*: "To her father white/Came the maiden bright/But his loving look, Like the holy book/All her tender limbs with terror shook." Now she's gone, somewhere, whisked away from Leland, Bob, Dale Cooper, Twin Peaks. So Bob, in hateful ire and frustration, made Leland kill himself, and Leland ends up in the Red Room, still without Laura. And as the murderer of Teresa Banks, he has his karmic debt to pay off.

To borrow the title of Pierre Péju's book, Laura is *The Girl in the Fairy Tale Forest.*

Peju sees fairy stories as narratives of female growth, evolution, and empowerment: the primacy of the girl encountering the magical forest that's a zone between worlds, to face challenges from without and within. From death to spiritual transcendence, Laura has certainly been the One of *Twin Peaks*, and Cooper has been the prime male. Yes, it's nice; it's gratifying that Cooper and Diane love each other. But *The Return*'s primal question remains: where will the Man in the Black Suit and the Blonde Woman end up?

At night Cooper emerges from the Red Room amid the pale, thin, leafless Sycamore trees of Glastonbury Grove, leaving the red curtains behind him. This is the smooth, easy egress he would have enjoyed if Mr. C/Bob had come back in when he was supposed to—but that would be some other movie. Cooper sees Diane in the darkness. In this universe of questionable identities, they touch each other as they did in the sheriff's office, to determine that "it's really you."

Then, in an eye blink of time, they're in an older American car, like the one Cooper came to Twin Peaks in twenty-five years ago, when there was the murder of young Laura to investigate. But Cooper seems to have saved her now, though she needs to be found. When Cooper drove alone toward Twin Peaks, he recorded tape messages for Diane. Now, she sits next to him, and they talk about their new adventure ahead, which will involve terms the Fireman spoke to Cooper about at the opening of Part One: "four three zero" and "Richard and Linda." They're traveling through a vast, dry, treeless landscape. Four-hundred-thirty miles from Twin Peaks would put them in Southeast Oregon or east in Montana, the state of Lynch's birth.

Diane has exchanged her cuddly, homey pink bathrobe for a black sweater top. She's a match with Cooper's black suit, and their manner is focused and serious, reflecting the gravity and danger of their journey. Are they sure they want to do it? They don't know what it's going to be like: "Once we cross, it could all be different." A space-time warp, some existential reshuffling like Cooper endured when he fell from the Red Room? Lynch's aesthetics indicate how high the stakes are: undulating next to the otherwise empty highway they're traveling on is a crackling, hissing line of tall high-tension wire towers, like an endless serpent of electricity. And a throbbing low soundtrack rumble indicates it could be bad electricity. Lynch has spoken of how you could stand blindfolded beneath such towers and feel the force field with your body, how invisible electricity can be "zapping us" when we don't know it. When they reach mile 430, Cooper gets out, and the energized air billows his unusually unbuttoned suit coat out from his body, his arms rise (a visual rhyme with Gordon Cole's [David Lynch's] arms rising when gripped by the South Dakota vortex, Lynch self-identifying with Cooper). Cooper and Diane may really be playing with cosmic, interdimensional fire, for the serpentine line of towers and wires resembles similar wiry forms in a Lynch painting from the 1990s called *A Figure Witnessing the Orchestration of Time*, as if to underscore the correspondence between Lynch's art forms. Cooper looks at his watch as his coat billows, beneath the wires in the humming air, suggesting that powerful forces can make time slippery, as Phillip Jeffries would say: a prefiguring of shifting times to come.

Back in the car with Diane, Cooper needs something solid, says, "Kiss me." Their love has sealed their decision to proceed, and the car pulls forward, toward us. The image looks in at them from the front, Cooper driving on the right, Diane on the left. Electricity flashes around them in the car. Lynch does some of *The Return*'s fastest editing, mixing in side profiles of each, producing that superpositioning feeling that they're both here, and there. Lynch settles on the image of them facing us, and as it becomes night outside the car, the flashes inside the car illuminate something disturbing, just for a few milliseconds. Diane's bobbed hair, whether blonde as tulpa Diane or ruby red as true Diane, is a rounded mound shape. But as the light flashes, almost subliminally fast, there's a dark shadow of her head shape superimposed on her face (it can be seen in slow motion), while Cooper's face is normal. What a subtle poet of dissociation, and foreboding, Lynch is.

In a frame of blackness, Cooper and Diane's black car finds a lit-up midcentury-style motel, strangely placed on unpaved ground: a horizontal left-to-right row of doors punctuated with dark bush shapes, office door far right. With the camera in the back seat, looking forward, Cooper parks, gets out, and walks left to right past the doors and bushes to the office. The camera pans to follow him, so the foreground black mound shape of Diane's head is huge in the frame, and as the camera gradually pans to the right, her shadow head is mirrored by the black rounded bush forms. The black bush smudges are like the evil black abstraction on Mr. C's ace of spades playing card and the black shape in Lynch's 2000 painting *Bob Sees Himself Walking Toward a Formidable Abstraction*. Maybe, deep down, our brains perceive a chilling echo of tulpa Diane, who could/couldn't be trusted. As Diane waits for Cooper, she sees, for a moment, her red-haired self standing by the motel entrance.

Things do seem different here. Since Cooper and Diane began their 430 journey, they've been cold and distant from each other, driving without speaking like some bitter couple long trapped in a soured relationship. In this part of *The Return*, Lynch directed Kyle MacLachlan to be harder, harsher than Cooper, but not at Mr. C's cold summit of severity. Is Cooper now some "Richard" without knowing it? And who is Diane? Are we in some parallel reality, the way that the exterior and the interior of the TARDIS space-time travel device in *Doctor Who* are in different dimensions?

Cooper returns from the office and stands in front of door number seven (not all of *The Return*'s sevens have positive associations). He's unsmiling, domineering, looking at Diane in the car as if to say, Don't you get it? Get out of the car and come here. He doesn't open door seven for her; he barges in first. She turns on the light; he says, "Turn it off." In Lynch's world, that statement is both simple and metaphysical, a "Now It's Dark" moment.

What's love got to do with it? Cooper and Diane were tender with each other in the sheriff's office, reuniting after so long. And there was a sense of regeneration and mutual caring as they embarked on their next chapter, the journey to 430. We all feel like we have many selves inside us, many roles and ways of being, but they feel integrated into a wholeness: I'm me. Cooper and Diane have lived their multiple selves out in the world and in various dimensions, and it's been punishing, fracturing. Cooper's bad self has been in Mr. C, merged with Bob, his good side in Dougie. And now he seems to be more pulled-together Cooper again, but Cooper in a realm where "it could all be different." Diane has been her regular self, stored away for safekeeping in Naido, and she's been a tulpa, in which her good and bad sides have warred agonizingly with each other. Now she's more her regular self, but haunted by otherness: the flicker of her shadow in the car, her doppelgänger seen momentarily outside the motel. It's felt like her and Cooper's love circuit has been rejoined glowingly—so why is he coldly ordering her around? He stands by the bed, says, "Come here." They'll be having sex, not making love.

When Dougie lay prone and Janey-E rode him in a supple rhythm, their union was joyfully loving. When Diane and Cooper are in the same position, it's torturous for Diane. Years ago, she and Cooper only kissed. Then he (actually Mr. C) showed up and raped her, made her a tulpa to do his bidding. At the start of the 430 journey it seemed like Diane was embarking with the good, trusted and true Cooper–but this sex is hellish. As she undulates on top of him, he's motionless, his impassive face and unblinking eyes staring up at her. Cold. Heartless. Like Mr. C. Her face twisted in grief and disgust, she weeps and covers his face with her hands so she can't see it. It goes on and on; she doesn't climax; the scene goes dark. Diane has lost the flirtatious innocence of twenty-five years ago, when she and Cooper communicated by audiotapes and phone calls, and kissed once. She now knows there are multiple Coopers, even in the restored one: there were dark thoughts and impulses in him that Bob only encouraged and amplified when he was Coop's passenger, in Mr. C. In *The Return*, Cooper and Diane ask each other, "Is it really you?"—meaning the safe, stable being each knew the other to be years ago but now seems hard to find. That illusion is gone. Now there are other personae aspects who seem real as can be.

In Lynch's 2006 *INLAND EMPIRE*, Laura Dern, in another stunning performance, enacts the timeless human story of emotional-sexual betrayal and revenge through the personae of the same/different women: Nikki, an actress whose life merges with Susan, the role she's playing in a film. And the movie she's working on parallels an old Polish folktale, so the familiar Lynchian multidimensional/multinarrative/plural identities layering is fully evident. Nikki hesitates to get involved in the project because an early attempt to film the story seemed cursed; people died. Nikki's hesitation parallels Diane's trepidation about proceeding on *The Return*'s 430 journey. In Part Sixteen, Tulpa Diane said, "I'm not me," and on the 430 trip, now seeming to be fully Diane, her sense of self is questionable.

At the nameless desert motel (Lynch already visited the Lost Highway Hotel in another movie), Cooper wakes up—and Diane is gone. The morning after their sexual encounter, she left a note: "Dear Richard, When you read this, I'll be gone. Please don't try to find me. I don't recognize you anymore. Whatever it was we had together is over. Linda." In *Lost Highway*, another story of shifting identities, a couple makes love in the desert. Before climaxing, she pulls away, saying, "You'll never have me." Like Diane, she's blonde, but this other fair-haired woman is a wicked hellion. Diane has our sympathy; we want her to come out of all this okay, with body and soul together. She doesn't sexually climax with this darker, harsher Cooper, this Richard. Lynch and Frost have given aspects of Cooper and Diane's personae the names Richard and Linda, or rather the Fireman has; he's certainly one of Lynch and Frost's muses, their cocreators. In the 430, Diane sees a different side of Cooper: debased, though not at the Mr. C level of evil intensity. She reacts negatively to this Cooper and takes herself out of the picture, perhaps as Audrey does with Charlie, snapping back to reality, leaving him behind in her memory/imagination.

What's sex got to do with it? English magus-author-cult leader Aleistair Crowley (1875-1947), a proponent of Tantric "sex magick," was referenced in Mark Frost's *The Secret History of Twin Peaks*. Crowley disciple Jack Parsons, founder of the Jet Propulsion Lab, collaborated with writer L. Ron Hubbard in sex rituals designed to invoke the spirit of the Book of Revelations's Whore of Babylon, Mother of Abominations, to open portals accessing hidden dimensions and astral planes. As we've noted, Lynch didn't read Frost's book, but some commentators feel that Frost worked the "sex magick" concept into *The Return*'s Part Eighteen. Meaning that Cooper used Diane for sex to generate the intense metaphysical power needed to transport Cooper to the realm of a second, different motel that he's in now. Crowley believed the highest concentrations of spiritual energy were in deserts, far from polluted, contaminating cities. And he studied the Kabbalah, with its conception of the universe as ten spheres connected by twenty-two paths. *The Return* seems to be an esoteric network of passages between various realms of time and space. And in Lynchian deserts, a young man discovers that he's a god (*Dune*) and one man becomes another (*Lost Highway*) and is starting to become someone else.

At at the start of *The Return*, Cooper was pulled from the Red Room for a briefing with the Fireman, and responded, "I understand" when the Fireman mentioned Richard and Linda. Now, in the morning in the motel, he's puzzled by the names, he doesn't seem to remember that briefing. To him, it's Diane, not some Linda, who's missing.

People presenting different identities, a motel that's not itself. When black-suited Cooper (Richard?) emerges into the morning light, he's coming out of a different motel, a two-story building with pavement, not desert earth, around it. Palm trees indicate the continuity of an arid climate. In *Lost Highway*, a desert cabin materialized out of reversed time, fire, and smoke; earlier in *The Return*, Naido's large living room was contained within a box in space: Lynch is a master builder of metaphysical architecture.

When Cooper emerges from the second motel, his FBI pin is on his suit. He seems to be Cooper, but he's puzzled by Diane's Richard-and-Linda goodbye note; he strangely doesn't even approach being emotionally devastated by her leaving his life. We never saw Cooper brief Diane on the nature of the 430 journey, but maybe the Fireman did so in some esoteric way. She doesn't forget the Richard-and-Linda aspect of the plan, but it confuses Cooper. Nonetheless, Cooper/Richard is enacting the Fireman's master strategy. The Fireman, who sent Laura's golden spirit to Earth in 1945. The spirit who was born as Laura Palmer in 1971, died in 1989, and was beatified, filled with pure light, and is now somewhere in the cosmic winds. She's the One; the Log Lady could sense her spiritual prominence, her ultimate value in counteracting a process of invading evil. Maybe the Fireman knew that Diane was a significant part of Cooper's emotional life and provided her for their sheriff's office reunion to help solidify Cooper's dedication to the mission. Then the Fireman, with the Richard-and-Linda ploy, removed Diane from Cooper's sphere, so he could focus on finding Laura and furthering her rise as a champion of righteous goodness. In the *Twin Peaks* universe, Laura and Cooper are the Ones.

We know that David Lynch's key artistic principle is contrast. And since he believes that divine mind results from a balance of opposites, Cooper must be on a blessed path when he leaves motel number two. He's driving a gleaming black Crown Victoria, Mr. C's ride when he defied the Red Room and a world away from the junky sedan Cooper and Diane arrived in. As Cooper/Richard (?) exits the parking lot, Lynch's camera lingers on a white globe light fixture next to a denuded tree, which, as a combined image, is like the spirit presence of the Red Room's benign electric tree with its leafless branches and white-blob head. This tree and the Red Room tree both have seven main branches from the trunk. Cooper may be on the right path to "the little girl who lives down the lane," but he retains his 430-region distanced hardness: no grinning exclamations about coffee from this guy.

When Cooper and Diane started to drive beyond the 430 point under the crackling power lines, it suddenly became night, and the car accelerated supernaturally. Who knows how far from Twin Peaks their desert motel was? But as Cooper proceeds in his big black car, we see that he and motel number two are in Odessa, Texas. It seems the 430 point was in the Twin Peaks plane of existence, as was the first motel. But overnight, a shift to a second plane occurred. As with the Richard and Linda letter, Cooper takes it in stride.

Cooper cruises through the town's outskirts: dusty one-story warehouses and a diner named Judy's. The Fireman's words: "two birds with one stone." With Cooper as the stone: kill Bob, find Laura? Or, bearing in mind Phillip Jeffries's directive ("This is where you'll find Judy"), is Cooper supposed to now find Laura and find Judy, these two being conjoined somehow?

Even though the Cooper we're seeing seems different, colder and harsher, he knows the name Judy when he sees it. He pulls in. As Cooper walks toward the glass entrance door, which has a horizontal push bar to swing it open, Lynch films his approach from inside the diner, so visually the push bar bisects Cooper's form, emphasizing his horizontal splitability; he may be moving upward, or downward, on the spiritual ladder.

As always, spaces and places are important for Lynch. Cooper, an oddly urbane man in cowboy country, stands motionless and takes in the scene. Big room, booths on the left wall, kitchen on the right; you could fit a country western hoedown in the wide central space. Cooper really is different, closed in on himself, no smile for the waitress, a bland response to the coffee she brings. But his sense of right and wrong is still hyper vigilant. Down the row from his booth, three cowpokes start hassling the waitress, grabbing at her. Cooper calls them on it: "Leave her alone." (These words parallel what Kyle MacLachlan, playing *Blue Velvet*'s Jeffrey Beaumont thirty years ago, said when a punk was sexually harassing a girl: "Don't force girls!" Female vulnerability is an abiding Lynchian theme.) Their macho egos inflamed, the three cowboys come to Cooper's table, and one pulls a gun on him. Over the years, Lynch has conceded that Kyle MacLachlan can be seen as Lynch's alter ego. It must be great to have your on-screen self be a martial arts expert. In a flash, Cooper disarms that man, kicks him in the balls, shoots another man in the foot, and leaves all three moaning on the floor. If this was good old Dale Cooper, the foot shooting and genitals kicking would be unnecessary, shockingly cruel gestures. But it's the way this FBI man rolls and is perhaps a politico-Mark Frost-influenced commentary on the coarse, aggressive, civility norms-abolishing socio-political climate of the Donald J. Trump era. Cooper has contained the three dangerous men, but now he endangers everyone in the room (waitress, cook, two patrons). He dumps the roughnecks' three guns in the hot bubbling oil used for frying fries, casually saying, "I don't know if this is hot enough to set off the bullets." He adds, "Better move away," without really knowing how easily the bullet might fire, penetrate the metal box of hot oil, and rocket anywhere in the room. Maybe this Cooper is actually Richard/Cooper in a transitional process of becoming fully the Cooper we treasure. Mr. C is dead. Cooper's dark-human-nature aspects, no longer Bob supercharged, are back home in his mind-body. Maybe now he's not repressing them, or can't, as much as original Cooper could.

Cooper, whether he's using logic (a diner this size should have two waitresses) or intuition, resides in a twinned world; he asks the waitress (Francesca Eastwood) where "the other one" is and is told she's out sick. In the car, he follows the waitress's directions to a dusty street with a pale, dilapidated ranch house. Has his whole 430 journey been guided by something in the air, an invisible electromagnetic beam that's tugging at his mind and heart? In the original *Twin Peaks*, Cooper once said, "I'm a strong sender," meaning telepathically, and he's a good receiver too. Decades ago he "met" Laura Palmer in a dream they shared. Here in Odessa, Texas, there's a telephone pole number 6, and crackling wires overhead, both linked with metaphysical energies and transports in *Fire Walk With Me*, as Cooper knows. And the Fireman knows that this pole number 6 in a zone other than Twin Peaks is very important; it concluded the image parade/montage he showed Andy, and now here's Cooper right under it. A single telephone pole in two places. Two people in different times and places, inside the same dream. In the *Fire Walk With Me* script, at the convenience store meeting of paranormal denizens that Phillip Jeffries witnessed, Mrs. Tremond (a mysterious woman in the original *Twin Peaks*) says, "Why not be composed of materials and combinations of atoms?" She's a spirit, an energy, that's taken on corporeal form. The Bhagavad Gita of Lynch's Hindu philosophy says that only one-quarter of the created universe is matter; the other three quarters is the spirit world, and it's all connected: Lynch's Unified Field.

Lynch can get a sense of this base unity while meditating, but an evolved yogi shaman like the Fireman feels it and knows it implicitly, every moment. Mrs. Tremond, with her "combinations of atoms," sounded like a scientist. Throughout the ages, common, primal human perceptions have been quantified in various belief systems and expressed with different words. The poet might be stirred by intuition, pulled by her heart strings, while the physicist would analyze data and speak of nonlocal access, string theory, and quantum entanglement. Atoms are composed of particles, and particles that have previously interacted remain entangled, outside of time and space. James Marshall sang, "Just you, and I; together, forever, in love." Cooper is entangled with Diane and Laura; he could say those words to either one, but right now he's in Laura's aura—or is it her? And is the love worldly, divine, both?

The things that Lynch puts together for us to see (paintings, films, the whole lot) are composed, colored, and detailed exactly as he wants them to be. Even if he can't, or won't, explain why, or how, they are "correct," they emanate what he wants them to emanate. His eyes and hands touch all elements.

Cooper walks toward the Odessa house. The dusty yard has no greenery: dead plants in plastic pots, sun-bleached tall weeds, a car wheel with tire (not much help if you want to get away). Now that we're closer to the house, we see that it's a pale pink, the symbolic color of love, linked in *The Return* with the Naido/Diane/Cooper bond; the Mitchum brothers' angelic Pink Ladies, ever offering loving sustenance (and little sandwiches); and the color of Lynch's own house. The Texas front door isn't red, *The Return*'s symbol for the vital force of life. It's white, like the pure, beatific spirit light within Laura, before Cooper "saved" her and she vanished from the Red Room. By way of the numerology that Lynch and Cooper practice, the house number 1516 adds up to four, equated with the square, the cube, signifying a minimal, limited awareness of the totality: the earth without the counterbalancing heavens.

In contrast to the rarified Laura of the Red Room, with her flowing golden hair, majestic black gown, and soft voice, the woman (Sheryl Lee) who answers Cooper's knock is certainly earthbound, in tight jeans and flowery white top, permed dirty-blonde hair, and pronounced Texas twang. In 2012, when Lynch and Frost were secretly thinking of making more *Twin Peaks* and starting to get ideas of how to proceed, Sheryl Lee wrote a poem, "Dear Laura," for *Bullet* magazine. Lee's beautiful, haunting words speak of Laura's decades-long prominence in her consciousness. In conclusion, Lee says she's "caught somewhere between my earth and your stars." We don't know if Lynch or Frost ever read these words, but this Texas woman standing in front of Cooper seems firmly earthbound. Is she the one he saved from death as a teenager, thus robbing her of the supreme blessings and bliss of heaven? If this is the "saved" Laura, having run away from her Twin Peaks pain (being raped, though not killed, by her father), has she lost herself in a new persona, a psychogenic fugue like Fred Madison's consciousness creates to escape his pain and guilt in *Lost Highway*? Or are we in the future, gazing at the reincarnation of Laura after her natural death?

When Phillip Jeffries was calibrating the cosmic mechanism that would send Cooper back to February 1989, he said, "It's slippery in here," indicating room for error (in the *Fire Walk With Me* script, when Jeffries materialized in Gordon Cole's office, there was a discrepancy between Cole date affirming that the month was February and Jeffries saying it was May). Cooper did arrive in February1989, as Jeffries said he would, but then he plunged into the space-time warp of his 430 journey. When Cooper and Diane moved on from the 430 point, and it instantly became night, their car whooshed forward supernaturally fast, so the time frame could have shifted farther ahead than it seems. In our Albert Einstein universe of relativity, which is not a changeless clockwork, space and time are inextricably bound; duration, length, mass are not fixed; an apparent position may not match the actual position. And Lynch and Frost add personal identity to the swirl of fluctuation.

Standing in the Texas woman's doorway, Cooper calls her Laura. She says she's Carrie Page. Cooper's homing drive is so strong. He's set it up so the tulpa of his best self, Dougie, can be husband and father to Janey-E and Sonny Jim. And maybe someday he can send the tulpa away, come home, and introduce them to the loving Dale Cooper. Or maybe, somewhere, somehow, he'll reunite with Diane, in the pink light. What is Cooper thinking as he tells Carrie Page he wants to take her home to Twin Peaks, Washington? Does he see Laura, Leland, and Sarah Palmer as the resonant archetype of a toxic, broken family that he can mend and make right? His ultimate Eagle Scout good deed that will somehow heal him too? Since he's taken Laura-beyond-death from her angelic spiritual realm, is he obliged to restore her earthly family? Or is this all part of the get-Judy plan? Restore Laura to earthly, corporeal existence, use her to get close to her mother, Sarah, now a Dark Mother in whom Judy resides?

Convinced that Laura is lost within Carrie, Cooper mentions "your father, Leland." No response. But when he says "your mother, Sarah," Carrie seems momentarily flustered, her shoulders slump a bit. But if this is Laura, you'd think that the word "Leland" would trigger a major response. Lynch and Frost have some fun with Carrie confusing Washington State with Washington, DC, a pet peeve of we who dwell in the state. Carrie doesn't quite realize the place is half a continent away, but she's been "wanting to get out of Dodge" anyway and agrees to go with Cooper.

Cooper stands alone in her living room while she gets her things. He takes in details that would fit a Laura-reincarnated-as-Carrie, or a Laura-in-fugue-persona-of-Carrie interpretation. Laura had been involved in lawbreaking activities (drugs, prostitution), and she was with one of her boyfriends (Bobby) when he killed a sheriff's deputy with a head shot. It was pretty much in self-defense, but neither she nor Bobby reported it. Cooper sees a head-shot dead man sitting in Carrie's living room. When she answered her door and Cooper said, "FBI," she replied, "Did you find him?" indicating that the shooter was running from the law. As with Laura, a man has head-shot another man in close proximity to Carrie.

Another signifier from the past is a white horse figurine on Carrie's mantelpiece. Mother Sarah is the one who saw a white horse in the Palmer living room twenty-five years ago, when Leland was upstairs abusing Laura. But Sarah may have mentioned her vision to her daughter over the years. And when post-death beatified Laura was whisked out of the Red Room (the moment Cooper saved her corporeal form?), we glimpsed the white horse on a dark plane that extended beyond the wind-stirred red curtains. Since Laura being pulled back to life, away from the Red Room, was linked to us seeing the white horse again (which links to the evil in Sarah's house), maybe the evil in Twin Peaks is strengthening and growing now that Laura didn't die. Or perhaps the horse is the divine mount awaiting its cosmic mission with the blonde rider, the female champion princess who will ride forward to battle universal evil, the Judy within Sarah. No wonder the horse appearing made Sarah/Judy uneasy. The horse on Carrie's mantle is a talisman of her destiny, but she'll have to travel far with her spiritual partner Cooper to come to that realization.

The night journey, one of Jung's archetypes, deep in the human race, a passage resonant with portent. Lynch, in his thinking and his art, likes having room to dream, and he likes to float us into it. The night view, penetrating blackness, headlights illuminating the dark road ahead rushing at us, has graced many of Lynch's films: *Wild at Heart*, *The Return*, and especially *Lost Highway*. This view, the mainline momentum of flying forward into some future, opens that film. It's a poetic representation of Fred Madison trying to outrun the guilty knowledge that he's killed his wife Renee. Renee, who betrayed him. He needs to forget, like it never happened, like he's someone else, Pete, who's got a different life, has no knowledge of Fred, gets to pursue a blonde beauty, Alice, who we see looks just like Renee. Lynch conveys the mystical transition of Fred into Pete by first showing Fred's face contorting grotesquely as he drives on the night road. Then we see his point of view: the road ahead and a figure on the right, further on, that becomes Pete. So for those of us who have seen *Lost Highway*, when we watch *The Return* there's a kind of subliminal memory jog when Cooper and Carrie's car's headlights reflect a little glimmer way ahead on the right side of the dark road. And there's a passage where the headlights of another car glare behind them, which recalls *Lost Highway*'s ending, where headlights bear down on Fred Madison as his body contorts on the verge of another persona transition, trying to escape his personal hell, very much in the spirit of Carrie Page's desire and need to "get out of Dodge." If Carrie really is Laura, this would be her second escape route, the second time she's fled a messed-up, victimized existence, this time in Odessa. As she and Cooper traverse the night, she says, "I tried to keep a clean house, get everything organized." But from what we saw in Odessa, the job was too much for her: the wasteland front yard, haphazard clutter in the living room (rolls of toilet paper, a dead body, splattered cranial fluid on the wall).

For fifty years, beginning in his 1970 *Gardenback* script, Lynch has seen the image/idea of the house as a metaphor for the human head, the mind, the psyche. Personally, Lynch likes to stay home, be self-contained in his sacrosanct place. And in his work, the house/the head is vulnerable to troubling disturbances, conflicts, warring impulses, physical and metaphysical invasions. In *Lost Highway*, things were bad at home for Fred, with Renee and her cheating ways, but he let his dark, angry impulses steer him into violence, a horrific act he can't admit to himself—so his mind flees; he becomes Pete. So if Carrie is Laura without knowing it, she's enacting a similar emotional-physical process. When Mark Frost spoke in Seattle before *The Return* aired, he mentioned the general principle of burying and self-erasing unacceptable memories, the mind's need to escape truths it can't face. At the point time-traveling Cooper saved Laura from being killed, she'd been living a life of bad choices and being victimized by her father/Bob. As Carrie and Cooper drive on through the night, she says, "I was too young to know any better." As Cooper led her away from her final, deadly, *Fire Walk With Me* rendezvous with bad people, death, and beatification, did the Fireman click-click her away to being Carrie Page, safe half a continent away in Odessa, Texas? Or did Laura, with the single-mindedness with which she sacrificed herself in *Fire Walk With Me*, make a break from her chaotic Twin Peaks life and get on a bus heading south? Maybe she'd seen Odessa on a map. Maybe she'd seen the movie *Giant* and was touched by James Dean, the sensitive, misfit outsider who ends up striking it rich in the limitless horizon of Texas.

If, as Mark Frost says, things in *The Return* "happen in sequence," then Cooper and Carrie make the drive from Texas to Twin Peaks in a single night, with just a gas station stop. (Did Lynch, after moseying across the Midwest at the speed of Alvin Straight's riding lawnmower [*The Straight Story*], have a burning need to really put the pedal to the metal?) Cooper and Carrie seem to be in some paranormal space-time. As Dorothy in Lynch's film favorite *The Wizard of Oz* says, "We're not in Kansas anymore," and she later adds, "People come and go so quickly here." In terms of screen time, Lynch makes the trip seem like a long journey; somehow, it's long in time and short in space. Once again, this artist's complex poetry is on display.

Cooper and Carrie are mostly silent, alone with their thoughts, and there's time for us to ponder this Carrie person. It's clearly actress Sheryl Lee, talking Texas style. We recall the way Lee showed up in the original *Twin Peaks* after blonde Laura was killed, playing Laura's black-haired cousin, Maddy. Maddy was Laura's blood relative, but Carrie is really different from Laura, though she could be fooling herself: Laura forgetting her past darkness, hiding in a new persona, a fresh beginning. Fred Madison ultimately couldn't lose himself, escape his bad karma, his sin of killing Renee. Lynch believes in karma and reincarnation, that there's "perfect justice in the world." Your misdeeds will revisit you over future lifetimes until you learn to do better, pay off your karmic debt, eventually breaking the birth-and-rebirth circuit/cycle, transcending the wheel of life in blissful oneness with the All, the Absolute, the "big home of everything," as Lynch once said to me.

With his deep spiritual beliefs, Lynch may instinctively see his screen stories as metaphors for the way people's actions generate karma; they then deal with the result ("actions have consequences," "a debt that must be paid") and keep incarnating until they can sing with the angels. The tagline for *Lost Highway* was "Time is dangerously out of control." In *The Return*, there is no Greenwich Mean Time, no absolute indicator of when it is, so, as Mark Frost says, "Reality is fungible" (in the dictionary: "one instance or portion may be replaced by another in respect to function"). Bearing in mind the One-Armed Man's litany of "Is it future or is it past?" and Lynch's artistic principle of valuing contrast, *The Return* has delved into the past (Cooper saves Laura) and could now be in the future. Could Carrie be a reincarnation of Laura, who died sometime after 1989, having been saved from death-by-Leland? Leland would still be in the Red Room saying, "Find Laura," qualified to be there for his years of raping her and killing Teresa Banks and Jacques Renault. Or maybe Leland's living his future incarnations, suffering for his many sins, having slipped much lower on the karmic ladder. And in the Hindu view, Laura's bad deeds (granting that she did many good ones) were amplified because she intentionally let herself be killed, a form of suicide, which is profoundly taboo. So if at the end of *The Return* we are in the future, there could have been multiple incarnations along the spiritual road of Laura becoming Carrie, whose Laura-like lifestyle is not that of a highly evolved being. If Carrie is Laura's reincarnation, she doesn't remember Laura's world, which fits with Hindu spirituality. But ironically, from the Christian point of view, keeping Laura from being killed by Leland and having Bob claim her soul for the dark side robbed her of post-death heavenly exaltation. Still, the Fireman sees all; the girl in the golden globe, the spirit he created and sent to Earth, is still a player in the cosmic drama.

Beginning with the *Twin Peaks* Pilot episode three decades ago, a singular nocturnal red traffic light has been a symbol of evil and dread, like a burning circular peep-hole into hell or the devil's red eye. We've seen it again in *The Return*, flaming in blackness. And in daylight, a different red light was linked to young Becky, foreshadowing the threat her husband Steven embodied.

Now, as Cooper and Carrie approach Twin Peaks on their epic night journey, they come upon a bridge so narrow that only one car can proceed across at a time. Lynch's life and art are about looking for signs and meanings, being a detective. At the bridge, there are no other cars in sight, no red light, but two green ones. For Cooper, this evidence further reinforces the idea that the universe is smiling on him and his mission. All systems are go; he's doing the right thing.

The sinning, remorseful Leland said, "Find Laura." The Log Lady said, "Laura is the One." The little girl lost needs to be taken home, to the house of her childhood, a place of joy and pain, where her mother grieves her loss. Cooper has made possible the restoration of Dougie and Janey-E and Sonny Jim's family, and now he will bring home the far-wandering Palmer daughter. The Palmer family has been more prominent, more galvanizing, than any gathering of souls that Cooper could call family. Laura was the Special One, to her parents, to the men and women who loved her, her whole town. The empty space where she used to be was a light-devouring black hole, a hungry mouth swallowing all goodness and vomiting back evil, birthing monsters. Laura was the woman with the golden head and blue eyes who could kiss Cooper in dreams and whisper things beyond comprehension. Cooper loved her, needed her, but the sorry, suffering world needed her more. He'd attended her in her angel-blessed state, seen the pure light filling her. But she was dead then, dead to this world. Cooper knew many worlds, but the world where flesh and blood are warm, where Donald J. Trump holds national power and there are border fences and refugee children in cages, where ancient glaciers are melting, plant and animal species vanishing, the world of springtime, coffee, pie, and cigarettes needs Laura, the golden seed of female divinity and wise power, to live and bring the light. Whether hiding from herself, her shadow side, in Carrie Page or manifesting as a reincarnation, she is the spirit essence, the golden one, who in time will learn, grow and thrive, teach and guide.

Cooper drives across the single lane bridge, signifying his single-track mission. They encounter no other cars, no indicators of what time frame they're in. It's late; the Double R diner is closed. The building doesn't have the "RR to Go" sign painted on it; we could be behind or ahead of the predominant time period in which *The Return* is occurring (2016). Lynch shows their car from an omniscient point of view, going past the front of the diner; there's no indication that Cooper notices the missing sign.

As they progress, Cooper asks, "Do you recognize this street, these houses?" And finally, with the Palmer house in view, "This house?" The white house is iconic, emanating many emotions for *Twin Peaks* aficionados, let alone, one would think, for the woman who grew up and suffered and dreamed there. But Carrie says, "No"; there's no flicker of recognition on her face.

In Part Seventeen, Cooper knew he had Laura by the hand as he led her away from death in the woods. Now, as he takes Carrie's hand, is he sure who this woman is? Emotion floods the moment as they cross the street and climb the front steps. Cooper and Laura have engaged and enchanted us for twenty-seven years. He's had a deep spiritual connection to her as a stone-cold murder victim, communing with her in dreams, attending her post-death beatification, sharing space-time with her in the Red Room, seeking and saving her before her death. No matter who the woman walking with him to the Palmer front door is, she's vulnerable, has suffered, needs help, and Cooper has dedicated his life to helping.

Cooper and Carrie stand before the white door with glass panels veiled with pale curtains. Cooper knocks softly, no response, knocks again. Lynch makes us so aware of time, suspended in pauses and silences. A figure behind the veil, a woman (Mary Reber) half-opens the door. No smile, neutral expression. In an atmosphere of time extending, with close-ups of Cooper and Carrie, we absorb information, learning that the woman's never heard of Sarah Palmer. She bought the house from a Mrs. Chalfont, and her name is Tremond. We and Cooper know where we are: the Palmer house in Twin Peaks. But the question of when it is is now up in the air. There's never been evidence to contradict the conclusion that the Palmers have been longtime members of the Twin Peaks community, and we know that Laura was born in 1971. So if we're in the past, the Palmers' residency in the house is still to come, and Alice Tremond looks too modern for that scenario. She's like the liberated 1970s neighborhood moms Lynch, Frost, and I knew in youth: long, straight, center-parted hair, a daring deep plunge to the ruffled neckline of her untucked blouse. She's with-it, au courant; maybe we're in the future, after Sarah's died, the house having been occupied by succeeding owners.

The names Chalfont and Tremond deepen the mystery. The Tremond house, the Chalfont house, the Palmer house: in the *Twin Peaks* universe, even a house (like human heads) can have multiple identities, all touched by the beyond. The 1990-1991 *Twin Peaks*'s Mrs. Chalfont (Frances Bay) was a quizzical little old lady with a magician grandson (played by David Lynch's look-alike son Austin): two prescient guide figures who helped point various characters in the direction of ultimate goodness. In *Fire Walk With Me*, Lynch made the Tremonds more enigmatic by linking them to the name Chalfont (the cast list says, "Mrs, Tremond [Chalfont] as Frances Bay"). And, at the Fat Trout Trailer Park, some force field emanated by the Chalfonts' trailer, or maybe the owl cave ring positioned in a ceremonial dirt mound beneath the trailer, caused Agent Chet Desmond (Chris Isaak) to vanish, and he's still missing.

The threshold of this white house in Twin Peaks, which Cooper saw as, at last, a portal to peace, understanding, and resolution for Laura, is closed. With the hubris of a born rescuer, he has presumed to know what she needs, and his complex, arduous effort to provide it has failed. The house door closes; Cooper and Carrie turn away from it, and Lynch floats his camera behind them all the way down the steps and into the street without a cut, in silence, as the two digest the situation. Maybe Alice is the mother of old Mrs. Tremond's grandson or is married to the now-adult grandson. Or maybe the spirit of Mrs. Tremond, who helped Cooper and Laura in the past, knows that Sarah Palmer is now allied with the Dark Mother and warns them away from the house by pretending ignorance of Sarah, the house shadowed even when the sun is out. We remember Lynch's conviction that "The house is a place where things can go wrong." The house, a symbol of the human head.

Since the original *Twin Peaks*, Cooper has known the Palmer house to be Bob saturated, Leland, Laura, and Sarah having the dark one, in varying degrees, a presence in their minds and lives. Pondering for twenty-five years in the Red Room, Cooper decides he knows how to make things ultimately, finally, right, to exorcise the Palmer family's demons. And whether he's conscious of it or not, to exorcise his own demons, heal his own wounded psyche, atone for his mistake of a lifetime.

When *The Return* introduces Diane as Cooper's longtime love, it's news to us, which is fine dramatically, plotwise; it's fun to be surprised. But it strikes a discordant note. The decades-long *Twin Peaks* saga has always positioned Laura as the primary female in Cooper's life after Caroline. Caroline, whose life bled away through stab wounds struck by her husband, Windom Earle, Cooper's partner in 1985. Caroline had witnessed a federal crime, and Cooper was assigned to guard her. With his chivalrous, white knight-protecting-humanity self-image, Cooper relished this "duty." He and Caroline immediately fell deeply in love and acted on their feelings. Cooper let himself get swept away by his emotions, violating his sacred professional code, resulting in Caroline lying cold, bloody, dead in his arms. This traumatic melding of love and death and guilt was Cooper's primal psychic event, which generated the remorse, sadness, self-disgust, and fear that enabled Bob to take him over at the end of the original *Twin Peaks*. Previous to that event, Cooper had kept his emotional wound, his badge of guilt, to himself. But once the Laura Palmer case was "solved," Cooper was talking to Audrey before leaving Twin Peaks. Audrey, young, nubile, willing, and in love with Cooper—so why didn't he answer her emotional call? "Someone must have hurt you once. Very badly," she mused. Cooper responded, "No, someone was hurt by me. And I will never let that happen again." In other words, "I thought I was keeping someone from being hurt, and I actually ended up making sure they were hurt." This last sentence isn't Cooper talking about his sorry past with Caroline; it's detective Jake Gittes (Jack Nicholson) regretting his past in Roman Polanski's 1978 film, *Chinatown*, a picture Lynch loves deeply.

Penned by the great screenwriter Robert Towne, plus (uncredited) Roman Polanski and Edward Taylor, *Chinatown* was supposed to end optimistically, with evil defeated and Jake helping a woman move hopefully forward on her life path. But director Polanski, who'd grown up in Nazi-occupied Poland, whose parents were in concentration camps, whose pregnant wife, Sharon Tate, was slaughtered by the Manson family, drove the film to a dark conclusion. All Jake's good intentions were like dry leaves scattered by a scorching Santa Ana wind. Just as in his past, he couldn't "always tell what's going on," and his actions contributed to the woman being killed, and evil winning. Jake is stricken. He's at a loss. He doesn't understand how reality could flip on him like this. He can barely stand up, and his friends lead him away. One says, trying to be comforting, trying to fend off chaos with words, "Forget it, Jake, it's Chinatown." This is one of the most famous, viscerally affecting endings in film history. Lynch once told me that "it's perfect; it opens everything up," meaning it leaves us room to dream. Mystery will always haunt the night air, tantalizing us, sparking our imaginations, the eternal wondering: What comes next?

The *Chinatown* ending, which Mark Frost also reveres, exudes the same sort of atmosphere of futility and existential vertigo that envelops *The Return*'s last moments. Urgently in his heart and mind, Cooper believed that saving Laura from being killed, enabling her to live on, would counteract some cosmic imbalance, reconnect a broken circuit, form a golden circle. Like Jake Gittes, he didn't understand what's going on; he says, "What year is this?" And Carrie, whether she's a reincarnation reliving a memory or Laura trying hard not to be Laura, hears the dwelling spirit of the house, Sarah, shout-moan, "Laura." And the blonde woman, the One of *Twin Peaks*, feels all the horror and pain of humanity's suffering and screams, screams her heart in two.

Laura, retraumatized, victimized by her hero, her champion, her "savior." Cooper, her protector, has harmed her like he harmed Caroline, whom he thought he was protecting. The mastermind doesn't know what time it is:"What year is this?" By Frost's and Lynch's conscious design or not, it's the show's "Forget it, Jake, it's Chinatown" moment. *Twin Peaks*'s icons, Laura and Cooper, brought low. Laura's scream is the last vocalization we hear in the show. This is where Lynch and Frost chose to leave the story. So what have these two deep-thinking and feeling men been showing us and telling us in *The Return*?

When Lynch's mother, Sunny, was killed in a car crash in 2004, I sent him a condolence card that was a reproduction of mystical Northwest artist Morris Graves's (1910-2001) painting *Lotus*. The lotus, sacred flower of ancient Egyptian, Buddhist, and Hindu spirituality, that is born from the mud, a single, clean, fragrant blossom that rises opening to the sun. Graves's *Lotus* is soft, misty pale, a spirit flower emanating pure white light into a golden atmosphere. This flower stalk crowned with an orb of luminance was like René Magritte's 1937 painting *The Pleasure Principle*, in which a black-suited man's neck is topped with a corona of white radiance. The image of a vertical form capped with a glowing circle was in turn like the conclusion of a short black-and-white film Lynch made for me to show at the Seattle Art Museum in 2008. A zigzag floor, dark curtains, two chairs. Black-suited Lynch in one chair, an effigy figure representing Laura Palmer in the other. As the *Twin Peaks* theme plays, he gets up, bends forward, and kisses her head, then stands tall next to her like Cooper in the *Fire Walk With Me* Red Room ending. A bright spotlight makes his head an orb of incandescence.

In 1953, *Life* magazine did a multiple-page feature story on "The Mystic Painters of the Northwest," centered on the work of Morris Graves, Mark Tobey, Kenneth Callahan, and Guy Anderson. In the years immediately following the horrific chaos of World War II, with its Holocaust and nuclear-bomb-melted Hiroshima, its massive acting out of the darkest human impulses, these Northwest men brooded on the war, talked, got their bearings, and painted. Callahan (1905-1986), who worked at the Seattle Art Museum years before I did, said he and his artist friends "contemplated the interrelationship of man and nature, the infinite, Picasso and cubism, Chinese painting and Oriental and Christian philosophies." Men listening to what the whispering trees, the owls, and the brooding skies tell them; pondering where this world ends and the next begins, or if they're both here and there; reality represented in multiple perspectives of space and time; the Chinese way of painting "the flight instead of the birds only"; Hindu thoughts of karma and reincarnation, light and dark goddesses, the *Book of Revelations*, Christian suffering, grace, angels (*Modernism in the Pacific Northwest: The Mythic and the Mystical*). *Twin Peaks: The Return* reflects the sensibilities of Kenneth Callahan, Morris Graves, and their fellow forest artist-mystics. The Northwest painters were fascinated not just by the inspirations of Asian spirituality and art, but also by Native American culture, whose design motifs blanket the walls of The Great Northern hotel and whose spirit lore and traditions are embodied in Deputy Hawk and the consciousness of actor-artist Michael Horse. Just as I was stirred by the art-life correspondence of my father having been a lumberjack in the *Twin Peaks* woods, Coast Salish Native American punk poet Sasha Lapointe was moved by Michael Horse's Deputy Hawk, and the show in general. In her book *Red Paint* she says,"I felt at home in *Twin Peaks*, I saw myself and my places on screen. Hawk was only the second Indian I ever saw on a screen," and he was a powerful archetype: "He was a tracker, he knew the woods." Lynch paints the hopeful, life-force color red throughout *The Return*, and red has spiritual significance for Lapointe, her tribe, and family. Red paint colors the faces of evolved leaders, and Lapointe matured into a wearer of red paint, which connotes "healer." Lapointe notes that "Audrey Horne switches from her saddle shoes to a pair of red pumps." *Twin Peaks* was also a romantic signpost for Lapointe: when she met her future boyfriend at a party, she thought, "Damn, a real-life Agent Cooper."

Morris Graves believed that works of art could transfer enlightenment from master to student, from the artist to the one experiencing the art. The spirit-formed artwork could be "loaded to the blissful limit with information for a mind in meditative evenness" (*Modernism in the Pacific Northwest: The Mythic and the Mystical*), that is, calm, open, receptive. Assuming that viewers of *The Return* are in the zone of attentive, enlivened "evenness," what information has the show imparted? It's shown us the great human value of living in nature in a community of people mostly dedicated to being friendly, kind, and helpful to each other. Really being there, present, talking and listening, not on the phone or watching screens. Not consumed in materialistic status seeking or exploiting people and natural resources for financial gain. Valuing gentleness, reading and learning, communing with trees and rivers and their spirits. The Native American tradition of living with the land is their primal nature, as is a willingness to tolerate, respect, and value people as they are: some damaged, wounded, sad, angry, some with damn foolish ideas—but they all breathe the same air; they pretty much follow the law; they get by together.

Twin Peaks residents manifest their commonality with each other and the place they live in secular houses of worship: the Double R diner and the Roadhouse. Music in the air, good food and drink, happiness shared, problems aired and worked out, and, sometimes, the prospect of new love. Twin Peaks is a quirky oasis far from America's urbanized rat race. No wonder Special Agent Dale Cooper, battered by all the troubles of the big world out there, saw this realm as a little slice of paradise and immediately felt at home here.

So the *Twin Peaks* saga imparts the values of goodwill and community and, through the exchanges of Cooper and his law-enforcing colleagues, the personal values that made teenaged Boy Scout David Lynch strive and reach the exalted, top rank of Eagle Scout. Looking through my 1950s Boy Scouts of America's *Handbook for Boys*, the same edition that Lynch had, I read characteristics that describe Lynch's alter ego Cooper. Be careful of your clothing; be observant; plan a route; find your way; seek truth and knowledge; be prepared; help others at all times; be kind, cheerful, loyal: pursue ways of helping our America. In short, be idealistic, pump up the good karma.

The *Boy Scout Handbook* is full of appealing black-and-white pen-and-ink representations of right-minded youths among forest trees, interacting with nature. There are images that evoke *Twin Peaks*. A circle of stumps: did someone cut down Glastonbury Grove? A steel circle, a bell suspended in the air that's been struck by a mallet, dash lines representing the ringing sound. Perhaps, buried in Lynch's memory, this inspired the Great Northern hotel's mysterious ringing. It also reflects "teapot" Phillip Jeffries's airy messages that float within a circle form.

The handbook's opening chapter is called "What to Do First," and the image above its opening words stunningly sums up Lynch's personal spiritual life path, his professional journey, and the aesthetic and narrative structuring of his work. We see a boy from an angle behind him; he's in a dark room, his back shadowed black. His left hand is on the room's black door, which is half-open into a space beyond that is pure white light. The light rays are illuminating his face and seeping into the dark space he's in. He's going forward across the threshold, into the light. Years ago, Lynch told me that in his art stories he likes to sink people down toward hell, where it's ugly and horrible, with torments for body and soul. But at a certain point, they stop sinking and start to rise; they learn the lessons of darkness and can choose to counteract it. Falling first, then rising, journeying from darkness to light; there is always a beacon of transcendent hope. An abused boy grows himself a grandmother and discovers a positive evolutionary path (*The Grandmother*). *Eraserhead*'s beleaguered Henry gets to embrace his heavenly Woman in the Radiator. In death, *The Elephant Man*'s John Merrick melds with the spirit of his beloved mother. *Dune*'s Paul Atreides realizes and embodies his godly status. After *Blue Velvet*'s dark night, the robins sing in the sunshine for Jeffrey and Sandy. *Wild at Heart*'s Sailor finally sings "Love Me Tender" to Lula. *Fire Walk With Me*'s Laura Palmer is blessed by her angel. *The Straight Story*'s Alvin Straight reunites with his estranged brother beneath an infinite star field. *INLAND EMPIRE*'s Nikki Grace enjoys the grace of fully integrated selfhood. In this film, a character tells a tale of a girl "half born," lost in the realm of surface appearances, seeing only half of reality, needing to discover and experience the deepest energies and forces at work in the world, and herself. Whether it's due to original sin or the way our brains have evolved, we all have a need for Something More, something to see further on, a way back to the Garden, an expansive consciousness of a blissful reality. Lynch samples it when he meditates; he lives a life receptive to the deepest messages. It takes work, suffering, generosity, love. Lynch and his characters are in a state of evolving, becoming, even beyond death: sleepers awakening, becoming fully born. Lynch doesn't feel he's attained enlightenment, but he's working at it, and his living example is inspiring.

Lynch's characters are at varying positions on the spiritual continuum of base metals becoming gold, lower and higher on the karmic ladder. *Lost Highway*'s Fred Madison and *Mulholland Drive*'s Diane Selwyn have been instrumental in causing the deaths of people they once loved/do love, but redemption, growth toward goodness, are universal possibilities for Lynch. He often says he loves "continuing stories" because that's the way he sees the world process of spiritual energies: on and on in an expanding universe. We leave some of his screen stories with characters in a bad place, but that's just an appearance, a snapshot, a fragment, the point at which the film ran out—but the story goes on.

In *The Return*, the Giant has become the wizardly Fireman. Sarah Palmer has become the Dark Mother, an aspect of Judy. Laura Palmer has become Carrie Page (the missing page of Laura's diary?) and is perhaps evolving toward being the Hindu "Mother Divine," as Lynch calls the Vedic literary personification of positive female energy, a name for the angelic women of his art. When the original *Twin Peaks* ended on June 10, 1991, David Lynch and Mark Frost felt they had more *Twin Peaks* to give. As Lynch says of the inconclusive, evocative *Chinatown* ending, "It opens everything up," creating the room to dream that he loves. Lynch and Frost's mystical Northwest continuing story enabled them to express their deepest ideas, feelings, and visualizations of good and evil, light and dark, matter and energy, world and spirit. *The Return* received almost unanimous critical praise, boosted the Showtime channel's subscribership, was named on international ten-best lists of both the year's best TV shows and films, and its DVD/Blu-ray release debuted at number one, according to Seattle's famous Scarecrow Video store. Showtime Programming President Gary Levine told *Deadline*: "The door's always open to David Lynch." But Lynch and Frost are older men; they spent four to five years of their lives on *The Return*, and they passed on making more. Still, *Twin Peaks* haunted their consciousness, as it does ours.

Lynch has told me that "things happen the way they're supposed to happen, and when they're supposed to happen." Laura-Carrie is on her way to a blessedness, a divinity more luminous than her beatification at the end of *Fire Walk With Me*, as ordained by the Fireman and Lady Dido. But what of Special Agent Dale Cooper, seeker of knowledge, helper of humanity? The shaman with the Eagle Scout values? The *Boy Scout Handbook* quotes from Edward Everett Hale's story "The Man Without a Country": "Never dream a dream but of serving her as she bids you, though the service carry you through a thousand hells." The "her" refers to the idea, and the ideals, of America as a feminine entity, just as the people of France call their national allegorical symbol Marianne; America was personified as the noble, gown-draped Columbia before the militaristic Uncle Sam shoved her aside. The scout handbook quotes Hale further, "You belong to Her as you belong to your own mother." You, Dale Cooper, your highest self, doing what your country, Laura's Queendom—Laura the Mother Goddess, the Good Mother—needs to be done. Judy and Bob, the psyche's subhuman shadows, are in us and in the world. Be vigilant, fight the fires, drain away the poisons, seek the light.

In the blackness of the street. The Palmer house has gone dark; Laura's scream echoes in the night. Cooper looks up into the starless sky, then at Laura. He says, "It's a feeling. . . I understand everything."

Of course, he could be wrong. But fifty years ago, David Lynch conceived of a parentally abused boy who knew that one particular seed would grow him a living grandmother (*The Grandmother*). Lynch's orientation, drive, and desire surge toward hard-won love and bliss, a transcendence of negativity, of "non-exis-tence." Standing in the dark street, Cooper and Laura emanate an aura of potentiality, a generative force field. They're on a road. They're alive. They need to choose which way to go. In a world where, as the Log Lady once said to Laura, "All goodness is in jeopardy," perhaps Cooper and Laura need to be fighters, fierce warriors trying to eliminate the darkness. Or maybe Laura can neutralize Sarah/Judy's power with a sudden Zen gesture—embracing her mother, Sarah, encompassing her, understanding that dark power will always exist, but channeling it toward creation, not destruction.

Maybe there's a flash of cosmic electricity, and we're high above the town of

Twin Peaks, then higher, with South Dakota, Montana, New Mexico, Las Vegas, New York, and Odessa in the same vast image. It's like a huge map or jigsaw puzzle, and bending over it are two men in robes the color of red curtains, Tibetan monks, delicately letting colored sand slip from their fingers to form the all-encompassing picture. It's a great circular form like a mandala, but it's not symmetrical. The monks leave a gap, like the entrance to a labyrinth, which is one of the most ancient cross-cultural symbols. The seeker enters the labyrinth's confusing tangle of many pathways and tries to get to the center, to a golden wholeness of understanding and integration. But it's a long, torturous journey. Forward motion ends in a blind alley. Your steps double back on themselves. Is this a new path or one you've already tried? You have to consider what you're learned and try another route. Your consciousness, your sense of what's real, is disturbed. Your linear, rational orientation is worthless. You're lost. To the ancient Chinese alchemists, attempting to understand and negotiate the labyrinth rationally "is not pleasing to the tao of the female principle and will lead to great danger" (*The Book of Symbols*). The seeker should approach the hidden, divine center point "free of thought and worry," like an intuitive detective (Dale Cooper) or a Transcendental Meditator (David Lynch) would. Reverence for the Female Divine motivates Lynch's life and art; it drives Cooper's quest. In Lynch's beloved France, at the center of one of the world's most sacred labyrinths, at the Notre Dame Cathedral, is a six-petaled flower representing the Virgin Mary, the feminine principle. Laura Palmer is "the One" at the center of the labyrinth that is *Twin Peaks*. Mortals of an evil nature perish in the labyrinth (*The Shining*'s Jack Torrance, *Twin Peaks*'s Windom Earle in the nexus of passageways that is the Red Room). Heroes like the storied Greek Theseus slay their monsters and emerge cleansed, purified. Cooper and Laura, our hero and heroine, are on the twisting and turning path to their golden potential, their arc from confusion, entrapment, and multiplicity to clarity, liberation, and unity. In the labyrinth, once the center is found, the way back will be utterly new, a discovery of what's around the next curve of the continuing story. As Lynch quotes the Bhagavad Gita regarding his own seeking and discovering Art Life: "Curving back on My own Nature, I create again and again." The monks finish their sandpainting and leave. Something stirs. A wind from nowhere blows the sand, the image, away, into white light. A wind that whispers in the fir trees, that ruffles David Lynch's hair.

Paris, France, calling. No, it isn't the minister of culture wanting to give Lynch another upgrade to his present Legion of Honor status (though Lynch did receive a career-honoring Oscar in October 2019). It's Parisian journalist Cédric Deville asking me to do something that does not thrill Lynch: put myself in his head, as I did in *David Lynch: Beautiful Dark*, speaking for the man, talking about what the woods, the waterfall, the cherry pie, the coffee of *Twin Peaks* mean to David Lynch. I said, "Sure, I'll do it."

The European arts channel ARTE's program *Invitation to a Voyage* examines the influence of particular landscapes, the sense of place, on the lives and art of various filmmakers, such as George Miller's (*Mad Max*) Australia and Wim Wenders's (*Wings of Desire*) Berlin. I would be filmed at some of the signature *Twin Peaks* locations, talking about how Lynch channeled the essence of this Northwest place into his art and what it all meant to him.

I've had Lynch's unique artistic sensibility on my mind for fifty years, since I saw *The Grandmother* in 1970. His thoughts, feelings, and views of the world are singular, particular, like *Twin Peaks* and its people and stories. But, in words Lynch wrote for the Log Lady's introduction to the original *Twin Peaks* pilot, the town of Twin Peaks (and Lynch's uncommon mind) "encompasses the all." The visions of quirky character Lynch are expansive, not limited. They show that the other is us; we fall and redeem ourselves throughout life; we seek freedom and love in a universe that is infinite and holy; people, nations, the world, the universe will be consumed, and reborn; the farthest reaches of time and space are within us in this moment; all is now; all is generated by one; we all build our own structures of subjective truth; everything is transforming all the time; no single viewpoint can encompass what happens; Jesus and Muhammad doubted.

Still, we get up in the morning; we have our coffee. Today I'll be filming on ground, in places, that were part of my boyhood, my life, and my father's life as a young man, ground that is simultaneously part of David Lynch and Mark Frost's imaginations, their Twin Peaks. The French connection means a lot to me. Like Lynch, I have long venerated France's relatively feminized culture, its respect for deep philosophical thought, sensual pleasures, metaphysical poetics, the amusements and the sacredness of romance and love, and the art of the cinema. My mother, Nona, though Russian, loved French things. I grew up admiring her post-World War II New Look French fashion sense and the Pierre Auguste Renoir prints and large Degas-like painting of ballerinas on our home walls. In my late teens and early twenties, I read Balzac, Proust, Baudelaire, Mallarmé, Verlaine, Artaud and absorbed movies by Truffaut, Godard, Chabrol, Rohmer, Rivette, and Malle. Their French films provided an emotional education, on the nuances of desire and restraint and the challenge of seeking unchanging absolutes in an impermanent world of relativity.

Those filmmakers have passed on, but Thomas Cazals and Cyrille Renaux were waiting for me in front of the Mar-T Café in North Bend. Cyrille, the camera- and sound man, was a jeans-and-T-shirt guy, while Thomas, the interviewer, wore grayish outdoor gear; both sported brightly colored sneakers. They mostly spoke French, I spoke English, and we made do pretty well. Thomas smoked American Spirit cigarettes "because David Lynch does" and called my book *David Lynch: Beautiful Dark* "a precious document," adding that it was "crazy, a crazy thing," which I took to be Parisian-hip praise.

I grew up loving Howard Hawks movies, in which professionals who knew their stuff banded together to fight wars, drive cattle, or confront alien invaders. So it felt great to instantly bond with Thomas and Cyrille and get to work. Cyrille set up his camera on a massive tripod by the café's front door,and had me walk toward him from way down the block of storefront shops. He shot multiple takes from different angles, one from across the street, so people in the little shops on West North Bend

Way saw me walk and linger, walk and linger on the sidewalk. When a couple of older local women looked at me quizzically, I said, "*Twin Peaks*," and they nodded and grinned. It was a busy lunchtime at the Mar-T, and there were *Twin Peaks* fans taking selfies outside. They tried to be cool and casual about paying attention to what these French filmmakers and I were doing.

The final product will have voice-over narration as I walk along the storefronts, enter the café, sit in a booth, study the menu, order cherry pie and black coffee, then leave the goodies untouched as I look to the left of Cyrille's lens, where Thomas asks me questions that launch me into riffs about trees in Lynch's life and work, his forest-researcher father, his lifelong sense of hidden forces at work in the world. I was wired for sound, with a microphone taped under my shirt, and at one point I made a gesture of tapping my heart, producing a thumping we didn't want. We paused, I rejoined my train of thought and gestured silently. Most of the time I made eye contact with Thomas, a perfect, intense listener, who rarely blinked and silently laughed when I referred to Ben Horne as "*Twin Peaks*'s toxic capitalist." Maybe, as I voiced that spontaneous thought, we were both picturing Donald J. Trump. Thomas and Cyrille never said "cut!" It was always a French-accented "*su-pair*!" or "*par-fait*" (perfect). I felt at ease and natural giving them (I hope) what they wanted. At the end of the day, Cyrille, driving us in a big four-door American car, gave me what I took as a compliment: "You must have done this a lot, at least ten times." I told him it was a brand-new experience.

During a break in Thomas's questions and my answers, I reflected that just being in this valley, nestled between two mountains, the moist, mild summer air scented with evergreen trees, evoked Lynch and Frost's fictional place. Then there was the concreteness of the cherry pie and coffee, resting on a golden Formica tabletop. There was the counter stool where Big Ed sat when his dream of Norma came true. And Norma's "office" booth and the one where Bobby, Shelly, and Becky sat when the bullet shattered the window. The patrons who were in the Mar-T on our French filming day could have fit right into any of the scenes Lynch shot there. It felt like somehow we were all part of his Big Picture.

Cameraman Cyrille fended off anyone who might intrude on any of his compositions, but one man came up to Thomas, drawn by the French being spoken. Tall, shaved head, bushy dark beard, black Pearl Jam T-shirt. He started speaking French to Thomas, and I heard Thomas mention "Greg Olson . . . *David Lynch: Beautiful Dark*." The fellow was Belgian, here to spend time in Twin Peaks with his wife and young son.

As Cyrille's camera rolled, Thomas asked me the core question of their film, "What is the importance of sense of place in Lynch's work, his life?" In my mind a portal opened into Lynch's world of correspondences and interconnections. Months after *The Return* aired, I was in a Seattle room where Northwest-born Lynch spoke of the forest as a "cathedral of trees." For over three decades, Lynch has lived in a Hollywood Hills house designed (1963) by Frank Lloyd Wright's son, Lloyd, who's most famous for his Wayfarers Chapel (1946-1951) on the Palos Verdes

Peninsula. Wright had been inspired by the idea of "a church as growing from and symbolizing a group of tall trees with the sky as the roof." Comprising mostly glass, and including chevron forms that are also prominent in Lynch's house, the cathedral is indeed a sacred fusion of human-built shelter, pine trees, and sky. As a Los Angeles architectural guide says, "Wright created a sense of a mysterious, almost fairy-tale forest." Lynch is well familiar with the chapel, since it's within a few miles of where his former wife and dear friend Peggy Reavey lives and where he visited his daughter Jennifer Lynch while she recuperated from a car accident.

Before Wright took on the Wayfarers Chapel commission, he designed the Institute of Mentalphysics in the California Yucca Valley desert. The architect's poetic sensibility was in perfect harmony with this spiritual-realization group that studied Tibetan teachings, and he designed a Temple of Reverence, a Caravansary of Joy, and a Preceptory of Light among the ancient Joshua Trees.

Another factor linking Lynch with the poetry and metaphysics of trees, nature, and Lloyd Wright the builder is the that Wright's Wayfarer's Chapel was commissioned, and is managed by, the Swedenborg Society, which espouses the philosophy of Swedish mystic Emanuel Swedenborg (1688-1772). I once told Lynch that William Blake could stare at a piece of wood until he was afraid of it. Lynch grinned and responded, "Sure, I love William Blake." We've noted how Lynch's work in many mediums shows Blake's influence: huge figures and head forms floating free of gravity in fields of stars; fictions of innocence and experience, good and evil; narratives built on unique artist-devised personal mythopoetic systems; a veneration of imagination, of intuition over proscribed rules. Swedenborg's visionary ideas, perceptions, and writings were nutritious food for Blake's thought. He was a member of the Swedenborg Society and wrote margin notes as he read the mystic's books, feeling attuned to the "instructing spirits" he sensed in the world. This is certainly Lynch's and Agent Cooper's approach to life, the attentive detective mode Lynch urges us all to adopt, attuned to signs and wonders.

Swedenborg, Blake, and Lynch perceive the interpenetration of the material and spiritual worlds, the correspondences, reflections, echoes: evidence of an underlying unity, an absolute oneness. They're attuned to duality, Jung's two-faced archetype; as Blake says, "Heaven and Hell are born together." Lynch, Blake, and Swedenborg understand the essential subjectivity of life, the way the external world is in the eye of each individual beholder, a configuration of their inner psychic states. As Blake says, "Though it appears without, it is within." And Lynch, "The world is as you are," which reflects Philip K. Dick's idea that we all, each one of us, projects the world.

These visionaries see beyond the supposed finality of death. Lynch believes in karma and reincarnation, and Swedenborg's words from two centuries ago could apply to Laura Palmer: "All have capacity to be regenerated, because all are redeemed, each one according to their state." Swedenborg believed that those who endure the most suffering are especially blessed. And Blake sees personal/universal consciousness as "Eternal Vision, that Eternal World the Permanent Realities of Every Thing which we see reflected" (*A Vision of the Last Judgment*). The soul-enriching words, writings, and images of Swedenborg, Blake, and Lynch are the evidence, the rewards, of their expanded visionary consciousness. As Blake said, "The tree a fool sees is not the tree a wise man sees" (*The Marriage of Heaven and Hell*).

Cyrille, Thomas, and I finished shooting in the Mar-T café, and I got to finally eat the cherry pie and drink the coffee that had been sitting in front of me. The camera wasn't rolling, but Cyrille and Thomas looked at me expectantly until I said, "Damn fine coffee!" Parisians aren't supposed to smile at Americans, so my filmmakers must be rebels. The way elegant Frenchman Thomas loaded up his big all-American cheeseburger with ketchup before tearing into it bespoke a Franco-American alliance, plus he seemed to appreciate the American version of french fries.

They wanted me to take them to the forest, so that they could film further conversations amid looming trees. But it started to rain heavily, so we decided to drive a few miles to the Salish Lodge (Great Northern hotel) and film by the cozy fireplace. It was a big tourist day at Snoqualmie Falls; we got the last parking spot. There were a lot of people strolling between the falls viewpoints and the lodge. Cyrille wanted to get a panorama of me alone walking toward the hotel entrance, past the stone pillars where Audrey Horne with her saddle shoes had sat waiting for her limousine ride to high school. Cyrille was a man of crisp, precise, brisk movements; in the café, he didn't hesitate to shoo people away from the shot he'd lined up. I was poised by the stone pillars, ready to walk to the hotel; Cyrille was thirty feet in front of me. Before he could say "Go," two women walked into the space between us. Oblivious to what Cyrille and I were doing, or willfully not looking at us, they took many minutes talking and posing for each other's cameras. I was a bit irked, and I assumed Cyrille was more so. As the two self-absorbed women finally walked off, without a glance at us, Cyrille smiled at me and said, "Funny." I smiled back. A good life lesson: don't be so wrapped up in yourself that you can't enjoy privileged moments of unscripted reality.

The dignified woman sitting by the Salish Lodge lobby fireplace did not have Cyrille in her plan for the day. There were two chairs by the fire, and one was occupied by this elderly woman in a tasteful cashmere sweater and pearls, quietly sipping her tea. Cyrille wanted me to come into the room, approach the fire, sit in the unoccupied chair next to the woman, and look at the fire until he stopped his camera. He had me go through this process three times (they felt identical to me) while he squatted with his camera in front of the woman, almost brushing her knees. She remained silent, but as we finally finished, she shook her head as if to say, "Oh, these crazy artists!"

Thomas's trust in Cyrille's ability to film good footage for him to work with was absolute; he never asked to see anything Cyrille had just shot. But now Cyrille flipped up the little view screen so that Thomas and I could look over his shoulder. In the small frame, we saw an image worthy of Lynch: a close-up of a burning log, almost incandescent with heat and flame.

We were done for the day. Thomas headed to the hotel gift shop; Cyrille went off to find "the toilet" (not the bathroom, the men's room); he also voiced disdain for "Americans putting ice in their water." Thomas looked over an array of tasteful *Twin Peaks* items (no garish T-shirts) and bought a refrigerator magnet showing Snoqualmie Falls. Earlier, he and I had talked about a linkage between the cascading water and Lynch's mystical electricity. As he pocketed his magnet, I said, "Electromagnetic power." He chuckled.

It was pouring rain again. The car was way back over in the parking lot. Cyrille grabbed the lodge concierge's umbrella and ran for it, got the car, and swung back to pick up Thomas and me. The concierge helped load in their filmmaking gear and opened the doors for us to climb in. As we did, he said "au revoir" to each of us separately. Unable to resist being seen as part of a French film crew, I said "merci" as he closed my door.

Thomas and Cyrille flew back to Paris, where Thomas edited the film for its late 2019 broadcast. Journalist Cédric Deville, (who first invited me to be in this project) and I have become email pen pals, and he's invited me to hang out in Paris, drink coffee and talk about books and movies. Interacting with these Frenchmen whose lives are dedicated to the arts has validated what I've done with my life: appreciating, learning from, and exhibiting moving images that touch our hearts, minds, and souls. It's easy to see why Lynch feels that the French "get" him, that they naturally acknowledge and endorse what he calls his art life, his essence.

Twin Peaks: The Return ended, but it's not over. Lynch and Frost stirred up, accessed, visualized, and dramatized all the micro-macro opposing forces and polarities of humanity and the universe, concretized as Good versus Evil, abstracted as Laura versus Judy (Sarah Palmer). Throughout history, humanity has been immersed in the Light versus Darkness conflict—on a continental scale, and when we look in the mirror. It's a constant battle. What to do? Where's Lynch's "magic door" between warring opposites? In *Moby-Dick* (1851), Herman Melville sought to portray "the enormity of evil" abstracted as the monstrous white whale and the mad Captain Ahab, who sheds his humanity pursuing the beast to the ends of the earth (*The Cast of Consciousness: Concepts of the Mind in British and American Romanticism*). Along on the sea quest voyage is Ishmael, the book's spiritually seeking protagonist who, throughout the monumentally long tale, notes almost countless examples of polarities. Within this mazy web of contraries, Ismael senses a hint, a vague "image of the ungraspable phantom of life . . . the key to it all." Ralph Waldo Emerson, Melville's transcendentalist contemporary, felt himself "adjacent to the One," saw Ishmael's "ungraspable phantom" as a glimmer, a whisper of divinity in the unconscious, waiting to be fully manifested: a calm center point, a harmonic wholeness in the midst of a chaotically fragmented world. Melville, near the end of his life, wrote a poem on the creation of *Art* (1891), comparing the arduous process of his creative way of life (his dharma) to biblical Jacob wrestling with the angel until it blesses him. It's a quest, a struggle, to find the right form, "pulsed life create." And that aliveness in art can only be created when the teeming, opposing forces and energies, "the unlike things . . . meet and mate." The inherent oneness is realized: you are an aspect of me; I am an aspect of you. Scholars feel that Melville stopped writing because he couldn't properly express his ideas in words; language was limited. Perhaps artists of the cinema are best able to project spiritual truths, to nestle us in metaphysical realms.

Lynch quotes from the Yoga Sutra in his book *Catching the Big Fish*, "Avert the danger that has yet to come." Try a new path, away from eye-for-an-eye violent "justice" that fruitlessly attempts to obliterate the Other. Shift to a make-love-not-war view that sees self and nonself, all dualities, as aspects of a unified whole, what Lynch calls the Big Home of Everything, smooth running, producing bliss on Earth now, in each eternal moment. Such thoughts are brand-new and ancient, always being discovered by those with inward vision. Many people, especially the young, in Lynch and Frost's midcentury America, experienced a mental-emotional-spiritual reorientation, linked to a centuries-long chain of inspired seekers.

Joseph Campbell, the great scholar of human nature and the mythic stories we tell, has noted common themes voiced by enlightened thinkers through the ages. From the Egyptian *Book of the Dead* (1550 BCE): "I am Yesterday, Today, and Tomorrow, and I have the power to be born again a second time. I am the divine hidden Soul who created the gods . . . Hail, Lord of the shrine in the center of the earth. He is I and I am He!" And Christ in the *Gospel According to Thomas*: "I am the All, the All came forth from me and the All attained to me. Cleave a piece of wood, I am there." And in the earliest Hindu Upanishad, *The Great Forest Book* (eighth century B.C.): "This self is the footprint of that All, for by it one knows the All . . . So whoever worships another divinity than his self, thinking, 'He is one, I am another,' knows not." Walt Whitman (1819-1892) adds: "to glance with an eye or show a bean in its pod confounds the learning of all times . . . there is no object so soft but it makes a hub for the wheeled universe . . . In the faces of men and women I see God, and in my own face in the glass; I find letters from God dropped in the street, and every one is signed by God's name, and I leave them where they are, for I know that others will punctually come forever and ever."

In 1872, London physician and psychologist Richard M. Bucke (1837-1901), after immersing himself in Walt Whitman's poems, had a mystical experience of feeling wrapped in a cloud of warm light, which was also radiating from inside him. It was "an intellectual illumination" (*Mutants and Mystics*), a "momentary lightning flash of Brahmic splendor," referencing the Hindu concept of Brahman, the blissful state of divine essence before space, time, causation, and the differentiated world were born, the zone Lynch gets a taste of when he meditates. Like the 1970s "pink light illumination" experience that sparked writer Philip K. Dick's creativity, Bucke's light immersion catalyzed his spiritual evolution, and in 1901 he published his seminal book, *Cosmic Consciousness*, which conveyed the feeling of being connected to the expanding universe, of *being* the universe.

Bucke felt himself to be a current in the river of transcendental thought and spiritual energy that sprang from Gautama the Buddha onward to include, among others, Christ, Muhammad, Dante, Blake, and Balzac, culminating in his contemporary Walt Whitman. The two met and became friends and took a trip down

Canada's St. Lawrence River. *Cosmic Consciousness* posits that the universalist insight-epiphany experience awakens and elevates the mind and spirit; it's an evolutionary force that unifies kindred spirits, putting them on an exalted plane like Hindu yogis.

Lynch and Frost are in this awakened cohort, facing east like Walt Whitman, whose poem *Passage to India* (1871) was the capstone of his poetic mythology. Whitman felt that "the poet of the kosmos" should chart the path between material reality and the soul, find the world in himself and of himself, the me within the not-me. Whitman plunges (David Lynch: "I go deep") down to the primal intuitions "below the Sanskrit and the Vedas" (*Passage to India*). In the poem Whitman's persona is the Poet who seeks to decipher and bring into being the divine plan, which is the business of Cooper, the Fireman, and Major Briggs in *The Return*. The Poet is "chanting our chant of pleasant exploration," echoing Lynch's composition: "one chants out between two worlds." Mirroring the Vedantic return to the All of Brahman, Whitman's poet masters the stars and planets, mates with Time, smiles at Death and fills "the vastness of space."

Lynch and Frost grew up in familiar, pleasant, sustaining WASP America, but Frost "felt there was more to the world and reality than what my culture was telling me, more here than meets the eye" (*Conversations With Mark Frost*). He read the Indian philosopher Krishnamurti (1895-1986), absorbing the message "Figure it out for yourself, use your inner resources to interpret reality and find your path." And English writer Aldous Huxley (1894-1963) showed Frost that "a basic unity lies at the heart of all spiritual pursuits." Frost was interested in "alternate theories about what the heck we're doing here," including the experiences of spiritual seeker Alice Bailey, who channeled a "Tibetan master" in her writings.

While Frost was reading and thinking about mystical doings, thanks to LA's sorely missed Bodhi Tree bookstore, Lynch was having a mystical experience over at the Los Angeles County Museum of Art. "They had this show of ancient sandstone carvings from India. There was nobody around, it was really quiet. I rounded a corner, and down the corridor was a pedestal at the very end. My eyes went up the pedestal, and at the top was the head of Buddha. When I looked at the head white light shot out of it into my eyes and it was like boom! I was full of bliss. I've had other experiences like that." Frost was absorbing a written record of mystical experiences, his mind evolving into cosmic consciousness, while Lynch was having a direct, real-time, sensory, Richard M. Bucke, cosmic-consciousness-conversion epiphany, complete with Bucke's flood of light and emotional-intellectual elation. While Frost kept reading, and writing in a mystical vein, Lynch kept having direct soul-bliss experiences in his daily meditations, and he's often manifested metaphysical white light in his artworks. Sizing up the public record, it seems Frost is more a cerebral scholar who thinks deeply and imaginatively about mystical experiences, while Lynch has had his body-mind-soul gripped and shaken by the *mysterium*, as has Lynch's alter-ego Dale Cooper in *The Return*. The experience is the whole-being essence, the totality; it's primary. Thinking about it comes later, or maybe not: it's what Lynch calls the nonverbal "inner knowing."

For decades, Lynch has, as expressed in *The Films of David Lynch*, felt himself to be "a fellow traveler with the heavyweight of surrealism," Jean Cocteau (1889-1963), whose seeking, evolving, expanding consciousness mirrors Lynch's own. Both Cocteau and Lynch grew up enthralled by the imaginative worlds that artists magically create. Lynch would subscribe to Cocteau's youthful mission statement: "We must learn the real world by heart and rebuild it above the clouds, from a blueprint that is poetry." In long careers that span the better part of a century, both men built worlds of poetry, drawing, painting, photography, music, stage productions, films, and acting. Young Cocteau's mind gravitated to deep matters of life and death. His father had committed suicide, and Cocteau experienced the horrific atrocities of World War I trench warfare firsthand. The French and German soldiers hated each other to the death; symbolically, the übertoxic male Kaiser Wilhelm of the fatherland was battling France's warrior mother figure Madeleine. Still, in the mud of the killing fields on Christmas Eve, Cocteau could hear his sworn enemies singing "O Tannenbaum," the song his family always sang at holiday time: beneath the surface hatred there was a common unity, something positive to build on. In his future art expressions, Cocteau often linked opposing contradictory elements in a dreamy center zone. Decades later Lynch would say, "We live in a world opposites, extreme evil and violence opposed to goodness and peace. There's a balancing point between opposing forces, a mysterious Door that we can go through when we get it together." Lynch said this at age forty-five, at the time of the original *Twin Peaks*. He's wrestled with this existential-spiritual equation for decades, and the full *Twin Peaks* saga (1990-2017) is its most resonant expression.

The first film Cocteau made, *The Blood of a Poet* (1930), showed Lynch the Poet as an heroic archetypal figure who encounters mysteries within, and beyond, the everyday world. Cocteau felt that the human face is "an oval mirror that reflects the world," and in *Blood of a Poet* he introduces one of the most resonant and famous surrealistic images, which reflects the human psyche and the sensibility of David Lynch. The Poet stands before a full length mirror, then slips into, and beneath, its quicksilver surface. The "mirror" is actually a pool of water that Cocteau filmed looking down from above, but the image is the threshold to magic, the passage to the labyrinth of inner space, the subconscious, what lies beyond temporal life; it's Lynch's idea that "the world is as you are," his Red Room as a mirror of its occupants' desires and fears. In Cocteau's film, the familiar laws governing space and time are reshaped according to dream logic. The Poet experiences death and a return to life, and his female muse leads the world toward the stars: a mirror of *Twin Peaks: The Return*.

Twenty years after *The Blood of a Poet*, Cocteau made *Orpheus* (1950). While his first film proceeded through a landscape of otherworldly, stylized abstract tableaus, *Orpheus* lives in more ordinary, realistic settings, with cars, cafés, wallpapered bedrooms, yet they're charged with metaphysical energy, like places and people in *Blue Velvet* and especially *Twin Peaks*. In *Orpheus*, Death is a woman in a black car; in *Twin Peaks*, Evil (Bob) looks like a car mechanic. As Cocteau writes, "Realism in the unreal is a trap set minute to minute." Cocteau's films may have taught Lynch how to personify demons and angels as our neighbors, the dramatic aesthetic power of figures moving down corridors and room to room, moving backward (though not speaking that way), even putting on a significant rubber glove. *Orpheus* may have inspired Lynch's love of minimalist, nonsequitur speech, declarative statements that don't fit the logical context of what preceded them; they float, glowing with poetic importance: "That gum you like is coming back in style"; "This is a Formica table"; "Where we're from there's always music in the air." In *Orpheus*, a car radio says things like "A bird sings with its fingers"; "Silence goes faster backwards"; "A single glass of water lights the world." Parisian expatriate American writer Gertrude Stein (1874-1946) may have started the ball rolling when she puzzled, amused and artistically galvanized her creative friends like Cocteau by writing "Dining is West" on a piece of paper with no explanation.

Lynch's and Cocteau's creative minds expand along parallel poetic paths. In Cocteau's cinema, mirrors enable transports between dimensions, this world and others; while Lynch's electrical flashes accomplish similar transitions. Cocteau's *Orpheus* Trilogy (*The Blood of a Poet, Orpheus, The Testament of Orpheus*), and Lynch's *Twin Peaks* saga each spans three decades (1930-60; 1990-2017), and Lynch seems to have absorbed some pointers from the elder poet-artist. On the evidence of Cocteau's *Trilogy*, which he called his spiritual-artistic autobiography, the two artists appear to be close kin. Both men's summary works, via doppelgängers, time shifts, motion backward and forward, explore the eternal struggle between life and death. They're especially sensitive to the life-death midpoint, which Cocteau calls the Zone, where a mortal man seeks his dead wife with hopes of her resurrection (Lynch's *The Return* Zone is a more fearsome interdimensional place, where good people are killed). For Lynch, the place between opposing forces, his "magic door," is the concept of relativity, balance, where moral/behavioral choices are made that cause one to climb higher, or slip downward, on the karmic ladder. Lynch's Hindu/Tibetan Buddhist beliefs posit an afterdeath in-between for the soul, a resting-place pause before one's karma moves them up or down in their next life, a place Laura Palmer is familiar with.

Both Cocteau and Lynch traveled in India, where Cocteau marveled at the goddess figures with one head and hundreds of arms to reach out and act with, symbolic of female power and the many selves within us, foundational concepts for the *Twin Peaks* saga. And Cocteau believed in karma: "Everyone has the place he deserves through a system of checks and balances that functions at a deep level." And Lynch would see himself in Cocteau's words: "I seek to live a reality that is truly mine and beyond time. Having discovered that this site was my privilege, I inspired myself and plunged deeper," words that could have come from Walt Whitman's *Song of Myself* or William Blake's musings: the inner space/cosmic artist-explorers.

The *Orpheus* and *Twin Peaks* epics clearly bear the heartfelt marks of their makers, right down to Cocteau and Lynch acting on-screen roles. And both epics feature an actor playing dual aspects. For Cocteau, Maria Césares portrays woman as Death (the doorway to evolving life) and the life-affirming Poet's muse, and for Lynch, Sheryl Lee is both sinning, suffering, self-sacrificing Laura and protogoddess, light-filled Laura. Cocteau's character in *The Testament of Orpheus* dies and is reborn, just as both he and Lynch will live on in their work, their ideas evolving in we who witness. For Cocteau, seventy years ago in *Orpheus*, Death sacrificed herself so that Orpheus could return to his reborn wife. But what of David Lynch and Mark Frost's Laura and Judy in 2017? The show's over; Lynch and Frost won't be making more episodes, but *The Return* is vibrantly alive in our minds and imaginations. Bob has been killed violently, but the personification of ultimate darkness, evil, death (Judy within Sarah Palmer) and the avatar of light, goodness, life (Laura) have yet to contend.

Showtime TV, September 3, 2017, the last moments of *Twin Peaks: The Return*. Sarah Palmer's voice: "Laura"; Laura screams; the Palmer house, everything, goes dark. Then a flashback: in the Red Room, Laura whispers in Cooper's ear something that jolts him alert, focused, galvanized—but the show's over. In the speculative theater of my mind, Laura said, "Find me, find my mother." In May of 2017, the week that *The Return* started airing, David Lynch told *Variety*: "I believe in intuition, optimism, and a Boy Scout attitude, and Cooper's got all those things." Just as Lynch, buzzing along on seven cups of coffee, is receptive to the electrified ideas that zap into his brain, Cooper takes Laura's words as holy writ. The usually taciturn Lynch, with his *amour de la France*, actually said some seminal things about *The Return* to the French journal *Cahiers du Cinéma* (which spawned the mid-century French New Wave writer-directors). The interviewer said of *The Return*, "Cinema can express abstract violence, but also how to find the energy to reach the golden age, but we end in the night, in front of the Palmer house, with a scream." Lynch responded, "If we lived in the golden age we'd be there at the end of *Twin Peaks*. But we do not live there, we are in front of the Palmer house." We, and the characters, are mired in the dark age.

Throughout his half-century career, Lynch has been celebrated and vilified as *un poete des tenebres* a poet of the shadows, whose emotional-visceral, soul-piercing art goes straight to the heart and mind, radiating darkness—but also intense light. He says, "Ninety percent of the time I don't know what I'm doing": he's a conduit, a medium for ideas that he reifies through an intuitive process of action and reaction, seeing himself as a lone painter with his canvas, even if he and his collaborators are making an eighteen-hour movie for TV. Kyle MacLachlan told *IndieWire* Lynch wants "to put you in a frame of mind," and *The Return*'s framed mind-picture is a vision of Vedic philosophy.

We've noted many references to karma, reincarnation, death as the passage to the next life, the wheel of life and death turning until all souls are united in divine being. *The Return*'s driving Vedic principle is the dharma of Cooper and Laura, their karmic mission path, their fate, which they are discovering as they go. *Twin Peaks* has brought Cooper intimate knowledge of his good and bad sides; he's matched wits with his shadow. Self-integrated now, he's the truth-seeker between polarities, able to marshal the power of both. He's better equipped to evolve and elevate than ever, and he's dedicated to integrating, balancing, empowering *Twin Peaks*'s female polarities, Laura and Judy (within Sarah Palmer) in a constructive way.

For the moment, in front of the Palmer house, time, as Lynch said of *Lost Highway*, is "dangerously out of control," but it's not beyond understanding. In interviews, Lynch has said, "Time is a conception to measure eternity." In our world of manifested matter, ideas that structure time help us navigate our lives, sequence our experiences meaningfully: William Blake's "portions of eternity." Lynch's belief system says that karmic-level advancement to higher dharma paths can speed spiritual evolution almost magically. Lynch took his "Time is a conception to measure eternity" quote from page 253 of his guru the Maharishi's translation of the Bhagavad Gita. In *Fire Walk With Me*, a project that Mark Frost did not participate in, it's the morning after Laura has realized that Bob, who's been having sex with her since she was twelve, is also her father Leland. She's in a daze of anguish and confusion. Reality is warped, dizzying, the clock on the wall seems to go fast-slow, suspended at the 2:53 mark. Lynch has said that 1992's *Fire Walk With Me* is a key to 2017's *The Return*, in which the Red Room's electric tree with its oracular voice tells Cooper, "253. Time and time again." *The Return* presents the designation 25 cents and a digital 3 on Dougie's winning slot machine; 2:53 is the time Mr. C is supposed to come back into the Red Room, and the time Cooper becomes Dougie; 2:53 is the time of Bobby, Andy, and Sheriff Truman's 253-yard trek to a vital forest site; and Cooper sends a message to Gordon Cole about "2:53, and that adds up to ten, the number of completion."

We've noted that Lynch, more than Frost, has encoded a numerical-spiritual system within *The Return*. All those sevens, Lynch's favorite number, usually with a positive connotation; and the 253s of both time and space, which add up to ten, a beacon of the highest good, for in Hindu thought ten signifies the incarnation of God, matchless and unparalleled excellence, completion indeed. This God is not faraway in the sky, it's an earthly, human incarnation that restores proper dharma, splendor and righteousness. Those who have an internal awareness (Lynch's "inner knowing") of the sacred ten God sign are awakened to the divine arrival, and Lynch, via his and Frost's poetic-artistic story system, has made us aware. Farther down page 253 of Maharishi's book, the sage speaks of "something that has the greatest longevity in the relative field of creation. The Divine Mother, the Universal Mother, ultimately responsible for all that is, was and will be in the cosmos." When "dharma is decaying, the path of evolution distorting, social rightness declining, the Incarnation comes to restore the true principles of life. The Mother takes birth, age after age."

In *Conversations With Mark Frost*, Frost has said that when working with Lynch "he's going to be the driving force and less collaborative"; it's "more Lynch's rodeo than mine." He admires Lynch's ability to "allow ideas to occur to you in the moment," even if "he doesn't immediately know how they fit in the narrative." And in *Lynch on Lynch*, Lynch has spoken of the euphoria when "fragments rush together"; "little proofs of meaning that keep us going"; "searching for magical combos of all the elements"; "you get the 'whole is bigger than the sum of the parts' kinda thing." Lynch began meditating and reading the Maharishi's words fifty years ago. Two years before he and Frost started writing *The Return* Lynch mentioned the Maharishi's "Time is a conception to measure eternity" in an interview. Did page 253 of the Maharishi's book, which emphasizes the quote and stresses female divinity, combined with Lynch's memory of the 2:53 stuck clock in his 1992 *Fire Walk With Me*, his numerological perspective that 253 is ten, the Hindu godhead number, give Lynch a resonant primal conception of *Twin Peaks: The Return*?

Hindu believers like Lynch know that beneath the surface of the materialistic, capitalistic marketplace world of patriarchal power, a female force animates all. But a greedy hunger for wealth and egotistical influence has tipped the world toward climate disaster, overconsumption of natural resources, war, authoritative male power structures. In America, there are more guns (an archetypal phallic symbol) than people; 78 percent of the guns are owned by men, and there are frequent mass shootings, 90 percent of which are perpetrated by men. Other cultures have plenty of guns, but their level of gun violence is minuscule compared with our oppressive flood. America's relative lack of social support services, abysmal discrepancies in wealth, racist and imperialist tendencies make our idealized "shining city on a hill" a hollow sham, a con man's trick. Fear and insecurity spawn irrational thinking, twisted conspiracy theories, and Frost recalls that he and Lynch imbued *The Return* with "an aura of dread and despair"; the Dark Age is in every breath we take, not just Dr. Amp's webcast rants.

For Frost, Donald Trump epitomizes the negative energy of the Dark Age: "He's a grifter, a moral vacuum, a sociopath, maybe the worst human being our country's produced on a lot of levels." Dr. Amp's angry broadcasts are a direct expression of Frost's passionate outrage. And he equates *The Return*'s conception of evil with Trump's wickedness. With Trump in mind, Frost says, "That's the frog-moth crawling into Sarah Palmer's mouth right there" (*Conversations With Mark Frost*): Frost's sense of current political reality as psychic energy, as artistic concept. Lynch hasn't made any such direct life-into-art linkage statements, but he certainly perceives Trump as a dangerous force of dark energy. In the most forceful political gesture of his life, Lynch wrote an open letter to Trump (*vanityfair.com*), going right to the core principle: "You're causing suffering and division." In Lynch's Hindu belief, aggressive, attacking words are bad karma for the speaker, so he characteristically accentuates the positivity of his spiritual outlook. "Steer our ship towards a bright future for all, unite the country, your soul will sing. With great, loving leadership, no one loses, everybody wins. Think about this, take it to heart." Lynch concludes with the sunny admonishment "Treat all people as you would like to be treated," the Christian Golden Rule, which over the years Lynch has come to view in karmic terms, as he told me: "What you do to others you're doing to yourself, action and reaction are equal." Lynch's teacher the Maharishi says, "Through every thought, word, and action we are creating some wave in the atmosphere, and discord, suffering, sorrow, and hatred have an intense influence on the world" (*The Science of Being and Art of Living*).

Both Lynch and Frost perceive and abhor Trump's monstrousness, and Frost calls him on it, aggressively, amusingly, and often, on his Twitter postings. Frost sees Trump, our everyday monster, as the frog-moth, Judy's evil injected into humankind, living within Sarah Palmer as Bob lived in Leland. And *The Return* showed us that their daughter, Laura, is the Fireman's agent of goodness, sent to counteract Judy. The show is over; Lynch says we're still in the dark age, but he sees the world, and his art, as structures of universal consciousness: he's a builder.

In his comments on Trump being an intensely negative entity, Lynch concluded, "No one is able to counteract this guy in an intelligent way." These days, Vladimir Putin, with his horrific war on Ukraine, can meld with Trump to signify primal negativity, what Lynch might call "an ugly ball of sludge," like the black smudge on Mr. C's playing/calling card. And with his karmic-retribution belief, Lynch tells *Variety* that Putin will suffer "lifetime after lifetime" for his evil deeds. In the world of *Twin Peaks*, Bob was Male Evil, but he was but a minion, born of Mother Evil, Judy. For Lynch, with his Hindu veneration of Mother Divine, held higher than heaven in ancient Sanskrit literature, Judy is ultimately perverse, sinful, abhorrent: a violation of natural law, so not the way women should be (Lynch's mother was named Sunny). The Maharishi Transcendental Meditation organization sponsors a Mother Divine Program, whose ethos is voiced poetically: "May peace on Earth be powerful/ May power on Earth be peaceful." The Fireman, a highly evolved, enlightened male, knows to fight the black-fire, A-bomb-portal evil-force invaders with divine fire, the light of illuminated consciousness, not the flaming sword of war. He walks with the warm, inspired fire of positive evolution and creativity. Cooper is FBI all the way, but on the cosmic-spiritual level, he's the Fireman's special agent. And Bob was Judy's agent-servant, like *The Shining*'s Jack Torrance, "taking orders from the house," the generator of murderous negativity.

If asked, Cooper wouldn't, maybe couldn't, write an official version of his high calling, what pulled him to Washington State years back, nudged him into the trees like a cold wind, the warm call of a dead girl, alive in his dreams. All the people he's met, all the adventures . . . but Laura's the One. And he's the one to protect her, guide her to her destiny, even if he can't verbalize what that is. Maybe Cooper has an origin story that we've not been privy to. When Cooper sits opposite the Fireman to absorb key information, it's like a tableau of a son at his father's knee. If the 1945 Trinity A-bomb test prompted the Fireman to create the counterforce savior spirit Laura, maybe the 1950s nuclear situation inspired the Fireman to conjure up Cooper. In the months preceding Cooper's April 19, 1954, birth, America decided to amass an arsenal of atomic weapons. And a South Pacific American H-bomb test on Bikini Atoll, one thousand times more powerful than the A-bomb, contaminated a seven thousand–square–mile area with radioactivity; the atoll is still not safe for habitation. Perhaps the Fireman realized that Laura would not arrive on Earth in an all-powerful state; she'd need help and guidance, time to evolve, and who better to aid her evolution than Dale Cooper?

I speculate that in the Red Room, Laura whispered, "Find me, find my mother."

Cooper did get Laura back to the time before her death, when her mother was alive, but then Laura vanished, moved on, changed, and evolved on some profound path. Cooper stuck to his path, found her, got her to where Sarah should be but is not. A setback, sure. Doesn't matter. In his online weather reports, Lynch touts the joy of "being on the fun work train," the energy and momentum of inspiration roaring forward. When Lynch gets an energized thought, a hint idea like "Laura is the One," he says, "I've been stirred, I've made a choice, and free will is gone. Once you have a film you've decided to make, it becomes a road and your road is set" (*Lynch on Lynch*). Sometimes when Lynch and I were talking about his films, I would mention some moment or point out a pattern of details or recurring patterns. He would say, "You would see that, but I wouldn't. Maybe years later, seeing it from more distance." In the act of creation, he's working way close up, in a fever of inspired intuition. As he told me, "Ninety percent of the time I don't know what I'm doing." In *Room to Dream*, looking back from 2018 at 2001's *Mulholland Drive*, Lynch can see that "*Mulholland Drive* is about Marilyn Monroe." And, a year after *The Return* aired, he added that "Laura Palmer is Marilyn Monroe." Laura and Marilyn, beautiful blonde women radiating sexuality and innocence, fervently loved in their worlds, both with vulnerabilities, weaknesses, shortcomings, abused by those they trust, choosing to give up their lives, in death revered like goddesses. In *Mulholland Drive*, Lynch presents the rise and fall of a troubled, downtrodden blonde woman as both the real her and her idealized dream self: one who is cinematically two.

Lynch shows us fallen worlds with divine essences that are obscured by bad thoughts and deeds, just waiting to be unearthed, like the divine potential within those who experience his work. He believes, as he says in *Room to Dream*, there are "the happiest of happy endings," waiting for us all, but getting there can be a bitch, named Judy. Or a witch, named Marietta. In Lynch's 1990 film *Wild at Heart*, Marietta was young Lula's maniacal, man-destroying, hyper controlling Bad Mother, who will do anything to separate her daughter from her boyfriend, Sailor. Fleeing with Sailor down the nocturnal American highway, Lula has a vision of Marietta as the Wicked Witch of the West from *The Wizard of Oz*, riding a broom on the night wind. And we see Marietta, in a fever of fury, color her whole face red with lipstick, a mask of blood lust like the red tongue of Kali, the Hindu goddess of destruction. If Mr. C's black-smudge ace of spades playing card is an abstraction of abiding evil (Judy), Marietta's red face is a sign of its active mode. For Lynch, Lula is another blonde manifestation of the Marilyn Monroe archetype: she presents sexy Monroe-like poses and small talk, and Sailor references a famous 1953 Monroe film by telling Lula, "Gentlemen prefer blondes." Consciously or not, Lynch signaled the Laura-Monroe connection with Laura's iconic crown-wearing Homecoming Queen photo, which mimics a shot of Marilyn wearing a jeweled crown in *Gentlemen Prefer Blondes*. In Lynch's mind, actress Sheryl Lee may always be Laura. In the finale of *Wild at Heart*, she's *Oz*'s Good Witch, with pink gown and magic wand, floating above industrial LA, entreating a benighted Sailor, "Don't turn away from love." She's presented in a glowing orb, as is Laura's golden face in the opening credits of every part of *The Return*, and within the globe of the Fireman's fathering spiritual alchemy. Right after *Wild at Heart*, Lynch made *Fire Walk With Me*, which concludes with Laura in an exalted, angel-attended spiritual state. From the time Lynch embarked on *Twin Peaks* and met Sheryl Lee, he's been exploring a full spectrum of female energies, from light to dark, gentle to ferocious. He and Mark Frost have evolved *Twin Peaks* to the point where in *The Return*, Laura and her mother, Sarah, are the Ones, the exponents of opposing polarities.

We're familiar with Judy's methods, her operatives Bob/the Woodsmen raping, murdering, and possessing brainier human beings. The Woodsmen are the most animalistic, pursuing a squash-heads-and-conquer mission. But Bob-within-Cooper forms an entity with complex criminal savvy and international clout. Judy herself may be a savant of evil; perhaps she telepathically influenced the Manhattan Project scientists to create an A-bomb stairway to the heaven of our world, a paradise of food for the alien invaders' bodies and minds, providing the grand sport of destroying our civilization from within. How can Laura even think of besting this dark superpower? She's shown no aptitude or inclination toward inflicting violence, and Judy's good at hiding.

Lynch and Frost, with their powers and abilities, their attentiveness and receptivity, how might they have proceeded?

In the early part of the twentieth century, Jean Cocteau felt he was a spiritual antenna picking up vibrations from the air, and Lynch and Frost characterized themselves that way in midcentury, when the vibes were coming big time. Was it the Holocaust; the Hiroshima and Vietnam horrors; mistreatment of Native Americans, African Americans, women, sexual minorities; toxic capitalism; the hypocrisy of politicians and organized religion; environmental degradation; the birth of rock 'n' roll; Elvis's swinging hips; Marilyn's curves; the birth control pill; bra-burning women and draft card-burning men; the Age of Aquarius; Asian wisdom which prompted young and young-at-heart Americans to question the status quo, reassess their personal values, and wonder if there was a better way of being?

In the mid-1970s, when Lynch was delving into Transcendental Meditation and Hindu spirituality and Frost was immersing himself in concepts like "thought transmissions from Tibetan masters," American comic book writers and artists were being stirred by an ancient Asian idea: some seed within a person, their unique potential, could be hyperevolved and blossom. As Professor Xavier of Marvel Comics's X-Men says, "You are a mutant. I can help you find your true potential." In *The Return*, Sarah Palmer carries the dark destructive Judy seed, and daughter Laura bears the Fireman's golden seed of creative divine light. In 2005 and 2007, Mark Frost wrote screenplays for the *Fantastic Four* Marvel films, narratives that showed his connection to primal aspects of Lynch's sensibility. "I was addressing things under the collective surface, issues of identity, anxiety; what is one's ultimate role? Is there salvation? Comic book characters that had archetypal identities."

Throughout the myth systems of world history, there have been female champions, both warriors and wisdom masters. In the 1930s, William Mouton Marston invented the lie detector, and after much research with male and female subjects, he concluded that women were "more honest, efficient and reliable" (*Mutants and Mystics*). Marston's imagination sparked and, concluding that American culture was "overly masculine-dominated," conceived the comic book character Wonder Woman (1941), the Amazonian warrior-princess who uses her special powers to battle "those wicked men." As singer-songwriter-author Jimmy Buffett (1946-2023) sang in "Only Time Will Tell (1996)," "Are we destined to be ruled/By a bunch of old white men/Who compare the world to football/And are programmed to defend/ I'd like to try a princess."

For centuries, a testosterone-fueled, entitled sense of territoriality ("I want what you have; you can't have what I've got") on personal and global levels has generated mayhem, misery, death. But the pop-culture estrogen brigade can be killers too. Reflecting the growing interest in Asian spirituality, TV's *Xena, Warrior Princess* (1995-2001) worries that her violent actions are negatively affecting her karmic future. Marvel comics wizards Jack Kirby (1917-1994) and Stan Lee (1922-2018)'s character Jean Grey (1963) became the most resonant embodiment of *X-Men* mysticism, evolving from a traumatized young woman to the cosmic goddess Phoenix, "celestial child of the Sun, child of life, the vision of cosmic harmony" (*Mutants and Mystics*). She becomes filled with the universe's all-powerful light, the Phoenix Force. As X-Man Wolverine says, "Last time you lit up like this, the whole universe peed its pants. Blind people saw it in Seattle, Jeannie." Marvel's Phoenix narrative has been alive for five decades, imaginatively manifesting *The Return*'s dynamics of evolution and return. Jean Grey has lived, died, sacrificed herself, been resurrected; the powerful Phoenix Force has been beneficent and evil, creative and destructive, on the most monumental possible scale. Lynch and Frost, with their human-scale values and personal immersion in the inner life, keep *The Return* on a relatable level. Vast, strong forces are at work, but they're modulated, present in everyday forms: the forest mist on your face, the bite of hot coffee, the look of love, the metallic smell of electricity, the fear in someone's eyes, a wind from the trees whispering, "Come in." *The Return* manifests the forces, spaces, and time-sense of the human psyche in a toned-down, matter-of-fact way, giving room for them to expand in the viewer's mind.

Lynch is receptive to "what's in the air," the zeitgeist, and in the world in which *The Return* aired, Marvel Comics brought Jean Grey back again in *The Hate Machine* book. She who can psychologically destroy people by showing them "the infinite reaches of time and space" (*Mutants and Mystics*) and can make reality an inferno. Jean's alive again, but "not content to return to the same life." She's evolved and grown: "We need to do better, be better." Once Jean could "scream through space as a destructive entity," but now, when hostile forces confront her, she admonishes, "Ignorance is never an excuse for hatred. Go home. Learn something." She doesn't say, "Go meditate," as Lynch might, but as Lennon and McCartney do say, instead of violent revolution, "You better free your mind instead." As Kyle MacLachlan adds told *IndieWire*, "David wants to put you in a frame of mind," receptive to positivity, and enacting it in the world. Jean Grey has a vision, "a beautiful idea" of a changed world that's like a Lynchian abstraction, a generative seed: a golden sun globe glowing over the whole world, like Laura's radiant face in the Fireman's fathering globe, all the potential of goodness. Lynch and Jean Grey have received their primal inspirations, sustaining image-ideas, and both need helpers to, as Lynch says in *Lynch on Lynch*, "tune into the original idea and make it real." Jean recruits her personal team of X-Men, and Lynch gathers his cowriter, actors, technicians, marketers, business people, and legal team to realize *Twin Peaks: The Return*. Since his holy creative mantra is "You must have final cut," Lynch will be blunt, imperious, sometimes angry and secretive to make his essential idea bloom like a blue rose.

The characters Lynch and Frost created must remain true to Lynch's core conception, especially Cooper, who, both Kyle MacLachlan and Lynch agree, is very Lynch like, as is MacLachlan's Jeffrey Beaumont in *Blue Velvet* (1986). And Laura, who is more Lynch's obsession than Frost's: "David didn't let go of Laura as a character; something about her possessed him," he says in *Conversations With Mark Frost*. And from Lynch himself: "You could say that Laura Palmer is Marilyn Monroe; everything is about Marilyn Monroe" (*Room to Dream*). Marilyn and Laura, resplendent, beloved stars in their worlds, full of secrets, vulnerable, in trouble, needing love, guidance, help; nurturers who had no children, who chose to let go of their troubled lives. In death, both are living legends. In the film *Gentlemen Prefer Blondes* (1953), Marilyn wears a diamond crown above her golden bangs, as does Laura in her iconic Homecoming Queen photo. In the same spiritualized America that Lynch matured in, Marvel Comics author Grant Morrison said,"The powerful Phoenix consciousness entered Jean Grey through the crown chakra at the top of her head." This locus of spiritual receptivity is near the forehead's third eye, which many Asian cultures see, in light of human suffering, as the enlivened capacity for spiritual evolution. In the *Twin Peaks* pilot's iconic close-up image of Laura's face, Lynch positioned a grain of sand in her third eye spot. In life with her crown, and her third-eye designation in death, Laura has been primed by Lynch for higher things. Even before the Log Lady verbalized it, Lynch's subtle visual messaging has told us that Laura is the One.

In temporal life, and the expansive world of spirit, Lynch believe in mystery, and happy endings. On Showtime in 2017, *Twin Peaks: The Return* ends mysteriously. How might Lynch have venerated his Marilyn muse with more story? In Joss Whedon's *Buffy the Vampire Slayer* (1997-2003), the righteous blonde killer says, "I may be dead, but I'm still pretty" (she also wondered, referencing a time disruption, "So that's why time went all David Lynch?"). With all due respect, way more people have read the Bible than seen *Buffy*, so when Laura says, "I am dead, and yet I live," in *The Return*, she would strike most viewers as echoing Christ's Prince of Peace ethos. Is the Fireman God? Is Laura the Second Coming? She is of the Christ consciousness spirit; she saw Christian angels in life and prayed to them (her bedroom wall picture), and in death an angel bestowed divine grace on her in the Red Room. All this is sweet and fine and uplifting, but Laura, whose weaknesses and shortcomings we know so well, has yet to confront her own mother, always a little off, a little strange, now the monstrous, murderous embodiment of universal evil.

Judging by Lynch's work, when he declared to my Linda, "I love the female psyche," he meant the full spectrum, all aspects from dark to light. Regarding mothers and children, in *The Grandmother* (1970), the Boy's mother is slovenly, abusive, quasi-erotic toward her son. He symbolically guillotines her head off and gets warm maternal love from a grandmother he grows from a seed, an early manifestation of Lynch's individualistic "find your own path to what you need" philosophy. In *Eraserhead* (1977), the mother of Henry's girlfriend transgressively nuzzles and nibbles his neck; he lets it pass. *The Elephant Man* (1980) first presents Lynch's Mother Divine-sense of cosmic female spirituality. In the film, which is based on true historical accounts from Victorian England, Merrick is a physically deformed, orphaned outcast who was exhibited as a carnival freak, then rescued by a man of science, Dr. Frederick Treves, who discovered and revealed Merrick's sweet soul and sophisticated sensibility. It's a telling statement for Kyle MacLachlan, who's known Lynch for four decades, to tell the Criterion Channel in 2022 that "David feels a strong affinity for the John Merrick character." The historical Treves's writings about Merrick, emphasizing his obsession with the idealized feminine, do sound like a portrait of Lynch: "Merrick had a lively imagination; he was a romantic; he cherished an emotional regard for women. He fell in love—in a humble and devotional way—with, I think, every attractive lady he saw" (*The Elephant Man and Other Reminiscences*). Merrick's path has been a quagmire of physical and mental misery, but it becomes a blossoming garden in Ladyland. He gets to behave like a refined gentleman, enjoys the patronage of Mrs. Kendal and Princess Alexandra, and sees the play *Puss in Boots* in which a floating Princess Sweetheart fairy waves her wand, sprinkles the world with magic dust, and declares, 'Happily ever after." In Lynch's heart, the surge of female love and guidance is manna from heaven. In death, via tender cinematics only Lynch can do, Merrick merges with his post-death mother in the cosmos, the female Soul of All that is the universe. She says, "Nothing will die. The stream flows, the wind blows, the cloud fleets, the heart beats," in the spirit of Lynch's Hindu life-death-rebirth beliefs, which he echoes in the lyrics of his song "The World Spins": "The sun comes up and down each day/The river flows out to the sea . . . Forever and ever/The world spins." In his stage production *Industrial Symphony No. 1: The Dream of the Brokenhearted* (1990), Lynch had Julee Cruise sing these words suspended high in the air, like Princess Sweetheart, like *Wild at Heart*'s Good Witch, in a shower of sparkling, consoling cosmic dust. And Cruise singing this song, and the words' sentiment, are essential to the original *Twin Peaks* and *The Return*'s final hours.

Lynch has spoken of the magazine ads and TV commercials brimming with "smiling female faces" he saw growing up, and mother Sunny's beneficent countenance certainly brightened his home life. For Lynch, Frost, and me, midcentury America was where "domestic goddess" homemakers were portrayed in the kitchen wearing sparkling crowns and brandishing golden wands, showing

US men returning from fighting World War II that the women had been running things just fine on the home front—maybe even spending their days riveting the wings of fighter planes. American women were capable, powerful, independent thinkers, expanding their horizons, moving into the workforce, the public sphere; questioning male dominance; seeking sexual freedom and political clout; exulting in female bonds of sisterhood, conceiving of the planet as female, God as She. But in Uncle Sam's patriarchal America, this all could be threatening, a devaluation and deflation of the manly male ego, an assault on the way guys have been doing things. As Lynch says, "It's all action and reaction." In this postwar sociopolitical period of female expansiveness, male filmmakers responded by flooding screens with shadow shapes of dangerous women, alluringly beautiful and full of promises, who could scheme behind your back—and maybe put a bullet through your heart. The delightful 1930s screwball-comedy "battle of the sexes" had turned deadly. Payback can be righteous, and American Film Institute graduate David Lynch knows his noir. *Dune*'s Reverend Mother Mohiam, the Bene Dessert Witch, schemes on a grand scale, seeking to topple the universe's patriarchy with a massive breeding program to produce a female messiah. Paul Atreides (Kyle MacLachlan) foils her plans, and his boon companion mother Jessica is his helpful partner in space-spanning adventures. *Blue Velvet* (1986)'s Dorothy is a good mother, but her husband and young son have been kidnapped, and she must submit to violent, sadomasochistic sex with the kidnapper to keep her family alive. In *Blue Velvet*, Lynch, for the first time, presents a person being invaded by the spirit of darkness: Dorothy says of Frank, "He put his disease in me." She wants to be slapped, and when she has sex with Jeffrey, she holds a knife on him and issues commands, and Jeffrey emerges tainted by darkness, potentially paying it forward like the Woodsmen creeping in our world. Sarah Palmer is not the first Lynchian mother to carry a dark partner, but the cosmic power of her Judy eclipses all temporal villains. Still, *Wild at Heart*'s Marietta is a fountain of earthbound maleficence; her transgressions are legion. She hires someone to burn up her husband, puts her boyfriend in mortal danger, exerts a raging control over her daughter Lula, tries to seduce Lula's boyfriend Sailor in a men's bathroom, hires a hitman to kill Sailor. How to combat this roaring personification of female evil, whom Lynch likens to *The Wizard of Oz*'s Wicked Witch? Marietta's machinations put Sailor in prison. When he's getting out, after Lula's had their son, Pace, Lula's on the phone with her mother. In *The Wizard of Oz* Dorothy kills the Wicked Witch by pouring water on her, and as Lula steadfastly defies Marietta by saying she's going to meet Sailor, she splashes a glass of water on a photograph of Marietta, which symbolically fades away. Lula, Sailor, and Pace will be a family, and maybe there'll be room for Marietta—but it will be on Lula's terms.

Lynch reveres the great, independent-minded, perfectionistic auteur Stanley Kubrick (1929-99), who, by example, showed Lynch the creative necessity of having final cut, the last word on the shape and presentation of his art. *Eraserhead* was Kubrick's favorite film, and Lynch treasures Kubrick's body of work, including his 1987 Vietnam War film *Full Metal Jacket*, which has a resonant linkage to *The*

Return. The Judy force, with her spawn Bob and the Woodsmen, is the Dark Mother essence of *The Return*. And in *Full Metal Jacket* a prominent male character, the squad's most hate-filled, cruel, and nihilistic killer, is called Animal Mother. On his helmet is the signifier "I am become Death," a shortening of the phrase "Now I am become Death, destroyer of worlds," uttered by the Manhattan Project's J. Robert Oppenheimer, "Father of the Atom Bomb," on the occasion of the Trinity test that in *The Return* provides a portal for Judy and her crew to run rampant into our world. Oppenheimer's words are quoted from the Bhagavad Gita, the sacred Hindu text that Lynch knows well. As a detective says in Lynch's *Lost Highway*, "No such thing as a bad coincidence."

Lynch believes there's goodness, a divinity within us all just waiting to be realized, but Kubrick was more pessimistic, feeling that deep down, we're more primordial killers than saints. *Full Metal Jacket*'s protagonist, Joker, projects a Lynchian sense of human nature's complex duality. He's a wiseass college boy in a sea of working-class gung-ho grunt soldiers. He confounds his doctrinaire drill instructor by having "Born to Kill" on his helmet while at the same time wearing a peace sign. When the dumbfounded, irate instructor wonders, "What the hell?" Joker replies that he "was trying to suggest something about the duality of man . . . The Jungian thing, sir!" Joker has a nuanced sense of irony about the world around him. The Make Love *and* War messages he wears reflect all those others, not himself. He tamps down, denies any sense of darkness within himself, any capacity for violence. Yet at the climax, Joker's the one who kills the sniper, just a Vietnamese girl with a big gun who's been picking off Marines one by one. Does he do it for revenge, to save other Marines, both?

The swirl of impulses, thoughts, emotions in our mind-bodies, the desires of the individual and the collective, are the stuff of centuries of human stories. Mythologist-sage Joseph Campbell, the spiritual father of George Lucas's *Star Wars* saga, understood that our stories and myths are externalized dreams, projections of universal psychic forces and energies. "In cultures throughout the world, there are myths and legends of the Virgin Birth, of Incarnations, Deaths and Resurrections, Second Comings, Judgements" (*Myths to Live By*). As Campbell's friend filmmaker and dancer Maya Deren said, "Facts of the mind manifested in fictions of matter," our insides visualized, experienced outside in the world. Throughout his life, Lynch has pondered ideas: As above, so below; inside and outside; self and not self. He feels that his self remains the same no matter the age of his body, and that the primal, universal Self of Being contains, is, All. Yet *Twin Peaks* is a panorama of splits, dualities, warring factions, on the temporal surface and at the deepest eternal levels. In our stories and lives, balancing warring forces, achieving cohesion and unity, is a high goal, something to keep working toward. This is Cooper the facilitator, the agent of the Fireman's mission of high goodness.

In the sheriff's office, Cooper's frame-filling face, overseeing all the players, including himself, intones, "We live inside a dream." When I presented Lynch at the Seattle premiere of *INLAND EMPIRE*, he spoke a few words from the Upanishads before the film: "We weave our life and then move along in it. We are like the dreamer who dreams and then lives in the dream. This is true for the entire universe." He has said that "we come into this world with so much already set": newborn, we are the sum of our karmic heritage, our actions and thoughts in past lives, but change and relativity rule, the ongoing balancing act, evolution is nonstop. So Cooper says, "The past dictates the future," but "There are some things that will change." Both, forever and ever.

On Gordon Cole's FBI office wall is a poster of Bohemian literary sage Franz Kafka (1883-1924), who Lynch reveres for his tales steeped in existential anxiety and alienation, oppressive dread, surrealistic imagery, and the primal sense that life is absurd. These are vital themes in Lynch's art, and they reflect today's generalized spiritual-social malaise, for since the 1950s media mentions of the term "Kafkaesque" have climbed yearly. Lynch's work dwells in darkness, but it seeks to attain the soul's transcendence, which Kafka sums up as "radiance" (*New Heaven, New Earth: The Visionary Experience in Literature*). Over the years observers have marveled at the contrast between Lynch's sunny personality and his midnight-bad-dream stories and images. Author-critic Joyce Carol Oates has noted that it is Kafka's literary vision that encompasses the anguish of human existence, while Kafka the man intuitively feels that we posses an inner radiance that we need to wake up to; he believes human consciousness must expand beyond the ego's "frozen sea within." Dualities can be transcended: "Evil does not exist; once you have crossed the threshold all is good" (*Conversations With Franz Kafka*).

Literary lioness Joyce Carol Oates has written that "the fantasies of childhood parallel, in essence, the fantasies of the race. Not 'realism,' but a kind of 'surrealism' is the mode of storytelling that predated all others. Legends, fairy tales, ballads, the earliest of preserved drawings, are not at all realistic but magical, with claims of divine or supernatural origin" (*The Faith of a Writer: Life, Craft, Art*). Oates's fellow literary light Joan Didion knew in adolescence that she wanted to be a writer, to find the words to decipher "What is going on in these pictures in my mind?" (*Let Me Tell You What I Mean*). She would start a book with a primal picture. "It was a picture of white space. Empty space. This was clearly the picture that dictated the narrative intention of the book—a book in which things happened off the page, a 'white' book to which the reader would have to bring their own bad dreams." In a Jewish parable, the student comes to the rabbi saying, "I've completed the lesson." He pages through, proudly explaining the text. The rabbi says, "Yes, you know the words, but what about the white space?"

David Lynch and Mark Frost are storytellers of the white space. That's where they wanted to leave the identity of Laura's killer in the original *Twin Peaks*, but marketplace pressures forced their hands, thus inspiring decades of more story. With total creative control in *The Return*, they ended the Showtime, September 3, 2017, final broadcast without a parent and child reunion, without Laura Palmer and Judy, Sarah Palmer, confronting each other.

In *Blue Velvet*, malevolent Frank Booth intones, "Now it's dark" as he unleashes his bestial urges in psychosexual torture sessions with Dorothy. In the *Twin Peaks* Pilot, Agent Cooper seems to evoke a metaphysical principle as he tells a town meeting, "These crimes took place at night." *Wild at Heart*'s Marietta is visualized as a Wicked Witch riding the night wind, and *The Return*'s evil invaders thrust into our world on a wave of nuclear fire while the sky is black, the sun asleep. It can feel like all of Lynch's film and TV work takes place at night. Sad, despairing souls, hateful murderous souls, soulless human beings populate Lynch's nighttimes and shadow the days: dark emotions, thoughts, and deeds predominate. But always deep within Lynch, the consciousness of the spiritual and temporal golden age, its possibility, the balancing point between polarities, black and white, the door between.

Perhaps there's a gray mist, soft electrical flashes, a circular table top; mother and daughter, Sarah and Laura.

> "Sit down, Laura. Listen to me."
>
> "No, Mom. You didn't help me. I was hurting, I was dying inside. Dad was hurting me. You knew, you had to know." Laura sits.
>
> "No, Laura. He was my husband, I loved him . . . But the house, something . . . fog in the room . . . can't sleep."
>
> "Mother, take my hand."
>
> "No, don't touch me. I'm shadow . . . hungry, I have to take you . . . "
>
> "Mother, stand up."
>
> "No Laura, you . . . Oh such light . . . "
>
> "Dance with me, Mother, you taught me to dance."

In *Fire Walk With Me*, when highschooler Laura, alone in her room, reaches across her desktop for the hidden key to her secret diary, we get a momentary glimpse of an image lying on the desk. An antique black-and-white photograph of a girl sitting on the curve of a crescent moon. The moon is a time-honored symbol of the divine feminine, protective and nurturing; but also of the dark feminine, hunting and reaping: lunar light and dark fluctuate.

We've noted that in *The Return* Lynch linked a crescent shape with Mr. C's helper tulpa Diane and the malevolent invaders the Woodsmen, Bob, and Judy, and that the Judy force is in Sarah. Even while young Laura is reflecting the evil influence of Bob, she is heroically like a caring mother toward those she loves. Laura, a child of parents infected by the dark ones, yet imbued with golden goddess potential. Perhaps the Fireman knows that sending her into a family of vipers will ultimately spark her divine self-actualization. The shifting balance of darkness and light, within individuals and between people. Next to the moon girl photo on Laura's desk is a clear glass tumbler holding pens, one red, one green. For a split second of Lynch's visual-thematic-narrative artistry, Laura's hands holding her diary, her intimate secret life, are poised above the moon girl photo that's adjacent to the tumbler and pens. Laura's hands, her written material existence; the moon girl of future metaphysical potential; red and green, two primary choices. Stop or go, stop *and* go; destroy and create, contract and expand. William Blake said it takes both to generate divine energy.

Maybe Sarah and Laura, darkness and light, dance in the mist of *Twin Peaks*'s White Tail Falls, my Snoqualmie Falls, where the falling water, dancing polarities, generate electricity that keeps the lights of the valley lit. And Cooper watches, smiling, the agent who persevered and made true his vision of Laura and Sarah, the Fireman and Judy forces, reenergized interplay, shifting balance, tipping toward positivity, keeping things spinning. Lynch and his partner Mark Frost, all the places and characters they created, the whole cast and crew who helped will certainly see each other again. Things will have changed, evolved; people will think thoughts, do deeds, and karma will shape lives and dreams, but everyone will be beaming at the curtain call.

Lynch invited Linda and me to the cast and crew screening of *Mulholland Drive*. We flew down from Seattle and had a transcendent cinematic experience in the Director's Guild Theater on Sunset Boulevard. The next morning, while Linda was bringing in coffee, the phone rang. I answered it and sat up in bed. It was Lynch's assistant Jason: "Hold on, here's David." He wanted me to sum up *Mulholland Drive* in a sentence. I took a sip of coffee and said, "Whether it was in life or in a dream, before death or after death, there was a through line of surging emotion." His voice was strong and loud: "Fantastic, Greg!" Lynch's core idea, in his mind and heart and the works he shows us, is one for the ages: death is the path to life.

Years later, after Linda had died and *Twin Peaks: The Return* had aired, I was showing the French filmmakers Thomas and Cyrille around *Twin Peaks* country. They wanted to get a good shot of Snoqualmie Falls, so they posed me at the viewing platform, with cascading white water over my left shoulder and the "Great Northern" up above my right. We were surrounded by other awe-struck falls viewers. Motorcycle travelers, foreign tourists (the Belgian Twin Peaks family from the Mar-T had caught up to us), some of whom saw this place as being the town Twin Peaks, a concrete reality: thunder in the air, mist on their faces. For me, it was a place near where my Swedish emigrant father had been a lumberjack in the woods. Where my parents and I had enjoyed lodge dinners as I grew up, and I'd celebrated my now-ex-wife's birthday in the first flush of our marriage. Where I'd had breakfast with the legendary British writer-director Michael Powell (*The Red Shoes, A Matter of Life and Death,I Know Where I'm Going!*) and his wife Thelma Schoonmaker, Martin Scorsese's triple-Oscar-winning editor (*Raging Bull, The Aviator, The Departed*).

Cyrille's camera rolled; the water fell and fell, and as I talked about the falls in relation to *Twin Peaks*, my eyes locked on Thomas's. Unexpectedly, he asked, "So, Greg, what do the falls mean to you?" Pausing, I remembered Julee Cruise telling me that when she sang Lynch's words to the song "Falling," which meld with Angelo Badalamenti's lush music and the image of the falls in the opening of *Twin Peaks*, in her mind she was singing the tender love song to her cocker spaniel Rudy. And I pictured Laura Palmer in *Fire Walk With Me* talking about falling in space. How she'd go "Faster and faster. And for a long time you wouldn't feel anything. And then you'd burst into fire. Forever . . . And the angels wouldn't help you. Because they've all gone away." And I thought of Dale Cooper in *The Return* falling from the Red Room through some hellish space, in danger of atomizing.

I said, "It's falling, freedom, letting go, the ego gone. Like when you're walking in the woods, really looking and hearing and smelling, and you're quiet, all your spinning thoughts have evaporated, and what you're breathing in and out is the moment here that's also everywhere, always. You are it; it is you. And the water flows downstream, out to the ocean. The water evaporates up to the clouds; the rain and snow fall; water feeds the rivers, flows down to the falls, over and over." Will I have such consoling, unifying thoughts in the last moments of my life? When my dear Linda was near the end, her thoughts, some essence within her, didn't flow in water, but wafted upward, into warmth and light.

Writing this book in the winter after Linda died, I would pause and look out the window at a tall evergreen hedge. Every now and then, after a rain, the sun would come out. One raindrop, just one in the field of green, would be at just the right angle. A diamond of light.

LA sunset: Linda and I with Twin Peaks Festival organizers David and Susan Eisenstadt.

—ACKNOWLEDGMENTS—

For Launching the Project: Fayetteville Mafia Press; David Bushman, editor; Scott Ryan, designer. John Thorne for his foreword.

From Another Place: David Lynch, Mark Frost, Peggy Reavey, Catherine Coulson, Richard Beymer, Josh Eisenstadt, Sheryl Lee, Wendy Robie, Gary Hershberger, Ray Wise, Naomi Watts, Richard Green, Michael J. Anderson, Julee Cruise, Anthony Slide, Anna Cottle, Thelma Schoonmaker, Brian Belovarac, Cédric Deville, Thomas Cazals, Cyrille Renaux and Grace Zabriskie for the photo on page 292.

From the Neighborhood: Matt Marshall, Mark Steiner, Janice Findley, Paul Hansen, Ricahrd T. Jameson, Kathleen Murphy, Jan Baross, Tova Gannana, Charles. R. Cross, John Trafton, Moira Macdonald, Robert Horton, Sean Axmaker, Jeannine Gregoire, Kendal Gabel, Suzanne Ragen, Rustin Thompson, Nick Thompson, Norm Hill, Aron Michael Thompson, Lindsey Dabek, and Chris Matthews.

–SELECTED BIBLIOGRAPHY OF KEY INSPIRATIONS–

Allen, Gay Wilson. *A Reader's Guide to Walt Whitman*. Octagon Books, 1990.

Arnaud, Claude. *Jean Cocteau: A Life*. Yale University Press, 2016.

Arnold, Kyle. *The Madness of Philip K. Dick*. Oxford University Press, 2016.

Bhaskarananda, Swami. *The Essentials of Hinduism: A Comprehensive Overview of the World's Oldest Religion*. Viveka Press, 1994.

Grimm, Jacob, and Wilhelm Grimm. *Grimm's Fairy Tales*. Grosset and Dunlap, 1951.

Bushman, David. *Conversations with Mark Frost*. Fayetteville Mafia Press, 2020.

Campbell, Joseph. *Myths to Live By*. Bantam Books, 1973.

Digby, George Wingfield. *Symbols and Images in William Blake*. Oxford University Press, 1957.

Gerwig, Greta. *Lady Saints & Mystics*. A24, 2017.

Greenberg, Alan. *Love in Vain: A Vision of Robert Johnson*. University of Minnesota Press, 2012.

Junker, Patricia. *Modernism in the Pacific Northwest*. Seattle Art Museum and University of Washington Press, 2014.

Kripal, Jeffrey J. *Mutants and Mystics: Science Fiction, Superhero Comics, and the Paranormal*. The University of Chicago Press, 2011.

Levy, Julien. *Surrealism*. Da Capo Press, 1995.

Lynch, David. *Catching the Big Fish: Meditation, Consciousness, and Creativity*. Jeremy P. Tarcher, 2007.

Oates, Joyce Carol. *New Heaven, New Earth: The Visionary Experience in Literature*. Gage Publishing Limited, 1974.

Pettit, Ted S. *Handbook for Boys*. Boy Scouts of America National Council, 1956.

Rawson, Philip. *Art of Tantra*. New York Graphic Society Limited, 1973.

Rushdie, Salman. *The Wizard of Oz*. British Film Institute, 1992.

Taylor, Beverly, and Robert Bain, ed. *The Cast of Consciousness: Concepts of the Mind in British and American Romanticism*. Greenwood Press, 1987.

Taylor, Tom. *X-Men Red: The Hate Machine*. Marvel Worldwide Inc., 2018.

Watson, Steven. *The Birth of the Beat Generation: Visionaries, Rebels, and Hipsters,* 1944-1960. Pantheon Books, 1995.

Yogananda, Paramahansa. *Autobiography of a Yogi*. Self-Realization Fellowship, 1999.

Youngblood, Gene. *Expanded Cinema*. E. P. Dutton & Co., Inc.,1970.

ALSO AVAILABLE

AT TUCKERDSPRESS.COM